30 Years of Hindsight

ROBERT PAUL

Copyright © 2019 Robert Paul
All rights reserved
First Edition

PAGE PUBLISHING, INC.
New York, NY

First originally published by Page Publishing, Inc. 2019

ISBN 978-1-64462-867-6 (Paperback)
ISBN 978-1-64462-868-3 (Digital)

Printed in the United States of America

Dedicated to Buttley

4~THOMAS
you can't change your past..
But you can make it change your FUTURE!
Rob

Introduction

I have a best friend whom I do not talk to as much as I would like anymore. When I do touch base with him, I am always the only one talking, because for some reason I always have way too much to say, I am very long-winded and tend to turn stories into other stories and elaborate until, apparently, it gets annoying. I have done this for years up until the point where one day he simply cut me off and said, "Shut the fuck up and write your stories down so I can read them if I want and I don't have to listen to you." He did not say that exactly, but I know what he meant. However, if you do know me and my voice, it would help to hear my voice reading the stories to you as you read because I wrote every word as close to how I talk as I could. I was asked to write a few stories, maybe five to ten pages; I went a little overboard, but most of the time I was having fun. I was not told to type it, but considering the majority of what was written was done after dark into the wee hours of the morning while smoking copious amounts of marijuana and drinking my face off, I decided to at least make it legible. If I had handwritten it, no one would ever be able to read it. Some of the best literature I have ever read was done by those in an inebriated state of mind, and I loved how you could tell what state they were in. They might start off quite coherent and even sober and then fade into a daze of whatever type of fucked up shit got them off. I think that is quite obvious throughout what I have written. I also decided to decline having it edited because it would be expensive due to its length and also the fact that many of the best books I have read seemed like they were never edited at all and I liked that. They were simply the raw, original writings of the authors…that's how it should be.

My First Memory

The first years of elementary school are arbitrary, insignificant, and unmemorable. Those years may as well have been forgotten when you look back at your life. However, I do remember one thing, I was a cow in a past life. It sounds really weird, but I had visions as a child of being a cow. I was spotted in black and white. I was at the end of a trail with my mom (a cow) that looked suspiciously similar to the one right by my house, which seems to be an easily dismissed factor in my story, but I had never seen this trail at this point in my life as I was way too young. I was three years or younger and very descriptive of the trail, my mom being a cow, and then seeing a snake. The snake bit me. Everything went black, and I woke up as a little boy.

I don't necessarily believe that this actually happened, but it is my first memory, and I guess it was pretty fucking real to me at the time. This may have never occurred, but it was real to me, and I still love milk! Although this is the time when you have nothing else to worry about and you are more or less forced to learn things that will inevitably help you throughout the rest of your life. This is around the time that my dad's dad got me into *Jeopardy!* which I still watch religiously to this day. I was way too young and didn't get anything right, but I thought it was fun and kept watching. Now I still watch every day, and friends come over to play with me. I kick ass every time.

We would go to my grandpa's cabin every summer, and it was gorgeous, and I learned to fall in love with and appreciate nature. We would go fishing every day, and the water was so clear you could see the bottom and the salmon as well as rainbow trout swimming everywhere, even where the water was around one hundred feet deep. We always drove out there, which sucked ass, but we made a lot of stops that were cool to say I have seen but will probably never go back to, like Mount Rushmore, Crazy Horse, and Sturgis.

I also fell in love with *The Simpsons* around this time in 1989 when they made their debut, and I know every word to every episode, but I still watch whenever they are on. I later fell in love with mathematics and still do it to this day; I do it arbitrarily for no reason. I find myself kept up, unable to sleep, because I am lying in bed, trying to figure out what a 15 percent tip for a $36.75 bill would be. I also like to propose hypothetical questions and present them to my mother, who is a doctor of psychology. I like to present my thesis, wait for some rebuttal, then blow her away with all the things I have to back up my theory. I love it when she doesn't have shit to say; it makes me feel really smart.

My mother is a genius, but she just doesn't think outside the box. These are things that I learned in my younger years that have stayed with me forever. However, college helped to progress this concept into a whole other dimension. I also remember a few first and foremost life lessons at this time from my mother. I learned, and will never forget what she said: "School is your job, and you cannot do anything else until all your work is finished." To this day, school is actually my favorite thing in the world. I know people don't understand that, but I really enjoy learning, and that is no bullshit. The other lesson I will never forget as my dad was fucking up hard core left and right but my mom wouldn't leave him is that you don't give up on someone you love. I never have, and I never will. I learned that the people whom you love and who truly care about you and your well-being are the most important aspect of your life.

It is not until puberty when all your attention is focused on the opposite sex and you forget everything else. I feel that many of these memories are lost because of the surge of hormones and desire for the opposite sex, which is why everyone most likely remembers the cute boy or girl in school. These aspects of growing up become obvious and come about around the time of puberty. This is when I found my focus and the beginning point of when I can remember or what I chose to remember.

I also remember my first theory that I presented to my mom that I feel was truly validated. I proposed that the concept of intelligence was based on a bias scale and should not be taken at face value. Just because someone can pass a test does not make them any more intelligent than someone who cannot read. I feel that true intelligence cannot be learned from books, because I feel that true intelligence comes from independent thought. Anyone can read something in a book and regurgitate it to a question that already has an answer to it. True intelligence comes from thinking outside the box and creating your own questions and proposing a new answer that has never even been conceived.

Theologians who have been condemned over the centuries for creating theories which were not accepted by most were considered crazy and basically stupid until hundreds of years later when their theories where proved to be correct. The IQ tests that are conducted rely on a test that has been used for years, and anyone who is anyone can find out the answers. I think that we should reward those with knowledge and open-minded thought about things that no one has yet thought about.

At ten years old, I had my first experience with death when my grandma (my mom's mom). She died from her third stroke / heart attack. The first two had left her paralyzed and unresponsive, so I really don't remember a lot about her, but I know that I loved her, that the ashtray in her car was always full to the top with cigarette butts, and the exact point when she died. I was playing Hot Wheels with a buddy when we got the call. I heard the news and grabbed the track and swung a section at the wall like a fucking baseball bat and shattered it while screaming like a pro wrestler. I then proceeded to punch the wall while screaming and crying. This was my introduction into the world of loss and my transformation into the emotional pussy I am today.

I was a pudgy little boy with glasses who got picked on occasionally and wanted nothing more than touch a boob, let alone get a kiss. I do remember my first kiss and her name and everything; it was under the twisty slide on the playground. She was kind of pug fugly, but we were good friends and talked about the whole kissing issue and decided to give it a shot and get it out of the way. We were good plutonic friends, so it was no big deal. Maybe she is hot now. I am not on social media, so I have never looked her up, but I was not done looking for tail. I had found HP's porn stash at a young age and knew what I wanted. Young boys did not have the privileges of the kids today, who can look up any porn you could possibly imagine on their phone in seconds. It took vigilant efforts to find your dad's stash or that of one of your friends, and even in elementary, I remember people coming over specifically to watch some porn. Even something as tame as *Playboy* was a goldmine to find to some kids. This is also around the time that I was told what I would eventually amount to in life.

Most parents tell their children that they can grow up to be whatever they want. They were told they could grow up to be a politician or an astronaut. I, however, was told that my father and his father before him were alcoholics and I would grow up to be one as well. It is hard to aspire to be anything when you are told you will be something specific. I embraced it and basically thought of it as my birthright. I drank my face off at a very young age and found out I was really good at it.

I hung out with my dad at this point in my life more than any other time; he was really good at drinking his face off as well. My dad was a sheriff but was laid off because he did some really stupid shit. He had many issues mentally, as well as the fact that he was a big-time alcoholic. He was in a library, studying for an upcoming bar exam because he was going to school to become a lawyer. He finished school and got his degree, but this day, he lost his cop job forever, and nowadays he was probably on some creep-show list. I was not there, but I read about it in the paper, and my mom told me about it.

Apparently, he saw a pretty lady in the library and thought it was a good idea to jump on the table, drop his pants, whistle at her, and shake his wiener around. I guess I know where I got it from, but I would not do it in a library. He had no job, and my mom was always out of town, which was the case my whole life, but now I would go hang out with my dad when not in school instead of work being alone. Actually, he did work as a school bus driver for a bit, and then he was a city bus driver.

I came along with him on his shift one time, and I remember it was between routes, so there was no one on the bus. I was lying down on the back bench, playing Gameboy, and all of a sudden, I got thrown off the bench and halfway down the length of the bus. I don't know if he was drinking or not, but my dad was a good driver, and I still have no clue how he hit that parked car. He lost that job, and we hung out more.

Around this time, I started hanging out with him at his man cave, which was a big garage that he called the Toolbox. I had fun there; my dad and his friends would get loaded and work on cars. I would just wander around and play with junk; this was a huge garage, and I remember one of the guys' stations had a calendar with naked ladies, and I would grab it and bring it to the bathroom. I figured out my body very early, and I had fun. I still do. Who doesn't?

My dad was part of a pit crew for a race car team. We went to the tracks a few weekends. It was fun at the time, but I would most likely hate everyone there if I were to go nowadays. They were always working on the car, so my dad told me to go around and find stuff that I would want to make something out of. I am not good with mechanics, but I looked at this like an art project. I grabbed some big-ass wheels, the front of a dirt bike, a bucket seat, and a bunch of metal. My pop's showed me the basics of welding and set me free to do whatever I wanted. I made a fucking three-wheeler. I did not and still do not jack shit about how to fix an engine, let alone make it work. I got a tractor motor, and HP helped me hook everything up. I did the artsy part, and I made it work. It hauled ass! Later I would lose that trike, and I have still not forgiven my dad for that.

It happened after my dad received his law degree and decided to invest in some sort of law firm with a lawyer "buddy" of his. After a while and all the checks were cleared, my dad's "friend" bolted on him, stole all the money he invested, and never spoke to him again.

We went to find him, and it was clear that he was gone for good. We looted all the shit he left behind. My dad ended up bankrupt and had to sell all his thirty-plus cars. His lot included my three-wheeler that my dad and I had made from scratch then I also lost the boat that we were working on…I really wanted to keep that boat because love fishing and working on it wit' my pops.

Before this happened, I would go to the "back to the '50s" car show at the state fair every year. He had a dope car every year, and he would always get plowed, but I remember one year that he drove us in Bigfoot, which was an old Willys Jeep with giant monster truck tires; it was fucking awesome and was going to be my inheritance, no dice. I remember my dad had damn near the entire bed of the truck full of beer. He gave a few away, but I swear he almost drank like two cases with ease and drove us home. Later on, when my mom could not put up with his drinking anymore, he told me he would not drink beer because it leaves too much evidence and smells. He said that he was switching to vodka because it doesn't smell, bullshit. I knew every time he was drinking, and I stole his liquor (on principal and out of spite). What the fuck was he going to do? Tell my mom I took his booze that he is not supposed to have?

So my dad had lost everything and did what anybody would do and drank his face off. He stuck to his theory of drinking vodka because you can't smell it, but he was not fooling anyone. This was still in the days of the Toolbox and the beginning of my parents' separation. I was always at the garage with my dad and noticed that he was spending a little too much time and being a little too close with this pug-fugly abomination. She was the most disgusting pig I have ever seen in my life, but I guess she knew cars, so they had something to talk about when they drunk. Fuck, she was a gross grease-monkey wench, but I think a big part of how I felt about the situation is what my pops was doing to my mom, the most important person in my life. I felt that he was doing her dirty, and she is the most innocent, loving person in the whole fucking world and did not deserve that.

Little did I know that a rotten apple doesn't fall far from the shit tree. Would I follow him down the same path? Yes, I would, but I did not know that yet. I was pissed, and I told my mother about the infidelity and the drinking and basically ratted him out on everything. I love my mother, and I did not want her to get hurt. They eventually separated, but my mother would not divorce him because as I learned in another of her life lessons, you do not give up on anyone, especially when you have made that big of a commitment.

I finally made friends I would want to hang out with outside of school in fifth or sixth grade. We had a little crew of ragamuffins riding bikes and doing what kids that age do. Then in came a new kid at school that we didn't know how to measure up. Whatever it was, it had long hair, a dangling earring, and a Metallica T-shirt. We were told that the mysterious being was named B——, but we swore it was a girl. Eventually, we found that it was true, and we hung out with all the time. In the end, friends and cliques go their separate ways as we did. However, I fell in love with the boy-girl with the dangling earring who now is and will always be my brother. I learned that you should never judge someone on first impressions.

People do not always grow up the way they are when they are younger. I was a fat kid with glasses, and I remember being picked on and punched by a popular athletic kid. Eight years later, he was a pudgy dork with acne, and I was on the other side of the spectrum. Girls, especially, a lot. Many of them just need to grow into their nose or face in general, but some of the girls that were homely or just went unnoticed became beautiful and vice versa. Everyone changes over time in appearance, but people with good hearts tend to stay that way, but some can change. However, assholes will always be assholes because that's all they know. It is like the cliché that you can take a kid out of the ghetto but you can't take the ghetto out of the kid. The same goes for truly good people. They will always be there for you. It is just a little tricky to pick out who is who at that age.

Junior high came next, which I was nervous about because I was still a fat kid with glasses and a broken arm I picked up over summer break. They still let me play football as starting middle linebacker; however, I was cut from the team for using my cast as a weapon. So I picked up a new sport along with a new crew and a whole new world of girls. Eventually, I dropped weight from skateboarding every day until you couldn't see, but I stopped wearing my glasses at this point, so it didn't really matter.

We would go downtown on special occasions. I was the dumbass that tried any and everything, but I did land a bunch of cool shit that

I still remember. My sister also brought me to my first real concert, Lollapalooza, which was more of a music festival. It had every popular band from the '90s. I continued to go to the show every year until they stopped having it, but my best memory was my first one when I was eleven.

My sister introduced me to the mosh pit, which was fucking nuts. I was fine at first, but then the music picked up, and it got crazy. I was slammed around like a goddamn pinball. My shoe fell off, and I got knocked all over hell trying to pick it up. My sister, who was sixteen at the time, jumped in and started pushing big-ass dudes out of the way, saying, "Get the fuck off of my brother!"

Nobody would fuck with her. She must have been terrifying, but she cleared me a spot. I got my shoe, and she escorted me to safety. I love her. This is when I learned if you have to or want to get somewhere in a crowd like that, you have to be an asshole. I like to go to the stage and actually see the performers, so in that situation, all ethics go out the window. Push women and children. Try not to knock them down but plow through everyone equally. Then you make it where you wanted to go, and no one gets hurt. They just think you are an asshole, but who cares? You don't know those people. I don't think I have been to a show once where someone didn't plow through the crowd like that, and when they hit me, I just say, "What the fuck?" and continue to watch the show; it doesn't ruin my night.

This also reminds me of the music that we listened to in the '90s. It was so fucking depressing; I cannot believe more people did not commit suicide. That would come later in life. Most were friends of friends that I smoked weed with but I was not super close to. That doesn't make it any less tragic, but it also did not make me lose any sleep. The first was the brother of a school friend. We didn't hang out outside of school, but he was a good kid. His brother hung himself in the woods right by a good friend of mine's house with a belt on a branch that was shorter than he was. This means he was very committed to committing suicide, and I have no idea what his issues were. I just gave his brother a hug and said, "I am sorry."

Another friends brother would later die of an overdose, which seemed be on purpose, but I don't know as did a handful of other people that I knew. I swear my high school has the highest suicide rate in the country. There were two whom I considered good friends. They had both spent the night at my house more than a few times, and we were on good terms. Some suicides do not surprise you, and some just come out of nowhere, and you don't expect it and start blaming yourself and wondering what more you could have done to stop this from happening.

One was a good buddy whom I knew was kind of fucked in the head, but I did not think he would do anything like he did. He simply started his car in the garage with every door closed. There was no ventilation, and his car windows were down. His dad found him too late. I assume he went peacefully, but it is still sad.

Like I said, in hindsight, I wish I would have known that something was up because I would have done whatever I could to help him. He was a grade above me, and I'm not sure if he graduated, but after he left high school, I only saw him at parties or whatever. The same goes for the second one, whom I considered a good friend. I am not sure if he graduated either, but he was also a grade above me. After high school, I didn't see him too much. I knew he was into some dirty shit, but I did not know to what extent. I know that he had more than a few guns, and at some point, there was a warrant out for his arrest. He was facing thirty-plus years, and they came to pick him up. He ended up running and apparently got somewhat cornered in the woods. So rather than go to jail, he shot himself in the head, sad.

There were even that I just heard that they had done it, just not how—once again, fucking sad. Everyone has bad days, but you have to look on the bright side. If you tough it out, there is bound to be a day down the road that is much, much worse. That is not funny, but it is true. There will be good days as well. "Just focus on those days" is my advice. I could personally never attempt suicide because I feel like I would not pull it off. If you are trying to off yourself because you feel like a failure in life, what happens to you when you even fail to kill yourself? That would be me, and I wouldn't know where to go from there.

Seventh grade. In junior high, you had to take an instrument or choir. I chose to play the trumpet. I was okay, but I hated lugging it back and forth to school every day, so I dropped it for choir. I was put into the "changing voices baritone section" with one other big-ass black dude. We later became friends, and he became the first Black Cat—that was actually his cat name. I have a deep voice, and I can't sing for shit unless it is some Barry White or something. The teacher literally told me that my voice was too deep, and I couldn't sing for shit, and I got kicked out. I was told to just quit and take study hall. The big brother did not get kicked out.

Later that year came my first school dance. I was awkward and had no possibility of pulling any tail even if I paid for it. I was just getting into drugs and whatnot so I was open to anything. I found out about some shit people were doing, which was basically drinking a bunch of Tussin (cough syrup) and tripping balls. About ten years later, thirty-six Mafia came out with a song called "Sippin' on Some Syrup" or something like that about drinking this Robitussin with soda and getting all fucked up.

They were not playing around. That shit gets you crunk, and I didn't even know what that meant at that age. You have to get the DM formula because anything else is a waste of time. I did that, and it sucked, but at this one seventh grade dance, I drank me a ginormous bottle of the DM, and I swear it was comparable to any horrible acid trip I have ever had, maybe worse. I remember drinking it in the bathroom and ending the night in that very same room and stall. I did not stop there. A fat friend of mine whom I would rob cars with who was an extreme kleptomaniac would steal Drixoral, which had the same necessary ingredients to get you fucked up, and you didn't have to drink the nasty cough syrup ish. We did that shit way too much. At the height of our use, I was able to swallow an entire package of gel caps in one swallow. That is not cool, and I am not proud of myself for accomplishing that sad horrendous capability. I look back and down on myself at where I was at in my life before I was even old enough to drive. I was a fuck-up, no doubt about it.

I played middle linebacker for the school, and I was pretty fucking good. I was a big boy and had weight to spare. In other words, I was fat with glasses, and if I remember correctly, my hair was fucked eight ways from Sunday. In the fall, I was riding my bike around the block, and I hit an acorn. I could have avoided it so easily, but I ran straight into it and flew over the handlebars. And did my patented "jelly roll" down the street, breaking my arm in a couple of places and the hooked me up with really sweet cast from my fingers to my shoulder. The school let me continue to play football for some reason, probably because I was fucking awesome, but in the first game, the opposing team said that I was using my cast as a weapon and they kicked me out of the game and eventually off the team. Fuck them, I was good!

I found a new sport, which came with a new lifestyle. I turned into a grungy skater fuck and embraced it to the fullest. I wore the baggiest pants and had every color hair under the rainbow. Once I dyed my hair purple, and my mom paid my sister to spike my shampoo with peroxide to get rid of the color. That way, she wouldn't have to feel guilty about doing it herself. This backfired because my hair was purple, and the peroxide just faded it until it ended up pink. I will never forgive her for that.

Skating completely changed my life. I dropped a ridiculous amount of weight, shaved my head, pierced my ears, and was an entirely new person. I later discovered and fell head over heels for my first love—sweet, sweet chronic. I, along with a few buddies, was curious and wanted to give it a try, so I asked the one person whom I trusted and I knew had access to the magical herb, my sister. She picked us up from school and brought us a *J*. We drove around smoking, and I was hooked.

Unlike a lot of people, I actually did not get stoned my first, second, third try. It was the twentieth time when I first got a taste of being high as shit, and I flipped my lid. I remember it well. I stole a joint of Mexican red hair from my sister and my friends, and I smoked it after school at my house because there were never any parents there. I got plastered, and I remember running around in a daze, feeling like I was on some kind of goddamn roller coaster.

One of my friends was drooling and shouting the same thing over and over. I had tripped on LSD previous, and I also experienced colors, melting walls, and sound that I knew were not there. Before long, it was dark out, and my mom came home. I am a pro now, but back then, my mom had to have noticed because I can only imagine I appeared borderline retarded. This was the year that I first tried powders. It was not my intention, but I called a neighborhood cat who was a well-known pothead and asked him for some grass. He drove his boat across the lake and picked me and my buddy up. We went back to his house and smoked. I grabbed some weed, and before he brought us back, he asked if we would want to try something. I said, "Sure, what the fuck?" My friend did not. I saw it and assumed it was cocaine, but I was wrong. This was my first lesson about why not to assume anything. It was speed, and I think I was up for the rest of the weekend.

I later tried coke and found that to be more enjoyable. At least it doesn't make you bite your lips and tweak out. I still enjoy that on occasion if it is free, but I don't mess with that crystal. I have seen it severely fucked up the lives of some good friends. I was also "turned on" to the world of LSD, which I continued to enjoy well into college but no longer indulge in. I did research into it as I do any drug I have tried and learned of the idea of flashbacks. My dumbass was like, "Hey, I like this stuff. If I do enough of it, I can have free trips the rest of my life." Bad idea, because I am pretty sure that it worked.

I discovered the magical world of mushrooms that summer, so much so that I tattooed one on my chest. You can't see it anymore because I turned into some kind of hairy ape over the years, but it is still there. I also tattooed a cross on my hand that I have to look at every time I reach for something. My best bud has one, too. What do you expect? We were twelve. We saw how people in prison did there tats, and I G'd some India ink from science class, and we did them ourselves. Hindsight is 20/10. Fuck 20/20…it is always easier to make the right decision after you have already made the wrong one. That is hindsight. I had a couple of girlfriends, but nothing came of it, at least I did not get to cum. But I would not be thwarted;

I would not give up until I got some action, just like every teen movie ever made.

I had my first encounter with the police this year, and it couldn't have gone worse. I had a friend sleeping over, and we decided to go outside and smoke some weed and then watch a movie. At this point in my weed career, I thought you were supposed to dip out and kind of hide to smoke it. Little did I know that the rules are the exact opposite. If you go and hide, people think you are up to something, which is what happened to us. However, if you just walk down the street, smoking a joint, no one is gonna say shit. Plus by the time anyone notices, you are already down the road. I have since smoked a spliff (a cigarette with weed in it), standing next to a cop, and I could see him smelling the air and looking around for the culprit, but I was right there.

When we got busted, someone had called the police because we went behind the apartment garages and they thought we were stealing. The cops nabbed us and took our smoking utensil which happened to be made out of one of my mom's old inhalers. They brought us back to my house, told my parents what we were doing, and showed my mom the makeshift pipe and asked her if it looked familiar. I will never forget the look on my mom's face. I got in a world of trouble, but it is kind of hard to enforce punishments when you are never there, so nothing really changed for me, but I did have to do some community service.

That summer, I got my next big injury. I was skateboarding on a "fun box" that I made with my dad. I did a nose slide, and when I came off, my ankle got cut by the metal edge. The entire back of my ankle was opened up like a bag of chips. It severed the tendon, and my foot was flopping around like a dying fish. I ended up with a butt-load of stiches and was skating in two weeks.

My sister had dropped out of school and wanted to get the fuck out of the house and do her own thing even though she was only like sixteen. At this time, my dad was getting the boot and got a duplex in East Side Saint Paul, so my sister shacked up with him. She was always really close to our dad. My sister lived on the lower level, and our dad was the grumpy old drunk man upstairs. My stoner friends and I would go over there sometimes and just hang out and do I-don't-remember-what, but I do remember that it was a place we could smoke weed openly inside, and it was all gravy. It was nice because even though my sister lived there for a long time, in every memory I have of the duplex, it is butt-ass freezing Minnesota winter. Smoking inside was a luxury.

The old man upstairs wasn't going to do shit, fuck him. She would have some of her friends over, but mostly her Mexican Gangster Disciple boyfriend. He was older and did seem really gangster at the time, but in hindsight, this guy was a fucking joke. He would always brag about gangster shit and tried to teach us the rules of the game. What real gangster is trying to recruit a bunch of fourteen-year-old white skater kids? Times must have been rough in the hood back then. I went with my sister to pick up the thuggy dun from his dad's house, and it was sketchy from the beginning. My sister did not want to go get him. I thought it was because it was really cold, but I would later learn that it was because the gangster's dad was a batshit crazy drugged-up nutcase. I went to the door and asked for the asshole, and his dad, who was clearly high as fuck, told me that he could go out for a minute but I had to wait in there with him. I was fucking terrified. I thought we were picking the douchebag up; I didn't know he was on house arrest. So I was being held hostage as collateral for the gangbanger. This guy was not right, and I just kept staring out the window with my fingers crossed. It was a very scary situation. That fucker came back, and I ran to the car. I don't remember what happened, but I am pretty sure I yelled at my sister—that sounds like something I would do.

This is when I first got interested in art. My friend's brother and his friends were all doing graffiti, so we obviously thought that was cool. We started by tagging. Everyone always had a fat black marker on them; eventually, we moved up to spray paint. We still tagged but moved up to murals. I remember the first that I did, the friend I got busted smoking with slept over again, and we had accumulated a lot of paint and colors. We had everything planned out so we could finish it and be out of there in record time. It was right on a busy road, so time was crucial. I made a STC piece that was about eight by ten feet doing all the lines, and then my friend helped me fill in all of the colors. It was beautiful and stayed up for a few weeks. What is funny about this is that friend went on to become one of the most skilled graffiti artists I have ever seen. It put me to shame.

However, I was still into art in a big way as far as I was concerned. It was a class that was fun and easy A and a class that you could get stoned ass beforehand and it would just make it more fun. I was right and did had a great time. I was in a few shows but never happy with my work; nothing was ever good enough. I did eventually decide that it was what I wanted, to go to college, not realizing that you really cannot do dick with an art degree.

This is also around the time I began carjacking with a buddy of mine, who to no surprise turned into somewhat of an unfavorable person to say the least. We did not pull people out of their cars and steal them; we simply walked around the neighborhood and went into unlocked cars, grabbed anything we saw, and moved on to the next one. It was mostly just CDs and money. Every once in a while, we would find some random cool shit. We jacked a ton of CD players, and once we got the subwoofers and amp too. One time, the person had a loaded bowl and a little bag of weed; it wasn't real good, but it was a nice find. I smoked that whole bowl in their car in their driveway; I was a fucking moron.

Later that night, I think we set off an alarm and then started hearing police sirens. We decided to go our separate ways. He was pretty close to his house, so I'm sure he had no problem getting there, but I had much further to go. I had to cross train tracks, a river, and a highly populated street that actually has the highest number of different jurisdictions, Saint Paul, Roseville, Maplewood, Ramsey County, and state troopers, not to mention that the K-9 training center for damn near the whole state is just a couple of blocks away. I bet they can smell my weed policing the area of anywhere in the state. There are five different forces that police the intersection by my house. I was crossing the train tracks, and a big truck drove down the road, shining a spotlight down the tracks. They shined it right on me. I ran my ass off and jumped down the trench into the river which was about ten inches deep. I threw everything in my pockets and lied down in the river. I kept my head up just enough to have my nose and mouth out of the water, and I would lay there perfectly still for at least forty-five minutes, maybe an hour. All the while, the police were on the tracks, shining lights when they would come close. I would go down and hold my breath and try to be quiet. I could hear dogs, too, but they didn't find me. When they got past me, I crept out at a snail's pace. As soon as I got to the top of the embankment, I took off like an Olympic athlete past numerous police cars, trailing water to right where I was, but I'm not stupid, so I ran onto grass as soon as I could to hide my trails. I no longer steal or commit crimes of any kind.

Eighth grade. We would go to First Avenue on Sunday for the all-age dance party. It was a place that a thirteen-year-old could go and smoke a pack of cigarettes inside the club with no issue and possibly sneak a drink if you were so inclined. I did exactly that and went out to dance and ran into my first young harlot. She was fifteen, which is only a two-year difference, but to a thirteen-year-old, it was like hooking up with an adult. We danced for a while, and somehow, she grabbed me and pulled me into a gap between two machines and mouth-fucked me. I instantly grew a pair and threw my hand down her drawers. I had no fucking idea what I was doing; all I knew at this point was that you are supposed to finger them, so I did, like I was digging for treasure. That is not the way to do it, but I was clueless. We swapped numbers, and she eventually took a bus with a friend of hers from about an hour and a half away with her friend. We met up and went to my room, hung out, and listened to music burning incense because that was cool in the '90s. Her friend fell asleep, so we started messing around and then just went to town. There was only my futon in my small-ass room, so we were right next to her, but we proceeded, and she deflowered me there with her best friend lying right there. I can remember looking at her as I was doing the damn thing for the first time. It was everything I had hoped it would be, and I wanted more.

Now I was on the hunt, and I wanted a hot cheerleader-type girl, and I found one who I approached with extreme confidence and landed her. She was an innocent girl, cute, and that was the beginning of my search to become the virgin surgeon. I succeeded in my first endeavor and we were together for a little bit, but I wanted more. I set my sights on the hottest girl in school, and somehow, I managed to get her to come along for a ride as well. She was innocent at the time as well as a cherry, but I took care of that. We were actually a couple for a long time, which is about four to five months at that age. We eventually broke up, but it ended up bad for me for no reason of my own. The person she dated after me was real pissed off because I got the honey pot and he could not.

In the summer that year, I went to a local party spot and got plowed, literally. I drank two 40-ounce, which is a lot for a thirteen-year-old, and someone asked me if I wanted to go smoke some herb, so I followed, as I would today. Then behind me, I heard someone say, "Hey, bitch," and to this day, I do not know why I turned around and started to respond, only to a giant fist that literally made me do a 360 and fall on my face. This was not the first person, and I was told there was a third. I later found out that one of them was also doing it because I was racist. I find comical because one of their mutual friends, who is black, picked me up and carried me over a mile to bring me to where this Mexican cat's car that was already waiting for me and who properly drove me to the hospital. This was a good thing because one or all of them jumped and stomped on my leg until they had broken all three bones going to my foot. So that was fucked, and I had to wear a full leg cast the entire summer, from my foot to my balls. On top of that, I got two black eyes, a broken nose, some broken ribs and cheekbone, and a lovely Nike shoeprint on my chest that stayed there for over a week or so. What is fucked is earlier that year I went to a rave (fright night) on Halloween with one of the kids whom I actually thought was a good friend. It would be the first time I did ecstasy as well as a copious amount of coke, and it was the first time I did nitrous oxide. That was fun. I could hear myself losing brain cells. I was really surprised he would do something like that.

I was down but not out. I hobbled around with my crutches wherever the posse was going, even long distances, and could run on my crutches fast enough to get away from the police, which happened, but that is a different story that will never be told. I never pressed charges because I was good friends with the main guy, and we still are which is weird, but I am a very forgiving person. I knew that if I did, I would have a red flag on my head for the rest of high school. I went out to parties, and I met a girl, a well-known virgin who was said to be unbreakable, but I broke her in. Regardless of the giant cast on my leg and the fact that it is a well-known faux pas to mess around with your friend's ex, I did that, too, about a week later. We dated for a bit, but it did not bother the hanging-earing boy. He didn't care, and it didn't last. This was also the year that I was first held up at gunpoint. My friends and I were walking to a friend's house to grab some herb, and this thuggy dun stopped me out of everyone and told me to run my shit. I was able to do the trick where you keep everything in your pocket and pull out the liner. It looks like you emptied your pockets although you hadn't. Unfortunately, I had a clip on my pager that you could see, and the motherfucker robbed me for it. My mom did not want me to have one because, in her words, they were only for pimps and drug dealers. I guess she was right because it got me a 9 mm pointed at my temple. When someone has a gun to your head, just do what they say, don't try to analyze the gun to see if it is real and then tell them to fuck off, you might regret it.

 Ninth grade. After my ass-whooping, I was no longer allowed in the school district I had attended my whole life. I was told that they knew about the incident and that it was the result of a drug deal gone bad, which is complete bullshit. I did not deal drugs at that time; I might have middle-manned a few transactions for personal gain, but I was not a dealer. Eventually, that would change. No public school would take me because they had heard about me somehow. In fact after being denied for all the private schools as well, we found one that would take me, but fuck, it was a Catholic school, so they have to be accepting, right? I was not very accepted for the most part, so every day for lunch, I would grab an apple and read in the library about drugs. I wanted to know everything because I wanted to have fun. This is what eventually turned me on to Hunter S. Thompson and unconventional journalism in general.

It is good to know what you are putting into your body before you do it. This is why I never have nor will I ever use any intravenous drugs. However, sometimes ecstasy (MDMA) is cut with heroin and/or speed, and I've done that a million times, but I will never pop a vein. I don't. It was an interesting atmosphere because it was a small school and everyone had been going to school together since kindergarten, and I was fresh fish. This meant that all the girls were into me, possibly because I was the bad boy, but that made all the other boys want to kick my ass. I was cool with that.

I remember in math class, the one black girl in the school, obviously wearing a plaid skirt, turned to face me and spread her legs, showing me the whole shebang. She must have been planning it for some time. I knew she liked me, but damn. I still wish I would have hit that. I started to flip weed at school because for some reason people came to me to see if I knew how to score any. It didn't take long to realize I should just buy a quantity, move it, smoke for free, and maybe make a few bucks. I would use a hand scale and weigh it out in front of them to show that it was all kosher, but I used my ring finger to tip the scale to add a gram or two that goes in my pocket. I met one friend out of that who was cool, and I saw him recently, but I couldn't bring myself to look at him because I had boned his baby's mama repeatedly.

I felt like a douche. Fucking an ex is one thing, but you don't bang your buddy's baby mama. I continued to do what I do, flirt and be hated, so it was only a matter of time before someone wanted to squab. Apparently, this one cat's old lady had a thing for me, and he was not cool with that. It was presented to me like some shit from a movie or old TV show where I was told to be at the bleachers right after school to have at it. I do not like to fight, although I do have a black belt, which don't mean dick when you get jumped from behind by multiple parties by the way. Either way, I tried to avoid the situation and got on my bus, but they somehow knew where I was, and four of them got on the bus and more or less forced me off.

I was nervous because I was alone and Capitan Dipshit had four friends with him, so if I whoop his ass, his buddies are gonna jump me. So we had at it, the one truly fair fight I have ever been in. It was clear that no one was going to win, so I stopped and said, "Look, if this is going to take forever, I'm gonna have a smoke." So I lit up my Newpimp and smoked a onie, and he said, "Fuck it, I'm done too."

I actually ended up hanging out with them later on. I actually went to a few parties with them. One of which I was able to pull off another first. She was a hockey player, but in fact probably the hottest girl in my grade, not what you would picture if you thought of a girl hockey player, petite, cute face. I went to a "party" if you could call it that, and I ended up being pulled into a side room to make out. Fuck that, I dropped the drawers and had at it. The entire party was literally inches away, and there was a hole in the wall (it was in an unfinished basement), and I remember watching these poor depraved Catholics attempt to dance, and I railed her from behind. What a way to lose your innocence, huh? Poor girl.

It was around this time that I realized that I was something that girls might actually want, and I did not need to put as much effort into pursuing them. I was at my buddy's house, and he had a sister who was extremely attractive. I had been friends with this kid for a very long time and always had a crush on his sister. She was so fucking hot. For some reason one day, she pulled me into her room and started making out with me violently, and I was blown away. After that, I felt like I could conquer any female that I desired.

I got my first real job at this time. I had been a paperboy and a busboy, but this job kicked ass. I worked at a meat store for lack of a better term. They had really good meat, but they eventually got bought out, and you can only buy their frozen meals in certain convenience stores. I did everything from the register, which was a first for me and stocking the freezer; I would even cut up and weigh out meats for distribution. I got the job through neighborhood kids who were about four grades above me, but I had known them my whole life, riding bikes and whatnot.

It was awesome. I can clearly remember one time while working the register, Ponytail from the neighborhood came and took over, telling me that I had to go to the back immediately by the door. I had no clue what the fuck he was talking about, but there was kind of a big line, so I was cool with that. When I got to the back, there was a huge chunk of hash burning and a cup filled up with smoke. We would put a chunk of hash on a push pin or any kind of pin and light it up, then cover it with a drinking glass and wait until it filled with smoke. You lift up the corner of the cup, suck it up, and get dusted off your ass. That was a nice surprise. I smoked the whole chunk, which was probably worth about twenty dollars. He was busy, and the hash was burning. I wasn't going to let it go to waste.

I ran all around that place and was climbing in the rafters that day. I had fun. I basically just cut up meat, weighed it out, ran the register, and then got really high, and played like a kid in a candy store for the rest of the day in back. There was an old lady that worked there, and she was so sweet. I worked with her all the time, and she was just so kind-hearted it was like working with your grandmother. She knew that we were always fucking around, but she just turned a blind eye to it and was such a sweetheart. She is probably dead now; that sucks. She was a good woman.

I remember that on the first and second of the month, the store was always overrun with people spending their food stamps. This was the money paid for with tax dollars that was intended to feed their family for a month, but that is not how they would use it, and they would always buy the same shit. It was like the first of the month was time to stock up for the block party with the staples like ribs and burgers but they would always load up on the expensive shit like lobster and shrimp. I am not labeling anyone, but it was always either a big fat black woman or a thuggy-looking black man, and they would both always have gold all over—gold rings, watches, more necklaces than any one person needs, and then they would take their free food, which the taxpayers paid for to their Cadillac in the parking lot. That money is intended for people who are truly in need, not drug dealers. Like I said, I am not judging, but I know one when I see one, and the majority of these people did not need any assistance whatsoever. I would actually get happy when I would see people come in who were clearly poor, buying staple foods that were clearly to feed their family. It made me happy and gave me a little more faith in humanity.

I got my longtime friend a job their when Ponytail quit and went to college or some shit, but it was awesome. We worked together all the time because I had to train him in, and we just fucking clowned around the whole time. We would have food fights in the freezer with all the individual frozen items, and one time, I got done dirty. I was not looking, and he said something, so I looked up. When I did, I got a one-pound frozen lasagna to the face at warp speed. He lived in the trashy apartments across the street from me that was also just across the parking lot from the shop. He could get there in two seconds, but it took me a few minutes. That doesn't sound like much, but the boss, who also had the same name as me, was a real hard-ass. He basically told me that he only needed one of us, and since I always stumbled in a few minutes behind my buddy, he was going to keep him, and he canned my ass. That's when I hooked up with another neighborhood kid and got a job at the liquor store on the other side of the street in the ghetto.

    I met a new friend around this time who lived right across the street, but I don't remember exactly how I began talking to her, but if I remember correctly, she initiated the conversation. She lived by herself and was very independent and basically intimidating, not to mention the fact that she was fucking gorgeous. You could see my house from her window, and she said that she noticed me mowing my lawn and saw that I wore baggy pants, so she figured I would be cool. I am glad that she did. She would hook me up weed and acid all the time and would go hang out with her all the time until one day shit changed. Some friends and I went over to her place to but some acid. We dropped the acid and just hung out at her place because there was never a parental figure there, and the possibility of one coming around was 0 percent.

    The dose kicked in, so we went outside to enjoy it. I remember at one point when we were smoking out one of my friends was tripping balls, and I remember the incident so well because he had a very distinct voice and way of speaking. Unfortunately, years later, he would kill himself, but these were happier times. He was high as fuck now on top of the acid, and he was looking at my other friend, a neighborhood kid. He said, "Dude, you look like a big fucking buffalo."

He was a boy of generous proportion, so that was funny enough, but then the big boy put his fingers up on his head and charged him like a bull. I know I was high as hell among various other intoxicating substances, but that shit was fucking hilarious. It was almost twenty years ago, and he still remembers it. We talked about it today, and he laughed his ass off, remembering it vividly as well as the memory of our friend who is no longer with us. I was tripping my ass off at this point, and it felt like I was in a completely different world even though I could see my house right across the street. I knew my mom was out of town, and I had nothing to worry about, but anytime I looked at my house, I would get this impending feeling of terror that almost sent me into a bad trip. She kept me calm, and I was having a great time, then as all my friends were fucking around and doing God-knows-what, she pulled me aside. She began pushing me and talking shit, trying to get me to fight her.

She was a feisty one and had a reputation for just that around the neighborhood. I did not know this when I met her. I just thought it was a really hot girl that happened to live across the street. I did not know she had a cult following for being a cute girl that would knock you out in a heartbeat. She kept fucking with me and would not stop until I punched and eventually fought her. I was way too high for this. I was seeing all types of crazy shit, and then this hot bitch who I did have a big crush on was pushing me and telling me to punch her in the face. I was unbelievably confused and scared as hell. I could feel myself falling to the dark side, which is a horrible place to be on LSD because some people never come back from that.

I was terrified and looking though a world of trippy-ass colors and weird shit at my friends playing around across the field, and I remember thinking, *Why aren't they helping me? I am going to have to fight this girl.* My heart was beating uncontrollably, and I thought I might wig out. This is when she grabbed me by the head and kissed the fuck out of me. Maybe it was the acid or the fact that I really wanted to kiss her anyways and she was too intimidating, but that kiss did more for me than ten orgasms with ten different girls. It was amazing. I still say fuck her for doing it that way. If she wanted to kiss me, she should have just done it. She didn't need to scare to shit out of me first because that shit was traumatizing.

We started hanging out a lot together quite a bit, which was nice, except she had some crazy ex-boyfriend/friend that apparently knew about me and was not happy about it. I only knew him by name. I had no clue what he looked like, so it was like being told the invisible man wants to kick your ass. I finally did see this guy who had been built up to be this big badass, and I laughed my fucking ass off. Either way, we got more than chummy and started messing around all the time. I would occasionally sleep over at her apartment. I don't know why we didn't just sleep at my house if my mom was out of town, but I guess it was fun to sleep somewhere else for some reason.

I remember going to the lake with her. I don't remember which on because there are kind of a lot of them in Minnesota, but it was a body of water with a lake. I do remember that she brought me a six-pack of Rolling Rock, and before I had even finished them, I was plowed, but I guess I was still a young buck. I remember swimming with her, and I remember making out and groping like we were teenagers. Oh wait, we were teenagers, so it was okay. I do not advise making out in public lakes. In hindsight, it is pretty fucking gross. Little did I know I would do much worse later on in life.

I only remember that day swimming because when we got out, I put my shirt on, which was white, and she hugged me with wet tits as if that was acceptable. I guess it was a new suit because she left a perfect copy of her boobs and bikini on my shirt. I kept that shit because at that point it was pretty cool. Later on, I would learn that things left behind like underwear is not that cool. One other memory from this time period with her was her getting me out of a minor consumption charge and contributed to the reason she sometimes intimidated me.

We were drinking at a park with a bunch of her friends, which reminds me, it is very difficult to date a girl whose only friends are guys. No matter how confident you are, that shit will drive you batshit crazy because no matter how much you trust her, you can never trust him, and it never goes away. The party got busted, and she just calmly walked away from the group, which was large. She made a big circle and walked up to the area, saying hello to the police because she was clearly not a part of the party. She walked up to me, kissed me on the cheek, and said, "When I say go run quietly to that tree, then run west, and I will pick you up at the end of the street." It was like some shit from a movie, but it totally worked. She pulled up and picked me up the second I got to the end of the street. That was another cool thing about her.

She had a jeep and would drive me wherever whenever. Nothing ever happened sexually at that point, and in hindsight, I know that is because I was not confident enough. We actually dated for a while when I was in college, and that bridge got crossed. Goddamn, she was tight. She even bought me a $100 pair of headphones for my turntables; I still use them. We had a falling out because she always wanted to go out. I don't understand the point of going to the bar just to go to the bar. If you are going to meet people, that is different, but I don't want to go pay ten dollars for a drink and just sit and talk when I can do that at home for much less, and no one has to drive. This was one of the first times that I realized I was getting old, and even though she was older than me, I just wasn't feeling it, to go out and party every night. I could feel the gray hairs growing.

Back to ninth grade, this is when I had my first pregnancy scare. It was another Catholic schoolgirl. I don't know, there is something about the little plaid skirts that makes me want to stick my toe up their butt. She was a Cambodian chick that loved to give head. I'm cool with that, but the one of the times I boned her, she got knocked up. I immediately remembered what a friend's brother told me once that Highway 35E goes straight to Mexico; I was planning on it. Luckily, she took care of it, and I felt like I was given a new life. I did not talk to her after that because she was far too fertile. I remember, only a couple of names, but I did learn the fun of "Tig-Ol_Bitties." Sometimes I write "BassAkwards" but I guess that is what happens when you are born feet first. She loved to bone; she had a car. She was twenty-one, and she would buy me liquor—not just buy it but pay for it. She had a pool and loved to fuck in it. She blew my mind when we were messing around, and she told me to grab a popsicle. I had no idea why, but I just went and got it. When I handed it to her, she sucked it and then jammed it in her business, took it out, sucked it, and did it again until it was gone. However, before it was gone she held it in her mouth for a bit then gave me a frozen BJ. Never had one before. It was scary at first and then very nice. It is always worth it to try new things.

The Cat Crew Begins & The Virgin Surgeon is Born

This was the year that that the Cat Crew started up. It was me, and all the boys, started by the earring boy-girl and another cat. It was pretty much just a joke, but everyone began to refer to us as the Cats. You had to be "scratched into the crew," and that means exactly what it sounds like, pretty dumb. Then we each got names and ranks. I was Krazy Cat, third in command, just under my brother. There was one course that we all had to take in ninth grade that I hated, but I would later learn that it was the most beneficial class I would ever take all throughout high school. That was the typing class, because I was at a shitty Catholic school we had to take the course on typewriters so we could not fix any mistakes and they were very strict. It always comes in handy, and I probably would not have ever turned anything on time in college if I did not pay attention in that class.

Every day after school, my friends would take the school bus routed to my house and meet me there because I got out earlier and there were no parental figures ever. One day, they brought over a new friend; he was our first Ecuadorian. We typically listened to the normal '90s shit, which looking back is so fucking depressing I am surprised that more people did not off themselves then. I still like that music, but this cat who had the cutest accent introduced us to Wu-Tang. We listened to hip-hop, but it seemed to open new doors, at least for me it did. He is still the reason why when my dogs fuck up, I put them on "punishment," because I thought it was funny when he would say he could not leave the house because he left the toilet seat up, or something really stupid like that, and his mom put him on punishment. Unfortunately, he got deported. By which, I mean his dad had a new job opportunity, and he had to move. No worries, there was another to fill his shoes.

This leads me to the next virgin, who was a real hottie at the time. Later she kinda fell off. However, one day I remember the busload along with her came over to kick it. I think we were dating. We were listening to Wu all types of loud, and we dipped out to my room, and I proceeded to take her flower with "Wu-Tang Clan Ain't Nuttin' Ta Fuck Wit." Another beautiful loss of innocence. However, later on, this proved to piss someone off. Apparently, they were best friends, but he had a wicked crush on her. Once again, I am in a situation due to boning a girl that someone else really wanted. Well, they should have stepped up to the plate. I did, but he was not happy. We happened to meet at the state fair, and he and his crew followed me and mine around forever because he wanted to fight. I was not on board because I had pounded two 40-ounces before the fair, smoked a bunch of cheeba, and was plowed. I tried to tell them that I couldn't fight then and it would be unfair. Not to mention the fact that he was like six inches taller than me and had a bigger crew.

I agreed to go in between some buildings and have at it. Both parties agreed that everyone would stay away except for my buddy who just came to make sure it didn't get out of control. I told my buddy I wasn't going to fight back. He said just to take one and fall down. I apparently forgot. I told him I wasn't going to fight, but if beating me up makes him feel like a big man, then go ahead. He clocked me in the grill pretty fucking hard, but I get hurt so much I brushed it off. He hit me again and again, but I would not go down. I had my hands at my sides. I looked over at my friend, and he signaled to me to just go down, so I did on the next punch, but I could have stood there all day. He kicked me a couple times and was talking shit, but clearly tired, I said, "Are you finished?" He kicked me again and said, "That's right, bitch." I laughed and said, "I hope you feel better about yourself." I got up, smoked a onie in the Bi-fi and got a corn dog.

Going to a Catholic school gave me a whole new outlook into the world of religion. I was baptized, went through Sunday school, and also got confirmed. I didn't actually go to the church where I was confirmed, but churches don't usually turn anyone away. I only went because every Wednesday there was nothing to do because everyone was at confirmation. I would go to confirmation with them even though I was not a member of the church, but I participated and learned if you can call listening to fairy tales learning. I only went because there was nothing else to do and everyone would get together beforehand and at break to smoke weed. The church people knew this and told this. They just said that they were just happy that we were there and paying attention. This began my interest in the mythology of religion.

I know that people who are religious do not like it referred to as mythology, but some of the most important stories of the Bible are scientifically impossible, and others are explainable through science, not divine intervention. When the plagues happened, frogs fell from the sky, and this was supposedly because God was pissed off and there is no other possible explanation for that happening other than an all-powerful being making it happen. Well, it has happened and has a scientific explanation. Tadpoles in shallow pools of water can be essentially lifted up into the clouds when the temperature, air currents, and other factors are just right, more or less the way water evaporates and goes up into the clouds, eventually falling back to earth. The tadpoles are so light that with the right conditions they can be brought up to the clouds as well. Once they matured and became heavy, they would fall to earth, and it literally appeared to be a rainfall of frogs, obviously brought on by God. However, it has happened in modern times and is scientifically explainable.

However, there are some fairy tales in the most published book of all time that I have a problem with and that every devout religious person just shrugs their head at and says, "No, this is how it happened," even though they had no way to prove it. I got detention for explaining my theory that went against everything they taught.

I will start at the beginning, which I might have mentioned earlier, and that is the story of Adam and Eve. If you accept the fact that Eve was created out of a single rib out of blind faith, that is fine, but that faith is exactly what it is called *blind*. If you have any idea how procreation and science works, you would know that for two people to repopulate the world is impossible. According to the Bible, they did procreate and had two children, both males. With only four people alive of earth and only one of them being a woman, not to mention the fact that they were all of one immediate family, there is no possibility to reproduce without the negative effects of incest. Either Adam or Eve had more kids, in which case they would just have more siblings, so in the end, the children would either have to procreate with each other or their parents. Either way, if that was the case, everyone on earth would be inbred, and we would not have lasted as long as we did. Not to mention the fact that in this theory, there is no plausible explanation for other races. Two Caucasians cannot have created an Asian child; it is simply impossible. The story of Noah upset me as well because three-hundred-plus cubits, which was the measurement of the supposed ark, could not physically hold two of every creature, and they would not possibly get along living in the same space. Once again, if it was of two of each creature, including humans, there would be no possibility of procreation without consequence.

My favorite discrepancy in the Bible actually got me in a lot of trouble because after I pleaded my case, they had nothing to say and gave me detention. I asked why I was getting in trouble because they could not prove the lies they were teaching us. The biggest one was about the origin of Catholicism, and that was the Virgin Mary. I proposed that she was nothing but a liar and that Catholicism was nothing more than a religion based on the Immaculate Conception. This was one woman who really stuck to her story, and people have believed her for thousands of years. Hypothetically, if your daughter came to you and told you she was pregnant but swore up and down that she had never had sexual intercourse, would you believe her? Hell no.

These are just three that I picked out, which are so obviously ridiculously fairy tales they were easy to explain. I got in a lot of trouble for proposing these theories, and I am convinced that it was because they could not prove me wrong, let alone prove their point, and that really pissed them off. I guess ignorance truly is bliss. This is the one reason why I can tolerate the Bible, which is that although it is a collection of made-up stories. If there is one good thing I can say about the good book, it is that these stories were created to teach life lessons, and if they managed to help some people live a better life, then they have served their purpose, and that is a good thing.

Tenth grade. At high school now and back with my friends. It was nice. All was forgotten, and my crew and I were well respected, except for the freshman kidnap, which was actually for the sophomores because we did not have freshmen at the school that year. I had no problems. I just hung out with the people that were supposed to be tying me up and hazing me. One of my good friends who got picked on all the time even though everyone went to him for herb got the worst that I saw. We had a little get-together at my house because my mom was out of town, which she always is. He brought over a paintball gun, and the older kids tied him to the tree by my driveway and shot the shit out of him. I thought the rules were that you just haze kids on school grounds; I guess I was wrong, but nothing ever happened to me. However, the next year, when freshmen were allowed at the school, we duct-taped the shit out of many kids.

There were many parties at my house at the time, and for some reason, I would tell like one person that my mom was out of town, my dad did not live there then, and at the end of the day at the spot, everybody met. It was yelled out loud, "Kegger at ——'s house, everyone invited!" People would show up, and shit got crazy. I cannot believe the cops didn't show up more often. One time we were all drinking outside, and we heard a noise that sounded like sirens, but it was a parade of the senior girls coming to the house. The first car stopped, and then the car behind it rear-ended it. All five or six cars ran into each other. They all jumped out in bikinis with little squirt guns because there was a war between the boys and girls. At this point, we heard another barrage of horns coming up, and it was the guys who came up with a big-ass bag full of Super Soakers, threw them down, and said, "Everyone grab one, let's get these bitches." Everyone grabbed one, filled up, and we soaked down the hoes. Everyone packed up and left. It was all over in less than a couple of minutes, and I remember looking around like, "What the fuck just happened?"

This was the year I met one of my friends whom I am still close with. He was a senior, but I was basically friends with everybody—dorks, jocks, and upperclassmen, whatever. I was invited to one of his farm parties, which were legendary. And it was fun as hell, just a bunch of drunken kids acting a fool on a farm in Wisconsin. I would continue to go to these parties whenever he had them even well after he graduated. The first couple of years went off without a hitch, but one year, the cops came, and many underage consumption tickets were handed out.

At this point in my life, I was in a tie for the most received by any of us with like eleven, not good. He grabbed me and pulled me into the cabin so I would not get into trouble. It was just me and the seniors in here. I felt privileged. They hid me and gave me some coke. It was awesome. We have been good friends ever since.

I also met another friend who would later become a lifelong friend who I truly love. He was our second Ecuadorian; he also had a cute accent, although he has lost a lot of it over the years. He is one of the nicest genuinely sweet guys I have ever known, but if you cross him, you better run for your fucking life because if you don't, you might be living the last seconds of it. I would go over to his house after school and just get stoned and listen to hip-hop.

One day I went across the street and jacked some beef jerky and candy because I was high and I was a hoodlum. When I got back, everyone wanted some, and I said, "Get back, you jackals," and I grabbed the biggest knife in the kitchen and started swinging it around like a goddamn samurai sword, cutting it into pieces for everyone. I damn near cut my finger off. It was long and really deep and was gushing blood. In fact, the blood actually squirted up to the ceiling and stained it. The bloody spot was still there when they moved out three years later. I ended up getting stitches and have a wicked scar on my index finger.

I am not a thief, but I do remember that it was around this time that I met up with some total fuck-ups, and I am pretty sure the only reason I was hanging out with them was to get some weed, but they were bad news, and I knew that. Either way, after we got herb and got high, one of them said that they had a stolen credit card and that we should go to the mall and buy a bunch of shit. This was well before identity theft, and they still used a roller and carbon paper to make a copy of the card, and they never asked for an ID. We went around and bought a ton of stuff. I was kind of the young buck of the group, so I only got a few things, but I stole a bunch while we were at it because I figured that if we got busted I would be fucked either way. So in the end, I got a bunch of stuff. Actually, in the end, I guess one of them fucked up at the register, and all I heard was, "Bail," and everyone started running. I was far behind, and the rent-a-cops were not far behind me. We made it out and away. I must say I would never do anything like this again.

I fell in love with snowboarding around this time. I was previously a skier, but around this time, snowboarding was the thing to do. I remember my first time, and I was riding, which in hindsight I can remember as being a big clunky piece of shit. If you strapped me onto it today, I could probably ride it all right, but it was no type of board to strap on a beginner. I rode the bunny hill for about an hour, and I said "Fuck it." I threw the board in the parking lot and rented some skies. Everything was so much cheaper back then and decided to do that for the rest of the day.

My board was obviously a big piece if shit that nobody wanted because it was still there. I brought it back home and would not give up, practicing on free hills that you had to hike back up to ride again. I got the hang of it, and eventually, Santa brought me a real board that I still use twenty years later. They started a ski club at the school, which I would go to later ever when I did not go to the school. I loved it and got so much better as well as the fact that I fell in love with the sport. I was in the club throughout high school and completely fell in love with snowboarding as well as the weekly trips to the hill. I cannot even remember how many girls I fucked around with on the ski-club bus, not to mention the fact that we brought booze and smoked weed in the back of the bus.

We got away with everything. I would continue to ride with my buddies just about every weekend, and my mom told me she would give me money to go snowboarding because I was doing something healthy and staying out of trouble. All we did is fuck around and get high. Later on, when we could drive ourselves, we would just go at night when it was cheap and pay for our own shenanigans. This is when I received my first snowboard injury. We were playing bordercross, which was not the same as the Red Bull or X Games version of the sport.

We would ride down the hill, and two people would face each other. You could slow down and switch your stance so you were on your good side. As long as you were facing each other, you had to go after the other one and try to take them down. I was pretty good at this game because I can ride both ways, but this time, I got fucked. I was faced off with my friend's sister, whom I always had a crush on, and we ended up riding down the hill, wrestling. We both went down, and I landed on the edge of her board with my leg. It hurt like hell, but I shook it off and kept riding. Years later, I would find out that it severed some of the muscle tissue in my lower leg, which resulted in it bulging up and creating a big bump in my leg right by my knee. I went to the doctor, and they basically told me that my muscles on that leg were fucked. They could take out the lump, but it would not make my leg work any better, and it would only be an operation for aesthetic purposes.

My next injury which happened in that same year was to the knee on the other leg. There was a big snowstorm, and school was cancelled, so a bunch of us got together to go riding. There was so much new snow, and there were not many hits or "jumps," so we built our own. The snow was very sticky; it was a perfect snowman or snowball consistency. I went first, and as I approached, the hit I came to an abrupt stop. However, my body kept going. This put all the stress on my left knee. It was dislocated. I could hear it, and it really sucked. Little did I know it would not be the last time I would have to do this. Since then, I have gotten it checked out, X-rayed, and other tests. They told me that I did a very good job resetting it for not being a doctor and probably saved myself from needing surgery. They told me that now it was still not aligned quite right and looked like a condition called runner's knee. I said, "You know what you're talking about, but I only run from the police, so let's just call it skateboarder's knee or snowboarder's knee."

I ended up hooking up with one of the older girls from one of the farm parties, and eventually, we got together every weekend to bone and nothing more. We would meet again later at the same location. I did, however, have my first experience with sleepwalking at this time. I was sort of dating her, and my friend that introduced me to Sage Francis was dating her friend. We went to spend the night at their dorm room. I have to say that I am glad that I would never go on to live in a dorm full-time; they fucking suck. We stayed there. We stayed on the top bunk, and my buddy and his old lady were on the bottom. This is also where my fear of bunk beds stems from. I fell out of bed in the middle of the night, walked around for a bit, then apparently, I jumped into bed on the bottom bunk directly in between my friend and his girl, and proceeded to snuggle with both of them. I have very little to no recollection of this, but all three of them remembered it in great detail.

This year, I had a teacher who was very important in my psychological development. He taught a speech class and was a really cool teacher. He seemed older at the time, but in hindsight, I think that he was like fresh out of college, which was maybe why he seemed so cool. My favorite memory was of one the end of the semester speeches we had to give. We could speak about whatever we wanted, but the speech needed to be at least ten minutes long. I fucked around and didn't do anything until the last day and in fact the last minute, literally. I had nothing to talk about, and I had an epiphany. I would talk for ten minutes about how to give a ten-minute speech when you are not prepared and have nothing to talk about. I just got stoned before class and talked my ass off like a drunk girl at a college party, and I was spectacular. I started by writing my name on the blackboard and explained in detail how doing this can take up valuable time and prolong your speech. By the time I was done writing my name, I was a minute into the speech and said, "Do you see that? I just spent one-tenth of my time, and I haven't said a damn thing." I saw my teacher smile, and I just went off and continued to ramble, but everything would always come back to my main point. It was completely scatterbrained and somewhat redundant, but I learned that as long as what you say supports your underlying thesis, it is relevant. It was this way of thinking that I would later use in my writing that allowed me to easily write papers that my teachers enjoyed, and I have never received less than an A on a paper.

I kept writing various things that I would say on the board and continue to waste time, but everything that I wrote would refer back to my main topic. By constantly repeating these points, I was wasting plenty of time while further justifying my main point. I ended up going over fifteen minutes and got cut off. I ended by saying to end up on a big note and go out with a bang, so I said, "I guess I'm done here, so let's all ditch next period and go to Taco Bell, I'm buying." I got a standing ovation, and the teacher said it was the best speech he had ever heard not only by an underclassman but overall in general. Needless to say, I received an A, and it changed the way I would write my papers. I found that I am a much-better writer when I am true to myself and simply write the way that I speak.

This was the year that I truly fell in love with snowboarding. I went to Colorado with a buddy to see his mom, but I just wanted to ride a real mountain, considering all that there is in Minnesota is hills. We rode like three times, and I was hooked. This is also when I got my gecko, which is still around somehow. He was about an inch and a half long and named Premiere. He was given to me two years later and renamed Mr. Bo Jangles.

At this time (even though I still had the same girlfriend), I was talking to a senior girl whom I had a bit of a crush on. We would hang out and do everything, like all types of weird drugs I had not read about. One was called the Dobber or something like that, and it was a powder that made you trip balls and had effects like ecstasy as well. That was really fucking fun! especially when you are with a girl that you can't believe would be sitting there naked, doing drugs with you and down to do everything else.

We would smoke herb and do a few lines of whatever. I was not opposed to speed at this point, but there were some crazy other crazy drugs I had no clue about but did them anyway because then we would make out like our plane was going down. I finally nailed it one night at a hotel party, and it was everything I thought it would be. One of her friends with huge tits walked in and kind of just stood there and watched us fuck. I was okay with it, but it was kind of weird. That was the one and only time, which is cool, because I have seen her since, and although she is still real hot, she is still into the powders. I can't deal with that.

It was this year that me and my father had a falling out. My best friend and I were drinking beer in my room. Maybe we were too loud, I don't know, but my dad came in and grabbed the case. He brought it to the sink and began to dump out the beer. My dad was a "recovering" alcoholic, but I knew that he was jealous that I was allowed to drink but he was not. I wasn't allowed to drink either, but I was sneaky. The only reason he busted us is because everyone can sniff out their own kind, and he knew what was going down. As he was wasting the perfectly good beer, my buddy tried to stop him and grab the beer, saying that it did not belong to us. This was true, but we were drinking it. My dad grabbed him by his throat, basically choking him, and all I could see was my brother being assaulted. I punched him in the side of the head, and then we wrestled. This went on for some time, and I'm not exactly sure how, but I ended up standing and my dad was on top of my friend, holding him down. Once again, all I could see was my brother being hurt, although my dad never touched him.

My buddy helped out when I was being fucked with, but as far as I can remember, he never struck my father. I snapped and stood over my dad and railed him in the head with both hands repeatedly. I remember getting my buddy out of the way and standing over my dad as he screamed for my mother to call the police. She did, and they were on their way. I kicked my friend out of the house and said, "Run the fuck home right now." I waited around because there was really nowhere to go. I got locked up for felony assault and battery and spent a week with some dude named Corndog, who got the name from stabbing someone with the stick from a state fair corn dog. Good times.

My dad eventually dropped the charges, and I know my mom made him do it, but whatever. I was on probation for some time, and we were not very nice to each other. In hindsight, I am really glad he dropped those charges and that nothing happed to my brother. That was pretty much the end of that year, but I remember having at it with at least two girls that summer. I don't remember exactly who, so I guess they were not that memorable.

My parents split up that year, which was an idea I had been promoting for a long time, and my mom finally accepted. My sister moved with him, so it was just me and Mom Dukes, who was gone about 90 percent of the time. I smoked a lot of pot at that house. It was a duplex, so my dad was upstairs, drinking his face off. Luckily, this didn't last forever, but he never stopped drinking, and we were still in the middle of our falling out.

My dad was also going a little batshit crazy around this time. In hindsight, I do believe it might have had something to do with the fact that he had quit drinking, yet he saw my little fifteen-year-old ass running all over hell, drinking my face off among other things and getting away with it while he was condemned to a life of sobriety. Once again, in hindsight, I totally understand now where he was coming from. However, this withdrawal eventually took its toll on him, and there were a few incidents, one of which I will never forget.

My dad served in Vietnam, and apparently, that eventually took its toll on him as well. I had asked him if he ever killed anyone, and he simply said that he did not know. It sounded like a lie to me. He said they would do flyovers and just fire rounds into various cities and he had no idea if he had injured or killed anyone, let alone women or children, and I think that got to him.

I was not in the shit as they called it or the frontlines, but I think randomly shooting at villages had an effect on him. One day, he freaked the fuck out and started screaming. He was yelling at my mom for something she never did, and she had no idea what the fuck he was screaming about. He ripped off all his clothes and ran around the house, screaming some random shit about the Vietcong. I can't remember exactly what he was rambling about, but it ended up with him lifting up the mattress and hiding in between it and the box spring and yelling, "You will never find me in here, you bastards." The police were eventually called, and he ended up in a mental facility. I did not know that this was a glimpse into my future, because I would eventually experience the exact same thing, except for the getting naked and yelling at the Vietcong. Mine would later be a much different situation.

Eleventh grade. This was the year that I met my first long-term relationship. We would exchange notes every passing period, and I fell in love with her instantly. This did not change the fact that I was a cheating asshole. There was more than I can't remember, but I know I did her dirty a lot, but she was the only one I cared about, and we are still good friends, and I still love her to this day and always will. She got booted out of the house at around fifteen. She would stay at random friends' houses, and I would usually come spend the night wherever she was. Otherwise, she would come stay at my house, which was cool because my mom was never there. I got accused of kicking her dog around this time, which is bullshit, because it was my friend that did it. That dog lived forever.

I needed a job, and I had a few neighborhood buddies worked at the local liquor store. I got started to work there, and there is no better job for an underage kid in high school total access to LQ. This is when I got my first real tattoo. It was to cover up a shitty one that I had done myself. I got it in Saint Paul with a fake ID. We had many a party at this time, and I think I tried everything in the store. I wasn't old enough to run the register, so I spent my time in the back doing stock or whatever.

I had sex in the storage room with about four different girls on the clock. Among those was one I met on a double date. A friend of my buddy who got me the job came to me one day and asked me if I would go hang out with him and this girl he just started dating. She was going to have a friend with her, and he wanted some support, just to go play cards or something stupid like that. I G'd some hooch and went with her even though I barely knew this cat. We played and drank for a bit, and I went outside to smoke a Black & Mild. When I came back in, the other girl was standing in the kitchen. She didn't say shit, but I swear I can smell pheromones, and I know when a girl wants to get down. So I didn't say shit either. I just walked up and grabbed her tits and started going at it. Huge tits, by the way, and a bangin' booty and a cute face. I wonder what happened to her.

We fucked right there in the kitchen with the other two a room away. The other one must have heard a good story because I got an invitation to play with both of them. I went out to big tits' house. The other one was super cute as well, along with being very well endowed. Goddammit, the size of these the tits on two who were quite fit was crazy, and they wanted to get down. So I grabbed some booze and went to her house. Bitch was rich as fuck. There was a goddamn half-pipe in her backyard for God's sake. So I spent the night and had my first three-way, which included the girl my buddy's buddy was trying to hook up with. So I got them both. Fuck, I wish I was still a teenager I was doing some straight-up XXX shit.

This year, I got my second taste of the mountains and fell deeper in love and knew where I wanted to go for college, not specifically, but I knew I wanted to be somewhere with mountains. This was for a school ski trip. My girlfriend was in the group, as well as a girl that I was good friends with, but what she didn't know is that I wanted to fuck her brains out. Well, it wouldn't happen on this trip. Unfortunately, we went to Salt Lake City, which I can only imagine is one of the lamest cities in the world. There are crazy laws, and you can only buy liquor for like a half an hour a day, two days a week. That is an exaggeration, but it seemed like that.

Luckily, we found the two people in Utah who were not Mormon and got them to get us some bottles of booze and some beer to last the week. It was tricky to get away with shit because the chaperones put my group of friends and me in the very last cabin far from the lodge and the other cabins, and they coincidentally had a cabin directly across from ours at the end of the resort. They could look right in our cabin whenever they wanted. Not to mention the fact that they would do random pop-in visits whenever they wanted as well. They wanted to bust us so bad, but they never did.

Some of our other friends were not so lucky; they did not even get a chance to go riding. They were not in the Cat Crew, but they were close friends in their own clique. They decided to roll a fat joint the second they walked in the door to their cabin. They didn't even go in a room; they just did it on the coffee table of the living room, so it would be the first thing you see when you walk in the cabin, fucking amateurs. They got deported back to Minnesota and had to buy new tickets, losing an ass load of money and probably getting their ass beat when they got home to their parents who were planning just one week free from those little bastards. Although the city and everyone there was pretty lame, the mountain (Snowbird) was awesome. We rode all day every day, and it was nothing but powder everywhere. It felt like floating or flying down this gigantic rock. We were also smoking some really good herb, and at this time, I still got high as a kite at times. Now it just kind of brings me back to normal and makes me hungry after a while.

This was also the year that I found another love, my love of floating down a giant cesspool in a tube. Some friends and I went down the Apple River in Wisconsin. I had been there the year before, but I did not know there was basically no age limit to bring a cooler full of beer down the river. This year, I came prepared with just that as well as a ridiculous clusterfuck of baggies inside a bigger zip bag holding my smokes, lighters, and herb. That was a much better trip down the piss and beer. That's how my buddy referred to it, and what is gross is as I looked around, I realized he was absolutely right. I saw lots of boobs on that river, drank a lot of beer, then one year, I ate a bunch of mushrooms. I couldn't tell you what I saw that year, but I remember it was fucking cool.

I have since found clean rivers to tube down that are not overflowing with annoying teenagers. I'm sure we were not like that, right? No we were probably worse, but now they are annoying, and it makes me feel old. I remember actually getting arrested and going to jail for a brief period of time because we were parked in a van down by the river. That is a joke if you are my age. Anyways, I was with the younger sister of a famous country singer at the time, and we had the van a rockin' and the police came a knockin'. I went in for being young and shitcan drunk, as well as having a minor in some creepy van down by the river. I think they thought she was being held there against her will because they kept asking me weird questions to that effect. She eventually came to the jail and got me out by telling them that she was there on her own will and we were just having fun.

They let me go, but I still got a ticket for minor consumption, and these were adding up, and with one or two more, I would have to do a bid because I was an adult but not old enough to drink. So in this country, I was old enough to be tried as an adult and put to death in some states, but it was not okay for me to have a few drinks and fool around in the back of a creepy van at four in the morning.

This year, they began a hip-hop Wednesday after school, which was for anyone who wanted to come, but it was mostly the hoodlums (my friends and I) that would play spades and a bunch of Asian cats that would breakdance. They played music over the PA, and we could use the microphone too. I did a little bit of everything. It was fun. I actually got halfway decent and breakin', but I mostly took on to rhyming.

In twelfth grade, I found out that freestyling came as naturally to me as looking for pussy. I started wearing tracksuits and going to breakdance every Wednesday, then freestyle and then play some cards. We would also throw dice. I met who would ultimately become one of my favorite rhymers of all time until he got arrogant and killed himself with pills. Michael Larson, a.k.a. Eyedea, will be missed forever. I still freestyle every day. I battle my dog, and I win every time. It must be because what I say blows his mind. He never has anything back.

One person who actually died that year was my mother's father. That killed me and still does. I am reminded of him every day, especially as my hairline proceeds to recede every day and makes me look more and more like him. That's okay though. He was a good dude who truly cared about his family. I don't think I ever heard him swear, and he was always doing special little things for the kids, like making us pancakes that looked like things.

The day he died was August 21. I know that because I still have the ticket from the Smoke 'n' Groves tour, which is where I was at when everything happened. I was with my best friend, and we were talking to these chicks. They were a bit older than us, but they were into it. I walked away for two seconds, and MOP, one of the headliners, stole our girls. I was pissed. Little did I know it would only get worse. But it did.

We were waiting for my sister who was supposed to pick us up. We waited forever and kept calling from the payphone, which was the only way to call back then, unless you were rich. The meter ran up to our limit, and we had to get out and walk. It was only a mile or so, but I was pissed off. We got back to my house, and I finally got a hold of my mother, who told me the news, and I felt like such an ass. I was only worried about myself and my inconveniences. I still feel bad about it, and I don't think it will ever stop.

Later that year was the first time I really cried in front of a friend. It was me and the same friend watching *Soul Food*. I spent the night at his house. If you don't know the movie, it is about a family that gets together every year at Big Mama's house (the grandma). Then one year she died, and it was really depressing. I started bawling like someone just cut my balls off. Ever since then, I have been ridiculously overemotional. I had to move on.

I was good friends with a girl whom I actually had a bit of a crush on, and we just hung out, got high along with other substances, and fooled around. It took a while, but I got her, just once in a shitty hotel. Even though I was fifteen and she was a senior, I got what I wanted. Although I was still in a relationship, I also ended up talking to this chick whose name I cannot remember, but I call her sty eye because she had a sty when I actually hooked up with her. We went to the fair and did a bunch of stupid shit, but then we went on the infamous make-out ride of the fair, Ye Ol' Mill. She went down on me like it was going out of style. I pounded her ass somewhere on the fairgrounds, but I don't remember where. That girl was really hot though.

Around the same time, maybe before, maybe overlapping, but regardless, she had a crush on me. She approached and seduced me. She was smoking hot but younger, which I usually do not go for, but what the fuck? Why not? Another V card taken. There was also one more time that I broke the rules and boned a friend's girlfriend—not ex but current. I still feel bad, but it was a high school hotel party, and we were the last ones awake. There were seriously around a dozen people passed out all around the room and nowhere to go, so we just boned on the floor in front of everyone. One girl woke up, but she just laughed and went back to sleep.

At the end of the year, I went on a trip to Florida, and a friend actually came with me. We met up with a good buddy from junior high who got shipped down there when his parents split up. One day, my buddy and I skated into town, and I got my tongue pierced. My mom loved that. This was around the time I started messing with this girl that was two grades younger than me. I am not usually attracted to younger girls, but this chick was fucking hot. To add fuel to the fire, my girlfriend told me she hated her because she knew that she wanted to fuck me. I could already tell that, but she confirmed it and probably should not have because then I perused and conquered it. One more V card for me.

4.0 GPA & High As Hell...Everyday!

Twelfth grade. By senior year, the Cats were on top of the food chain. We didn't fight or sell drugs or anything. We just got along with everyone and got away with everything. The school was renovating, so it contently had construction workers all over. One of the hardhats left the keys in the door to an unfinished room that had a giant hole in it. It became known as the hole, and I had the only key. The door was always locked, but the Cats could get in. This was the smoke spot, but even after we got busted in there 'cause the whole hallway smelled like pot, I hid the keys, which was a good thing, because after some trial and error, I found out it opened just about every door in the school. I was like the fucking dungeon master of the school. Everyone, every pastime would come to me to get the keys to the smoking spot. You could also get access to any classroom, gym, bathroom, etc.

    The school had recently put in a security checkpoint, and no one was allowed to leave campus. You needed a pass to leave the grounds, but we would just pull up to the checkpoint and ask them what they wanted for lunch, and they would let us out. We always told them we were going to Taco Bell, but we actually went to Willow Gate and then grabbed the guards some burritos on the way back. Our one cool science teacher would actually let me and my buddy dip out early as long as we brought him back C-4 (sesame chicken). I got away with everything because I had a 4.0 GPA and the staff knew who I hung out with and what I did but could not understand how I did it.

I was in advanced mathematics courses, which brought me to calculus, and I realized that I had just enough credits to skip a class, so I took study hall. I was the only one that did schoolwork. I figured that while I'm trapped in this cage, I might as well make the most of it and finish the shit that I would inevitably have to do eventually, which allowed me to party like a fucking rock star and maintain my GPA and graduate on the dean's list. That's a life lesson from a pothead—pay attention in school.

There was a girl, a gymnast, that my girlfriend hated. She thought she wanted to get with me. I swear they can smell that shit. But she was right, and I was all about her tight body, big boobies, fat ass, and she loved nothing more than to give head. This bitch could suck a golf ball through a garden hose. My girlfriend completely knew what was going on but seemed to turn a blind eye to the situation. My mom happened to be going to a conference in Mexico that year the exact time of spring break. She had frequent-flyer miles to spare and invited us both to come along. We went down there for a week, and I have to say that I was a little disappointed because I did not get laid the entire time. We fucked before we left and right when we got back, but she would not hit the skins while we were out there because she didn't want to get caught. I didn't see what the big deal was because my mom had caught us before, not visually, but you would have to be and idiot not to know what was going on. I used to jam a knife in the door so it would not open, and I remember us having a loud session and my mom coming home and trying to open my door. There is no way she did not hear what was going on. I didn't really care because I didn't go down there to have sex. I just wanted to get drunk underage in front of my mom, play in the ocean, and have a good time. I could fuck my old lady anytime I wanted when we got home.

The place we stayed was all-inclusive, so you could get an XX whenever you wanted and not just from a bartender. They would leave the bars unattended, and you could just go up to the tap and pour your own pint even at three in the morning; it was awesome. There was a swim-up bar, which was the coolest thing I had ever seen. You never had to go to the bathroom. You could talk to people, drink, and urinate all at the same time; it was amazing. I entered a drinking contest outside that pool for two reasons. One, I was pretty sure I could win, and two, I knew it would piss my mom off. I love my mother more than anything, but it is fun to get her goat as people in their nineties would say. I was against a bunch of a few Americans, some Germans, and a whole bunch of Canadians for some reason. We had to race, slamming mugs of XX, which were really big, but I won every round.

In the final round, I was up against this woman from Canada, if you could call her a woman. She looked like a fucking lumberjack. We had to slam a mug and finish it off with a shot of tequila. She was incredible, but I won. However, it was really close, and I give her credit for keeping up. She would have won honestly if she wasn't up against me. We finished at relatively the same time even though I was first. When she finished her tequila, they announced that she had won, and then she jumped up and threw up all over the place. I saw the whole thing, and it was hilarious. They told me that they knew I won, but regardless of the outcome, they always let the girl and said that I spilled or something. They gave me double what she got, which were just two stupid shirts and a couple of glasses that I don't even think I brought home. All I know is that I smoked all those Nazis, Canucks, and the fat guy from Texas. I am a quarter German, so it is okay for me to say that.

The day before we left, we were scheduled for a fishing trip. The fishing company had a clause that said you could not cancel your trip without more the twenty-four hours' notice, and no trips would be refunded due to weather conditions. The weather was completely fucked this day, and the company actually said that they would refund any deposits for this day because it was so shitty. It was our last day, and I knew my girlfriend would really love to go deep sea fishing. She loved fish in general, so we were going fishing no matter what. The waves were unbelievable. It was like the boat would go up at a ninety-degree angle and slam down, and it was basically unbearable. I was doing okay until the one other person who chose to take the trip got sick. He was a big fat guy, and he got up and went to the bathroom, if you can call it that; it was more like a closet.

I was doing all right until this point. When he opened the door to come out, the entire boat was engulfed in the smell of nasty vomit. I instantly got sick, and it would not stop for the rest of the trip. Seasickness is worse than any flu you could ever get. We had our lines in, and mine hit first. Mind you, I had just thrown up about thirty seconds earlier, and there was more on deck. I had to strap on a belt with a holder for the pole, which means if this fish was really big, it could possibly pull me over the rail and into the ocean, and considering the weather I would have been fucked. It was a mahi-mahi, and it was the biggest thing I had ever caught. It took almost an hour to reel in with the pole, pushing on my belly. The belly pushing along with the conditions on the water, I was throwing up over the edge about every thirty seconds. It fucking sucked, but it was very gratifying once I pulled the fish out.

My mom's line hit next, and I think she was terrified, but she was a trooper. My girlfriend took the pole for a while, and they basically took turns, bringing in the fish, and it took longer than mine. When they pulled in the fish, which was also a mahi-mahi, it was a little bigger than mine, but fuck that—it took two people, and I did it by myself. My girlfriend eventually got sick as well. The only person that didn't was my mom, but she is a tough lady despite the fact that she looks quite fragile. The fat guy that puked right away did not catch anything, but I do not think he would have been able to in his condition. We were all done, so we headed back. When we got back to the pier, they weighed our fish, and mine came in at a little over forty pounds, and theirs was around forty-five pounds, so they beat me. However, in hindsight, considering the fact that they split the chore of catching the fish, they each only pulled in 22.5 pounds apiece, which makes me the winner. They offered to filet the fish and give it to us for a small fee, and it would have been a really good deal, but even the thought of fish made me want to vomit in my mouth. Mahi-mahi is fucking delicious, and it would have been nice to have some filets later on in life, but at the moment, the thought of eating fish made me want to keel over.

We also had to fly home the next day, and it was an ass load of fish. After cleaning and gutting, it would have still been over fifty pounds of fish. What the fuck are we supposed to do with that? We gave the fish to a local restaurant and felt like we did our good deed for the day and went back to the hotel to die. We made it out alive, and within an hour or two, I was back down by the pool. I was going to put as much free alcohol in my body as humanly possible before we left. I am pretty sure I succeeded because I ended up cutting myself off, which rarely happens. I was not too drunk; I had just reached a plateau wherein my level of intoxication could not have possibly increased. Maybe if I had some other recreational drugs, but it was just booze for me and maybe some weed.

Hallucinogens Will Come Back To Haunt You!

This was the year that I discovered Sage Francis, who would later become my all-time favorite MC and poet. He won the Deaf Poetry Jam so many times they wouldn't let him compete anymore and made him a judge. The same thing happened at the Scribble Jam competition. I was listening to Atmosphere and other local hip-hop. I saw them both at the U of M–Saint Paul campus. I was totally immersed in the world of hip-hop and going to shows, getting up close and personal and meeting the performers. There was an event that all the local groups would perform at, and it was only five or ten dollars in a small club, and you could talk to them. I even freestyled with some of them, including slug (Atmosphere).

Twenty years later, that same concert is held outdoors. Tickets are seventy dollars, plus parking, and a beer is like eight bucks. Not to mention the fact that it is infested with little kids that bought the ticket with their parents' money and have no knowledge of the music that is playing; they just come to party. Even Lollapalooza was only twenty-eight dollars. I have one ticket stub right in front of me right now; I don't know why I still have it, but I do. That was a concert filled with only headliners, and everyone in the crowd was a die-hard fan. This completely ruined this type of concert experience for me; I will not pay that much to wade through a sea of adolescent idiots who are in my way and preventing me from actually enjoying the show. The beer is too expensive as well; I hate that. Now I will not go to a concert just to go; I will only go if I actually like who I am going to see and if it is in a decent venue and not a stadium. While I am on the topic, Weird Al is the best performer I have ever seen in my life.

I have seen him five times, and he just gets better. He is dorky, but it is true, he puts on a good show.

This was the last year that the high school would have two-hour gym. It was a coed class that was such a joke it wasn't even funny. All we did was get high and fuck around. We listened to music over the PA and danced around acting like idiots. Then every Friday, we would go bowling, which was awesome. The teacher would stay in the bar, and we were free to do whatever we wanted. We would sit over by the arcade games and smoke our faces off, smoke herb in the bathroom, and every once in a while, someone would bring a bottle or something, and we would get tipsy. That class was fucking awesome. For some reason, they cancelled that class after that semester. I'm glad I got to take advantage while it was still around. As a matter of fact, I have been in more than a couple fights at that particular bowling alley. There were two that I remember quite well. The first happened when this guy was eyeballing me and wouldn't let up. I noticed, but I wasn't feeling froggy, so I didn't jump. My good buddy, however, noticed as well and was not cool with it. He stood up and looked at him and said, "So you think my boy is pretty cute, huh?" They conversed, and my buddy mentioned that he couldn't keep his eyes off me. This guy was so stupid and kept running his mouth. He had plenty of boys with him, but they were fucking toys.

It was a simple agreement. Outside? Okay. We went outside, he tried to throw a punch at me, and I moved out of the way. That was the end of that. My friend clocked him in the ear, and we proceeded to whoop his ass all over the parking lot. The police came, and he was screaming about how we jumped him for no reason and robbed him for his necklace. One of the police picked up his chain and was like, "Do you mean this one?" Then they put him in the car, and he went to jail. We were just told to drive home even though we were drunk and underage. There were other fights but not as interesting, just "Fuck you! Well, fuck you," then punching, no story to it, kind of boring.

The other one that I remember was on Christmas Eve when I went to the same place I went with my best friend, my other buddy, his brother, and his girlfriend. The night was relatively uneventful until we went out to the car. There was a group of guys walking out to their car at the same time, shouting some nonsense. My buddy's brother shouted out, "Jesus is the reason for the season!" I don't know why that would piss anyone off, but I guess it did, and they charged us. I wasn't in the mood for this, so I turned into what I would call my "angry drill sergeant" personality. I was yelling at everyone. I grabbed the girl and threw her ass in the car and told her to stay there. Next, I had to save my best friend. I screamed at him and told him to get the fuck in the car. I helped my buddy get the douchebags off his brother and screamed at them to get in the car and start it. I don't know what I said or did, but I was screaming at the bad guys, and they took off, so did we, and everyone had a merry Christmas.

Toward the end of the year, I had two of the most terrifying hallucinogenic episodes of my life. The first involved LSD, having fun with my friends and then everyone leaving me at home alone to trip my balls off. I was literally alone, no friends, not family, nothing. I thought I could just watch TV and relax, so I put on some animal show, which happened to be all about bees. I watched the whole fucking show, which seemed to be about ten hours long, all the while tripping my face off and seeing a whole other world of melting walls and colors. All the shit they make, it seemed like in the movies. I was in a fucking cartoon, and it was awesome. Then for some reason a realized I was all alone for the rest of the weekend, and my cartoon world turned sinister. The fluffy bunnies all turned into bees, and eventually I was surrounded. I freaked the fuck out and had no one to go to. I am absolutely terrified of bees to this day and have even jumped off a boat in all my clothes and shoes, screaming like a girl to get away. I have been stung tons of times, and I know it does not hurt, but it triggers something that makes me really anxious and basically have a flashback.

It is not fun and not like a child running from a bee. I see shit and it is fucking scary. Around this time, and I am not sure exactly what year it was, and I know why. I was fucked up out of my brain, but it was a much different experience.

The science classes at our high school would have a field trip every year to the only outdoor amusement park in Minnesota, Valley

Fair. One incredibly drug induced occasion at a very young age occurred at Valley Fair while on a field trip when I was in middle school. I had never taken so much acid while doing schoolwork… it was only a matter of time before I would surpass that milestone. There was much more to come! The point of the trip was to do scientific experiments involving various rides and figuring out things such as velocity or whatever. My friends and I were only there to have fun, but I never forget that school comes first. If your ride to the party is about to leave, then you go party like the world is about to end and try to make time for whatever it is you got to do the next day. If you don't pull it off, don't be a bitch about it.

I cannot remember a party I was at, no matter how shitty, that made me rather be at home doing research. I told the group that I would take care of the work, so we got stoned, and I finished the work for everyone in our group quite quickly, and then we went on to our main objective. The park had just recently opened a new roller coaster that was the biggest in the park, so we had to ride it. Since it was the first year, the line was long as hell, so I dropped a good amount of acid while we waited in to ride the new coaster. About the time that we were halfway to the coaster, I began to feel the oncoming of what would inevitably turn into severe hallucinations and the possibility of me freaking the fuck out. I got really nervous, but my buddy held my hand, not literally, but he talked me down, put his arm around me, and told me it would be all right. By the time we got to the ride, I was tripping my balls off and scared for my life. I got on the death machine only because I had waited so long to do so. I remember the climb up to the initial drop, and I was hyperventilating and seeing everything pulsate and various colors but no sound. The ride started, and it was like the scene in *Charlie and the Chocolate Factory* on the boat when it gets really freaky, except it did not get scary for me this time; I was having a blast.

I should have purchased the picture that they take at the end of the ride because it was fucking priceless. You could clearly see the look of true terror as well as the look of a little kid at Disney World. Later we rode the coaster again before the trip was over because we wanted to pass around a joint as we rode. I was still tripping really hard, and hallucinations had become commonplace. We did what we had set out to do and passed the jay around while we rode the coaster. I knew we were coming up to the spot where they take your picture, I grabbed it and was hitting it while we passed it. I wanted to buy that picture. I had long bleached hair, which was okay in the '90s, and I had the doobie in my mouth and looked just about as fucked up as I did in the picture when I was peeking. I went to buy the picture, and I heard a loud deep voice yell out, "Look, that little cracker has a joint in his mouth!" We ran away, and I have nothing to remember those two pictures by, aside from the fact that those psychedelic memories are just a sliver in the tree trunk of drug-induced adventures, some of which I will probably never remember.

The second was toward the end of senior year. *The Matrix* movie was released, and it looked like a trippy, fun film to go see. There was a half-day, so a buddy and I decided to go see it after class. We went to my house first, and I had an eighth of shrooms, which I ground up and mixed into a glass of orange juice because I had read that vitamin C increases the effects of psilocybin. I had never been so fucked up, and I was excited to see a movie full of trippy special effects, which were groundbreaking at the time. However, I did not know that it was dark and not a happy movie. I actually had to leave at one point to throw up, but I didn't. I came back and was terrified the entire time.

I have seen the movie since, and it is not scary at all, but a little dark for doing shrooms. You should be outside in the sun like a hippie having fun. I, however, was shaking and just happy to go back home. This was until I was brought back home and my buddy said, "Okay, I gotta go to work," now and my fucking world crumbled. I was so scared, and the flashback of bees had nothing on this. I was seeing and hearing all types of ish, and it was all very dark and scary. I called my two go-tos, my best friend and my girlfriend. I was literally in the corner in a fetal position, crying, watching the gates of hell burn down all around me. I had never been so terrified before and have not been since. My two angels came and saved me; they sat with me, held me, talked me down, and in hindsight, possibly saved my life. I love them.

My girlfriend and I went to every dance throughout high school like the Sadie Hawkins dance, which was funny because you are supposed to wear matching plaid and jeans; I guess that is so you look like a farmer or something. My girlfriend and I wore matching FUBU outfits. What made it even funnier is that we were wearing a brand that white people are not supposed to wear. We didn't give a fuck; we thought it was hilarious. We always got a hotel room although I can't remember how because I didn't have a credit card and I was not yet eighteen.

One time that I remember very well was the snow dance because that was a crazy night. I don't remember shit about the dance because they are all so stupid I was always either intoxicated, high out of my brain, or both. We would usually pregame until we were good and fucked up, then just go to say high to friends and take pictures. After the dance, we went back to the hotel where most of our friends were staying as well and partied for most of the night, but I remember retiring early to our room because we were drunken teenagers with raging hormones and we had business to take care of.

We went back to the room to do the damn thing, and I will never forget what happened next. About halfway through, she made a very awkward request that was really kinky even for her because she was a bit of a freak. She told me that she wanted me to pee inside of her while we were fucking. Not on her, which I have heard of before, but inside. That was new to me. I was up for anything, so I figured I would give it a shot, but it was not as easy as it sounds. There must be something inborn in me that tells my brain not to let my penis urinate on people, let alone inside of them. Besides that, I had learned when I was young not to try to pee with an erection because if your dick is set at high noon and you pee, you pee in your face, so it is best not to piss with a hard-on.

It was not working, which I thought was weird because I had been drinking a lot so I figured it would come naturally, no dice. I had an idea. I would pull out, run to the bathroom, and start to pee, pinch it, and then run back to jump inside and finish the job. It was not as easy as it sounds even though I had the super wiener powers of a teenager and could keep an erection while walking naked in a snowstorm. There was no problem there, but it was hard to get the flow going, not to mention the fact that I was still kind of weirded out by the request. I had to try a few times before I got the flow to go inside the love muffin, but when I did, she fucking loved it. I am glad she had fun because I still think that was messy and weird as fuck. It was a good thing we put a towel down because we only had one bed in the room and I didn't really want to sleep in a puddle of my own piss. If it was someone else's pee, that would be okay but not my own.

The next dance was the prom, which I had never been to because I thought it was too expensive and dumb, but my girlfriend wanted to go with me before I graduated and moved away. We got together a big group. All my friends went together, and most of them did not have girlfriends. But there was a group of girls that we all talked to, so I guess they just divided them up within the group. I wonder if anyone got left out. My best friend, the boy-girl, did not go, but he had already dropped out of school. We had at least eight couples, maybe more, so we all got a suite downtown with two floors, a Jacuzzi, and a bunch of rooms even though no one planned on sleeping. That was a lot of people, but it just ended up being a big party. Two of my friends in the group worked at the liquor store with me at the time, and we had all been stalking up on booze for quite some time. We had plenty of beer, multiple bottle of hard alcohol, and more champagne than we could possibly drink, even with over sixteen people.

Money was obviously a concern of mine, considering I stole all the alcohol and said absolutely not to a limo unless someone else was buying. I drove my car, and I don't remember exactly who rode with me besides my girlfriend, but I do remember that it was designated, and the pot-smoking car and I were okay with that, whoever I picked up. I drove to the house where all the girls were, and I made a grand entrance. As I pulled down the street, I had my music obnoxiously loud to a window-rattling level like most dumbass teenagers. I was honking as well as we rolled down the street, and they were all standing outside and waiting for us so the old people could take pictures, but when we got to the house, I could not stop. A soda can had rolled down around my feet somehow and gotten lodged underneath the brake pedal. They all watched as we sped by bumping annoying music and not stopping, eventually driving into the schoolyard. There was a park at the end of the street, and I drove into it a little bit, but I got it figured out, the brake situation, and was able to get back on the road without calling a tow truck. I turned around and pulled up to the house with my tail between my legs, feeling like a jackass, and proceeded to take some stupid pictures. That went quick and was relatively painless, so we hit the road to set up shop in our room before the dance.

Since I was driving, one of the smoking cars, we needed to pregame on the way to the pregame, but everyone's pipe was either packed in the trunk or nonexistent. I had a cigar, but no one knew how to roll a blunt. I manned up and rolled the blunt as I drove on the highway in a tuxedo. It is not easy to roll a blunt and drive real fast at the same time, but I pulled it off. I don't think the fact that I was in a tux makes it any more difficult, but it is funny. We smoked the blunt and got to the hotel no problem and were stoked because now we did not have to drive anymore for the rest of the night because our hotel was right across from the Marriott, where the prom was being held or so we thought. We brought all our supplies up to the room, which was huge and really fucking nice to drink. We eventually were all there and got loaded until it was crunch time and we decided to cross the road and go to the dance.

I don't remember who booked the suite. Part of me thinks I did it, but I don't think so. Whoever it was, they really dropped the ball because it was really a nice room that was supposed to be right across the street was in Minneapolis, and the dance was at the Marriott in Saint Paul. When we walked into the hotel, there was some other occasion going on, and we were quite overdressed. Everyone looked at us like we were fucking crazy. We turned tail and realized that we had to get the fuck on the road, or we were going to miss the whole thing.

I drove to Saint Paul, and we just barely made it. Somehow everyone got there at around the same time, so we all agreed to go take a group photo first because it was literally the last minute. They took a picture, and that was it. Prom was over, and we weren't even able to take couple pictures because they kicked us out. All in all, I was at my senior prom for all of five minutes, if that. We all went back to the suite and began the drinking and debauchery. I think I remember other substances besides booze and weed, but I am not sure, which is a good sign that there was. However, I do clearly remember when two of the girls who happened to be the ones with the biggest tits got butt naked and took a bubble bath. They left the door wide open so anyone could come in and get a peek. I dated one of them in middle school, and the other one lived about a block away from me. That was nice, and I got some good pictures. I know the one from my block was bisexual, but if they did any actual sex stuff, I missed it. I was happy just seeing some huge soapy boobies as well as the rest of their bodies. They were hot and got me in the mood for what would inevitably happen later that night or early in the morning. I don't remember when we passed out, but we had our own bed and made good use of it that night as well as the morning. When we did get up, there was still an ass-load of champagne and alcohol, so I had some mimosas and packed up all the good shit before anyone noticed, and we went home. She stayed at my house a lot since she was kicked out a year or two before that.

My first introduction into gonzo journalism was when I took an ass load of acid and went to see *Fear and Loathing in Las Vegas*. I just saw it and loved every minute because of the effects. Because of that, I watched it a bunch of more times once it came out on video. I fell in love with Hunter S. Thompson immediately and now have the double thumb fist symbol of gonzo journalism tattooed on my wrist. I realized that in writing there is the traditional approach of regurgitating facts and then there is another approach which involves looking outside of the box and proposing new ideas, or better yet just random shit that has nothing to do with the original story.

Fear and Loathing was supposed to be a piece about a political campaign; however, it turned into a drug-fueled rant about everything but the story, and it became a phenomenon. I found that when I would take copious amounts of various substances, my mind would race, and I finished my paintings in minutes and could turn out papers like I was simply writing a letter and I never received less than an A. He turned me on to the world of journalism and taking my own approach to writing, basically ignoring everything I have learned about it.

The Only Books That I Like Are About Drugs!

There were a couple other books, which coincidentally are the only other books that I have read front to back that were also focused on excessive drug use. One was *Go Ask Alice*, which was a fucked-up little girl's diary who described everything she experienced in great detail as she overdosed left and right and had incredible hallucinations. I wish I would have kept a diary so I could explain every one of mine in such detail, but if I did, this would be a fucking novel. The others were *Trainspotting* and *A Clockwork Orange*. They taught me to pay attention to context while reading because sometimes there is foreign and slang and shit that it is almost impossible to be familiar with, let alone understand. I have been to both Scotland and England, picked up the gibberish just fine, but these two books were a little tricky and taught me a few things about writing. I have read more books than three, but these stuck out to me in particular and I think got me interested in writing.

At the end of senior year, they have this thing called the senior sleepover or overnight or some dumb shit. You basically go to school and get locked in all night. You are supposed to sleep in the cafeteria, but that wasn't in my plans. I was still working at the LQ and brought a bottle of booze as well as a full dugout of some chronic, so I was set to go. This was at the very end of the year. No more classes, and a handful of chicks that I would have boned in a heartbeat told me (to paraphrase) that they really wanted to fuck me but I was in a relationship. *Fuck!*

There is a couple that really pissed me off because I would have torn that shit up. Oh well, no matter, I ended up talking to an old friend, and for some reason, she had a big bag of coke. Somehow we both snuck off to the bathroom and did a bunch of coke and drank a ton of hooch, which is pretty cool for being seventeen and in school. We never went to sleep, so we mingled and would then run back to the bathroom for drinks and yea-o. Eventually, I wanted to smoke, so I tried my magic key on the girl's locker room, and it worked. We went in. I can honestly say I am the only person I have ever heard of from that high school that has smoked stinky weed and got it on in the girl's shower room.

Eighteen years. Three days after I turned eighteen, it was time to move out. I was accepted to CU in Colorado. I could have gotten a full scholarship, but I did not apply myself for one, and I missed out. I actually found out I most likely would have been accepted at some more-accredited big-name schools, but I just wanted to go snowboarding every weekend and possibly learn some shit while I was there. I had always been a latchkey kid, so I was used to being alone, but it was so cool to be on my own for real. Not that being able to come and go as I pleased and doing whatever the hell I wanted. My first realization of the fact that I was really on my own came after a day or two after I had moved in when I was high out of my fucking mind and was having cravings for I-don't-know-what, but I guarantee it was stoner food. I also needed to stock a few things for my fridge, cupboards, and just regular shit that you have to get when you go to the store, like toilet paper. It had never become a problem in the past because there was always TP in the house growing up, but I never had to buy it. This is when I learned that if you live by yourself and don't buy toilet paper, it will not magically appear, and if you do not have TP and you are by yourself, you are literally shit out of luck (pun). I also learned that if you ever bring a female back to your place and you are all out, she will be pissed (pun). Some girls will drip dry, but some cannot live without it. It is also important that if you are having a different girl over to spend the night, you need to check the garbage for tampon wrappers or any other incriminating evidence because it will be found. Even if whatever it is might be buried deep, it will be found, and they can tell if you have recently had sex by looking around the room once, sniff the air, and then you are busted. This has happened to me one too many times.

This was the first time that I ever had to go grocery shopping. I had gone to the grocery store before, just to grab a thing or two for a barbecue or something like that but never to stock up. So I got really dusted and went to the store. Bad idea, but it was so fun. I went batshit crazy in that place and finally realized how much delicious stuff I had been missing out on over the years. I bought anything and everything I had ever wanted growing up but was denied. I remember subconsciously asking my mom if I could have this or that and then coming to the realization that I was on my own and I could do whatever the fuck I wanted. I don't have much of a sweet tooth anymore, but I bought all types of crap food and of course the standard college kid stuff, like ramen noodles and what have you.

It was a big change, but I had just turned eighteen and if I wanted I could go grab smokes or a new pipe, or since I had a fake ID, I could go grab a six-pack, some lottery tickets, and walk around the apartment naked if I wanted. However, I don't like to walk around or sleep naked even if I don't need to be wearing clothes; it is like a security blanket. Yet every girl I have ever fucked with apparently has no problem walking around butt ass naked with the love dripping down their thigh. That has nothing to do with where I was going with that, but it had to be said along with this complementary fact: not all women should feel comfortable enough to do that all the time. Just because we just got finished fucking for like an hour does not mean that I want to see you ass naked just hanging out walking around the place. In fact, a lot of the times, that is when I want you to leave.

I just wanted to be by the mountains or snowboard every day, so that is what I did. It took two months for me to fuck it all up. I went to see my buddy's brother at their mom's house in Littleton because she was a professional cook and I was good friends with both of the brothers. The one who was in my grade was actually moving to Colorado that day, so we were going to do a whole get-together thing. I was bumping my music, which was obnoxiously loud, and driving way too fast. I got pulled over and I was honest. I told them I had two beers, which was actually true. I passed all the field sobriety tests as well as the breathalyzer. However, I had accidentally handed the cop my ID with my smoking hand, and he could smell the herb and knew I was dusted ass. So they told me to take a piss test or spend a week in jail. I said worried, "You know I have been smoking. I will pee, then let me go."

In hindsight, I might have rather spent the week, but jail sucks donkey balls. If you have never been, try not to go. They did not tow my car and gave me my keys back as my friends from Minnesota came and picked me up. They made sure to tell me not to drive it that night, but I was not going to leave it there. My friends brought me to my car and followed me back to their house, where I spent the night, and that was a very scary couple of miles. I realized I was so close to safety that I would have had a great night if I just did not speed. I always go the speed limit now. It is such a stupid reason to get in trouble when you could have otherwise just drove right past the cops with like ten pounds of whatever contraband floats your boat. Making sure that your tabs and everything is up to date and not speeding or swerving can be the difference between a good time and spending time…in jail. I got probation and lost my license, but I still drove because I had to get to school, parties, and to the mountains.

The brothers introduced me to one group of friends who I seemed to really fit in with although I was the only white boy in the group, and they constantly would make light of that or try to rip on me and make cracker jokes. I stood up one day and informed them that I would be happy to be their cracker if they wanted. They did not know the origin of the word and, like most people, just assumed that it was because I was white and so are crackers. However, I was actually darker than a few of them; I get tan in the winter and am the darkest person in my entire family even my extended family. This is part of the reason I thought I was adopted for so long until I found a picture of my dad at my age, and it was like looking in a fucking mirror. I explained to them that a "cracker" was the name given to the slave master back in the day by the slaves themselves because he was the one that cracked the whip. So I said, "If you want me to be your master, then I will take the position."

I was more than a few years younger than most of them, but I moved up a peg or two and was basically accepted and not just considered a little white boy. Later on, they were all freestyling one day, and I jumped in which I think they thought was a joke. I stepped up to the plate and blew them away; I guess they did not know that white people could not have rhythm or rhyme to save their life. I even stepped up to the biggest one, Black Rob. I ripped him a new asshole, and they were all surprised. They said, "We need to give this crazy cracker a gangsta-ass name. And because I was already called T, they decided to start calling me Tiggah the White Niggah."

I hung out with them for the rest of the time I was there, and they took me in and brought me around to parties and stuff. We did a lot of freestyling. Every once in a while at these parties where I stuck out like a sore thumb, someone would try to start shit with me because I was the only white boy there. They would step in and protect me. The name stuck and still follows me. However, later on my softball team, they didn't quite get it and took it too far. When I would do something good, they would yell, "Go, Tigger!" I had to tell them they were putting too much *-er* on the word. I was experiencing African American racism as a white person, and it was a little confusing. We played in the "hood" and I had to explain that word could easily be misheard as the N-bomb, and we didn't need that kind of trouble in that neck of the woods. I still got called Tiggah on occasion, but my name basically evolved into Tizzle. This was much more acceptable.

Talking to my buddy, he had mentioned that one of our friends from junior high was living in Colorado. I immediately asked if he could find out her number. We were best friends back then, and I had a crush on her from the moment I saw her. We would exchange heart-folded notes every day and talk on the phone for hours. I eventually got a hold of her, and it turned out she was going to come to Denver that weekend. She said she would stop by before whatever it was she had to do. I obviously said okay, so I was happy. When she arrived, I was blown away. I wanted nothing more than to tear this girl apart with my cock, but we were plutonic friends, and that's not right, right? Well, she asked if she could take a shower before she did whatever, and I replied, "Only if I can join you." She said, "Let's go," and I jumped in.

I was eighteen so I was up and ready to go in about two seconds. I could not believe it, but we got down and went to town for a long time and then some. We started dating. She lived in Breckenridge right by the mountain, so I went and stayed there every weekend in the winter. She had two friends that would party and ride with us—the super-hot one and Walt Disney's granddaughter. We would do ecstasy, coke, and smoke a truckload of herb and fuck around. It was awesome. They had a lot of money and funded pretty much everything. We were all under twenty-one, but someone left their ID at the liquor store I worked at my senior year, so I used that and was able to supply alcohol for everyone.

The dude did not look anything like me. He was a lot older and probably had around fifty pounds on me. I would always go to the LQ down the street with this Korean man working there every day, and every day, he would look at my ID and say, "Oh, no this not you." However, he would sell to me every time. I would always get Fat Tire, the Colorado brew at the time, and I really wanted the giant bottle of tequila with a cobra in it, but it was like $200. The store was just a couple of blocks from the mass shooting that happened at a theater 2014. I lived in southeast Denver, and right across the street from my apartment was the straight up ghetto. This is where the shooting took place. Someone even got murdered in the courtyard by the pool, which I never used, and I am a heavy sleeper, so I didn't wake up, but the thought is somewhat disconcerting.

I did not live in a nice neighborhood. My apartments were called Britannia Heights, and I lived on Bell Air Avenue. Yet the neighborhood was a fucking cesspool, full of garbage people. In fact, there was recently a mass shooting at a theater literally a block or two down the street from where I lived. Garbage people come in all colors and are not restricted to any race; they are simply the people that have no respect for society. That pool had a flag of Great Brittan painted on the bottom, and I love swimming, so I am still pissed that I did not ever use it. However, I did use the Jacuzzi one time. When I went there, a girl was already using it. She was about my age and pretty cute. I got in and relaxed. We talked a little bit, but I kept thinking about the girls I actually cared about and could not pursue anything. When she got up and left and went over and sat where she was, I instantly noticed that there was a jet blowing right on my balls. This means it was blowing up her crotch, and she was getting off hydraulically the entire time she was talking to me.

My junior high crush and I hung out all winter. I went out to the mountains every weekend, and we would go riding all day. She originally drove down there from Seattle and lived in her car using a guest membership at a gym to shower and whatnot. She found a place to stay with some guys whom I never met, but she just rode the couch. Some buddies and I, one flew in from Minnesota, all stayed out there with her to ride one weekend. We all slept on the floor, and she was on the couch. I was called up to the couch and proceeded to do the damn thing with my friends sleeping right there on the floor. It was slow and quiet, but my god, it did the trick, and it was awesome. A few weeks later, all the roommates went out of town, and she had a room all to herself that one of the guys said she could stay in. We took some really good E and spent twelve hours doing all the things you would expect people to do on ecstasy.

We listened to trippy instrumental music, rubbed each other, and fucked like rabbits. She gave the best massages and being tweaked out of my gourd made it all the better. She later went on to become a professional masseuse. No bullshit about the twelve hours. We went so long one time that we burned down a whole candle and burned a big hole in the dude's dresser that was a gift from his grandmother, whoops. We rode and fucked all winter until she had to go back to school in Seattle. We actually combined the two for the first time, which we would later do in three other states. I like to ride in the back country through the trees because it is always fresh snow, and you can park and smoke a bowl without worrying about the wind or anything else, you just want to try not to get lost. We stopped to smoke and I just got frisky and told her to drop her snow pants and bend over. This further confirmed my theory that a woman will do whatever you want if she likes you and you are very assertive. Confidence is the key. You might think that would be cold, but we actually ended up sweating our asses off, and it was a great experience. I found the joy of smoking a bowl while a girl is riding you on the side of a mountain with people skiing all around. It was fucking awesome. We would do it again later in Tahoe, Idaho, and Minnesota.

She was in Seattle and wanted me to visit, so I got my shit in order and bought a ticket. I did a little planning first. Throughout the year, many drugs came in and out of my apartment. One was new to me. I had never heard of GHB (date rape drug). You just take a shot, and you are done, not in a drunk way but you get fucked up eight ways from Sunday. There was also ketamine or special K (cat tranquilizer). I learned how to make it. You need a bottle of pharmaceutical ketamine and a stove. Place an upside-down teepee of butter knives in a pot of water and place a porcelain plate on top with about a half-inch gap to let the steam out. Bring the water to a boil and pour the liquid on the plate. Eventually, the liquid will turn solid, and you turn the stove off. Wait for it to cool off, and then scrape it off with a credit card, and it magically turns into a big pile of profitable powder ready to be bagged and brought off to a rave. This was knowledge that would become valuable later in life.

At this time, there was also a butt load of acid going around; my friends that I had met at the apartments would come over with a fucking bottle of liquid acid. You only need one drop, and they had a goddamn bottle. They would empty out, then fill up little breath-freshener bottles with the acid, each one holding about two hundred drops. We would dispense the LSD into individual little squeeze bottles the time in my apartment, but one day while cleaning my apartment, I found that they had filled and lost one bottle under my chair. I kept that and had my own personal free supply of dose for the rest of the year, and that is if I did copious amounts and used it frequently.

There was also a lot of blow and speed around, and there was this one cat who would steal pharmaceuticals and sell them or give them away if you got him high enough. There was actually an apartment on the bottom floor that was up to some dirty shit. I went there with a friend one night, or I guess you could say early in the morning after a party, to give him some green in exchange for some speed. I had nothing to do with it, but it is customary to smoke a bowl or two when cheeba is exchanged, so I came along for a free ride. When I got there—mind you, this was like 4:00 AM—this dude said, "Do you want some breakfast?" He handed me a saucepan full of god-knows-how-much meth, and my mind was blown. My first thought was, *Fuck no, and I don't think I want to know you.* I could see and smell that they were cooking it up in the apartment, so my second thought was that I needed to move out of that building because he was below me, and I wasn't ready to get blown up in a meth-lab explosion at that point in my life—maybe later, but not yet.

I had everything ready to go to Seattle for two weeks. I gathered supplies and filled a box. This was before 9/11, and you could do whatever you wanted. I filled the box with a bottle of GHB, some coke, some special K, a quarter ounce of really good chronic, about fifty drops of LSD, and some really good fresh mushrooms. I shipped it out urgent because of the fresh shrooms. However, when I got there, she had them in the freezer because one of her roommates told her, "That is what you're supposed to do." I yelled at him, "Fresh shrooms are awesome."

She had seven roommates, and every day was a party. One day I decided I wanted to go up to the Space Needle and apparently trip my balls off. I took the frozen mushrooms, which I was upset about, and dropped twelve hits of acid onto an eighth of fungi. Just a heads-up to anyone keeping track, this is way above an acceptable amount of hallucinogens to ingest. It was stupid, but I had a fucking blast. There was some kind of festival out there, and the whole park smelled like fucking hippies and that hippie perfume that they all use. Everyone was smoking herb, and there were cops all around. This was totally new to me. I have never been so high and happy; I went down to the shoreline and up to the top of the Needle, which was cool.

Nothing went wrong; we went home and banged, and I tripped my balls off all day. The next day, we had a party, and there were a ton of people. We were in a college town, and everyone showed up, everything was cool until a couple guys started acting up. We were standing at the top of the stairs out front, and one of them came up, hit him in the back of the head, and kicked him down the stairs. I was standing right next to him, and that could have been me. Frenzy and fighting broke out. I spent my time getting all the girls inside and safe because I thought it could get worse. Just after I got all the girls inside, gunshots started going off. No one was hit, but there were close calls, and the house was hit. I am just glad I could get the girls out before shit hit the fan. The next week, she had classes, so I decided to go get my second tattoo. I had drawn up a little spiral design that I liked, so I went and got it put on my neck. I still really like that one. I skateboarded around all day and acted like I belonged there. No one noticed that I was out of my element.

It was time to go back to Denver, so I got right back into riding while I could. I still went out every weekend. I had nowhere to stay, so I had to drive back to the city, tired as fuck, and that sucked donkey balls, but whatever. I eventually remembered that one of my second girlfriend's friends lived in Breckenridge, so I called her up to go riding, and I was straight forward. I said, "Let's go ride, and then I need to crash at your place." She said, "Cool," and then it was on like donkey.

I don't know how that whole "it's on like donkey" phrase found its way into my vernacular, but lots of cats say it, and I guess I just picked it up, sorry. She was beautiful, so sexy, and she could ride. It was fun. We drank and got high at night and messed around a bit. One night, we candy flipped (ecstasy and acid) and ended up doing the damn thing. She had her clit pierced, and that was fun to play with. The winter was almost over, and it was T-shirt weather on the mountains. People would look at me funny, snowboarding in short sleeves, but I simply said that I was from Minnesota. Enough said. I went out riding one day and hit the half pipe. I went in fast and launched up pretty fucking high. I meant to push out to do a 360, but I pushed straight out and fell in the middle of the pipe about fifteen feet onto my shoulder. I dislocated it pretty bad and had to punch it back into place. It hurt like hell, but I kept riding for another four hours.

I worked out at this time and was very fit. Eventually, I noticed that I was able to lift thirty pounds over my head with one arm and having trouble lifting five pounds with the other. I made an appointment to have it checked out the next time I went home. I had numerous scans and tests done, and I was told that I had snapped my nerve and that it had filled up with scar tissue, preventing it from working. My left arm was basically broken. I needed surgery, and I had no insurance in Colorado. On top of that, I could not be a resident of Colorado because you cannot gain residency while attending school. This meant that my tuition rates were a bit more than three times the in-state rates. I was running out of money and had to come home if I wanted to fix my arm.

I needed to fix my arm, but I wanted to finish the year in Colorado, so when I got back to Denver I was going to raves or parties every weekend. My buddies from the apartments knew a lot of people on the party scene, and they always wanted to go. I would say "Okay, you can drive my car and bring me there and back and give me some free acid and ecstasy or at least for really cheap herb," and we got a deal. I never paid for my drugs and always had a free ride both ways. It was a nice agreement. I went to a ton of very memorable parties and couldn't reiterate the majority of them if I tried. A few of them were also shows. I saw and met some wicked DJs, which eventually turned me on to turning tables. There were also breakdance contests where I met a couple of legends on two different occasions. Both signed the hat that I was wearing. They were Crazy Legs and Mr. Wiggles. Both were some of the forefathers of breakdancing and were in the film *Beat Street*, one of the first films to address the underground world of hip-hop.

One party that I can remember like it was yesterday, although I cannot remember the name of it, I could swear was a party just for me. It was outside in the mountains in somewhat of a valley, so there were cliffs on both sides of where the action was. I was drinking for the whole car ride into the mountains, so I was pretty plowed when we got there. I quit drinking and ate some ecstasy and washed it down with some acid. As I began to sober up and come down, I was starting to come up into an entirely different world of reality. It was the smoothest transition ever, and I was in a really good mood. I remember dancing all over hell with a bunch of people I did not know. It is amazing how nice people can be when they have ingested copious amounts of the right narcotics.

I remember dancing with this one girl right next to the speakers, and she was a really good dancer, always on beat and fucking sexy. I spoke with her for a minute, and it was the weirdest thing because she responded to me in ASL, and I do not know sign language. I did my best to communicate using primitive hand gestures, and I think she could read lips. I blew my mind when I realized she was completely deaf, and I could not figure out how the fuck she could dance so perfectly to the beat. Later that night, I talked to my friend's old lady who was legally deaf, but she was a very good lip reader and she could hear a little bit. She told me that she was standing so close to the speakers so that she could feel the vibrations. She said that she does the same thing. I had never thought about that, but it makes sense, yet I go by the speakers because I like the music, and it makes me deaf, not fair.

By this time, I was tripping my fucking balls off. There were a lot of horny girls, and it was a great atmosphere. I was not alive at the time, but I would compare it to the "free love" attitude of the sixties, making out with three or four girls at a time in a sloppy grope-fest of titties in my face and getting my wiener rubbed, then it was on to the next circle. I continued to dance around going from place to place in a world full of colors and trails of every light around. I remember I was zoning out to some cat swinging around a bunch of fire, and it was all one big trail to me. At this point, I was tripping so hard I could have seen trails of a snail. The music began to mix and incorporate a new beat. I stopped dead in my tracks and dropped my jaw because I knew that tune. It was the theme song from *The Simpsons*. It was mixed in perfectly over whatever crappy raver shit that they were playing. Sometimes if you get fucked up enough, it really doesn't matter what kind of crap is playing. Just look at any group of drunk girls at the bar; they will dance like total whores to a fucking line dance.

I was still zoned out on all the crazy colors and fire trails going around my head when someone smacked the shit out of my head from behind. Normally, I would have turned around ready to throw down, but I am positive that this X was caulk full of heroin, and I was so happy and lethargic I just slowly turned around like, "Huhhh?" It was my buddy's girlfriend, and she just turned me around and pointed at one of the mountain sides and said, "Watch." She rubbed my head or back or something as I stared at the blank side of a cliff, and then a laser light show started, and it blew my fucking mind, especially because *The Simpsons* was playing and actually sounded well mixed with whatever it was. The light show started out as a simple circle which grew and turned into an eyeball. It continued to grow, and it was trippy as fuck. That could be because of the acid and X and chronic, but someone that was sober agreed that it was trippy and pretty fucking cool. After that, the eyeball continued to grow until it was a pulsating Maggie Simpson about 150 feet tall on the side of the cliff. This show continued throughout the song as Maggie morphed into Lisa, into Bart, then Marge, and eventually Homer. I was in heaven.

One night, I went to a hotel party, which in hindsight was so stupid, considering the way that we were acting. Let's get together a bunch of underage kids, rent them a room, and have them do cocaine, ecstasy, acid, pot, and pills because nothing bad could possibly come of that, right? We were partying, nowhere to sit down, but all of a sudden, we heard a scratching at the door. Someone said, "Hey, ——, I think your mom is at the door." We all laughed for a second then looked at each other, and you could read everyone's face, and it looked like, "Oh shit, we are fucked."

It was exactly what we thought, the police, and they came in, and there was like an ounce of really good herb, some cocaine, alcohol, and around fifty pills of ecstasy that we couldn't find to hide. They busted in and held us up for a bit and gave us tickets for drinking while underage. I have a picture of everyone in the hallway of the hotel, and in hindsight, it is pretty funny to look at everybody high off their asses, waiting to see what they were going to do with us when they found everything. They had a dog, so it didn't take too long, and we all got very lucky when my best friend out of that crew that I had met at the apartments yelled out, "Everything in there is mine. These guys had nothing to do with that." What a fucking trooper. I still thank him for that because if they wanted to be dicks, we could have somehow gotten in a lot more trouble than we did.

I was so happy when released because they did not give anyone a breathalyzer. I realized this and told everyone not to pay the ticket and go to court because they had no evidence that we were actually drinking, and it is not illegal to be in the same room of alcoholic beverages. Everyone got off with no repercussions except for one. All the guys decided to stay at one apartment and ride a couple cars to court together. This was a good idea in theory; however, there was a bottle of tequila staring me in the face, and I could not resist. I woke up before everyone else and had a liquid Mexican breakfast along with a couple joints, one of which I smoked on the way to the courthouse.

I stunk really bad of tequila and herb, and I was eighteen. Needless to say, it did not take long for them to smell me out and put my ass in jail, but not before I went in front of the judge. He made an ass of me, telling me that I smelled like a brewery and that my eyes looked like New Jersey State road maps. I was locked up for contempt of court and had a nice five-by-eight-foot concrete resort for the weekend. They never really let me out. I got no recreation time, but I was able to see the TV in the common area. I could not hear it, but they did play *The Simpsons* every day at five, so I would stand at my three-inch wide little window and watch every day. It didn't matter that I couldn't hear because I knew exactly what they were saying. That was the only good part of my day. Some of the people were scary. I don't care for jail too much. When I was set to be released, they put me in a holding cell for way to long I had to pee really bad and my stomach started to hurt really bad. I thought I was going to puke, so I started banging on the door and yelling that I was going to get sick and no one came, so I threw up all over. I thought I would get in more trouble, but I did not. However, they did put me in arm as well as leg shackles and paraded me into a courtroom in front of what must have been a whole party of teenagers who must have been in trouble for the same thing.

I was a hot mess and looked like shit. The judge made a fool and an example out of me and told the party that they would turn out to be a piece of shit like me; it was embarrassing. My buddy that took my car picked me up when I got out, which was really nice. After a while, that same day, we got a call that our buddy who took the blame for everything was being released. We went to go pick him up and found him walking down the street. He got in the car and immediately started digging in his butt. We were like, "What the fuck?" and he pulled out a baggie with the fifty pills of EX out of his ass. He got lucky because that is a felony, bringing contraband into a lock-up facility, especially something like that. I know it is gross, but they were in a baggie, and yes, I did take some. I ate ass ecstasy, and I loved it, although it was on my mind that it had come out of my buddy's butthole.

I took a semester off because it was a pretty big surgery what with the cutting up my nerves then sewing them back together and everything. It really sucked, and there was a lot of rehab. It took a while to even be able to drive, not to mention that I was on a bunch of painkillers. Aside from not being able to move and having to wear this weird cold cast thing, it was nice to be home to the frozen tundra. It was also nice to hang out with my friends and be with my girlfriend again. My mother had since moved into her parents' condo because that is where we had always had family get-togethers, and she couldn't bring herself to get rid of it. My sister moved into the family house, and I moved in with her, I think I partied too much for her. In fact, I know she did. She had a roommate that I did not get along with, and it escalated to the point where I peed in his coffee and tormented him until he moved out. I was happy, and I started to mess around with spinning records and being a DJ. I bought two turntables and a mixer. I had headphones, a microphone, and some records, and I started from scratch (excuse the pun). I did in fact practice as a scratch DJ, mixing instrumentals and scratching the hell out of them. As my collection grew and I had lots of hip-hop instrumentals and a microphone, I began to freestyle all the time, and I fell in love. I don't even think when I do it, yet I am thinking four bars ahead, so I say something that will rhyme with whatever it is later, and it is totally involuntary.

My sister did not care for my newly found love, and I think I was a bit loud, and I know I was disrespectful, but I was nineteen years old and didn't really care. I feel bad about it now. Like I said, I was back together with my girlfriend even though I talked to the other one almost every day. I also got together with her over the holidays, and we had fun, but it was short-lived. I hung out with my girlfriend almost every day and went bowling and shit and watched movies. She was able to just stay over at my house all the time now because it was just me and my sister.

On New Year's Eve, there was the whole hoopla over Y2K; we decided to spend it up north at a casino because what better place to be if the whole economy crashes? Maybe the slot machines start throwing out change or something. We just got a bunch of coke and weed and had a good time. There were a few others up there with us, but society did not fall. I stayed with my girlfriend, although I cannot say there were no indiscretions during that time, but I don't really remember. In fact I know that there were, I am a bad boyfriend.

One day, my old lady and I were hanging out in the basement where all my stuff from Colorado was because I never unpacked it. She started going through some pictures, and then all hell broke loose. She found a few pictures of me and the new other girl. I guess she could tell the pictures were new and from while we were together and while I was in Colorado. They were not suggestive or pornographic, but I guess this was my first life lesson in the fact that women are not stupid. Quite the opposite, they always know what is going on, and you cannot fool them. Only tell the truth and leave out anything that you did that you know is wrong, then you never lied. However, I had not learned this yet, and I was a fucking dear in the headlights. I got grilled for a while, and she pushed me around until she got up and left. I followed her into the streets and whistled really loud. I learned how to do that watching a children's show when I had chicken pox. That has nothing to do with anything, but it is true. She threw the car in reverse, and I was like, okay word, but she didn't slow down. She kept coming, and I stood there like a dumbass smoking. It became crunch time, and I realized I had to jump out of the way. I tried, and the bumper clipped my leg. I rolled through the back window, and the next thing I knew, I was lying down in the back seat of her car with blood and glass everywhere. I crawled out and told her to drive back to my house because she couldn't drive with her car like that. I stumbled back to my house dripping blood and feeling faint. I guess we woke up my sister because she came out, and what did she do? She consoled her because she was crying. I just got hit by a goddamn car and went through the window. I needed stiches and was bleeding everywhere, but she was making sure she was okay.

Needless to say, we broke up, and my middle school crush and I were still active, vocally however, although she still lived in Seattle. That was a bit of a problem, so I just played around campus. I got a studio apartment / shared living arrangement. It was all right, but I learned that in those living arrangements, you cannot leave you food in the fridge or your toilet paper in the bathroom. My room held my bed, computer, and about two square feet of walking space. It was small, but it was right on University Avenue, and all my classes were walking distance. The first girl I played with was my playdate from the senior overnight. She just came over, had some drinks, and ended up cuming all over. I loved that place though, and I brought a few others over, but honestly, college was like Caligula, sex all the time.

The next one I remember well was a really hot brunette. She was riding me and saw a Vikings poster I had over my bed and in mid coatis just said, "Oh, I am Daunte Culpepper's daughter's swimming instructor." I just remember thinking, "Yeah, that's great, now get back to work." She did, and it was awesome. She was so fucking hot and did some crazy shit, but when she would talk, I just wanted to pour hot wax in my ears or punch her in the face, something to shut her the fuck up and apparently having sex with her didn't work although I know she got off because she squirted all over my bed. Unless she just peed on me, in which case I found her more annoying, but I know she came because she just about pinched my dick off when she got off.

I continued to mess around with my turntables and freestyling and got pretty descent. I went to a lot of hip-hop shows in Dinky-Town every weekend and met this one cat who had a crew and did shows. I hooked up with him, but I didn't DJ. I just came, and they would spit their written shit, and I would just freestyle, but people seemed to like it just as much sometimes more if I went off on a tangent and pulled it off. Later that year, I had to take a literature course as part of my graduation requirements. As much as I like to write, I fucking hate reading. I would self-diagnose myself as being mildly dyslexic. I am okay with letters, but I mix up words, and it makes no sense, and I have to read it all over again. It's kind of funny sometimes because whatever I mix it up into usually has some sort of underlying sexual connotation. However, it is also very annoying because it takes me forever to read anything.

I took a Native American studies course because it seemed interesting and easier than the other options. It was. There were only thirteen students in the class and thirteen books to read. Everyone was supposed to read every book and give one oral report on the one they were assigned. I didn't read shit, even the book I was supposed to. I just read the back of the jacket, and I still got an A. I met two friends in that class, coincidentally the only other two people in the class who were not Native American, and they were into the same hip-hop that I was. They apparently wanted to do something along those lines and were writing lyrics, but they needed a DJ. I stepped up, and we started doing shows as Minneapolis Junction. It was fun as hell. All the money went to the group. I just played for free drinks because it was so fucking fun. We would mostly have their set playing and have beats and random stuff to scratch lined up, so I would scratch and throw in beats every once in a while throughout the set, and then at the end, I would play instrumentals for them to freestyle to.

This is when it got cool because after a little bit, they would tell me to get on the mic, and I would blow up like I was fucking 2Pac. The crowd would go nuts because it is rare for the DJ to step from behind the decks and rip shit up, just as good if not better than the main attraction. I never toot my own horn, but I know what I heard. We did a couple albums, and I had a few versed on them, but I did do one song for a Christmas album in which I graphically described how I killed Santa Claus so nobody else would get any presents. After it came out, people would look at me and say, "I heard your Christmas song. What the fuck is wrong with you?"

That winter break, I wanted to go riding again, and I somehow found out some friends from high school, the same dumbasses that got busted five seconds into the ski trip, were living in Jackson Hole Wyoming. I got a hold of them and set it up to go stay with them for a week during winter break. It was fucking awesome, like spring break on snow. It was so sunny and nice. I was riding in a T-shirt, and I experienced the worst sunburn I could possibly imagine. I have dark skin, so I don't really burn at all, but it was so hot I was sweating through the padding on my goggles and had to take them off. I rode all day with no goggles. At the end of the day, the whites of my eyes were blood red and felt like they were covered in leather. If I opened my eyes wide, there were two clear lines where it was bleach white on either side, but the middle was red as hell and hurt like a bitch.

They lived in what had to be one of the oldest cabins in America. Maybe Daniel Boone lived there, I don't know, but it was all slanted, unbalanced, and old as shit. They had made a lot of friends, and it was like a campus party every night in the mountains. I got along with this one cat, and we would freestyle like every night. I recorded some of it, and it wasn't bad. This was the best mountain I had been to. We went riding every day, except for one day when everybody had to work. That is the day I burned the shit out of my eyeballs. They had these little snow huts that you would never be able to find if you didn't ride the mountain all the time, but they are just holes off to the side in the trees. You drop down into the hole into this little igloo type of structure, and it has buttresses and benches, it is fucking cool as hell and they are not approved by the mountain but they obviously look the other way.

We went into one to rest and smoke a bowl when a ski patrol came to the entrance and asked what was going on. He was clearly fucking with us because he slid in and said, "That smells good, but try this shit." We smoked, and I was blown away, not because his pot was so good but that in Minnesota the ski patrol will fuck with you for riding into the trees. There you go into the trees to smoke trees with the ski patrol. They also did not have a bar at this hill; however, they did have a convenience store at the main chalet. However, they sold forty ounces of Blue Ribbon for like two bucks, and you could drink them out on the patio.

They had the wickedest park, with all types of shit to slide and jump over, but the best was like a fucking trailer home in the middle of the park. There was a jump in front of it, and I hit it, did a 180 onto the trailer, and immediately fell on my ass. I sled the entire length of the trailer but managed to twist another 180 as I slid off the edge and land it. It felt so awesome. My buddy actually recorded it, but I lost that camera and the footage is no more. But I remember that shit, and it was cool as hell.

We partied every day, and there was actually a hip-hop show one night that was decent. They knew the bartenders, and somehow we got on the mic at the end of the night. I got into a zone and went off. We did a lot of back and forth, which was fun, but at the end, I flew off the handle talking shit. I'm pretty sure I talked shit about everything and everyone then finished up with a perfectly timed punch line, ending in Minnesota when I unzipped my hoodie to reveal my Minnesota T-shirt. I did not know that my friend whose room I was staying in was also a heavy sleeper, but I ended up missing my flight back. I bought a ticket for the next day, a little latter in the day, and went riding all day again by myself and had a blast.

When I returned to my studio in Minnesota, I got a big surprise. As I walked up to the house from the parking lot in back, I started to notice that all of my things, basically my entire room, everything that I owned and a bunch of expensive text books strewed all over the lawn as well in the dumpsters...I would have sold those textbooks if I were them...and an asshole. Those things are, or were fucking expensive, not that anyone reads actual books anymore. Now you can do all your research, find the answer to any question on the planet and look at porn all at the same time. I wish I had a cell phone when I was a kid. I had to ride a bike to the fucking Library and use the Dewey Decimal System and search through a stinky maze to find some book that that predated the printing press to write a paper. Ow you can do all your research on your fucking phone. I began to recognize the textbooks and thought, *Huh, I took that class and that one, and fuck, that's my notebook and all this paper is all my notes from since*

I started college. I walked up to my room, passing a bunch of guys I didn't know, which was weird because everyone that lived there always stayed in their rooms. I walked into my room, and there was a jockey-looking kid who seemed really confused. I looked around, and everything in my room was cleared out. All my textbooks, all of my notes which had a lot of good information. The only thing left were my desk and computer and my bed. I said, "What the fuck is this happy horse shit?" I think he was the only passive frat guy I have ever met, either that or frat guys are a nocturnal race that only turns into loud annoying douchebags after dark or a few drinks. Either way he was very apologetic and placed blame for the books and said that his frat brothers had fun throwing them all around and destroying it.

I clearly remember saying that they were obviously dumb as fuck and they could have easily sold all those textbooks back to the school and got enough money for a keg or something, then I realized they are probably spending mommy and daddy's loot, so fuck them. I was also pissed because he had neon bar signs up and a big rug. It looked so much cooler. Mine looked like an actual art studio. Oh, and a ton of my artwork got thrown out as well, fucking assholes.

The nice guy in my room was very apologetic, so I couldn't do anything with him, and I hadn't had enough to drink to start shit with a whole frat house even if they weren't in their asshole phase, I would have gotten fucked up. I told him I would pick up my stuff ASAP just don't have sex on my bed, but his bed was coming that day, so I really had to get my shit out soon and was lucky I came before that got thrown out as well. I just needed a place to put it, and when that happened, he actually helped me bring my stuff out to my car. I just put my bed on the hood of the car like they do in the hood because I moved three blocks away.

Finding a new place was not as easy as I expected because I almost ripped the leasing agent's head off when he told me that they transferred the lease to a fraternity because it was more profitable. I don't know how I did it, but I just left because I did not want to go to jail. I did what any young man who is put in a difficult situation would do, and I called my mommy to come save the day. She actually has the ability to keep her cool and the intelligence to get the job done. She was able to find me a place in Dinky Town. It wasn't on University Avenue, but it was cool. She got the rent lowered and I think some money for all the books and stuff that the fuck-heads destroyed. I remember clearly that later that day I drove past my old house, and it had those big Greek letters for the frat like right under my old window, and I really wanted to burn that fucking house down, but I did not.

I moved into my new shared living house. It was basically the same as before. I never saw anyone else, but I know they will use all your toilet paper if you leave it in the bathroom and eat your leftovers. You could not leave anything in the common areas, or it would disappear. I also did not ever take a shower. I think I did twice, but one time someone walked in while I was in the shower. I guess I did not lock the door. Instead of realizing that the bathroom was occupied, he just went to the bathroom. I wanted to beat his ass, but I was ass naked, and I feel that you would be a severe disadvantage if you tried to fight someone naked.

I did get to know one guy that lived there; he was a real piece of work. I could tell from the first time that I talked to him that he had an addiction, and it included but was not limited to powders. Later he confirmed my theory and told me he was a heroin addict. I didn't really care. He was someone to talk to and smoke a bowl with, plus I wasn't worried about being corrupted. I vowed never to do shit like that, and you cannot make me do anything I don't want to. He accepted that and never offered my anything, although we did do coke and stuff every once in a while, but I was relatively good. Although I know he still used H, I don't know to what extent because I told him early on that if he ever tried to do that shit in front of me, I would knock it out of his hands and punch him in the face. I assume that's why he never did it.

I was lifting weights every other day and in good shape while he was the poster boy for heroin addict magazine. I thought he started to get his shit together when he asked me for a ride to the methadone clinic. I would give him a ride whenever I needed to because I felt that I was helping someone and doing a good thing. Later I learned that this was something he had to do and was court ordered. For some reason, I try to believe that everyone is still genuinely good at heart, even the assholes. He would take it sometimes, and I would make him take it in front of me. Then he tried to trade me his methadone for some weed. I'm not going to do synthetic heroin if I don't have any desire to do the real thing. I found out he was actually selling/trading it, so I confronted him, cut him off, and told him I didn't want any part of it, and he needed to figure out his own transportation if he wanted to commit felonies.

There were a lot of parties at this time, and we actually did a lot of shows, mostly in Dinky Town, but some in Saint Paul and downtown Minneapolis. I found my "Cheers," where everybody knew my name. It was Dub's Pub right next to the Dinky Towner in the middle of Dinky Town. I got to know all the bartenders really good, and I together with whoever I was with owned the upstairs with the pool table, and no one would come up there. It was awesome—except for one time when me and a buddy who would always go there with me and the whole upstairs was full, so we just sat at the bar and talked shit.

Unfortunately, at one point my buddy pointed out a picture of the U of M wrestling team with this big gorilla-looking guy in the front. He was huge. The picture was signed by all the team members and in front of the behemoth; it looked like he signed "Buck." We started talking shit about him really loud if I remember correctly, and the bartender told us to keep it down before we get fucked up. Apparently it was in fact the wrestling team upstairs, and they could hear us, and Buck was there. The only thing is his name wasn't Buck. It was Brock Lesnar, who would go on to become a professional (if you can call it that) wrestler and a MMA champion.

We got pretty lucky on that one, and it seems like he is a bit of a hothead, so he probably would have tossed us around and whooped our monkey asses. We hung out there all the time. I would even go there by myself sometime on the way home from school for a pint or a cocktail. It is okay because I was friends with the bartenders, and I would talk to them, so it wasn't like I was really alone, maybe that is how severe alcoholism begins. Either way, it got to the point where one day I ordered an appetizer and he just brought me back to the kitchen and showed me where everything was and how to do it. He said if I wanted something at that time of day to just go ahead and make it for my damn self and I wouldn't have to pay. That was cool with me.

    The beginning of the next year began, and I was pretty happy with my place. I had more room to work on my art. The modem was faster, and I actually had a TV. I did not have cable, but it was better than nothing, which reminds me of the most memorable phone call I ever got and will never forget. My mom called me at whatever time it was, way too early in the morning for me. I said, "I am fucking sleeping, what the fuck?" I try not to swear when I talk to my mom if I can help it because I know it upsets her, but it was too goddamn early. She said "Turn on the television." I asked what channel, and she said it didn't matter. I turned on to see Tower 1 on smoking, and she told me that a plane had flown into it. It was a shitty way to wake up. I can remember when I saw people hanging out the window, and then when the first one jumped out, my heart fucking dropped. I said, "Did you see that?" and just then the second plane hit. Although I was nowhere near New York, it was crazy and even a little scary to watch even though we did not know what really happened and may not to this day, but that is another much longer story that I am not even going attempt to get into.

    Everything was different after this if you didn't notice, but there started being cameras everywhere, and you cannot bring weed on an airplane anymore because they inspect you for nail files and clippers for God's sake. That was the most disturbing phone call I have ever received. Calls about a death in the family sucked, but they were expected, and I knew it would happen soon. This came out of nowhere. School was out for a little bit, and every class had to have a little pow-wow about the tragedy when classes where back in session. This was arbitrary, and everyone said the same thing, but it is just lip service, and all of a sudden loving America when you hated it a week ago is not going to change anything. This approach to what happened makes me sick to my stomach. Before 9/11, the majority of Americans disapproved of the direction the country was headed. After the incident, everyone and their mother was rocking a flag and all about America. The one thing that pissed me off the most was a thirty seconds infomercial for a Patriot Pack. You got some American flag sticker and a flag and probably some other worthless crap for twenty bucks plus shipping and handling. Not one penny of the money from these sales went to help the city of New York or the families of the victims. I hope whoever kept all that money dies and goes to a personal hell where he is on fire and suffers for a while then has to kill himself by jumping out of a skyscraper. I watched the whole thing and smoked some weed, but that was one shitty morning.

    I kept going to school every day, but I had to get a crappy old bike to ride to class. It was such a piece of shit; I didn't even lock it. Bike theft is a huge problem on campus. It worked out fine and saved money. One day it was sleeting out and very slippery. I was coming up to the main entrance of campus, and I had the choice of trying to run the yellow light or wait. I gunned it at the other end of the intersection two Asian girls were crossing right in my path; I slammed on my brakes, which in hindsight was the worst possible thing to do. I flipped over and slid down the street into them and knocked them over like bowling pins. I apologized, and I think they were a bit hurt. I know they were pissed off. I still rode my bike to work out every other day and ate healthy.

    I still drank beer, but I would drink an equal amount of water for every beer I had. I don't do that anymore; maybe I should. I eventually took over more a hops-filled diet, lots of beer. So I went to a lot of parties at this time, not like in Colorado, just regular Minnesota kids drinking way too much at whatever location they could occupy. I was full of piss and vinegar at this time, so I would just go out by myself sometimes and find the party. It isn't hard. Just follow the drunk people. I went to many a frat party that I was not invited to, even one at the place I used to live. I wanted to pee on the wall, but I did not, considering all the drunken rowdy frat boys all around. They definitely are more docile in the daytime. I would just walk into random parties and act like I belonged there. The same as walking down the street smoking weed, the audacity of the action negates any possibility of being caught. I had girls on my jock at frat parties because they thought that I was part of the frat for some reason. I even have something on tape to that effect.

One day, I did just that because I could hear a lot of yelling and commotion down University Avenue, so I went down there. I brought my video camera because not everyone had a phone that could moving images at that time. Apparently, the Gopher Hockey team had won the championship, and everyone was batshit crazy. They were throwing bottles and lighting stuff on fire. A few cars even got tipped over; it was a good time. I recorded the majority of it; they had like a mosh pit with everyone chanting some shit I didn't understand. Then I heard some loud bangs, and a battalion of Minneapolis PD came down the street, covering it from wall to wall. They had shields, batons, beanbags, and as ass load of mace.

I ran into the middle of the street as everyone was running away. I stayed there as long as I possibly could. I was forced to move to the side even though I could not see because I had mace in my face. I continued to roll film, and I stood on the sidelines with some other photographers. I was rolling as an officer walked right up and deliberately sprayed down all of us even though we were just standing off to the side with cameras. The officer got hostel and started to hit and chase us. I was able to catch footage of the officer cross-checking one of the camera up with his nightstick. He then grabbed his camera and threw it on the pavement. After the incident, a group of girls brought me a flash component of one of the camera of one of the guys I was standing next to. They thought we were friends. When I looked at it, it said "Daily #3," the newspaper for the U of M campus is the *Minnesota Daily*, so I contacted them and asked who assigned camera number 3.

They knew exactly who it was and were so happy I had their equipment. I told them I had footage they might want to see. We set up a time to meet later that day. We did and I presented them with the footage in a meeting room, and the guy in the footage was there, and I could tell it was him. They asked if they could have the tape, and I said, "Of course." They used it, and a still from the footage I took ended up on the front page of the *Minnesota Daily*. It was a shot of an officer spraying everyone that had a camera with mace. I was really proud of that. However, I was more proud of the fact that they brought my footage to court and made a case against the Minneapolis police department for singling out and assaulting those with cameras. The result of this case was that all professional and freelance photographers were legally allowed to take pictures or record at any event and that any retaliation by the police due simply to the fact that they were taking pictures would be considered unlawful and punishable by law. I received no credit for the picture or the resulting legal changes that followed, but I know what happened and I am happy that everything worked out and that I was able to help. You don't need to get a trophy for everything, knowing that you did the right thing and helped somebody should be reward enough.

One day a friend of mine called me out of the blue and said he was in the neighborhood and was going to stop by. I said, "Okay," and he did. He was working for a moving company and had a nightstand and a small entertainment center from his last move that he was going to have to trash, so he asked me if I wanted them. Considering that I had basically no furnishing in my room, I took them and still have them today. He also asked if I was working, and I said I was not. He said he could get me a moving job with him and we could work together. I started working there the next week, and I had a blast. It was just me and my buddy in a truck, working alone and making good money.

The job was also very interesting. You would be amazed at the things people just leave out in the open even though they called a company to move all their shit. I cannot count how many dildos and other random sex toys I have seen by simply lifting up a mattress. One time this lady was very adamant about the fact that she needed to be out by a certain time, and she would tip well if we could do this. She was smoking hot, like model style, and there were framed naked pictures of her all over the house. I soon realized that she was only taking about half of the stuff in the house and also all the baby stuff. This bitch was dipping out on her man and taking their child without telling him. I wanted to slap her. My friend said that these things happen and you just have to do your job. I did, but I still wanted to slap her, and I dropped her dildo in the dirt on purpose. That shit isn't cool with me.

There are a million stories because every job was different, but one of my favorites was some rich motherfuckers in a high-rise in Minneapolis. When we got there, the guy showed us the situation and then said, "Take a look in the bathroom." I left a little something in there to help you work faster. There was a big fucking Scarface size pile of blow right there, and it was super clean and really good. I am glad I was working with the crew I was because everyone got down, and yes, we worked out asses off and knocked that shit out in like half the time. This has nothing to do with anything, but I have a very distinct memory of one of the movers using the bathroom and obviously taking some sort of epic shit because I could smell it down the hall.

It was really bad; however, right after he walked out of the bathroom, which was probably flammable, the lady of the house (who was really hot) walked into the same bathroom and started sniffing like it was going out of style. I still have no idea how she went in there and was inhaling all that funk and coke cocktail when I had to hold my breath when I walked down that part of the hallway. I had to pee like twenty minutes later, and I swear it was still so bad it made my eyes water. This is when I learned that whenever you have a group of men working together, the daily contest is to have the biggest smelliest shit out of the whole crew. I never played that game. Sorry about that; it is just a funny-ass story.

We had another buddy from high school working with us eventually, and we had a nice little crew. We would drink all day, which was okay because we were young and invincible for some reason. Those were good times. We worked together for a long time, but one day me and our other friend who hadn't worked there as long got pulled to the side and basically accused of a monetary discrepancy, and we had no clue what the fuck they were talking about. To this day, I do not know what they were talking about, but we did nothing wrong. Well, we drank a lot, and I smoked weed all day, but that was not the issue. So we got canned, but no one else did. Our other friend did get canned a few weeks later, however. Curious.

I went back to school for a bit and met up with someone somehow that hooked me up with another moving company. It was a really small operation, but they paid me, so whatever. I eventually talked to one guy I worked with, and he was talking about quitting his second job. At the end of the day, he dropped me off at my house and just said, "Damn, you live right here? This is just a few blocks from my other job. Do you want to take it?" I said, "Why not? Hook me up."

He had mentioned that it was a cake walk, but he was just sick of the job and the boss. Later on I would learn what he meant. The boss was dim-witted to put it nicely. I was at least ten times more intelligent than this man, and that is giving him more credit than he deserves. The job, however, was really fucking easy; all I had to do was play janitor on two floors of an animal-testing facility. It sounds like a fucked-up place to work, and it was. All I had to do was empty the trash in the offices and labs, vacuum, and mop. It only took like two hours, but I could only work between 8:00 PM and 8:00 AM and nobody was. I got paid for eight hours of work five days a week as long as it got done regardless of how much time I actually spent there.

Sometimes I would go out to the bar until close and then stumble to the lab, sometimes so plowed that I would ride my bike because I would get a DWI just by rolling down the window. No field test or breathalyzer needed. Sometimes I wouldn't even go till like 5:00 AM and still be there when the scientists were coming in for work. Other times, I would be so trashed I would just go and empty all the trash bins and be out in like thirty minutes. And a couple of times, I didn't go at all, but it was eight hours paid in my pocket. I would park in a heated garage that had a pressure washer, soap, and scrubby brushes for washing cars, so I would get a free car wash every week. It was kind of a mood point, considering my car was garbage, and it was like polishing a turd.

Although it was an easy job, it was a really depressing place to work. The offices were no big deal, but the labs were filled with horrible sounds of suffering mice, hamsters, rats, birds, all kinds of animals. I am not an animal enthusiast of activist, but it was even upsetting to me at times. One that bothered me a lot was the mice and rats. They would have these headpieces on with bolts screwed into their head, and they looked so miserable. I learned to ignore it, but I still felt bad. I had no clue how they could actually physically do this to these animals without them going nuts and running away. I would later find out that there were copious amounts of ketamine in all the labs as well as some offices that would do the trick, considering it can knock out a grown man.

I also found the monkey room. This was the saddest room of all, and I will never forget it. Outside of the mammal room, which I was not required to clean and not really even supposed to know about, they had a sign that said that all who enter must be wearing the required "scientist" clothing, including goggles shoe covers, and blue hairnet thing. I went in there wearing all that, and the monkeys went fucking bananas, and yes, that was sort of a joke. My dad would have liked it. After a few weeks, I decided to do somewhat of a social experiment and went in with the monkeys in my street clothes. It was very bittersweet in that the chimps were so adorable and nice they took to me like one of their own, maybe because I am so hairy. They were calm and collected and would even hold my finger and smile at me, at least it looked like they were smiling. I would smoke some herb and go play with the monkeys after that, and it made my day except for one aspect of the situation. They too had headpieces on with bolts screwing into their fucking skull, and they looked like they were in pain. However, they got happy as shit when I would come in with plain clothes and not torturing them. They got even happier when I noticed that they had a TV/VCR in their room and figured out that every movie they had was a monkey movie. *Tarzan, George of the Jungle, Dunston Checks In*, and a ton of other monkey-focused movies they apparently loved to watch. After I was done, sometimes I would smoke and then watch a movie with the monkeys. It was very therapeutic for me, and I believe the monkeys as well.

I hung out with a friend one night, and at the end of it, he couldn't go home for some reason, so I told him he had to come help me at work for a couple hours, so he did. We half-assed everything and got done really quick. While we were there, I wanted to further my social experiment involving the monkeys. I had my buddy put on the entire scientist garb that you are required to wear, and I kept my street clothes on. I won't say bananas again, but the monkeys did not like my friend at all to put it nicely. They were throwing their food and other stuff at him, and they loved me. This concluded my study, and I came to the conclusion that the animals are hostile toward anyone in blue scrubs, goggles, and gloves because they torture and hurt them, putting hardware into their cranium.

I really hated this place for this reason, but it was the easiest check I have ever gotten. I fucked around a lot and probably could have gotten in a lot of trouble. I was pretty much still in my prime and would do whatever it took to get high, except for anything intravenous…that scares the fuck out of me. So I would take the dust cleaners for the computers in the offices and fill up a rubber glove, then I would huff it like it was nitrous ox and be totally fucked up. However, one time, I did that around one or two in the morning. There was a lot of weird noise in my head, then everything went black. I woke up about 5:30 AM on the floor of the office with a glove in my hand and a bottle of keyboard cleaner right next to me. I got really fucking lucky because people started coming in about ten minutes later. I finished my business and tried not to look at them as they came in, but I never did that again.

The other significant and stupid thing that I did while working there involved ketamine (cat tranquilizer). As I stated, they had copious amounts of the drug around the building and had half-used bottles just sitting around. Sometimes I would G them, but at first I would just G a syringe and fill that up out of the bottle. Once you cook it up, you have a whole little crack baggie full of special K that could knock you and three friends out.

I eventually started grabbing whole vials, but I was careful I never got caught. One time I brought home a half a syringe of K and gave it to the crackhead downstairs. I tapped him, injecting it into his leg, and recorded him fall into a K hole almost instantly. It was fucking hilarious and very hard to watch at the same time. I was working on a film project, and it was supposed to be artsy and depressing, but it was a bit too sad, and I couldn't put it in. Eventually, I learned what the guy who got me the job was talking about when my boss got fired. He was totally incompetent and lost the account, so I was out of a job again. It was not long before I got a call from my first moving job. They were on a really big move and needed help. I said I would come help them out for cash if I could have my job back, and they agreed. I was happy because it was always interesting; however, in hindsight, I am pretty sure my back was pissed off at the situation because after a while I began to feel myself getting old. Who would have thought that after a while, bringing big screen TVs and pianos up- and downstairs would start to add up and take a toll on my body? Which brings me to one beef that I have about big screen TVs. What the fuck took them so long to come out with the flat screens? They are so light. When I was moving, more people had big screens than I would have thought they were bug fucking tanks. It was like a whole piece of furniture, and they were heavy as hell. However, I never got hurt on the job, just extremely sore afterward.

This was when I began playing softball. A few guys from work were playing in a D league, which basically means everyone pays more attention to drinking than playing well. That was fine with me because I hadn't played baseball since I was twelve and I had never played softball before in my life, but a player didn't show up one day, and I lived close by, so my buddy from work called and asked if I wanted to play. I was living on campus, so I didn't have a glove or cleats or anything. He asked if I was right-handed. I am, so he said, "Get your high ass over here quick or we have to forfeit." They would all say shit like this because they couldn't comprehend smoking copious amounts of weed and still being functional, but when you have been doing it every day of your life, you get used to it or develop a tolerance, whatever you want to call it, but I pretty much just smoke myself back to normal.

Some people need a cup of coffee to wake up and feel like themselves. Well, I chose to smoke a bowl. I dipped over to the field and was somewhat of a joke because I walked up with no glove, wearing skate shoes (no traction), some raggedy shorts, and an old skate shirt. I think some of them thought it was a joke, like this is who you called to fill in for whoever it was. I think I was in the field most of the time, which I hate, but there was one good thing besides getting plowed that happened in that game, which was I hit a home run in my very first softball game. That was cool. In hindsight, I really should have celebrated that moment more because it would be the only home run I would ever hit, ever. What bugs me is I didn't even hit it over the fence. We were on a field with no fence, so I had to leg it out, and there was a play at the plate, but I still got a fucking home run, goddammit. I also batted a thousand, that day, and every time I got on base, I scored.

That ended up being my thing because I was clearly not a power hitter, so I just swing at like half strength and uppercut just a little so the ball would go just over the infielders' heads and out of reach of the outfielders. I guess they changed their mind about me because they asked me to come back next week, and I ended up playing every game for the rest of the year.

After a few years, they brought me to Austin, Minnesota, the birthplace of Spam, for a weekend-long softball tournament. The whole town smells like Spam by the way. After the first game I played, they started putting me in as catcher, and after my first game in that position, I never played another one. That was until the first game of this tournament. The short stop for our team could not make it in time, and they wanted me to take his spot, and I said, "Hell going no, I play catcher, not infield." To this, they responded, "Biggie is going to play catcher, so it is either him or you at shortstop."

Biggie is a friend of the team and comes to watch all the time, weighing in at well above three hundred pounds and not quite the guy you want at short stop. This was a tournament, so for the good of the team, I took the infield. I batted really well, and we had a runaway game. However, toward the end of the game, I had a chopper hit right to me, but it took a wicked hop at the last second. I already had my glove hand down and did not have time to bring it up and stop the ball from hitting me in the face. I had to use my other hand to block my face, and the ball hit me right on the tip of my index finger, shattering the bone. It hurt like hell, but I finished the game as well as the game after it. It was getting very swollen, but I still played six more games throughout the weekend. This was a beer tournament so when you bought beer at the concession stand, it came in a rack of forty-eight beers that helped with the pain a lot. However, with the fact that we were all plowed, it was no mystery why we did not win the tournament.

I was also getting high as shit with this one cat from the team. When I got home, I showed my dad my finger and asked him about it. I trusted his medical advice because he did medicinal work in Vietnam. However, I would later learn that the best idea they would give the injured is just to tough it out. This was not good advice. Eventually, I could not bend my finger, and my mom said to go see a real doctor. When I did go and get X-rays, the doctor's first question was, "Why the hell didn't you come in sooner?" It turned out that a chunk of bone chipped off and got wedged in the joint and was in the way and would not let the finger bend. I told him my dad told me it was fine, and in a nice way, he basically told me my dad was a dumbass.

I had surgery where they took out the chipped bone and put a screw in my knuckle as well as a long pin down the length of my finger. This ruined my summer and fall. Then I had to do physical therapy, which really sucked, but my therapist was really hot and looked like my out-of-town girlfriend's sister. Once winter hit, I learned that this injury would bother me the rest of my life. I could no longer bend my finger, nor can I straighten it because the tip of my finger is more or less dead; it just flops around. The pin came out, but they left the screw in, and when a real Minnesota winter is in full effect, I can feel it in my finger, and my knuckle gets cold as fuck.

I played in this tournament every year without injury, but sure enough, it would happen again. I was playing catcher because they realized I wasn't joking when I said that I did not want to play infield. I was catching, and we played four games that day. It started raining, and we were done, but one of the teams playing after us on our field was short a catcher, and they asked me to play. I have no clue how many beers I have had at this point, and I know I was stoned as fuck, but I said, "Hell yeah," and jumped in. This is the beginning of my second injury at the Austin drunken tournament.

The minute the game started, it began to pour, and it got really sloppy. I actually played pretty well, considering how much I had to drink. There was a guy on third, and the ball was hit to the shortstop. The play was obviously at the plate, and I was ready. However, the shortstop threw a 90 mph fastball like he was in the outfield throwing from the fucking fence. It hit the ground right in front of the plate and bounced up right into my chin. I had no time to break my finger, trying to save my face. My chin opened up, and the game got put on hold. I went to the concession stand, and for some reason, I wanted duct tape, and they actually had some. I knew it was pretty bad, but I did not have any health insurance and would not go to the hospital. I duct-taped the gaping wound and stepped back in the game. I had to bat by the time I taped my chin up, and as I was standing there, I began to dump blood all over the plate. It was pretty bad; I got kicked out of the game.

The whole team got on my ass about the fact that my face was fucked and I needed to go to the hospital, but I would not go because I had no health insurance. If I didn't mention it, I was by far the youngest person on the team, but one of our guys just said, "Take this," and handed me his insurance card. The brother of my buddy from work basically grabbed me and brought me to the hospital, which was not far away. He came in with me to check me in, which is a really good thing, considering I couldn't even remember the guy's name, let alone his address after I gave the receptionist the insurance card.

Luckily, my buddy's brother knew all that shit and got me out of it. He blamed it on me being contused and that was very believable because I was losing blood like my chin was a faucet. I went in and got my stitches right away. It was really deep and wide, like my ex-girlfriend, ba-dum-bum. But seriously, they had to put nine stitches on the inside and fifteen on the outside. It was real horror show. I looked somewhat like a drunken Frankenstein. The doctor said he had to get some paperwork and I could be on my way, but I couldn't ever remember the guy's name who I was supposed to be. He left the insurance card on the counter, so I grabbed it and ran out the back door. I am very surprised that I did not collapse because I felt weak as hell. I ran to an intersection down the road and called the team and told them where I was. Someone picked me up in a few minutes. I went back to the park and continued to drink until the beer was gone; I wish I was still in my twenties.

For the next two weeks, I played every single game in the tournament, usually four games a day. Everyone seemed to know me because as they came up to bat, they would look at my chin and say something along the lines of, "Hey, you're that kid that got his chin spit and tried to duct tape it, aren't you?" This got old really quick because I had a ton of stiches in my chin and it was swollen as hell. It was pretty obvious that I was that guy. I played eight more games after my stiches/concussion, and I actually hit pretty good. I did what I do and go on base and made it home. I also caught well and made a wicked play at the plate.

My third and final softball injury was the beginning of the end of my softball career. It also happened to be the first pitch of the first game of the season. I was the leadoff hitter, and I don't know why, but I hit a looper over the infield and ran it out and had to slide in for a double. The next batter hit what I thought was going to be a home run, so I was already about a foot away from third base. The fielder caught it at the fence, and I had to run back to second. I had no time, so I had to jump in head first. I just barely made it, but I was safe. After two hits, I made it home, but I never noticed anything was wrong until I got high-fives at the bench. Something did not feel right, and then I noticed that my pinky finger must have gotten jammed on the slide because it was bent in three different ways. I can't believe I didn't notice it, but I have come to learn that after years of fucking myself up, I have an incredibly high pain tolerance. I told the coach that I had to go, and he told me to fuck off because they needed me. I showed him my hand, and he said, "Take your ass to the hospital." One nurse tried to reset it for a while then called in another nurse, and it took them way too long to reset it, but they did. However, they did set it, but it was still all fucked up and didn't quite bend right like the finger on my other hand.

During the softball days, I played around quite a bit because my out-of-state girlfriend was back in Seattle, so I was free, and I can only assume she was doing the same thing. I was also not really on good terms with my high school girlfriend. I went to a rave in a really odd location; it looked the kind of place you would bring someone to kill them, not that I would ever do that, but it was pretty creepy. I did some ecstasy and danced around like a jackass and eventually started messing around with some girl. She was fit and obviously high as shit, so she was fun. We messed around and exchanged numbers. We ended up dating I guess for a while; we even went to Mexico together, where I won my second drinking contest down there. We had a lot of fun. She was a big sexual freak, and she liked to party. We went to many, and she also liked coke and speed, which when done in moderation is really fun to do and fuck all night.

While we were dating I met another girl at a party on campus, and we had messed around more than a few times. One day in particular, I forgot that I had told my sort-of girlfriend that I would be down to hang out later. I had the other girl over, and we were fucking pretty loud so there is no way to lie your way out of that even if I had locked the door, which I did not. She stopped by and slammed open. I stood up, and she properly punched me in the forehead like a fucking man. She had a ring on, and I ended up with a hole in my forehead that was dripping blood. She almost beat the shit out of her, but she ran away. Fuck, that girl was really hot, but I never spoke to her again—I wonder why. The angry girl and I fought it out for a bit and inevitably ended up boning that night, and I didn't even wash my wiener.

Later I met a girl who looked almost the same as that girl that got me punched in the head. Fucking beautiful; however, she did have a kid that was like seven or something. I messed with her for a while, and when that little shit came around, it was fucking. I can remember him being around one day and her bringing him in the other room, yelling his name and yelling no very strictly. Then I heard the loudest smack in the world, followed by a horrible scream from the child. I told my best friend about it because it blew my mind. Later that year, he was over at my house. She came over, and she let the kid run around and went down on me till I finished, then brought the little shit machine to the lake down the street because she promised him she would.

My buddy and I hung out and smoked while she was at the lake, and I told him the story of her smacking the shit out of him, and just then she came back and stormed in the house, bringing him to the bathroom. Apparently, he shit himself while in the lake, and she was pissed. She brought him in the bathroom to clean up, and I looked at my friend and told him to be quiet and just wait. Without fail, there was the yelling of the name and then the inevitable sound barrier breaking smack that hurt me to hear it, and I think my buddy as well, because he cringed, saying, "I thought you made that up, yo." I did not, and I do not make things up. It is not my style. We messed around for a while, but I knew that would never amount to anything more than a good blow job and a willing and awaiting pussy that would come over at the drop of a hat.

Then the first cheerleader girl whose virginity I stole and who subsequently got my ass beat eight ways from Sunday met up somehow and started hanging out. She got a boob job and looked incredible. We would get together and drink, and I obviously was smoking my medicine. We did ecstasy more than a few times, but it would become very clear what she wanted to do every time we would hang out.

This girl evolved into a sexual deviant freak that blew my mind. She was loud, very loud, and would say some really dirty shit as well as wanting to tie me up and have her way with me. I almost had a threesome with her and some girl she had over. We were all rolling and horny as shit, then that bitch fell asleep. It was too much for her; it was really good X. So we just bucked up and had to fuck for around six hours, and once again, *fuck*, I wish I was twenty something again. That was fun.

One time she called me over to her dorm because her roommate was gone, so I went over there to a big surprise. My ex-girlfriend, the one right before her that she picked on and tormented until she left the school district, was right there hanging out with her. I had no clue what to do, so I just went in there, got fucked up, and played with both of them. I did not ask any questions. We played for a while, and then once again the third party fell asleep. There were two separate rooms in the dorm, so we were alone, or at least we thought. We were fucked up and had an all-out fuck fest, which included tying my ass to the bed and having her way with me and screaming things that could possibly get you kicked out of that Catholic girls' college. This went on for a couple of hours until the other girl (my girlfriend before her) walked in the room, saw and heard everything, then broke into tears. She freaked the fuck out for about an hour until she left with a huge bug up her ass. We said, "Okay, what are you going to do?" So we went right back to doing what we were doing, and I am still surprised she did not get into trouble because we were in a girls' dorm at an all-girl Catholic school and she was really loud and fucking nasty; it put porn to shame. I have seen her since, and she is married with children, but I could see it in her eyes, she would still let me hit it, and she is still hot as hell. I have since met up with quite a few old bones and had basically the same reaction from most. However, some could not forget how I did them dirty and wanted to kill me. I guess you can't win them all.

    Around this time, I was still frequenting my local pub every night and making good friends with the bartenders. One day, one of the older guys was bitching about how he was going to move, but he was going to get fucked if he left before his lease agreement was over. I was on a month-to-month deal, so I told him I would just take over his lease and promised to always pay it on time. He was stoked because he was able to get out of his lease early, and I was happy because the rent was actually cheaper. It was a win-win situation. On top of that, the room had free cable and a fucking air conditioner; I was so happy. There were a couple of weeks left on the lease, so before I left, I actually got into a bit of an argument with the druggy downstairs. I don't remember what he did, but he really pissed me off, and we exchanged words. I could have broken him in two, but I decided not to. Later that night, he went out, and me and my friend from work slammed a bottle and got rowdy. We went down to his room, broke in, and destroyed it. We broke his bed, desk, and well, we basically broke everything in the room, and my friend pissed on his bed and took a shit in his desk. When he came home, he flipped the fuck out, but he didn't have a chance against either of us, let alone both of us. I know that he was high as shit because the next day, he talked to me like nothing had happened. We were civil after that. I am not one to hold grudges, and I think he had more of a right to, considering his bed got pissed on, and there was a hot dookie in the room that I'm sure he had not found yet.

Later that month, my buddy that destroyed the room was smoking a bowl in his room with me. Actually, my friend wasn't smoking; it was just me, but that doesn't matter. He had a friend stop over, and she was really cute for a doper. After a bit, me and my buddy decided we should go to the bar and asked them if they wanted to join us. He said no, but she jumped at the offer. So the three of us went up to my bar and went upstairs to play pool and have some drinks. We had the whole place to ourselves until these two girls in their early twenties who from a mile away looked like nothing but strippers. They were. Apparently, no one told them that I owned the upstairs of that bar, but they were hot, so I let it slide. We played a few pickup games of pool and got pretty fucking drunk until things started getting frisky.

We collectively decided to go get a motel room and all get naked. It was so casual. Everyone was like, "Okay, I'm down," so me and my friend left with this hot drug addict and two hot strippers to have some sort of orgy in a gross motel. I didn't really know what to expect. We got to the room, and I just thought, *Fuck it*, and I took my pants off. I still had my drawers on, but my boy was right there, and I figured it was up to the girls to take the next step. There was no delay, and I got jumped on.

There were two beds, so I told my friend to stay on the left bed and I would stay on the left. No bed jumping except for the girls. All good things come to an end, and everyone was taken care of and finished, so we just decided to go our respective ways, considering none of us knew each other and we just wanted to sleep in our own beds.

On the way out, my buddy found forty dollars of stripper money on the floor. He should have split that with me but whatever. The druggie was a real good fuck, but I snatched up the two strippers numbers' to go, just in case. I ended up calling them a week or two later, and they lived like five houses down from me. They were an odd pair. One was a tall, fit black girl, and one was a regular-sized white girl with big fucking tits. They told me to come over, and it was clear what I was going there for. I got over to their house, and there was no bullshit about it. It was like a fucking porno. The second I walked in the door, I was attacked and stripped. They got butt naked, but they put on a bit of a show and played before we got down to business. They actually played with each other first, I guess for me to watch. I didn't mind, plus that warmed up the playing field for me before I jumped in. After they had clearly each got off, I threw them down on the bed, and they linked their legs together so I had a black-and-white sex buffet lying down in front of me. I went to town. They smelled clean, so I ate that pussy like a fat guy at an all-you-can-eat restaurant. I love that shit, and if I may be so bold, I will say that I am very good at it. I got them both off and then went to town, switching from black to white repeatedly until I was done, which was inside the black one I pulled out and made a Jackson Pollock painting out of their stomachs. I did not feel bad because they both got two for sure and possibly three. As soon as I was done, it was unspoken, and I just picked up my clothes and left. I never spoke to them again, but it was awesome.

The lease agreement was up at the bartender's place, so I moved in, and it was awesome. I had forgotten how cool (not a pun) that air conditioning is. I lived without it for the last three years, but once we were reunited, I think I cried a little bit. It gets so fucking humid and gross in the summer in Minnesota, you almost wish it was subzero temperatures again, and then two months later, you miss the warmth. The older bartender had obviously moved out, but the younger one who told me to cook my own damn food at the bar still lived there. I was on the second floor, and he was way upstairs, but it was a big room. We became good friends and hung out a lot. Another good friend of mine had graduated before me, but that is only because I took two full semesters off for surgeries and he was a year ahead of me. He would come over damn near every fucking day and want to go to the bar until closing time. I had no problem with that unless I had a guest in a dress. He would just stay on the couch the other guy left in the room. I should have made him pay rent or at least buy me a few drinks every once in a while. This is when I had yet another experience with sleepwalking when one night I apparently got up in the middle of the night and stumbled up the rickety-ass spiral staircase and went into the upstairs big room where my friend and former bartender was sleeping with his girlfriend. I don't remember any of this except for when I woke up, but I apparently walked in, pushed him out of the way, and once again crawled in between him and his girlfriend. What is even worse, I cuddled with her until he woke me up, and he simply said, "What the fuck are you doing?" I will never forget that. We hung out a lot, and I took a shining to one of her girlfriends and was told not to waste my time.

She was a little bit older than me, she was twenty-two and the oldest virgin I had ever met. The four of us would go out to the bars and party, but you must remember, I was not yet twenty-one. We messed around for a while, and she was into some crazy shit but would not have vaginal intercourse. That would soon change one night after a show, and we went and did the damn thing. She loved it and called me the next morning asking for seconds before work. I was cool with that and actually kind of liked her. She was innocent, and that turned me on. I had fucked older women, but none that were virgins, and I felt like it was an accomplishment to some degree to deflower this woman who had waited so long to eventual give into the temptation of sexuality, and I was the one to turn her over to the dark side.

Unfortunately, my friend had moved, and for some reason, at the same time, I lost, broke, or actually it might have been one of the many phones I have dropped into a lake. I no longer bring my phone out on boats as long as someone else has one because these days you really do need to have a phone with you. Even if you can't make a call, they can track where you were and find your dead body. So I lost many phone numbers and friends. There is a comedian whose name I can't remember that said something regarding this topic and asked the crowd if they had ever lost a phone with all their numbers on it and suddenly stopped being friends with a lot of people, and it is totally true. This has happened to me more times than I can remember, but I usually know a friend or a friend of a friend, and I can get that person's number if I need to, not to mention social media, which I am not on but have access to through friends and family.

However, finding the name of the one-night stand you had last weekend whose name you can't remember is a lot harder to find. What made it worse is that I took her V-card and the next day my buddy picked me up for work in the moving truck and was like, "What the hell? Your hand is all bloody," and it was. I was a little freaked out and had no idea where it came from. Then he pointed out that my shirt was covered in blood as well and the majority of the blood on my hand was on my thumb and palm. I have no recollection of sticking my thumb and or whole hand into the virgin, but apparently, I did and found the cherry pit, and I picked it. I had to wash of for a while when I got to work, and my shirt was fucked, so they gave me a new shirt for the day, and I was with my buddy or somebody else who got fired.

I had helped many a virgin pass through the doors of celibacy into the world of uninhibited crazy sexual exploits that most people will never experience, but I never made anyone bleed like that to the point that I would call them back to see if they need a ride to the hospital. This is why I brought up losing your phone a subsequently loosing numbers and eventually friends or booty calls, whatever you are into. I did not think of this as a booty call by any means, but I had no idea where she lived, and the only people that I could possibly get her number from had moved away, and because I lost my phone, I no longer had their numbers either. I really wanted to see her again, but I never found her, and I have lost a lot of friends that way. It sucks.

That year before I lost contact with that girl, I was at a party with her, my roommate, and his girlfriend. Earlier in the day, a big ghetto ass motherfucker sold some weed to my roommate. He was buying an ounce, and after he left, it came up one-fourth-ounce short. After I got done slapping him for not weighing his purchase before paying, I wanted to hurt this asshole even though he was twice my size and ripped. This guy was really big is what I am trying to say.

We ended up going to a party later that night, and he happened to be there. There was music playing, and a little freestyle session broke out. Of course, I jumped right into that, and so did the big brother who had done my buddy dirty earlier that day. It went on for a while until it inevitably turns into an all-out battle session. We were all having fun going around the circle. Big dude was up, and he talked ish at me. It is cool because it is all in fun or at least I thought. He didn't say anything that could possibly be interpreted as coherent. Not only was I feisty and drunk as hell, but I was still pissed at this big-ass dude for ripping my homeboy off. I don't remember exactly what he said to me, but it set me off, and I let him have it. And not to toot my own horn, but I cut him down to size in a heartbeat. I started off by telling him that he had a little big-man complex. I then proceeded to let him know that his style was weak and he only felt like a big man because he was clearly on steroids. Then I called him out on the fact that he had shorted my friend.

I remember it being very articulate and relevant to the situation to which I was referring to. Every previous punch line was nothing but butter, and my timing was immaculate. I fucked this dude up to the point where he was literally speechless. Everything rhymed perfectly and was on time, and I proceeded to tell him that he needs to get out of the game. I "rapped" that no respectable dealer would come up one-fourth short on a deal, especially when it is an ounce of supper good chronic. This was all while I was in this big man's face while I flowed that either he ripped my boy off on purpose and he obviously knew it or he didn't know how to work a scale and should be kicked out of the game on principal.

I remember that shit crystal clear, every line was on beat and the rhymes fit perfectly for the hurt that I was putting on this big ass mother-fucker. When I called him out on ripping my boy off and not knowing how to work a scale, he hit me like a Mack truck. I went down like a ton of bricks but was not out. He did not get the best of me, and in fact, no one has ever knocked me out. I may have just jinxed myself, but whatever, if it happens, it will be another story to tell. I have had many a concussion but never knocked out.

I stood up and watched be escorted down the stairs and kicked out of the party. I later figured out that my tongue stud had broken a tooth that I would later lose, and I got a wicked black eye, but this was not my first rodeo; I got right back up and continued to talk shit to everyone and never got put in my place. Actually, I was already in my place because nobody could beat me, and my place was on top. Not always, but this day, I was the hands-down champion even if it cost me a tooth and gave me a black eye. I know I came out on top. I ran into that gentleman a few weeks later, and he confronted me, and I wasn't sure what to expect. He shook my hand and apologized for what he had done. He said that he was embarrassed that a little white boy tore him apart and that I had mentioned shit about him dealing.

First of all, it was weed. Nobody cares about that, and he was a very well-known dealer in the Dinky Town area. I let it go because as I have mentioned, I try not to hold grudges, the douche-bag admitted that I smoked him on the MIC…that was good enough for me.

I Love Water!

As I was living here, I would go over to my sister's house (the house I grew up in) and would just hang out because you don't realize how nice it is to relax outside in actual grass and have a yard. My dad and I had also purchased a boat that winter, so I would go out fishing whenever I could. I went out one time with two buddies of mine, and we ran out of gas in the middle of the lake, which was one of the biggest in the Twin Cities. There were no other boats out to give us a tow, so we agreed to swim it back together. With all three of us working together, it couldn't be so hard, right?

I told them to hang off the back and kick while they pushed the boat; I jumped off the front of the boat with a rope that was tied to the front. I held it in one hand and swam my ass off as I switched arms while swimming, I was burning out fast. We had made it a long way and were almost to a little island in the middle of the lake. I had to take a break and figured I would just tie it to me and float on my back and keep kicking. Once I turned around and caught my breath, I saw my two "friends" sitting inside of the boat, smoking and laughing at me. I wanted to kill them and planned to; however, I wanted to get on some sort of dry land first. I went and took a drag off one of their smokes and yelled at them to get their lazy asses back in the water and start kicking. They did, and we made it to the island about probably a half an hour that seemed like five hours. I worked out my anger, and no lives were lost that day, at least not by my hands.

We relaxed for a while, and not too much later, some Minnesota nice came to the rescue. A sweet old man saw our situation and started up his boat coming to our rescue. He towed us back to the launch site and saved the day because I don't know if we would have made it back. My friends were wearing life jackets, which is always smart to do, especially on children. I, however, was really drunk and pretty fucking high. I consider myself to be an excellent swimmer, so I just dove in and went to work. In hindsight, it was not necessarily a good decision, considering I later found out that the area of the lake I was towing the boat was deep as fuck and up to one-hundred feet deep. It is also a big Muskie and Northern Pike lake, and that would not be fun to be bitten by.

I eventually sold that boat because although it was a project for my dad and me to work on, you need to recognize when something is a lost cause, and we could buy a new used boat for the price of fixing that one. We did just that and bought a new used boat with the money from selling the shit box. We went crazy on this boat; my dad put a goddamn air horn on this thing that sounded like a fucking semitruck. We put a detachable-face CD player in (which was still cool at the time) and speakers all over inside, including two really nice six-by-one feet on the in the back as well as speakers on both sides of the dash and two 8-inch subwoofers under the dashboard. We put custom seats in that converted into small beds; it was fucking sweet. It bumped like a low-rider to the point that it would actually shake the water around the boat. It was kind of a dumbass thing to do on a lake when people are just out there trying to relax, but I was in my twenties and just did not see it that way. I thought I was cool as shit. I lost a wallet, around five cell phones, and plenty of jewelry and ruined watches while I had those boats. That boat eventually crapped out as well and could not be fixed because I had no clue how to do it, and paying to have it done would cost about as much as I paid for the boat. I said, "Fuck it," and sold the boat for the price I bought it and just called the speaker system a loss. I stole the entire stereo system anyways, so it was no loss to me.

Around this time, I just moved back into the house I grew up in. My sister was living there with some douchebag; I more or less kicked his ass out because he couldn't handle living with me, so I took the master bedroom as well as the entire house. My sister met another douchebag on the internet and honestly was into him. I had my concerns, but I said as long as you feel comfortable and you really like him, whatever, you are a grown-ass woman. She eventually wanted to move to Detroit with this shit bag, and since I was still a mover, I loaded up a truck for her and moved her there. I only offered to help because if I didn't like him, I was going to kidnap her ass with all her stuff and bring her back home. I love my sister. She always looked out for me. I'm pretty sure I should look out for her. I stayed out there for a few days, and it was all right. I guess I was okay with Capitan Dipshit at this time. We smoked some weed, and I had beer, so I figured whatever; as long as my sister was happy I am happy.

I met some dumbass friends of Professor Dickhead's brother who thought they were straight out of the ghetto and knew how to flow. I said I was down to freestyle, and they laughed at me because I was from Minnesota and I can only assume that they thought I lived on a farm and not somewhere that people get shot like a block away all the time. And by the way, being from a shitty neighborhood does not give you any lyrical ability whatsoever; it clearly did not work for these assholes. They clearly did not understand my style of hip-hop, which is more underground and actually has intelligent lyrical content, a message, and sometimes jokes and shit, battles raps, and relevant thought. These guys "rapped" about nothing but all there hoes, money, cars, and dope shit that they had.

I was sitting with these dorks in the basement of one of the guys parents. It was quite clear that none of them had any money. These guys were all fat and so ugly that not one of them could pick up a girl if they paid them. I could honestly see them getting turned down by a prostitute. That's why when I flowed, I just talk shit about other people rather than talk myself up, especially if it is clearly not true. I was going to start to do just that until I realized the atmosphere that I was in, and these guys were not big ballers, but they were clearly hoodlums who were much bigger than me, outnumbered me, and would whoop my monkey ass at the drop of a hat if I insulted them. Canada was just a short drive out of the motor city, so my sister and I drove there to go to a casino. We were almost not allowed into the country because we did not have our passports, but they let us in anyways. We went and just played slots for loonies, and I got ahead a good amount, at least in Canadian money. I got a coin stuck in one of the machines and couldn't get it back. I was a little loaded and kind of mad a big deal out of the situation, and this resulted in me getting kicked out of the casino and the country in general, over a fucking quarter. The same thing happened to me in England, but they did not deport me.

Having the boats renewed my love of swimming. When I go out, I would frequently jump to get someone's lure back or to save a fish, but I also would swim recreationally. My girl from middle school moved back to Minnesota. I would later find out it was only for the summer, but I was blind to think otherwise. Her family was and is rich as fuck. Her dad is one of the top heart surgeons in Minnesota, which is crazy considering the MAYO clinic is here. Either way, he is paid, and her parents live in a goddamn mansion on a really nice lake right up the street from me. I would never eat fish out of that lake because it is too close to the cities, but it is really nice and has two of my cell phones. The fact that her family was clearly in a different class than me, I did not feel comfortable, and later on in the relationship, I had thought about marriage. However, there were two flaws in that plan. I did not feel comfortable around her family. I felt like I was the punk-ass ghetto trash that their daughter brought home while her two sisters were married to fucking doctors. I did not feel like I was good enough, but in hindsight, that is bullshit! I was just as intelligent as anyone of them aside from the doctor part of it, but more importantly, they were boring and had the personality of a retarded cat. I feel that my personality is the only way I have ever gotten laid because I have never had any money or anything to offer other than me.

Later, at the end of the summer, when I found out she was moving back to Seattle, she told me that she wanted me to move there with her. This was crazy because I was still in school and would have to transfer to U-Dub (University of Washington), and I didn't want to lose more credits because the last time I transferred, I lost half a year of work and had to repeat it. Before she left, we decided to just have fun, went to parties, and stayed out on the lake. I would fish every once in a while, but the extracurricular activities were much more enjoyable. We would take the pontoon out and just dive off the boat and skinny-dip after dark in the middle of the lake. Again, no life jackets, but we were both good swimmers. One day, it was really nice outside, so we just tooled around the lake, smoking weed and messing around. I ended up getting a raging hard-on. Remember, I am like twenty and ready to go all day for hours. I sat at the wheel and dropped my pants. I told her to take a seat, and she jumped on. We rode around the lake with her slowly riding me and then eventually bouncing up and down until we passed a group of boats and families. We slowed down, and I still remember waving at them while I was still inside of her and we were still fucking, just very slowly. We kept going until the end of the lake, and she rode me like a mechanical bull.

We went back toward the middle of the lake to cool off and swim a little bit. We swam around for a while and went under the pontoon and messed around. I had to just hold the underside of the boat as she was wrapped around me. This was, once again, in hindsight, a very deep part of the lake to be doing something like this while impaired with no life jacket. The inevitable happened, and I was ready for round 2. We got ass naked, and I held myself up under the boat as she held on for the ride. It was such a rush possibly because we could see her parents' house from where we were. We both came at the same time, and my arms and whole body for that matter was so fatigued I almost sank. We made it back flushed but just fine. I will never forget that pontoon trip.

She moved away again, and I continued on with my lifestyle. I still did the occasional recreational drugs but still did not mess with the intravenous and never will. At first, it was because I was nervous about getting an air bubble stuck in there and killing me. Later I came across people who decided to indulge in that lifestyle and saw what they ended up looking like; I wanted nothing to do with that shit. Anytime blow would come around, I was down without question. I still never bought coke, but I would chip in a buck or two on occasion, but then I would not do it for months. This is around when I hit a low point in my consumption career. There is no easy way to put it; I was curious about crack. I did not understand how one substance could become more addictive by cutting it, mixing in water, and then cooking it. I got some premium-grade coke and followed the directions that I had learned from ghetto movies to a T and mixed myself up a nice little crack rock. I was not impressed, nor did I start sweating and shaking craving more the next day. As far as I am concerned, it is not anymore addictive than freebasing cocaine.

One time during college, I stayed out all night, forgetting the fact that I had a class at 9:00 AM. We were doing a lot of white, but I had to go to school. My friend needed a ride back to Minneapolis, so for some reason, we bought some yea-o and left for the city. My buddy was too high and didn't have anything to do, so I said he could come to my class with me because it was an auditorium class with like three hundred people and no one would notice. The class was called human sexuality and was basically a sexual education course for college students. I saw and learned a whole college tuition's worth of information about female genitalia that I figured out in middle school. There was a lot of new information as well that was interesting and some really gross stuff that I wish I never would have seen.

If you ever get the chance, do not watch a video of a woman giving birth inside of a glass cage filled with water. I know it is a hippie way to deliver your child, but that shit is fucking disgusting to watch. It may be seen as a beautiful thing, bringing a new life into the world, and I agree with that to some degree, but regardless, it is just really gross and hard to watch. I don't care if it is my child. I do not want to watch my wife bleed out of her love muffin and shit all over the place just to watch a "beautiful moment." My coked-out friend and I walked into the class. The entrance was at the bottom of the auditorium, so everyone noticed us walk in incredibly late. The door was right by the teacher's desk, which for some reason was filled with dildos, vibrators, and all types of other shit, some of which was new to me. We laughed out loud when we walked in as the professor was stroking a dildo. We walked to the back and continued to watch the instructor show you how to make people have an orgasm. She was only a couple of years older than us and looked like a few girls I dated in the past and a few that I had dated after that. She was hot and was instructing how to properly use dental dam, and all I could think of was her going down on the super-hot girl that was sitting right next to me. We sat there for an hour, watching her stroke rubber dicks and sticking her fingers in rubber lady parts, trying not to pretend that it wasn't really hot. I loved that class, and I did get an A. How could you not pay attention when it is an entire class about sex?

At this time, my best friend and a couple other guys were living in a loft in Minneapolis where I would frequently spend the weekend. One of them was somewhat a DJ, and he spun house music. He actually taught me quite a bit about the trade and how to mix and match beats so that there was a smooth transition. I went out with him and his girlfriend one time to go to a party. I ran into some chick whom I may have mentioned before but not to this extent. It is kind of hard to freestyle write and just remember events off the top and then put it in order. We made out and shit on the dance floor and just exchanged phone numbers. We eventually hooked up later and eventually became somewhat of a couple although I was seeing other people at the time. She was big into drugs, so we did a lot of cocaine, pot, ecstasy, and although I am not proud of it, meth as well, she loved that shit. I would get ridiculously fucked up and spend a weekend with her and go back to school with no homework done and feeling like a shell of a man. It was okay because I spaced out my classes and I had plenty of time to catch up; I just had to work really hard. For some reason, she wanted to go on a trip and said that she had a time-share in Mexico that we could use for free, so I was all about it.

We went down there for a week, and it was awesome. Everything was free. I think we paid to go out to eat once because it was a party spot. The first day, they had a drinking contest by the pool, and I remember saying that I would smoke anybody. She got up and talked to one of the staff that she knew from previous years, and when the contest started, they called my name to come up. I guess I should have realized what she did, but I didn't. There were a bunch of big guys up there, so I wasn't too sure, but I was still young and was confident. I don't remember where they were from, but there were a couple of Mexicans in the mix. I blew them away hands down. Fuck, I could have drunk another round before they finished. So that is two trips to Mexico and two drinking championships.

There were tons of college-age kids around there, and it was pretty wild. I was able to score some weed within a few hours of being there. That made me very happy. One of the bars we went to had a wet T-shirt contest which my girl entered. She was a freak with tattoos and the clit and tits pierced. Obviously, she pulled up her shirt and showed off the twins. She was clearly in the lead until the last girl who had boobs about three times the size of my girl's flopped those cannons out and started sucking on them, but I think the kicker was when she dropped her pants and began to rub her pussy. My girl came in second, but I think the huge-titty chick should have been disqualified for illegal use of a vagina in a booby contest.

My girl was fit, and this other chick was quite the opposite, but I guess if you stick a finger in your twat, then you win the booby contest. I took a picture with the top 3 and even though I had my arm around my girl, when they took the picture, I reached over and sucked on the big tits, which felt fake to me. This means that she used to be a big girl with little boobies. Gross, she had a cute face, but still, gross. My assessment of her breasts was confirmed when we got the pictures back because she had big-ass scars under her tits, she got fucking butchered.

Her boobs looked really nice, but they didn't do too well patching up the job. The picture was on her camera, and she saw the picture before me and was none too happy about it. She wasn't mad that I did it. She was mad that she wasn't included. We had fun with another girl in the mix before so that wasn't the issue. She was simply jealous, and I think that is funny. After that bar, I wanted to smoke a bone down by the ocean, so we went down there to burn one. I remember there was a lifeguard tower, and I climbed up it to smoke my joint in the tranquility of this atmosphere. The sounds of the waves crashing, the moon and stars, they were all so clear. It was beautiful; I was in heaven. That is until I saw a flashlight coming down the beach; I knew what that meant. I swallowed the roach and hopped off the tower and thought I would be okay because I did not have anything more on my person; I was wrong. I am pretty sure that you cannot get in trouble for simply smelling like weed in the States unless you are high out of your mind and being a public nuisance, in which case you could possibly be arrested for public intoxication.

I was very intoxicated from both the herb and the liquor, but I kept my composure. They were not interested in that and told me they smelled *mota*. They spoke in Spanish, but I understood. I thought that I was fucked, but the lady had things under control. I think it helped that she had nice tits, but she handed the *policia* a bill of some denomination, and they walked away. I had heard that you could pay off the police, but I did not know it was that easy; however, I don't think I would have been as lucky if I were by myself—my tits are not that nice.

I bought a month's supply of everything you need for White Russians, and I drank them first thing every morning and would go smoke a blunt on the balcony. It is the breakfast of champions. We would spend most of the day down by the pool, which also had a swim-up bar that you could sit down and pee at. It seemed like everyone who worked there knew her and a bunch of other random people as well. I found this curious, but I had always had some idea that she had a past of being a trollop. That was okay with me because I, too, was a slut growing up, and years of experience had clearly made her a professional in bed, bent over the dresser or on the balcony.

The balcony was unforgettable. The sky was even better than at the beach. It was completely clear, and we were high up and had an overlook of the whole bay. We just got butt naked and fucked like rabbits while she rode me, and we looked out at the moon, stars, and ocean. And although no one could possibly see us, there is something about being outside butt naked that is exciting, only to be elevated by the fact that a girl has my dick in her mouth as I look out at the scenery while drinking a beer and smoking a cigar.

She loved cum. There is no better way to say it, but she did. I remember her talking about how much protein there was in semen, so she thought of it like a protein shake and did not let a drop go to waste. She knew how to work the equipment as well; she was a pro and could not get enough. While I was living on campus, I still saw her, but I saw many others as well. One time, I fucked up hardcore. I guess I had talked to her earlier in the day and said that she could come over later and we would hang out. To me, that means that if she was going to come over she would call and touch base first. I had not heard from her and walked to the bar alone, which is okay at this point because I was friends with all the bartenders. Not just like the local drunk whose name they all know and talk to being nice. They would call me for weed every once in a while, and we would hang out.

I met a girl there who was a real cutie and was down from the get-go. She even ditched her friends and came back to my shithole with me. The second we walked in the door, she jumped on and proceeded to fuck the hell out of me. My phone rang a couple of times, but I did not answer because I was "fucking" busy. In hindsight, this was a big mistake because that was my girl calling, and she was planning on coming over, which she did. She did not live close, and I would never drive that far unless I knew that the person was going to be there. However, she did come over, and due to another hindsight mistake, I did not lock the door. She obviously heard what was going on because she busted in like Wolverine and punched me dead in my forehead like a goddamn man, and I could literally see blood because it was pouring down my face. She was wearing a ring, and it left a fucking hole in my head.

She almost beat the shit out of the girl, but she ran out butt naked, which was funny because it was winter and the temperature was well below zero. We fought for a while. There was no way of talking my way out of this one, but somehow, she ended up getting naked and sucking all the other girl's flavor off my dick and riding me like a horse. There was another incident that brought me to the hospital. I have no idea who I was with exactly, but it was another I had met at a bar, and I was at an apartment fucking her when there was a knock at the door and my heart dropped. I did not tell her where I was; I just told her I was going to the bar, which at this point I guess was a red flag.

She must have driven all around Dinky Town, looking for my car, which would not be hard because it stuck out like a sore thumb. She also must have knocked on every door in that apartment complex because there is no way she knew which unit I was in. The girl opened the door, and sure as shit, it was her. I was more or less busted, but I did not get caught in the act. I could talk my way out of this one, no problem. She was being fucking batshit crazy and basically kidnapped me because I guess we had plans or something, I don't know. What really fucks with me is, How the fuck did she find me?

She basically pulled me out of there my by ear, not literally, but she might as well have. I never saw that girl again. She didn't give me time to get her number. We talked shit all down the hall, and she said some shit that pissed me off. So I went to my time-tested approach to this situation and got mad at her. I don't know exactly how I do it, but when I am in trouble, I am somehow able to flip the script and make them the bad guy. It works every time if you play your cards right.

I have gotten bust with sexting and really dirty naked pics. In one, the girl had her dildo shoved in her pussy and a finger stuck up my ass, my girlfriend saw it and freaked out. I got my girlfriend to apologize to me for looking at my phone without permission. Back to the most recent incident, I had turned the tables and yelling at her for tracking me down like a fucking stalker, and I was letting her have it. She was in front of me and went out the door and slammed it on me when I yelled, "Fuck you, bitch!" In retrospect, I should have just stopped the door with an open hand, but I chose to punch the door with a closed fist. Normally, this would not have been a problem; it might have hurt a bit, but it would not have been a big deal. However, this was a solid steel door, and I swear it weighed a thousand pounds if it weighed an ounce. I am really glad that for some reason, I punched the door with my left hand because when it hit I could hear the cracks and shattering of my hand; it was pretty loud. I was also glad I did not go with the right because I was still doing art and I am right-handed. I would have been shit out of luck because it literally did shatter two bones in my hand, so I spent the rest of the winter and some of the spring in a cast.

It is not as bad as missing out on the summer, but it still sucks. I hate casts. I did talk my way out of this conundrum and fucked the shit out of her after we left. Needless to say, we had a bit of a falling out after this incident, and I did not see for years. I eventually called her one drunken night when she was living in downtown Minneapolis and so was my girlfriend at that time, who was coincidentally once again my crush from middle school. She had passed out, and somehow I remembered her phone number out of nowhere and a blow job really sounded nice, so I called her. I did not know she was living right down the street, but without a pause, she gave me her address and told me to come over and hang out.

People of the opposite don't get together at two o'clock in the morning to hang out. They meet up to have nasty dirty sex, and that is exactly what we did. We messed around for a while, and she went down on me right away basically as soon as I walked in the door. After she had her protein shake, she pulled out a couple of pipes. The first one was herb, and I was all about that, and then she pulled out the glass dick. I debated for a minute, but I figured, why not? It was free, and I wasn't doing anything, plus I knew this bitch was a freak when she was sped up. We smoked some meth; I prefer to smoke because it doesn't fuck up your nose, and after you're out, there is still residue in the pipe that you can smoke for a pick-me-up when you would otherwise be out.

I had forgotten how much of a freak this girl was. I had a second wind and was down for anything. She asked me if she could fuck herself for a minute with her dildo. I did not have a problem with that. I just said that it was cool as long as I could watch. She got butt naked and still had a banging body. She went to town and teased me until my dick was harder than arithmetic. We fucked well beyond when the sun came up. We were at it for at least six or seven hours; it was amazing. This would be the last time I would ever see her.

I met up with the farm girl once again at the farm. I had not seen her for a while, and for some reason, we ended up down the road from my buddy's farm and started to mess around. I was holding her tits while we were making out like we were in middle school, and when I squeezed them, they seemed a bit firm and a quite a bit larger than before, although I had not yet made that connection. I honestly said, "Have you been doing a lot of pectoral workouts or pushups? What's going on here?" She laughed her ass off and thought I was making a joke, but I was fucking clueless. This was the first time that I experienced fake boobs, and to be honest, it was a bit awkward, but I will never forget what they feel like even though they would not my last pair to play with

I got a hand job in the middle of a deserted gravel road in the middle of nowhere Wisconsin. We exchanged numbers, and I hit that a few more times, and then I stopped caring. On one of those occasions, there was another girl thrown into the mix. I have no idea what her name was or if I ever heard it, but I remember that I had a good time. This is just a small story out of left field that has nothing to do with anything, but I think it is funny.

Around this time, I was riding my bike to school, and I was a little late to a class, and I had to turn in a paper that day. The teacher was a real dick, and everything had to be on time. I was hauling ass to class, but the roads were shit. It was sleeting and the roads were icy as hell. I rode up to the main entrance of the university, and there were two girls walking directly in my path. I had no back brakes on this shitty bike, so I hit the only one I had, the front. I basically flipped over the bike and slid across the intersection on University Ave., taking out the two girls like fucking bowling pins. This was first thing in the morning, so all the good kids were out, and the intersection/entrance was packed, and I was embarrassed as hell. I brushed it off, picked up my shit, and kept riding because it was almost the end of the semester and I had a class to pass.

My sister had since moved out of the house because she could not deal with my lifestyle. I would have random girls over and spend the night all the time as well as a dozen or more friends over for kegs and bonfires. In hindsight, I do not blame her; I was a dick. I was still going to school; I just had to drive from Saint Paul to Minneapolis every day, if I wanted to go to class.

Big boobies. There is a relevant story I can remember about boobies. I had just gotten off work at a bar and grill where I worked and was enjoying a mug of beer when I saw the biggest tits I have ever seen in my life, and that includes porn videos or internet. I had never seen anything like it before and have not seen anything like it since. I could not keep my eyes off this enormous set of tits across the bar and considering that I had been drinking all day, so my inhibitions were three sheets to the wind. I smoked a bowl and finished another beer, and they were still there staring me in the face. I walked right over to her and said that I needed to know what letter she had on her chest because I had never seen anything like that before. She knew exactly what I meant and proudly told me that they were Is. No joke they were ridiculous. I talked to her while constantly staring at her chest until she said, "Well, do you want to see them?" Obviously I said, "Word up," and took her in the back. What happened next blew my mind. She lifted up her shirt, and no word of lie, I swear that her tits almost hit the floor. Okay, that is an exaggeration, but they were ginormous. I had to feel them, and I did. They were incredibly heavy and spectacular. I mumbled that I had to taste one, and she was all about it. She said, "Go to town," and I did. Each boob was bigger than my fucking head; it took two hands to even lift one of them up to my mouth. I could have done anything that I wanted with that woman in the backroom, and she would have loved it, but for some reason, I did not. I touched her pussy and said those are really nice, finished my beer, and went home to my girlfriend.

Another really big-boob experience that I had was also with the same girlfriend. We were up at the same bar, and I had since quite working there. I later learned that my decision to quit was perfectly timed because two weeks later, the owners, my friends, sold the bar, and it took over new management. I went to my old workplace for a few drinks with my lady and a few of her friends. We were at that same bar because it was very close. The bartender was very nice, especially to me. We decided to go to the Limp Lifter, a strip club down the street. I am not big on strip clubs because when you apply yourself you can see that shit for free, and you can touch it. They had really good drink specials, and if you looked around, there were titties and pussies everywhere. However, the vaginas were all dancing behind bulletproof glass. This gives you a good idea of what type of place this was and the kind of neighborhood we were in. Mind you this location is about two blocks away from my house, which happens to be the highest crime district in Saint Paul.

I would go to this club every once in a while with a friend, but only to play pool and because they had a really cheap happy hour.

Eventually, they took out the pool tables, and I would only go there with girls and if the mission was to get plowed. One time, one of the friends and I were talking, and somehow the topic of sodomy came up. She mentioned how she loved to get fucked in the ass, hard. This girl was pretty cute and had some tig ol' bitties that I could not stop staring at as she talked about how she really liked to take it up the ass.

I noticed her looking at my pants, directly specifically my junk, which I will admit was somewhat erect due to the atmosphere and the conversation. I asked if she was interested. She looked over and my girlfriend, who was sitting right next to me, but she was looking the other way. Instantly, she grabbed my cock and squeezed it like a fucking tube of toothpaste. She showed me her titties. I squeezed them for a second, and then we stopped at the perfect time, about a second before my girlfriend turned around. The bartender that had served where we were at before the girls decided they wanted to go to the strip club came into the strip club and sat right next to me. My girlfriend's two friends were with us, and they were all talking about god-knows-what, so I was shooting the shit with the bartender from the other bar.

I am not big on strip clubs, but I have learned that it is always better to go there with a group of girls rather than horny drunk guys. You get much better service, and surprisingly enough, you get hit on a lot. It is like wearing a wedding band. She had the hugest tits, which I didn't notice at the bar because I was looking at the boobs of my girlfriend's hot friend while we were at the bar before. She grabbed my thigh, including my wang, and asked if I liked what I saw. I said that they were huge and asked what letter they were. I don't remember what she said, but they were a few over Ds. I think they were Gs. When me and my old lady left, she was walking out to have a cigarette and stopped me for a lighter, which is bullshit, because I knew she had one. She asked my lady if she would mind if she showed me her tits, and she said okay for some reason. She must have been drunk. So on this busy-ass street, this chick flopped out her ginormous mammaries, and I just grabbed them and squeezed the hell out of them. My girl had no problem. We went back home and fucked like teenagers.

There are actually many more giant booby stories. There is no point in writing about ever set when you have seen so many, just the ones that make you say, "Goddamn!" I met up with a pair, and I don't remember where, but she was a bit older. Anyways, I brought her back to my buddy's house to play. I used to ride to school with this kid every day. He had a PA and speakers hooked up to his truck, and we would fuck with people and pull them over. We were good friends since seventh grade, and I knew everything about him, including the fact that he was still a virgin. His parents were gone, so we decided to drink tequila off his girl's amazingly huge tits. The look on my friends face when she stripped down to nothing in two seconds was priceless. We laid her down and did body shots everyway you could possibly imagine. There was a lot of booby licking going on, and then she poured the tequila on her business and wanted it sucked or licked off. I could tell that this would be a first for my friend, so I showed him how to do it. She refilled the snatch, and he went muff diving for the very first time. It was a beautiful moment to watch. She had tried to call a friend, but she was too drunk to drive. I was down to tag-team her, but considering he had never even done anything before, I totally understand why he neglected to join in that activity. The big-breasted trollop and I went back to my house, where I ravaged every orifice on her body. That bitch was a fucking freak.

I was living alone in the house I grew up in at this time, and that same buddy needed a place to stay, and he became my first actual roommate. He moved in, and we had a kick-ass time and partied every weekend. I had set up my turntables and the microphone in the basement, so we had a lot of very loud fun down there. In the summer, when I would mow the lawn, I would mow crop circles into it while my roommate was at work and would deny any knowledge of it. People would actually slow down and look as they drove by. He would always end up finishing mowing the lawn because he couldn't stand it. I thought it was hilarious. I also made a gigantic snowman with a massive cock and balls, incredibly detailed, as well as an igloo with a fire pit in the middle that could fit ten people. The neighbors loved it. At this time, we would also get kegs for the events and hang out in the yard being loud and in our twenties, not giving a fuck about anyone else. If kids did anything like we did around my house these days, I would walk over to their party with a fucking baseball bat.

I do not know when it happened, but at some point, I turned into a really grumpy old man. I just don't have a shotgun; I don't like guns. If you know what you are doing, I guess they can be a lot of fun, but there is too much room for error and the possibility of hurting an innocent person who happened to be in the wrong place at the wrong time, and they scare the shit out of me. So we would have loud keggers and bonfire parties with a fucking loud-ass hip-hop show in the basement that you could hear from down the street. I cannot believe that no one ever called the cops on us. These activities were fun, and my buddy always had a good time, but I think that it was when those get-togethers ran into the workweek that he got a bit annoyed and decided to move out. I do not blame him either; it was probably annoying.

One night, we had a good amount of people over, and everything was going well until I heard some commotion and went to see what was going on. I found my best friend and my friend from when we were really young yelling at each other and basically at each other's throats. I pushed them both outside and told them I wanted to have a smoke, and they were coming with me. We got outside, and I lit up my cigar as they kept barking at each other. I stood in between them because they were both my close friends and they were also really close friends. They fucking lived together for like two years for Christ's sake. I have no clue what the hell they were arguing about, but they were both pretty pissed off. I remember exactly what was said either, but the boy-girl with the hanging earring basically told my friend from the ghetto across the street to fuck off. The ghetto child punched old Metallica T-shirt dead in the face, and it really didn't faze him. He is one tough cookie, and I did not know that.

We had wrestled around in the past, but he was my best friend, so I never punched him in the face and did not know how he would react. What happened next was some of the most gangster shit I have ever seen in my life. The punch was really hard and had to have hurt, but he just shook his head and said, "I dare you to do that again."

My heart dropped, and I knew that I had to get in between them, so I did. They kept talking shit, but I was trying to separate them. The big one was at the top of the stairs, and my little buddy was standing in the lawn. Boy-girl told him to fuck off again, and the ghetto child reached over my shoulder and punched him hard in the face again. My best friend did not think twice, and within one second, he slammed his lowball over the other one's eye. He did it just right, so there was a huge gash in a perfect circle around his eye. I thought his eyeball was going to fall out. He left, and I can only assume he went to the hospital because his face was seriously fucked up.

Nazis breaking cars. I was moving a lot of furniture around this time and doing a lot of long-distance moves, which was fucking awesome because I was simply a workhorse and never had to drive. Every once in a while, I would take the wheel for a couple hours, but for the most part, I just shot the shit, had a freestyle session, or just slept. I liked to sleep, and then I also loved stopping at random swap meets and flea markets. I know that it is garbage, but it makes you feel like a kid again. They fucking sell nunchucks, swords, and switchblades, and you can't forget fireworks. There was also different local jerky at every stop, so knifes and local jerky every day. What man wouldn't get wet about that? There are not many if any places to buy dorky shit like that in Minnesota. We went all over hell, but the two trips that I remember the best were to Florida and Chicago.

On the trip to Florida, I did not drive for shit, which was awesome because I was tired as fuck. I just slept the whole fucking time and woke up there. However, I did wake up and stretch, take a piss, and smoke some stinky green when we had to stop, and then I would stay awake for a bit and talk or whatever, but then lights out. We get a paid hotel stays, depending on how long the job takes, so if we drove fast and skipped the telly, we would make a lot more money because we were paid at a flat rate for long-distance moves. We would always skip the telly and tough it out, make it home early, sleep in our own beds, and end up making a lot more money if you measured it by hour by skipping the hotel.

However, sometimes the jobs were really hard, and driving across the country was not an option. When this would happened, we would talk about just getting back to the room and lying down and nothing else. This never happened, ever. We would stretch out our backs for a bit and then start figuring out, which was the best bar to go to that we would be able to crawl back from. This was one of those times. I cannot remember what city we were in, but I know we were in Florida. We got plowed ass somewhere close and made our way back to the room, where we had more beers and cheeba, but he didn't smoke, so it was more weed for me. We furthered our intoxication and freestyled, which for some reason turn into violence against the hotel furniture. The only thing that did not get broken, surprisingly, was the television. We were throwing chairs and tables at each other.

The lights were all gone, beds were turned over, and it looked like a fucking bull went batshit crazy in that room. My buddy threw a chair at my head. I obviously ducked, surprisingly on time, and it crashed into the wall. It left a hole in the wall to the point that the chair was hanging on the wall and we had to rip it out. We agreed that we should probably stop and get some sleep because we were on the wrong side of the country. Our minds were blown in the morning when we saw the carnage and we got the fuck out there as fast as we could. A year later, we heard about it because it came back as a security deposit infraction on the company credit card. We were both fined fifty dollars; it was worth every penny.

The next trip that brings back memories was Chicago. The move was not actually in the city, but we could see the skyline from where we were loading. It was just a little bit outside of the city. The move was relatively easy, and we headed home, but this time, we just wanted to get drunk, and we were getting tired, so we stopped at the first place we found when we realized we were running out of gas and either needed a drink or a bed.

We found a spot next to a little shitty bar; shitty bars are the best by the way. The bar was completely empty except for one older guy. He was probably in his early thirties, but he was older than us and thought that meant that we should respect him. Fuck that. He made small talk and asked us where we were from even though we had our work shirts on and where we were from was clearly marked.

He laughed at Minnesota and said we don't know shit because apparently Rockford, Illinois, is gangster as fuck.

Later I did come to learn that he wasn't bullshitting. A lot of crooked shit goes down in that area, but I doubt he had anything to do with the gang problems in the area. He was a very big guy and clearly looked feisty, but we just kept drinking and talking to the bartender. She told us to ignore him. We tried, but he kept talking ish to us about how gangster his city was and the Twin Cities was nothing but bitch-made. We just kept drinking until last call, and at this point, I have had enough. The bartender could tell what was brewing, so I just told her to watch when we walk out in case she needed to make a phone call. I asked my friend if he was down to roll on this fool if he tried anything stupid. He said yes.

We were obviously getting booted out, so I told my buddy to stand right behind me because in a rare lapse of judgment, I decided that I was not going to let this motherfucker get away with talking shit about the Twin Cities. I guess I took it personal. We all left at the same time, and I specifically told my buddy to stay right behind me because this guy was pretty fucking big, but I was feisty as hell and he was talking ish about my cities. He turned around in the parking lot and continued to run his mouth, and I wanted to close it. I walked right up to him and delivered what from that moment on would be known as the Rockford hook.

This big ass motherfucker was snoring before he hit the ground, and I continued to rail on him as he was going down. He was out and snoring, but I continued to pummel him with lefts and rights like a fucking pendulum until I had knocked out all his fronts and he was choking on his own blood and teeth. I stood over him and screamed, "Twin Cities, motherfucker!" as I spat into his mouth that was quite vacant of teeth and had an abundance of blood.

In hindsight, he sounded quite peaceful. It sounded like a very peaceful state of sleep that I have never experienced, and nothing could wake this bastard up. When I got up, I expected my friend to be right there, but no, he was huddled up by the entrance of the bar with the bartender like a little bitch. It didn't matter because I took care of business with one punch, but the fact is that he was not there when it went down. When your boy asks you to stand behind him, at least do that, even if you don't do anything you are supposed to be there in case shit hits the fan. That guy could have killed me if he had got the upper hand. That is some fucked-up pussy bullshit that would get you kicked out the gang if we were in one.

I got a little bloody out of the incident that would leave a scar I can see every time I reach for something. My watch was loose on one hand, and the dial kept slamming into the top of my fist as I was swinging my fists like a goddamn monkey pummeling the asshole in the mouth. It bled like hell, but now there is just a little round indent on the top of my left fist as a constant reminder to never let anyone talk shit about the place you call home.

It was not long after this, maybe six months, that I got fired from the moving job for not telling the bosses whose bottle was on the truck. Yeah, I drank from it, but it wasn't mine. I was smoking weed, too, and they knew that. They didn't care; you are just not allowed to get caught. I know I did not slip up, so it wasn't my fault. Considering I was the only one to get fired, I can only assume that everyone else that was drinking just said that they weren't, and all the blame got placed on me. In hindsight, I don't give two shit because that job was breaking my back and I am still paying for it.

I took up a job at a temp agency after that and was doing basically whatever shitty job they sent me to. After my friend from the moving company got fired a month or two after me, I told him about the temp agency because he needed money as most people do. He began working for them, but they set him off in a big warehouse, industrial position that was permanent. It was a plastics recycling company, but I didn't care. I just wanted to have one place that I go to every day. I was sick of switching jobs every couple of days; I drove to the wrong job once and was late to the one I was supposed to go to for God's sake. I talked to the temp agency and got transferred to that factory. It was nice because then we could carpool. This meant that I got picked up in the morning; I didn't have to do shit.

There was a younger pudgy little fuck of my line, and we talked to him a couple of times on smoke breaks and eventually brought him back to my house. He had no idea what he was in for. We made up a game, or maybe we saw someone else play it and we just came up with a better name, but either way, we would play Edward Fortyhands. We would get forties, preferably malt liquor, and two per person. We would then duct-tape the bottles to our hands. This involves teamwork, and the last player needs to use his teeth and get help from the others, but we had already opened our bottles and we can't spill or that is cheating.

It is a big advantage to pee as much as you can before playing this game, or you are fucked seeing as you cannot take your forties off your hands until they are both finished. There is no killing one hand and taking it off, so you can take a piss. You have to finish them both before you can do anything.

The game is pretty self-explanatory from there. You just need to be the first one to finish both of your hands, and you can go pee if you can get the fucking tape off. It is usually just a moral victory, but we would put dollars down every once in a while. I think we broke this kid in a little too fast because it was a little too much for him, and that is okay. We all had fun. I liked my position at the plant. All I did was listen to music and throw dumpsters of plastic into a wood chipper. My buddy was at a station that was somehow even more boring, so he asked to be transferred. He was eventually transferred to a job as a groundskeeper at a Catholic cemetery.

I eventually asked to get a transfer as well, and I got very lucky because there was only one spot left. My friend had talked about how much better it was, being outdoors and on your own as opposed to stuck in a factory, and I jumped on that shit. It was much better except I had to be the driver this time because I had to drive by his house on the way to work. Whatever, that job was the shit if you ignore the fact that we were run by a militant ex-marine who apparently never got his discharge papers. I swear that motherfucker still thought there was a war going on. We would have to line up each morning and be briefed as though we were going on a mission, but then we were sent out on our own.

I had a problem with walking over graves at first. I felt that I was being disrespectful until I realized that some of the jobs we had to do required even driving big fucking backhoes over graves to get to where we need to be, so I got used to it. But I still tried not to step on graves if I did not have to.

There was one grave site that I did pay particularly close attention to. My sister's best friend had a baby girl who was buried there. Unfortunately, she was born with epilepsy among some other condition that I can only assume made her short life a living hell. She was adorable. Couldn't talk, but she was still cute as fuck, and it was a tragedy when she was taken from us. In hindsight, after learning more about epilepsy, I can't imagine what life was like for her at that age, living with that affliction. Every year since she left, I have gone along with my sister and mother along with her friend's whole family on an epilepsy walk. We donate money and just do our part in support of her friend and to raise money for the cause.

My buddy and I made two friends out of the crew that was working the yard. It was a tall white guy and a shorter black dude. It doesn't really matter what they looked like, but it makes it a lot easier to decipher between the two if you are trying to explain something. They were as different as day and night or black and white, as it were, but they were good friends. They would play this game on the yard, which may or may not have had a name, regardless it was clearly homoerotic. The game's origin was from a movie called *Waiting* about a restaurant, and we played a version of what they played at work.

We all worked in different areas throughout the day but would cross paths every once in a while. The game was to get the other person to openly look at your scrotum. You never pull your wang out, just the beanbag. There was a fine art to this game; you would manipulate your sack in many different ways and shapes for which there were names. There was the bat-wing, the goat, and the killer was "the brain." You got two kicks for that one. The point was to be in some location within eyesight of the victim and have your balls out in one of the trademark shapes and just wait. You could not call attention to yourself, or it did not count. When or if the victim looks at you and you can see it on his face that he saw it you had to go up to them, make them bend over, kick them in the ass, and then call them a fag.

The little black guy would creep up on you, which is even more unfair 'cause that motherfucker knew I had music on and could hear shit, so I saw many a black nut sack that summer. My approach was to wait until I saw someone driving down the road coming my way, so I would hide behind a tombstone and set up shop. I usually prepared the brain because then I got to kick them in the ass twice. I don't know why, but whoever was working, they always looked over and got busted. No one broke the rules; no matter what they were doing, everyone would stop the vehicle, get out, and assume the position. It was a fun way to pass the time, and you got to degrade your colleagues as well as yourself by exposing yourself in a fucking graveyard. It did not take long for me to go from being nervous about walking over gravesites to pulling my genitals out while holding on to a tombstone.

Some people had to mow, and others did landscaping. I was always on dirt detail, which was fucking awesome because I was all by myself. I rode around in a little ATV that could load a ton of dirt and could tow more if I needed to. It was cool; I would just listen to music, smoke occasionally, and every once in a while, I would bring a little flask. Fuck that, I brought tons of liquor and got high off my ass every day. We had walkie-talkies, so me and my buddy would meet up every once in a while at the dirt pile and have a nip, shoot the shit, and take an unauthorized break from what we were being paid to do.

Little black dude and tall white guy would join in every once in a while if they ran into us at the pile (freestyle). They came over to my house a few times after work for beers and to smoke our faces off. The white guy kind of scared me because he would talk about his guns and how he had a lot, it sounded like he had a fucking terrorist compound. I did not believe him at first until one day he opened his trunk to grab some beer, and I was fucking scared.

He had AK47s, sawed-off shotguns, pistols, and all types of scary shit. I was actually surprised that the motherfucker did not have grenades in there. I got related much better with the little guy. We would freestyle and shit. He wasn't that good, but it was fun. He stopped by the house one time when my best friend and I were hanging out, and we all just kicked it and listened to music. Then this motherfucker pulled out some synthetic devil grass that I will never forget. It was called Salvia, and I have done it since, but nothing can compare to this incident.

We smoked it, at least me and my buddy did. Maybe the cat who brought it didn't smoke any, and he brought it over as a cruel joke, which I know is not true. However, as I was tripping my balls off, he was just standing there laughing at me. I had read that LSD gets trapped in your spinal cord, and I think whatever this shit was that I smoked unleashed any latent acid that was trapped in my spine, along with other controlled substances, causing me to hallucinate beyond anything I had ever experienced on acid, ecstasy, ketamine, GHB, nitrous, mushrooms, meth, cocaine, marijuana, alcohol, various pills, and every other drug that I have indulged in mixed together at one time. It is like it unlocked something, and I was gone. I don't think my friend was in the same boat, but I remember hearing all types of crazy shit, like I had super hearing, and could hear things from other dimensions. I don't usually think crazy like that, but whatever was going on was weird as fuck, and I was scared.

So as all of these noises and voices are going on, there was a world of beautiful colors dancing everywhere to the beat of some nonexistent music. My friend from work started talking to me, and I saw two of him. They eventually multiplied into vertical images of his face like they were on two separate movie reels. The left reel began to spin downward as the right one was going up. I remember this image so clear; it is like it just happened. The audio was all fucked up, and it was so trippy like when you see hallucinations being interpreted in movies, and you think it wasn't really like that, but it was, and it was fucking scary.

I felt like every possible flashback I had stored in my spine got released at the same time. I came back to normal eventually, and it was clear that my friend did not have the same experience as I did. I continued to attend to the final resting places of the Catholic until I pissed of the drill sergeant for the last time. I had come late to work. Mind you this was never over five minutes late; it was just the simple fact that I was late. He yelled at me like I had broken some sort of military protocol. I shut him out, put a hand on his face, said,

"Whatever," and boned out. I was driving a Lincoln Mark VIII at that time, so I did a few doughnuts and peeled out of the parking lot with my middle finger out of the window screaming, "Fuck you, Patton."

From there, I went back to the liquor store right up the street that I had worked at in high school, but I had a different job title. Apparently, now I was supposed to be security as well. I had put on about sixty pounds of muscle since the high school, and the neighborhood had turned to garbage, so I guess it made sense, but in hindsight, I think I should have gotten paid more.

A lot of people from Chicago now occupied my neighborhood, and they were not all bad. Some of them were very nice people like dude with the glass eye. He was scary as fuck, but I didn't see it like that. I would always talk to him occasionally, go have a smoke with him or something, and I still talk to him anytime I see him around the hood. I had to ask him to take the eye out because I had never seen that before. I will never ask him to do that ever again.

The Chicago people turned my neighborhood into a real ghetto whereas before it was just a little bit ghetto—nope, now it was full-blown. It did not really matter to me because I have grown up with this and nothing is going to change, and little did I know at the time, but it would only get worse. I worked at the store with an old friend whom I had worked with there in high school. He was an old man from the neighborhood that I believe my best friend's dad knew and had shared a beer or two with up the street at the bar. He looked like a grandpa, but I shot the shit with him like he was my age. I talked to him like he was one of the boys with no respect for his age, and I think that he liked that. We would tell dirty jokes and just fuck around. I swear I could see him feeling young again when we played around, and that always made me feel good. He knew what I would do as far as drinking and getting high, and I think he thought it was awesome when I would fuck someone in the stockroom.

We never said anything about it afterward, but he would always give me a high-five. It was an unspoken understanding and a dirty old man condoning the debauchery that frequently occurred in the backroom of the store while I was still on the clock. I will never forget that old man. He was fucking awesome. I would see him every once in a while around the neighborhood after I quit the liquor store, and he was just such a happy camper, to word it as he would have. I learned that he had died. I don't remember from what, but I did receive the information through my best friend's dad. They actually lived only a few houses away from each other. He will be missed by many and never forgotten.

I made a "friend" while working there this time. We got along mainly because we both smoked herb and liked to drink. He was usually at the register, but he would come in back every once in a while to drink loosies while I was watching *The Simpsons*. Loosies are the beers that fall out of six-packs and are just lying on the floor, or sometimes we would just grab a forty-ounce and say fuck it. My lady friend from middle school and then Colorado moved back home and became a staple in my life once again. This came out of nowhere but was accepted with open arms. I missed her. We began being "a couple," and I was okay with that. I cannot say that no infidelities occurred, because they did, but I was completely all about her. We stuck together like glue, but that is a story in itself. Back to dude from work. We made a habit of hanging out after work and drinking copious amounts of brandy. Every day, brandy, brandy, brandy; it began to get old. He would get feisty sometimes, and when he would run his mouth, he was racist as fuck, and I am not really cool with that. I have been to his house, so I can somewhat understand where the hatred was coming from, but I don't necessarily like to hear it. As I mentioned, we would get shitfaced just about every day after work and do stupid shit, and sometimes he would come over on days that we did not work. This is when he had me come over to his house for some reason, and I was introduced to his wife and kids.

After the first meeting, I dubbed his wife the dragon whore, and that name stuck. I did not mean to say it, but I referred to her by that title once while shooting the shit, and he loved it, so the name stuck. There is no better way to describe that disgusting waste of human flesh. She looked like a meth-head on crack, drunk, just really needs a haircut and some makeup. His kids were cool, except the little girl had somewhat of a little-girl crush on me. This was confirmed some years later when she called me from her cell phone and was apparently seventeen years old. She wanted to hang out, and I have no idea what I made up, but I declined the invitation. It was kind of weird.

Back when I was still working at the liquor store, he had a cat called Boots, and they were going to get rid of it. I think I was just drunk, but I said that I would take it, and I did. The thing would not shut the fuck up. All day long, he would just *mao, mao, mao,* so I renamed him Mao. He was an outdoor cat and very active, always knocking shit over and being an asshole. One time, he attacked Mr. Bo Jangles. I forgot to put the top back on his cage, and when I woke up, I could tell something had gone down. Bo J. was not in his cage, and the cat looked guilty. I threw the cat out of the house because I knew that he had done something dirty and then found Mr. Bo Jangles under a couch, and his tail was missing. I found his tail, and it was still moving around and really creepy. He eventually grew back a new tail, and he is still around, well beyond his expiration date. I kept Mao for years until one day he just did not come back; I didn't lose any sleep over it. I hung out with that guy from my work for a while, but I got sick of him being so blatantly racist and the mundane relationship based solely on getting plowed and doing nothing. I had to enforce the very rare guy-on-guy breakup. I told him that we should not see each other anymore and that I was sorry but I could no longer talk to him.

One day I was just hanging out with my roommate, and we heard a bunch of ruckus outside, so we checked it out in the swamp across the street that was no longer a swamp. There were two pit bulls tied to a tree in the middle of the clearing. The swamp had dried up, and apparently, it was just a place for the apartment people to throw their garbage after they had overflowed their dumpsters. There are always mattresses and recliners thrown back there among limitless amounts of random garbage, even used diapers. It is fucking disgusting. It used to be a big nasty swamp, but it was clean if that makes any sense. "There wasn't any garbage" is what I am saying.

The neighbor kid and I, as well as some of my friends from the apartments would play in there. We would climb up the trees that would branch out over the swamp. We would climb really far and then jump into the swamp below. We sank into the nasty putrid funk up to our armpits. It was really hard to get out but always did, and we did exactly what any disgusting dirty boy would do in that situation—we climbed the tree again and jumped back into the muck. Later my friend's dad told us that what we did was very dangerous because sometimes there are sinkholes in swamps and they can suck you up and kill you. We heard what he said, but we went right back there the next day and did it again. The swamp dried up, so now it was just a dry clearing with a single tree in the very center.

The two pit bulls that were tied to the tree seemed really scary, and they were barking super loud and fighting each other. There was no way in hell I was going over there. I called the police and watched them while I waited for them to get there. They actually got there really quick, and that never happens even though they are all over the place in my neck of the woods. The police were two younger guys who had no fucking clue what they were doing. They were clearly scared as they should be. Who knows how they have been tortured in this neighborhood? I was scared, and I was across the street right next to my front door. The cops walked up to the dogs, and they both had their mace out. The second that they started to spray the dogs, karma came and slapped them in the face. A huge gust of wind came and blew all the mace directly back at the officers. None hit the dogs. They stumbled back to their car; it was obvious that they could not see, and they were coughing their asses off and spiting all over. They deserved it. They got on the phone, and I assumed it was to call animal control. I was right, and they arrived really fast. In fact, it took less time than when I first called the police. The animal control people walked right up to the dogs, and they did not bark once. They had the poles with the lasso at the end to round them up, but when they got close the dogs were completely passive, so they just walked right up to them and untied their leashes from the tree and walked them to the van. They brought the dogs to a shelter or whatever they do, but they took off and the police were still in the parking lot, throwing up and rubbing their eyes. It served them right.

Around this time, my roommate's aunt and uncle would go out of town a lot, and they had an incredible mansion. He would watch the mansion on occasion, and it always happened to be on a holiday. My girlfriend from back in the day and Colorado went there all the time. They would have theme parties like a "pimps and hoes" party or just regular costume parties and there was always something on Halloween. We would dress up as a pair, and two years definitely stand out.

One year, we went as Mario and Princess Toadstool. I was the princess. I put a lot of work into the costume although I did not shave my chest, which made me look like a lazy drag queen. We won best costume at that party. The next year, we went a Popeye and Olive Oyl. This was perfect because she already looked like the character, but she just needed the outfit. I used skin-toned panty hose and colored anchors on the forearms, and it looked perfect. I had a corn-cob pipe, the right hat, and everything. We went to a costume contest and were going to win hands down. Then at the last minute, this bitch that was in the finals basically got naked, and needless to say, the whore won. We got second place and some free drinks. I wish I had tits.

We did a lot of drugs of all types there at that time. We would hang out in the sauna room, which had a sauna and a nice hot tub and get drunk and high because, honestly, what else are you supposed to do in that room besides fuck after you gets high? We did this, but one day I was in there alone and decided to do some looking around. I instinctively went to the medicine cabinet, and I found a gem. It was in a bottle of some kind of erectile dysfunction medication. I don't remember the name of it, but whatever it was in there, it was not for getting a boner. They were unmarked or unpressed pills that were clearly not pharmaceutical grade. I bit one in half and instantly knew what I was dealing with. This was the exact equivalent of ecstasy, only it was like super charged. I stole so much of that shit; it was like finding a thousand dollars' worth of X out of nowhere.

I did it for a long time and had a lot of fun, I know that, but it must have been even better than I can remember because all I can remember is the beginning after taking it and then it all goes blank. The same goes for the girls that I was with. My girlfriend had moved away again at this point, so I was alone and was just having fun.

There were many more parties, and I fooled around with many a girl involved, but two incidents stick out to me.

One night I, along with a few girls, had taken those pills, and we were all tripping balls and horny as hell. I did not do anything that night, but there was plenty going on. I was sitting in the Jacuzzi with three or four naked girls while there was a fucking orgy going on in the sauna. This was great because there was a big glass window in the sauna which was right next to the Jacuzzi. It was better than watching porn. Pheromones were in the air, and everyone wanted to fuck the closest thing to them. I was sitting next to my good friend's sister whom I had a crush on since seventh grade. We kissed and messed around a bit until she reached down and grabbed my cock. Our eyes met, and it was the most fucked-up feeling in the world; it was like my sister had my dick in her hands. We stopped kissing, she let go, and we never spoke of it again.

The other interesting encounter involved a friend's sister as well. She was quite a bit older; I think she was a senior when I was in eighth grade. I had a little crush on her, and at the end of one night, I couldn't find anywhere to sleep, which is complete bullshit because this was a mansion, and I have slept just fine in a bathtub at a motel 6. I just wanted to sleep next to a big pair of boobs. She was sleeping in a big bed with another girl, and I crawled in the middle and spooned up with her without saying a word. I just passed out and held on to her tits all night. In the morning, I had a raging boner and had I do something about it. I moved her hand into position, and she instinctively began to jerk me off. I eventually fucked her for a little bit, but we were starting to wake up the girl next to us who was also an older girl, so she just went back to whacking me off until she took a load in her hand like a champion, and I just grabbed her big-ass boobs and went back to sleep.

That year, I was just sitting at home alone, and I got a random phone call that to this day I do not know why I answered. It was the mama of my friend's baby who was so unbelievably hot, and I wanted to fuck her from the moment I met her. She was very forthright and said that she wanted to come over and hang out. I had nothing to say except *okay*. She came over, and it took little to no time before she came right out and said that she wanted me to fuck her, hard. I jumped on board, and we started fucking around. I had her up against the wall, fucking her from behind when she said the words that no woman should ever say unless they a really down to go through with whatever the answer may be. "Do whatever you want to me." I have heard this a number of times, and it is always awesome every time I have heard it, but you don't know what you're in for.

I was joking and I said that I wanted to fuck her up the ass. I was not ready for the response. She was all about it. She arched her back, spread her butt cheeks, and begged for it. I plowed her in the ass all night long, and she kept giving me head. She would not stop; it was amazing. Apparently, she really loved in the ass. I guess you don't know unless you ask. I continued to talk to her every once in a while for a while.

She lived just over the river in Wisconsin, so I would go over there every once in a while. I would drive over and hang out now and then. It was weird because she had a new kid as well as the kid she had while I was still good friends with the dad. I saw the girl in the hospital when she was only a few hours old. She was given the same name as my girlfriend at the time she was born, and that was kind of weird, not to mention the fact that she was big now, walking and talking, which made me sort of feel bad about what I was doing. However, it was so fun I would do it all over if the opportunity arose. I would go over, and we would play. I recorded all of it one time, something that in hindsight I would never do again. I cannot find that tape, and I know that it will be seen by the wrong person if I ever go through my tapes to look for something. What I did record was priceless, however, and I would love to find it. I just don't feel like watching hours of random footage just to find myself wrist deep in her love nest.

Fucking her in the ass was obviously not enough, and I raised the bar. When we were fucking around, I saw this massive rubber cock under her bed. It was pink and the size of my forearm. I asked if she could take the whole thing because it was ginormous and looked like it was just a toy like you would give for a bachelorette party to be funny. She picked it up and inhaled it like it was a pinky finger. I was amazed and started recording. Once again, in hindsight, I would never record anything like this ever again because nothing is sacred these days, and anything you do or say is recorded and will be brought into the light if need be, and you will get fucked. I had to find out the limits of this vagina, so I made a dart out my hand and dove in, not tickling the clit or playing around; I dove in that pussy like I was in seventh grade again.

She inhaled my hand with her business, and before I knew it, I was wrist deep in vagina. It was crazy; once I was up in there, I could completely open my hand and feel around, hitting every spot that I never knew existed. I could just grab the bean inside the pussy, not the clit, I mean deep inside there, and just torture it until her legs shook. I recorded all this as well as her using her absurdly large dildo with her pussy and ass at one point at the same time; it was a double-headed dildo.

I turned off the camera while I fucked her and plowed her asshole. She also sucked my dick a lot, and no one needs to see that. I continued to mess around with her for a while, but other situations came about, and she was no longer needed. It is nice to have someone that you have no respect for and that will willingly allow you to do whatever you want to them, but after a while, that is not enough.

At this time, I began to hang out with my girlfriend from high school again. We were always close and got along as friends, aside from the sexual relationship. We hung out a lot and watched movies and shit like that. I remember I had to let her stinky little dog out every morning, and the little bitch wore diapers because she never got fixed and she would bleed all over if she didn't wear it. They were cute though. They looked like daisy dukes. Regardless, I hated letting that dog out every morning.

One day we were just lounging around because we were up late and just lying down on the couch. I had my head on her stomach just kind of holding her, and I guess over time my head moved south. I was half asleep. When I regained consciousness, my head was directly on her crotch, and she was gyrating and holding my head, smashing it into her pussy. She pulled down her pants, and I was ears deep in the danger zone. There was no turning back now. I did what I had to do and took care of business with the lingual. We ended up fucking, and it was amazing. I had no idea how much I missed her. I continued to spend the night there for a long time and was very happy. It was not to be, however, as she was one of those girls whose friends are all guys, and I was still playing with any hot piece of ass on campus. I loved sleeping with her—actually sleeping with her not just recreating Caligula. We stopped doing the sex thing, but we never separated and are still very close to this day.

My first roommate and I went to a cabin party up north one summer. It was mostly friends from high school, including my friend's sister and mostly just girls, some of which I was friends with in high school. There was also an older couple there, and the guy was wicked rich because he invented Zoobas. It has nothing to do with the story, but it was interesting. Other than that, it was just a bunch of little shits in their early twenties. In the first few moments of being there, a little blonde girl was distraught because she had popped a tire and did not know what to do because we were out in the middle of nowhere. My roommate and I stepped up to the plate and changed her tire; she was really cute in a very innocent sort of way.

The whole weekend was full of binge drinking from sunup to well past sundown, as it should be in your early twenties. We played a bunch of games and spent a lot of time in the water. I challenged my roommate to race me across the lake. He was an exceptionally athletic individual, much more than myself, and had the clear advantage. The lake was pretty fucking big, and it was a long way to the other side. I don't even want to think about how deep that lake was because in hindsight, that would probably freak me out and make me wonder why I was so stupid when I was young.

We raced with no life jackets across this lake, absolutely drunk off our asses, and I kicked his ass. I knew that I loved to swim and I was comfortable in the water, but I never thought I could beat him in a race; he was built like a goddamn Navy SEAL. When we got to the other side, it became clear how far we had swam. We could barely even see the others at the campsite across the lake, and they were tiny. We rested for a bit, and then I remember saying that we needed to get back somehow, and I yelled, "Round 2, bitch!" and we raced back.

I vaguely remember being really fucking tired and wondering to myself how deep the lake was in case I ran out of steam. You should never think about things like that if you are ever in a situation like that. Somehow I beat him again on the way back; I would never let him live that down. We took a shot, I smoked some weed, and then it was back to the party, which coincidentally consisted of doing the exact same thing. There was a cabin, but I never went in it, and I don't think anyone ever slept in it. Everyone brought a tent. We stayed up pretty late, and everyone sort of crashed at the same time without anything substantial happening. We woke up. I think they ate food, but I stuck to my liquid diet and drank whiskey at 8:00 AM, washing it down with stinky, stinky weed. This is how the day would go—swimming, smoking, drinking, and listening to loud obnoxious music, exactly what you are supposed to do at that age.

I was fucked out of my gourd all day, but after dark, another controlled substance found its way into the mix, and the whole vibe of the party changed. I don't remember a whole lot after that point, but I remember that my roommate took me aside and told me that he had somewhat hooked up with this brown-haired chick that was up there. I knew her from school. She was older but kind of straight edge. She was cute, so I told him to go for it, considering at this point in his life he had barely kissed a girl aside from when I made this chick fucking let him do body shots and lick her tits. I told him to take the tent with her and I would find somewhere to sleep. I have had a great night's sleep in a motel bathtub for God's sake. I was sure I could figure out something, plus it was about time he lost his cherry. I stayed up for a long time. Now I was drinking and smoking in addition to the fact that I was rolling my ass off. When the night had clearly come to an end and everyone was in their tents, I realized that I needed to find shelter.

My tent was occupied, so I looked around, and I went to the tent of the girl whose cabin we were at. I asked if I could crash in there, and she said, "Sure," but there was someone else in there. It was the girl from the day before whose tire we had changed. I had left my sleeping bag in my tent, but I jumped in and was just high as hell. I had been friends with the cabin girl since middle school and knew her well. I knew nothing about the other chick, but the possibilities seemed endless. I plopped down in between the two of them, and it did not take long for touching to occur. I began making out with the cabin girl, and it was not long before I was inside her as I was making out with the flat-tire girl and had half my hand up her business. I fucked her for a while, but I can't forget how weird it felt because she was just a friend and it just felt wrong. I know I got her off, but I think she felt awkward as well because after she came, she just said, "Go take care of her now."

I was not one to argue, so I fucked the hell out of her as well, then rolled over in between them and fell asleep, taking turns spooning the two. I have a feeling that I boned the tire girl again, but I am not positive. It was time to head back to the cities, so me and my roommate packed up all our shit, and then he told me he was going to give that girl a ride home. He had a truck, so that basically meant that I needed to find another way home from two hundred miles outside of the city. What a dick. I don't mean that I completely understood and I did not have any problem hitching a ride.

I rode back with the cabin girl and my roommate's sister. As we were leaving and literally pulling away, I yelled for them to stop the car. I said that I forgot something. I went back to where the flat-tire girl was and got her phone number. I went back to the car and told the girls that I lied and that I just wanted to get the blonde girl's phone number. For some reason, they were both happy and said that it was awesome. This was weird because I had become known as somewhat of a womanizer at this point. I was stoked because the only thing I knew at this point was that I got another lady who would spread wide at the drop of a hat. I did not know her that well, but I knew she could be manipulated easily, a mind-fuck waiting to happen. I thought that the number in my pocket was simply just a booty call, and it was for a long time. In hindsight, the decision to stop that car and get her number would eventually change my life forever.

We returned home, and I continued to commute to school in my shitty $200 car that to this day was still my favorite until it broke down. My dad said that he would bring me to a car auction and split the price with me if I found something I liked. He bought a truck out of nowhere, and I knew my mom was going to be pissed off. I know why he bought it, because he had to sell all his cars and trucks when he went bankrupt. I remember watching him as he won the bid, and he was shaking uncontrollably. He was super happy and giddy like a little girl. I did find a car that I liked, and I told my dad to bid on it. My dad had incredibly shitty hearing, and he was not wearing his hearing aid. By the time he realized what I was saying, the car that I wanted had been sold for less than my limit was, and he bid on the next car and bought it. I never let him live that down.

It was a blue sports car that if you stereotype would only be driven by an Asian person. I had no business driving it. I hooked it up with big subwoofers and custom six-by-nines, and it was a stick. I prefer sticks because it keeps you focused on what you are doing. I grew to like it until an Asian destroyed it. Isn't it ironic, don't you think?

I was coming home from school; I had just purchased a twelve-pack and just gotten off the highway. I was going to crack a beer because I was on the home stretch, but for some reason, I decided against it. I had driven home without my seatbelt on and decided at that point to put it on, and I don't know why; I would normally be taking my seatbelt off as I approached my house. While going through the last intersection before my house, this kid did not yield with his left turn and hit me head-on. My car was totaled, and I was so lucky I did not open that beer because it would have been all over me, and I would have gotten in trouble even though I hadn't drank anything yet. No one was hurt, but I needed a new car. I found a shitty old Jeep somehow for mad cheap, and that was my new whip. I decked it out with a wicked sound system as well.

My girlfriend from Colorado/Seattle came back to Minnesota, and we continued just where we left off. We would go to shows and spend the night together damn near every night. She and the flat-tire girl were a big part of my life for a while. I would hang out with the one all day and at the end of the night, sometimes at like two in the morning, I would call the flat-tire girl, and she would come over without fail. They both knew about each other and let me know about it, yet they would keep coming back, even though they knew I was fucking them both on the same day, they came back. They were around so often that my dad kind of fucked up my game every once in a while. Because they were always around and my dad had a really shitty memory, he would fuck up their names and call one by the other's name and vice versa. I had to pull him aside one day and tell him to never address them by any name ever again because he always got it wrong. He did. I also had to reprimand him because he would come and knock on my bedroom door every morning, early as fuck because he wanted me to play with him in the garage. For some reason, he never noticed that there was an extra car in the driveway, and I had a naked visitor lying next to me in my bed, and I would rather play with that than whatever the fuck he wanted to do. I yelled at him about that as well and still feel sort of bad because I remember that it looked like I hurt his feelings.

I Had To Leave the Country In Order To Graduate!

I was getting close to being done with school, but I needed to fulfill my second-language requirements. I would have to continue taking language classes and pass an equivalency exam or study abroad. I obviously chose to go on a vacation while getting school credit on the side. In hindsight, I really should have done my homework on where I was going to spend the next four months of my life because where I went was not what I was expecting. I chose to go to Buenos Aires, Argentina, expecting it to have sunny beaches and shit. I had no idea where I was going.

We went down during the June, July, August months, which I know to be summer. My dumbass did not realize that once you go south of the equator, summer is actually winter. This was not a big deal because a cold winter day in Buenos Aires is like a warm fall day in Minnesota. I would walk around in a tank top and shorts while everyone else was wearing sweaters and even parkas. One thing that I found fucked up is that I was darker than the majority of the locals, not to mention the fact that I was a lot bigger, and I am not a big dude. Sometimes people would ask me where I was from, and I would say Minnesota, not realizing that people in South America did not have that much knowledge of the states in North America. They would say, "Oh, Venezuela, that makes sense." Then I would have to speak in English and tell them that I was American and Minnesota was a state very far up north.

That was one nice surprise that I was not expecting. Everybody spoke English. The surprise came when I realized that Buenos Aires was not a tropical paradise but a metropolis similar to Manhattan.

There was no beach but simply a sea port with water that I could tell was way too fucking cold. I did not go swimming one day the entire time I was there, not even indoors. We stayed in a hotel, which was really cool but kind of weird. We had room service and maids; however, I never let them clean the room because I didn't want them to steal my money or my weed. That was the next mission. I had to find a source of marijuana, or I would go fucking crazy.

This is also when I learned of the second pleasant surprise about going down there as well learning another very valuable life lesson. If you travel out of the country, find out the exchange rate before you go. It could mean the difference between getting a case of beer or a single can for the same amount of money. A pack of cigarettes was one American dollar down there, and I would buy forty ounces of Quilmes (the national beer) for around seventy cents. I drank that shit for breakfast lunch and dinner for four months.

After everyone had gotten acclimated to their new surroundings, the group decided to go out to a bar and have some fun, but I had a different agenda. It had been four days since I had taken a hit of weed, and I was starting to get anxious. I noticed right away that was the one that had to lead the party. They were all a little socially awkward; that was fine with me. I was standing at the bar, and a girl came up to me and told me I had a nice watch. I was looking at it, and it lit up when you press the button, but I just took it for what it was worth. I just seemed like a really shitty pickup line. I liked that watch, too, but it wasn't that cool. She was pretty transparent in the fact that she wanted to fuck me, but first things first. I simply asked her if she could get good herb and if she could get it whenever. She said yes, so it was on like donkey.

I brought her back to the telly and rocked her world. She was from Brazil, but she spoke very good English, although she had a heavy accent. I had her help me with my homework, which she pretty much did for me, so I wasn't learning a whole lot. She did not have any herb on her that day, but she came through with the goods the next day. Apparently, Argentina does not get *High Times* magazine because their idea of really good weed differs from mine greatly.

I tried to get good herb the whole time I was there from many different people, and it was always mundane even though they would swear it was the shit. I just thought, *Damn, yo, you don't know what you are missing out on.* Regardless, I kept hanging out with this girl, and she supplied me the whole time I was there. It was not the best herb, but it was weed nonetheless. I tried to explain the concept of chronic to her and her friends, but they just did not get it. I even looked it up on the internet, and it blew their minds. They would go to rave-like parties all the time and do pills as well, but it was not ecstasy, nor was it a pharmaceutical-grade pill. It was some weird press of god-knows-what, but it fucked you up for the whole weekend.

I went to a rave with her and some of her friends and did that shit. I felt like I did an eight-ball of meth and coke, and I was fucked up out of my brain. After the party, I took the train with them far away to what can only be described as a ghetto. I didn't make it back to the city until Monday just a little bit before class. When our director who was not that much older than me and really cute asked where I was all weekend, I told her, and she was surprised and terrified. They tell you not to go off by yourself, but I was not scared and we were not supposed to take the trains by ourselves, and apparently, the neighborhood I spent the weekend in was one of the biggest shitholes in Argentina.

I was only scared one time while I was down there, but it was never by myself or at night. The first night that we arrived, I went out skateboarding. I was a little disappointed in the quality of the sidewalks. The roads were smooth, but the city was clearly not made for skateboards. Nothing was scary to me; my neighborhood is much scarier, and this is one of the biggest cities in South America. I stopped at an intersection, and some guy came up to me and asked me if I wanted a free drink at this bar right around the corner. He said some other stuff, but I didn't understand because he talked so damn fast and he only spoke to me in Spanish, possibly because I was darker than he was, and maybe he though I belonged there.

Nothing happened, but in hindsight, you probably shouldn't follow strange people in a city that you are not familiar with. When I got there, they gave me a whiskey and Coke, and I sat down on a couch. I heard the guy say, "I think he could use two," and clapped his hands. This is when I noticed that I was not in the sort of bar that I was expecting. Two women came and sat down on either side of me and began rubbing my thighs and shit. They were saying all types of horny shit in my ears. I couldn't make it all out, but it was pretty obvious what they were getting at. I have never paid for sex or a sensual massage, and I was not about to start in South America.

I slammed my whiskey and spoke in English for the first time. I grabbed my skateboard, slammed my drink down, and said, "I am not doing this. You hookers have a good night." In the same way that the Spanish language sounds really fast to English people, they say that Americans talk fast, so I don't think the whores understood me, but it was fun and funny to drink free whiskey and then call them hookers to their face and walk away. Our director told us on the first day of school to avoid those places, and I just thought that was a bit too little too late. She said it was good that I got out of there because sometimes they rob tourists. I was never intimidated in that place. I was bigger than the bouncer, and I had my skateboard with me, which I can swing like Babe Ruth.

Every day I would go to the market and get whatever I wanted to eat for the day. I would just go every day and get new shit, plus I had to bring back my forty-ounce bottles and get full ones. I usually would get stuff to make sandwiches, some chips, and a bag of milk. I love milk and drink it with just about every meal. However, the milk in Argentina comes in bags for some reason. I remember the milk because it was so fucking delicious. It was like sweet and just really good. I couldn't put my finger on it, but I wish they sold something like it here. I would pass this store on the corner that was clearly for rich women, and there was this girl out front, and it was her job to get people into the store. I never talked to her, but I could swear to God she was giving me the "knock me down and fuck me" eyes. She had really nice eyes, but damn, she had some really big ol' boobies and a nice ass.

I would talk about her every once in a while with the kid on the crutches who was my only real friend while we were down there. I felt so bad for him because he was on crutches the entire time we were down there, so I would walk slowly with him to class so he had someone to talk to, and I would go to the store with him so I could carry his stuff for him.

One day, he needed to go to the store, and he saw her looking at me and said to go and talk to her. I am not shy, but she was working, and I didn't want to be that creepy guy hitting on women while they are working. I got to the market when I noticed he was not with me anymore. When I looked back, I saw him at the corner, talking to her. He waved me over, and I remember thinking, *What a dick*. I told him not to do this. I would later thank him.

When I walked up it was clear even before she spoke that she would have fucked me in the street if she wasn't working. We made plans to get together at the park when she got off work. She spoke English. It was a little broken, but she was really good, and she had the sexiest accent ever. I loved how she would say my name, especially when she would call me Booger and talk about the Froggies. Somehow as we were talking, the topic of nicknames came up, and I told her that my sister used to and I guess she still does every once in a while calls me Booger. She has done it as long as I can remember. This girl was very amazed by this word and loved to say it, and I loved to hear it. I fucking loved her voice. The Froggies came from when she saw my baby blanket and asked about it. I told her that it is the blanket I was wrapped in when I was born, and I bring it everywhere. It has been to many states and something like seven countries. I sleep with it every night, and I am thirty-four now, but I don't care. The blanket is green, and one side has a ton of little frogs on skateboards. She thought that was cute and always wanted to sleep with the Froggies right away, which was coincidently the day that I met her.

We did everything, but this girl really loved to give head. It was weird because she would just grab my business and go to town at any given second, which I had no complaints about. She loved it. She was amazing at what she did. It was unbelievable, but she did something that I was not familiar with. Every girl that had ever gone down on me my whole life has swallowed. This girl loved to finish the job and take a shot in the mouth, but then she would get up and go spit it out in the bathroom sink. It was really confusing because she sucked dick like a seasoned porn star; you would think she would take jizz all over her face, but I guess not. I was happy regardless. I was taken care of every day; it was just weird. She also fucked like a champ and would come over all the time for some of that, and then she would do my homework for me. That was nice, but once again, I was not learning very much.

The girl from Brazil still came around all the time, but I just timed it right. This was not my first rodeo. So what I had to have sex with two different girls a day? I was young and able, plus I got As on all my homework. They would do it in like two seconds, but in hindsight, that shit was probably like elementary-school level homework to them, so that makes sense.

I continued to juggle the two for the majority of my time down there. The girl from Brazil did freak me out a bit because apparently at some point I had mentioned that I thought it would be awesome if a girl shaved my name into her pubes. I was totally joking; I just thought it was funny, but this psycho bitch actually did it. She didn't even just shave it into her bush; she trimmed the hedges all around so that it actually spelled my name out in pubes. She actually did a really good job, and it looked cool, but it also scared the fuck out of me. I was now terrified of this girl, but I still needed weed, so I had to keep her around.

The program that we were in gave us dinner every night at the hotel. It was good food, but it seemed like we had chicken-fried steak four days a week, which was actually delicious, but it became like that dish in high school that it seemed like they served every other day, and you would say, "Not this again." The other food was really good too. I think they gave us breakfast as well, but I never ate that. I just drank beer every day in the morning.

I remember one time I was cutting it for time and needed to get to class, so I grabbed a tall can of Quilmes and walked to school. I was drinking too fast and got a bubble in my belly while I was walking. I did not stop. I simply turned my head and projectile vomited as I walked. I wiped my mouth and continued to slam my beer. The streets were full just like New York, and I can't imagine what the people behind me or anyone who saw that were thinking, but I made it to class on time. I went back to get something to eat around dinner time. I only occasionally ate with the group, so I got my own meal and brought it up to my room. I brought my plate back because I never had them clean the room, and the woman who served it to me told me that she could just bring the food up to me if I wanted to eat in my room and to just call.

She was the cousin of someone we knew from the school, but I don't remember exactly who or why that even mattered, but someone pointed it out to me after hearing about us hanging out. One day I called down to have her bring up my dinner. I asked specifically for it to be her that brought it up. She was about ten years older than me, and I don't know what was going through my head. Maybe I was drunk or just feeling really frisky, but I remember what happened next. She brought my food to the door, and I told her to come in. I grabbed the food and put it down on the counter in the kitchen. I didn't say shit. I just grabbed her and kissed the hell out of her she was all about it.

Once again, I do not know what came over me, because I am not usually dominating. Sometimes I am, but it isn't necessarily my thing. I pushed her into the kitchen, turned her around, and bent her over. She was clearly into this and was actually getting off on it. Obviously, she was still in her work uniform with a cute little skirt I just pulled that shit up, dropped her drawers, and went to work. She liked it kind of rough and loved having her hair pulled, as she talked dirty as hell, which is incredibly sexy in another language. She continued to bring me food and fuck me for the rest of the time I was there, but she did notice other girls coming to stay with me and got salty about that, but she would still come around. Once again, I had to time out my visits so as not to overlap the booty calls. We would hang out at the park on her breaks sometimes and drink *mate*, which makes you horny. I never fucked in the park like the couple I saw one time, but I did get a couple of hand jobs.

Around this time was the first scary time that I had in Argentina. The group went to Mendoza, which is wine country, and just a simple fifteen-hour bus ride away. That shit sucked ass. We spent a weekend out there and basically just slept on the bus. We did a wine tour, and when we would get to the vineyards, there was way too much wine and all different types of cheese and meat that looked like it was recently living. I drank so much wine that weekend I can barely drink red wine anymore. I will taste it, but that's it. I will drink chilled white wine if that is the only thing around; otherwise, just pass me a cheap-ass beer in a can, and I am happy. After we drank ourselves good and stupid (keep in mind that the majority of the group was under twenty-one; only me and the crutches kid were over twenty-one), we went horseback riding. Crutches did not get to go, and I felt bad for him, but whatever. We went out and rode around the hills and valleys with the *gauchos* (cowboys), and we were riding bareback. I had never done this before, and I just remember it hurting my balls. I also remember that any horseback riding trip I have ever taken in the states sucked donkey balls because you would never go faster than a slow walk, and the horse in front of you was always pooping all over the place along with the fact that my horse was always an asshole. This time, my horse was awesome and always wanted to be the leader of the pack, so we went pretty fast. It was fun. Toward the end, I was riding along with the girl from our group who was unbelievably cute and had some of the biggest titties I have ever seen. She was still young, so they were amazing. I could tell by how she was looking at me that I would see them someday. We got to the home stretch, and I could see the stable. I just wanted to get back and smoke a little bit of herb. Before the group got there, Big Boobs and I were out in front, so I figured that I had time. I kicked the horse like jockeys do and said, "Let's go home." The horse took off like a bat out of hell. I had never been on a horse at a full gallop, let alone without a saddle. There were no reigns, so I was squeezing the horse with my legs and had my arms wrapped around his neck, holding on for my life. I was terrified. During this run, my testicles were subject to extreme torture that left me walking and sitting funny for the rest of the trip. I prefer saddles.

We were going to go into Chile because we were right on the border; however, we were not able to enter because Crutches forgot his passport, so everybody missed out. What a dick. I just wanted to go so I could say I had been there because that is where my dad was born. I took a picture of the border along with everything else while I was there as well as parties and stuff that probably is not legal, but that camera got stolen, and the memories are lost forever.

The group went to our last stop on the trip before the awesome fifteen-hour ride back to the city. This stop would change my life forever. We went for a hike, and obviously, my friend could not come with, and he had to sit in the bus, which must have been really shitty. We hiked for over an hour, maybe two, I don't remember, but I remember coming to the end of the trail at the edge of a cliff. There were backpacks and ropes up there, and I had no idea what was going on, but I figured it out. We were supposed to rappel down the cliff to get to the bus. There was really no other option because I was not paying attention as we hiked and would never be able to find my way back to the bus. I have never been afraid of heights. In fact, just the opposite. I had an incredibly unstable tree house that was super high when I was younger. I had gone bungee jumping a couple of times, and I can remember leaning over the edge of the Grand Canyon, and I was having fun. But this was different. It might have been that I was a little stony, but this shit was scary as hell. I think the whole idea of walking vertically with your back to the ground did not appeal to me.

I believe it was one of the girls that went first so there was no way I could bitch out. I did it because I had to get down and nothing else, because I wish I had not done it. I have never been so scared in my life. As I looked down, which you are not necessarily supposed to do, and looked at the rope that was supposed to hold me and how it was all hooked up, I was not that confident. I waited until the fat girl in the group had gone because I am positive she weighed more than me, but I was still not sure. I needed some coaching as I rappelled, and I was unbelievably scared and having what I can only describe as flashbacks because I was seeing all types of crazy shit. When I got to the bottom, I could barely stand up. I was shaking so badly. All the girls except the fat one came to comfort me and were rubbing my head and telling me it was okay. It was very comforting because I was in a bad way. The big girl didn't do anything, but she didn't like me. I found her quite annoying, so that was okay. All the other girls were actually really quiet, but I liked Jugs. They were huge, and she also gave me the "fuck me" eyes, but I did not act on it in the same way you don't want to fool around with someone at your workplace. Even though I made it down safe, to this day I am terrified of heights and avoid them at all costs. I will still go up a mountain on a chair lift, but that is the cutoff. You will never find me dangling by a little rope ever again.

 I little while before I went to Argentina, my dad was diagnosed with colorectal cancer as well as some prostate issues. They gave him six months to live. I had already signed up for the program, but I was going to stay home. I was told to go because I needed to finish school, and that was only for four months so I could still make it back in time to watch my father die. It was a really shitty way to think about it, and I don't think that is exactly how my mom put it, but it was the truth. I went down there and tried to talk to the parents when I could. My dad decided that he wasn't going to last much longer, so he wanted to get out and travel somewhere. He decided that he wanted to come visit me in Argentina. They would use my mom's frequent-flyer miles and came out for Thanksgiving. They came and stayed at a nice hotel that looked over the park I would go to every day. I hung out with them every day and helped them around the city. It was funny because my dad spent his adolescence in South America and he was having trouble remembering his Spanish. That will happen if you are not around it all the time, so I took care of the talking. I had developed a pretty convincing accent by this time, and people just assumed I was Hispanic until they started talking too fast and I would stop them in English and say, "Hold on, let's start over."

 They were always surprised and would then speak to me in English, and I remember thinking, *Why the fuck didn't we talk like this to begin with?* You could clearly see that the old people I was with were fucking Yankees. That was the derogatory term that they would use to refer to Americans, although they said it in Spanish. They thought we didn't know that, and I guess most tourist do not, but I did and I almost beat the shit out of this little guy when I heard him say that in reference to me.

In Spanish, I told him I understood every word that he just said and I was going to rip his fucking head off. The look on his face was priceless. I couldn't understand what he said next 'cause he was talking so fast and he was scared out of his mind. My parents were down the street when this happened, so they never knew about it. We would go out and shop and shit. It was like an overload of cool shit for pennies, and if I could have, I would have brought back suitcases full of stuff. I had one suitcase and a backpack, so I was pretty limited and didn't really buy anything down there.

In hindsight, I could have gone down there with an empty suitcase and bought a whole new wardrobe for the price of one outfit. My dad was hell bound on getting a leather jacket because Argentina is famous for their leather. I remember saying something that I still regret. I asked him why he would spend a bunch of money on a nice jacket when he is just going to die soon? I still want to kick my own ass for saying that. He brushed it off because he knew it was going to happen. He just said to help him pick it out because it would be mine someday. I could obviously not brush it off so easily because it is still bugging me now. In hindsight, there were a lot of things that I said to him that I really wish I could take back.

We got him the jacket and had a good time around the city. They saw some sights while I was at school, and I think they had a good time. In hindsight, I wish I would have gone out shopping with them. My mom is the type to buy you a T-shirt or something if she can tell that you like it. I never take advantage of that; she is too nice. However, I will let her put down loot for school because that shit is fucking expensive. I still owe her money for that, but it is a lot nicer to owe money to your mom than the student loan people. I have heard that they are not very nice. She has offered to buy me a car so I have reliable transportation and I was driving a shit box. I have never accepted and drove the shit box into the ground and bought another one for less than five hundred bones, and I was happy because if I crash the shit out of it, it is no deal to me; I just go get a "new" one.

The parents and I were having a good time, and then Thanksgiving came around. The group had talked to the kitchen staff and set up a turkey dinner for Thursday. Considering they do not celebrate Thanksgiving in South America, it was kind of hard to find a whole bird for the harvest. However, they were able to wrangle up a good amount of turkey and gravy, mashed potatoes, basically all the staple foods, and it turned out to be about the best that it could be for a makeshift Thanksgiving in a foreign country. My parents ate with the whole group, and everyone seemed to have a good time. They would leave the next day, but I was not worried like I was before because my dad looked really healthy, and I was sure I would see him when I got home.

The school I was attending was primarily an art school. I had to walk through a museum to get to the classroom. I thought that was cool because the art kept changing with different exhibits. It was also in a wing of a huge building that was also a mall, so there was a food court with all types of different food that I would hit up during a break from classes. Sometimes I would go home, but by the time I got back, I only had time to inhale a sandwich and run back to class. Instead, I would eat Chinese food at the mall, and people watch, which was always a good time and much more interesting that in America.

There are apparently no social mores when it comes to public displays of affection. I would eat some fried rice and whatever else I ordered, go burn one, look at some art, and go back to class. The school was artsy school/museum and had many large areas in which they would have exhibits or rent it out for other functions. One time, they hosted a tattoo/piercing show. I had a sun tattooed on my right shoulder, and I am all about symmetry, so I was hell-bound on putting a moon on my left shoulder. The show was at the school for the weekend, so I went back to the room and drew up a circular moon design so that it would even out with the sun. It took a little while but not that long. That tattoo, however, took about an hour and a half. My mind was blown when after the exchange rate it only cost about twenty dollars, and that is nothing. I went back on the last day and got another tattoo on my back that was circular and went under my neck tattoo and fit into the theme. It took about an hour, and he charged me around twelve dollars. I could not believe it. If I was really high and had a bit of money on me, I would have tattooed my whole body. I also shaved off my soul patch and got my labret pierced for some reason. The piercing and jewelry was like half the price of the jewelry in the States, so why not? I liked it for a while, but eventually it started fucking up my teeth, so I took it out, and the soul patch returned.

I had gone there with my roommate for some reason, but that was what we did, and we met, or I should say I met these two girls who clearly belonged there, piercings and tattoos all over. One of them spoke perfect English and was in fact American. I had my eyes set on the other one who was a dark-skinned, dark-haired princess. I had to have her. There was one problem; she did not speak one word of English. This was going to take all my skills. Luckily, her friend helped me out a little bit as I struggled to pick up a girl in a language that I do not speak. Somehow my roommate got the American one to talk to him, which I still don't understand because he was such a dork. She was actually really sexy, and at any other time, I would have hit that in a heartbeat, but I wanted the dark meat. She was not that dark, but she was clearly Latina and could not understand a word I said. I did my best with my Spanish, and I guess I did good enough because I eventually got her butt naked and doing anything I wanted. Body language is truly universal because I could get her to do anything with simple hand signs, and she was down for everything I would imply with my hands. There is nothing hotter that fucking a gorgeous girl with a hot accent talking nasty when you can't understand a word that she is saying. I later found out that she was actually a virgin. Taking someone's virginity is an accomplishment, but to do it with someone who doesn't even speak the same language as you is incredible. I pride myself on that story.

I was still talking to the flat-tire girl. I called her one time while I was sitting by the phone and just hung up with my parents. I had nothing to say, but I was looking for anything else besides my homework. I basically called to say hi because I was high. I had mentioned that they did not sell Black & Mild cigars down there, which was all I smoked. I eventually found some, but they were expensive, although after the exchange rate, it was about what they cost in the States.

However, cigarettes were much, much cheaper, but I rarely smoked cigarettes, which would soon change.

In the meantime, she found out where I was staying somehow and sent me a care package. It had all types of shit, even *The Simpsons* toys, but the most important was a fucking case of Black & Milds, which I assume she though would last me the rest of the summer, but that was not to be. I went through those like a hot knife through warm butter. I really appreciated it though, and she was the only person to send me anything; I saved a couple packs for going to parties. That did not help them last any longer. I started to smoke cigarettes, but I didn't know what to get. I tried a bunch of them and ended up sticking to Lucky Strikes. This isn't the reason why, but I really liked hearing them say Luckys? Most of the vendors had a very strong accent, but Lucky Strike is the same in any language. Now that I think about it, I think that a lot of the vendors did not even speak English, but there was something about the way that these old men would say it that I thought was adorable. Eventually, I was smoking a pack a day; they were so cheap I felt like I had to take advantage of the situation. I would get three 40-ounces and a pack of smokes for under five dollars.

At this point, I was still having fun with all the girls that I had hooked up with, especially the girl from Brazil, because God knows I needed access to weed at all times, and she was a failsafe. One time, she even took the train into the city at like two in the morning, which was not a short trip by any means, just to bring me a bag. Yes, I had to have sex with her, but it was a small price to pay to have weed around when I needed it. My crippled friend and I would frequent the Temple Bar, which was literally crawling distance from where we stayed which was a good thing. We made friends with the bartenders. One in particular spoke very good English. He ended up hooking up with one of the hookers from our group. I only say hookers because I know which one it was, and we did not get along that well. I think it is because she was from Texas. In retrospect, there were two girls that I did not get along with out of the group, and what do you know, they were both from the South.

One of those girls was such a buzzkill; everyone hated her, and we all wondered why the fuck she was even there. We all came to party and have a good time, and I don't think she understood that. She had the most annoying Southern accent that you could even hear when she spoke Spanish. After a while, the group got hip to where we were going every night, and they all wanted to come with. Our sanctuary had been tainted and would never be the same. We would drink this shit that was basically a tradition and good luck, I guess. It was Ouzo, which is clear black licorice that is fucking diesel. They would put exactly three coffee beans in the bottom of a shot glass, fill it up, and then light it on fire. You would blow it out and make a wish if you want, or it would supposedly bring you good luck somehow, but not if you forget to blow it out before you take the shot, and yes, I did make that mistake one time. I never did that again.

One night, the group went to the bar to play some pool and do what you do at the bar. It was always funny because they were all under twenty-one and out of the league when it came to drinking and even partying for that matter. At one point, I was sitting on a couch with some of the biggest natural boobs on a young girl I had ever seen. She was only eighteen years old. It was the girl from my group that I knew for a fact had a thing for me. We sat and talked, looking at these postcard-looking things that were actually more or less flyers for a play/show that was going on at the time. It was called *pene*, which means penis, and it was exactly that.

The show apparently consisted of guys on stage manipulating the cock and balls so that they would form various shapes, and they all had names. My favorite were the Loch Ness monster and the hamburger where you bend your wiener in between your balls, squeeze them together, and twist it sideways, and it does in fact look like a hamburger. It sounds like it would hurt, but it does not. We sat there and got drunk, and I could read her eyes like a fucking comic book; she was so obvious. I had this one in the bag. There was the typical moment of silence, and she jumped on me like I was dying and she had to give me CPR. We made out for a while, which I do not like to do in public, but it was apparently the norm down there, so I wasn't too concerned.

We dipped out and went back to the hotel. I told the cripple where I was going because when you go out in a foreign country, you always have to tell people what you are doing or where you are going; otherwise, people freak the fuck out and expect the worst. I have never been good at following this rule, but I understand it. I never worry when I go out by myself. I am not a badass; I have just never felt in danger simply for the fact that I am in a foreign country or big city. If something happens, it happens.

On trips, I would often go out after everyone fell asleep and wander the neighborhood, drinking and smoking, and I always had a good time. Big Tits and I headed back to the hotel and went to her room, which was a horrible idea in hindsight; we should have gone to my room because I would kick my roommate out all the time. I would just say that I got the bedroom. "The couch is your new home. If you ever get a girl to sleep over here with you, I will gladly sleep on the couch." That never happened.

We went to her room and went to town. Throughout the ordeal, we obviously took off our clothes. I cannot possibly describe how immaculate these tits were; they were fucking amazing. They were huge and firm but not hard like a boob job. They were just perfect, and her face was just so cute, so as we made out, I gradually slid my wang in between her fun bags, and it was on. I titty-fucked her for a while and played with her business until at the absolute worst time her roommate walked in and fucked up everything. It was made even clearer Big Tits was all nervous and fun time was over. I just thought that really sucks, and then I remembered there were girls I could call on, which I did so. I had a full night and slept well.

Nothing really happened after that between us. She still looked at me like she wanted me to jump her bones all the time, but there was never a good moment. Plus I got to see the boobs and have my way with them while checking out the undercarriage, so I was happy and I had a bunch of other tail to take care of daily. She would see these girls come and go all the time I did not want to deal with another one in the mix, especially one who is staying in the same building as me.

The mix of ladies would inevitably get larger. I was at the Temple Bar with Crutches, and we were just sitting up at the bar, and two girls came up, and we started talking. One of them had clearly taken a liking to me. She had a beautiful face, nice boobies, but what I can only refer to as a "tragic" ass. It was so big. I like butts and everything, but I am not Sir Mix-A-Lot. I usually look at someone's face when I talk to them, not their ass, so I would rather be attracted to that. I might look at the tits every once in a while. One thing I have found funny about just meeting girls is that whole "my eyes are up here" thing. The girls with natural breasts don't seem to care, or they may be flattered. It is the girls that either have boob jobs or wear barely anything and pushup or pad their boobs so they look two cup sizes larger. Those are the ones that complain about people staring at their tits even though they push them up, push them out, or have paid to make them bigger for the purpose of their appearance.

This girl did had nice titties though. We spoke for a while in Spanish. I was doing my best, and then I turned to old broken foot in English, and the girl I was talking to said, "You are American?" She spoke perfect English, and it sounded familiar in some way, but I couldn't put my thumb on it. I told her I would prefer to speak in English, and as she spoke, I figured it out, she had a Midwest accent, so I asked her where she was from, and the bitch was from Minnesota. I couldn't believe it; she was from St. Cloud and was down there teaching English to Argentine kids. It was fucking amazing. What are the odds? We hung out until bar closed, and we went back to our hotel.

We went to the cripple's room because apparently his gay roommate was drinking wine with some of the girls. He never came out, but we all knew he was gay. He could not have been more obvious, even wearing a rainbow shirt Elton John glasses a fanny pack and holding a sparkler. Crutches and I introduced the two girls to the group, and we all just drank a lot more; however, they drank wine, and I was slamming a forty-ounce. I remember how the girl from Minnesota was looking at me, and I know that look, but I had no idea how it would pan out. I decided that I wanted to smoke some herb. She said she wanted to come with me and see my room, which was bullshit because we were in a fucking hotel and all the rooms looked more or less the same. The second we got into the elevator, she fucking tackled and mouth-raped me. She took off her pants to show me her underwear for some reason; they were blue and gold and had the Boca Juniors (the soccer team) symbol on them; I had the matching hat. I told her to put her fucking pants on and follow me. I didn't want anybody to get on the elevator because that would have been weird. We got to my room, and she took everything off down to her Boca drawers and was ready to go.

I said, "Don't you remember why I said I wanted to come down here? I am going to smoke this before anything." I was wrong because after I packed up a bowl and started smoking, she ripped my pants off and went to town. Luckily, I had opened a beer when we got down there and had it right next to me, so I was smoking dope and drinking beer as this girl I just met was swallowing my cock like it was water and there was a drought going on.

Inevitably, she took those drawers off, and she wanted it bad. She was a real dirty talker and a loud one. She told me exactly what to do like a fucking porn star and wanted me to fuck her really hard, and she loved it from behind. I thought I was taking a big risk when I pulled out and tried to go in hole number 2. Usually, if they are not into it, they will just say, "Wrong hole," and that is the end of it. This was different. She grabbed my dick and slammed it in the glory hole and wanted to be fucked hard. I was willing to comply. She was so fucking loud and screaming dirty shit, I was nervous and thought we might get in trouble, but fucking it was fun.

The next day at school, the fat Southern bitch who had no business being there talked shit to me. Her room was right above mine, and there was a courtyard outside the windows, so everything echoed, and I guarantee that she heard everything. She said that my "guests" were too loud, and it was inappropriate. This girl was clearly jealous because she knew that she would never experience anything like that in her entire life. The girl was very loud and said a lot of nasty shit, and when it is super loud and you can even hear the sex noises, that can be very annoying. I have experienced the same thing before even to the point where they the people in the next room were fucking so loud and hard they were moving our headboard. It was obnoxious and awkward because I was on vacation with my mom and sister in the same room, but I just thought to myself, *Be happy for them, they are having fun. Just go to sleep.* I asked the girl's roommate if it bothered her, and she said absolutely not. It was loud, but it sounded like fun. I asked if her roommate was so pissed because she was pug fugly and annoying so no guys would touch her with a ten-foot pole. She said I did not have to be such an asshole about it, but yes.

I continued to see this Minnesota girl, which meant that I would have to cut back on my contact with the other girls severely. That did not mean cutting off all ties, because I would still have the hotel girl come to my room every once in a while as well as the girl on the corner, and I obviously had to keep in touch with the girl from Brazil because I had to have my weed/medicine. Unfortunately, the Minnesota girl and I ran into the corner blow job queen, and it goes without saying that it was really fucking awkward and thought I was going to end up getting hit and hurt because those Latinas can be very feisty.

Nothing happened, but I could not help but notice that they were not mad at me; they were mad at each other. It wasn't either of their faults. I was the asshole. I was the one who should be in trouble, but I was okay with that. I did see the girl on the corner a few more times, but I was seeing more and more of the Minnesota girl, so I basically cut that off. If I went to the market, I would take the very long way all around the buildings and come up to it from behind, so I did not have to pass her. I would see her, but she did not see me. The hotel girl also ran into her, but she was older and very mature in addition to the fact that she saw me bring different girls to the room all the time, which is actually why I believe she wanted to fuck me in the first place. It is kind of a double standard, but when girls see a guy with a lot of girls all the time, something in their head says that he must be good at something because those girls are always happy. That or he must have money; it depends on what type of girl you ask.

When guys see a woman do the same thing, they simply think, *What a slut.* I would buy as much weed as possible from the Brazil girl whenever I saw her, so I did not have to see her for a while, and that seemed to work out somehow without confrontation because I had a connection for the entire time I was down there. I saw the girl who did not speak English a few more times, and it was fun to just meet and fuck without really talking, but it got old. In addition to all these things, I was really getting into the Minnesota girl. She was very sweet, and I guess the adage that men want a lady in the street and a freak in the bed would apply to her because she would be a poster child for that. She had to work teaching English in the day and would come see me at night. Unlike the Argentine girls, she would not simply do my homework for me, but she tutored me and made me learn, which was kind of annoying, but I understand why she did that, and it was the act of someone who really cared about me. That was cool. So there was a little bit of mandatory study time if I had homework, and then it was time for a reward, which she was quite good at.

By this time, we were basically dating, and she would come hang out with the group when we would go out every once in a while. She also introduced me to something I had no idea about, and that was a *tay-low*. I am sure that is not the correct spelling, but I just typed it out phonetically because that it what she called it. It was essentially a hotel that you rent by the hour, which was clearly for the use of prostitution, extramarital affairs, or just fucking when you have nowhere to go and don't want to get naked in the street or mess up your sheets.

The rooms were really nice, and you could fuck them up eight ways from Sunday with no regret because you did not need an ID to take out a room for an hour. When you got in the room, it was like the set of a cheesy '70s porn flick. There was a Jacuzzi right next to the bed and mirrors everywhere. They even had mirrors on the ceiling, which I thought was somewhat of a joke, but apparently it is a real thing. There were condoms on the night stand and what I would call porn music on tap that you could play while you played. The mirrors on the ceiling were actually cool as hell and introduced me to the fact that a lot of women like to watch themselves being fucked like they were in a porno, at least a lot that I have been with. It is usually not the slutty girls either. It is the innocent ones who love to watch themselves being ravaged; however, the loose girls like to watch as well, so I guess it is a universal pleasure. I actually thought it was kind of cool as well, and I got a kick out of it. We just set a timer and cleaned off in the Jacuzzi, which is stupid because Jacuzzis are frap traps of bacteria and fucking disgusting. Yes, we did have sex again in it, but it is still fucking gross. The whole experience was fucking amazing if you didn't think about all the shit that has happened in that room before you, possibly even that day. We did absolutely everything you could possibly do with only two people. I don't know how much she paid for the room, but it was worth every penny.

We kept dating down there, and I was eventually kicking it with her all the time, except for the occasional visit from the weed lady and the hotel women and the blow job queen, so I guess nothing had really changed, but I did hang out with the other girls a lot less. I still did my own thing as well, which was basically going to random parties and raves with whoever. I was very trusting because I never felt intimidated, at least not while partying.

There was this one time that I was intimidated to say the least; in fact, I was terrified. The majority of the group had decided to go watch a Boca Juniors soccer game versus Riviera Maya, and as we all came from Buenos Aires, we were on the Boca side, literally. The two teams were neighbors and rivals just like Green Bay and the Vikings, but I don't remember having to go to a specific side of the field at one of their games. The tickets said Boca on the side so we had to walk around and go to the Boca side of the stadium, and there were dividers so that you could not go into the opposing team's side. Boca is blue, and Riviera is red, and I hate red, so I was very happy to be on the blue side. The only people out of the group that wanted to go were me and every girl in the group. They had talked to the director and were told that they were not allowed to go outside of the city without a man. I was forced to go. I did want to be able to say I went to football game in South America, so I went even though it was incredibly boring. We could barely see anything because we had standing-room-only tickets, or maybe it was because I forgot to wear my contacts. Either way, it sucked.

The shittiest part was that we were surrounded by thousands of horny Argentine men that loved American girls, and I was alone and had to protect seven of them. I wish we would have had seats so guys wouldn't walk by and try to hit on them. I barely saw any of the game because I was watching out for the girls the whole time. I had to intervene and push guys away from them the whole time. No one tried to hit on the fat girl for some reason; I wonder why.

I was exhausted and really needed something to eat. I hadn't eaten all day, which was dumb, but I figured I could just drink beer at the game. They did not serve beer at the game, but in retrospect, that is probably a good idea because then it would have really been scary. I told the girls I would be right back. I was waiting in line to get a burger, and I felt something graze my ass. I am always aware of anything or anybody touching my pants because I have caught people trying to pick my pockets before. I felt something on my pants pocket where I usually keep my wallet; however, this was not my first rodeo, but it was my first soccer game. I had been to crowded functions in other countries before, so I knew better than to bring my wallet. I just had a little bit of cash, just enough to get by.

I felt something on my ass that was clearly more than the person behind me bumping into me. I whipped my hand around and caught an arm attached to a hand that had four fingers in my pocket. My wallet was not there, but even if it was, he would not have gotten it. The thieving hand was also attached to a very young boy. I felt bad about it for a second because I grabbed and squeezed his arm pretty hard, but then I remembered that the little bastard was trying to rob me, so I wish I would have broken his arm. However, looking back, that would have been a really bad idea because after I got my burger, I came out of the waiting area, and that little shit was standing in front of six guys who were about my size, which was pretty fucking big compared to the majority of the men down there.

The little bastard pointed at me and was saying something to them. I couldn't tell what because they were a ways away, but their eyes were all dead locked on me. There was a lineup of riot police just standing by the wall, and I went and told them the situation and that I was scared. I asked them to walk me to my spot so those guys don't kill me. Although it may have been at the level of a five-year-old, I know I spoke my Spanish correctly, but the *policia* literally told me to fuck off and get the fuck out of there. Curse words were one of the first things I wanted to learn when I went down there, also how to tell if somebody is talking shit about you. That is exactly what that cop was doing to me, and he knew those guys were going to kill me because when I told the 5-0 the story I accidentally pointed at the little thief that tried to G me. I watched these "putos" watch me point out their nephew or brother or whatever the fuck he was. The cop saw this as well and walked the other way. This was a group of half a dozen scary ass gangster looking motherfuckers and I was alone, responsible for eight white girls in South America in the fucking ghetto. I have never been so terrified and I will never go to another soccer game in my life, at least not in South America. Somehow I walked right past them looking them in the eyes, and absolutely nothing happened. After the game, which seemed like about ten hours later, we left to go where we agreed we would catch a cab, but the exits were segregated as well. Not only that, but they had barricades to divide the streets, so we had to go to the complete other side of town and figure out another place to get picked up at. We could hear and see a bit of drama happening between the opposite sides of the barricades, so we got the fuck out of dodge.

    The only other time I was scared of other people was when the group went on a school field trip type of thing to some barrios (ghettos). They were painted all types of pretty colors to make them look nice, but it does not fool anyone when you have chickens and feral dogs running all over the streets, not to mention half-naked children. Most of the hoods that we went to mainly had vendors on the side of the road, selling handmade goods and random shit, little trinkets, and whatnot. Since the majority of our group was female, we had to stop at every one of them. I did not necessarily want to buy a bunch of stupid shit. By looking back, I wish that I would have because they had a lot of cool stuff. However, on this day in particular, the field trip was mad early, and I did not have time to get my fix. I was able to take a couple of puffs and smash a tall can, but by the time we got there, I was well overdue for a refill.

The instructors were very adamant about staying on the one street and to not go anywhere else. If the buildings were not colorfully painted, you needed to turn around and go back to the colors because that is where it is safe. That did not work for me because I walked all the way down that fucking street, and I did not find one store that sold beer. I really wanted my breakfast and take another hit or two. I left the ghetto street of colors and entered the real ghetto. I passed many shady characters and just tried not to make eye contact. I strolled around the hood for quite a while and saw a lot of sad things and situations that people had to live with and live in.

I found a *mercado*, and I got me a forty-ounce and a tall can for the road. I knew that it would probably not be acceptable to walk down the strip of colors with a forty-ounce in hand, considering it was somewhat of a touristy place, so I continued my detour. I walked into what was clearly the heart of the ghetto; it had all the clear red flags. There was graffiti everywhere and sellers on almost every corner, along with hookers and street people.

I was approached by two Argentine men that looked like they just broke out of prison. They were tattooed up like it was going out of style. I have my fair share of tattoos as well but not on my neck and face. They were scary gentlemen to say the least. They stopped me, and I did my inventory, and once again, I did not bring my wallet with me and my loot was in my front pocket. The only thing they could snatch would be my watch, which I was not going to let go of. They did not speak a word of English, so that was a bit of a problem because I thought they wanted me to give them my forty-ounce and I was like, "Fuck that, I would not give it up." Thinking back, that was incredibly stupid. People get murdered on those streets all the time, and no one ever hears about or even cares. I would not give them my beer, but then he said, "Just let us have a sip please." He said *please* and sounded polite, so I handed him my forty-ounce. I was ready like a fucking ninja in case he tried to bash me over the head with my own bottle, but he did not. He and his buddy just took a sip and gave me my beer back. They were pretty gross, so I wiped the bottle off the best that I could, but the thought of it was still gross. One of them barely had any teeth, but I was not going to let the beer I had walked around for an hour go to waste.

I walked away shaking. I think they were just testing me, but whatever, I got my beer back, and nothing went down. I crushed my forty-ounce in the ghetto without any further confrontations and returned to the group. I don't know how I found them, but it was right as they were getting on the bus to leave. They were going to leave my ass there.

The next field trip was actually just people from the group; it had nothing to do with school. It was going to be to Antarctica. My problem with this was it was a longer bus ride than to Wine County, about seventeen hours, and after that, you had to take a boat for fifteen hours to Antarctica. Fuck that. Travel would take up the whole weekend, two full days of driving and boating, and maybe a few hours at the most on Antarctica, no dice. However, looking back, it would really be nice to say that you have walked on Antarctica, because honestly, how many people can say that?

I have watched a lot of nature documentaries and seen many on Antarctica since coming back, and half of me regrets not going, but the other half just thinks about the travel time and how much I hate that shit. I don't even like driving to the store; I don't think I could deal with thirty-two hours of travel each way as well as being in the open ocean half the time. I would freak the fuck out. In addition to this, it was not through school and definitely not free by any means. In fact, nobody ended up going, so I didn't necessarily feel left out. Instead, they went to Uruguay because apparently it was something we had to do before we could get back into the US. I did not know this or maybe they told me and I forgot. That is more likely. I went out and partied all weekend, fucked up out of my brain, and when I got to school on Monday, they basically told me I was fucked and I would not be able to return to America because my visa was going to expire in one week. I talked to my Minnesota girl, and she knew exactly what the deal was and what I had to do. I had to take a ferry to Uruguay to renew my visa, spend the night, and then return to Argentina, allowing me to legally return to the States.

We planned to go there for the weekend, and I never would have been able to do this by myself; it was really confusing. We got on the ferry and took the boat across an open ocean, which is very scary. She noticed that I was a little uncomfortable, and somehow I talked her into giving me a hand job to relax me. I was trying for a blow job, but she said that it would be too obvious and we could get into serious trouble. I was fine with the HJ. I busted a nut and fell asleep until we arrived in another country. I guess it was close to the ocean, equivalent of the mile high club.

The closest I got to the actual mile-high club was the same thing, a hand job on the airplane on the way to Mexico and then once again on the way to Idaho with my middle school crush. We got to Uruguay and had to find a place to stay, which I thought she had already arranged, but she said that we would just drive around and find I hostel.

I had never stayed in a hostel before, and I was confused about what the fuck we were going to drive around in. They had mopeds for rent when we got off the boat, and they were like ten American dollars per day to rent. I wasn't too sure about it because the roads were mostly cobblestone among other random surfaces that looked unstable and had no upkeep since the early 1900s. We rented a bike anyways, but then did not know who was going to drive it. I wanted her to drive because it did not want to be responsible, but she would not drive. This was a problem. I had a motorcycle back home that my dad and I took on as a project, so I had experience riding a bike. It was one that was about four times the size of the moped, so I was okay, but the roads were fucking scary.

I drove the scooter with her on the back, and it was, as I predicted, scary as hell, but it was also pretty fun. I was dipping around those streets like a local after a while. We drove around and found a hostel in no time that was really close to where we had to board the ferry in the morning. It was cheap as hell, and I soon found out why. I did not know that sometimes you have to share the room with other people who are not in your party. There were two bunk beds, so there were four beds. We decided to spend as much time out of the room as possible and just go back to pass out.

We drove around, got some drinks, and just had a good time in another country, one that I will most likely never be in again, so that was cool. I cannot believe I did not crash driving drunk as fuck a little motorbike on roads built by children one hundred years ago. When we got back, the other people staying in our room were there, and they were sleeping. You would think that you wouldn't be able to have sex in that situation, but I wanted to do it in yet another country, and things have a way of working it out. It was a good night. We had to get up early and leave, so we never met our roommates, but it was a good time. We made it to the ferry, where I received another hand job on international waters. We made it on time, and I didn't even crash the moped, so I did not have to pay the fifty cents for the replacement fee.

When I got back, everyone was surprised that I had done the trip and renewed my passport and visa all by myself. I am not a liar, so I told them the truth and that I didn't do shit. I did a lot more partying when I got back. I still went to raves with the girl from Brazil and got herb from her because Minnesota girl did not really live down the block so there were no drop-ins.

I went to parties with all the girls in my harem and did not get in too much trouble. I rolled my ass off one night and chewed the inside of my face off. I went to a party spot called Pacha, and it was an outrageous rave that went until the sun came up as most raves do. I found some actual ecstasy, but it was chalk-full of speed, and I could tell right away.

When I do speed, I grind my teeth, and sometimes bite my tongue and check although I am not aware of it until the next day. That place was crazy, and I don't even remember who I went with. It was either the girl from Brazil or the Minnesota chick. Regardless, I had a fucking blast. I was dancing like an idiot and making out with a bunch of random girls, which makes me think I was with the Brazilian because she was totally down with throwing another girl into the mix. I was fucked all weekend, and when I went to class on Monday, the director could tell that I was still messed up and asked me what I did during the weekend. I told her, and she said, "You went to Pacha by yourself? Are you fucking crazy?"

She also asked me what happened to my cheek because it was swollen as fuck. She was only like two years older than me or something, so I was honest and told her I did some X that had too much speed in it. She understood. I had no idea that she was a party girl, although she did look like she would be a freak in bed. She knew exactly what to do. She told me what prescription to get and take them right away. In America, you would have to see a doctor and get a prescription, but down there, you can just walk in like it is a gas station and you want cigarettes. You just tell them what you want; they disappear for a minute, then bring you your pills.

What would have probably cost me $50 back home and a lot of bullshit was $5 in the BA. The Minnesota girl brought me to the store and bought it for me so I didn't have to deal with it, so looking back, I definitely did not got to that party with her because she would have known why I ate my face. I told her what I did the night before but not with who or anything that went down. We were there to party, and she knew that, although I think she knew that I was more down than anyone else in the group because I was always out and about.

I did a lot of other things while I was there that did not have anything to do with sex and drugs. The class would go on field trips within Buenos Aries, which has a strong cultural heritage, as well as traveling outside of the city on longer trips. We visited many churches within the city, and I remember the first one very well. We did not visit the churches to learn from a religious standpoint but rather to get a better understanding of the cultural heritage of the country. We were entering the first church, and I took off my hat out of respect. I am not religious by any means, but I do have respect for the beliefs of others. I noticed that my roommate still had his baseball cap on, so I smacked him in in the back of the head and knocked his hat off, saying, "Show some respect. We are in a church."

He held his hat and from the whole time and from that moment on, I noticed that he would take his hat off right away at every church we would visit before the doors were even open. I taught someone a life lesson, and I bet he still respects that to this day. There were also many nice restaurants in the city. We ate as a group at nice places a few times, but for the most part, everyone just fended for themselves. I just had salami and cheese sandwiches and sweet milk when I was hungry; it was a lot cheaper.

Speaking of sweet milk, they had something there that they called *dulce de leche*, which they translated into "sweet of milk." They claimed that it was an Argentine creation. It was just fucking caramel and no different than what we use in the States to dip our apples in at a fair or carnival. I laughed at that. Food was not expensive in comparison to the US, but I didn't need to eat at a nice place every day just because it was affordable. My roommate would actually go to McDonald's every day and get a McQueso. This was just cheese and a bun. They do not sell them in the States. It was only a peso for a McQueso, which translated at the time into thirty-three cents for a cheese sandwich. They also had big-ass hot dogs and chips for two pesos, sold by vendors all over the city. I can happily say that I never ate at McDonald's or a food cart the entire time I was there. When my parents were there, my dad also wanted to eat a cow in addition to wearing one.

He had found his leather jacket, so now he wanted some steak. Argentina was famous for its beef as well as its leather, and I guess they have really nice cows down there. What I found funny and something that PETA would probably protest was the fact that the big fancy steak houses had actual dead cows that had been stuffed propped outside of the entrance. My dad had a blast and loved the whole experience. They had good steak, but I prefer to cook it myself because everyone's idea of rare, medium rare, or well done is always different, and I don't like my steak to moo when I cut into it, so I cook the hell out of my meat.

I hate looking like a little bitch because I did not finish my steak even though it is because it was not cooked to my liking. I also do not like to send it back to have it cooked more. I cooked at a bar and grill for three years, and when that would happen, I wanted to spit on their steak. I never did. Needless to say, I did not eat out that often unless it was under a skirt (bah dum-dum). I was happy with my daily liquid diet of herb and cigarettes washed down with Quilmes and whiskey.

Out of the blue, one day the director said to me that she knew I liked to party and we should all go out to one, meaning the whole group, and I just said, "Whatever, pick a place." I have no idea where we went, but it was fun. Everyone was fucked up. Even the fat Southerner was the leaning on the wall. I danced with the director a couple of times, and she was grinding on my junk like she wanted it bad, but I did not make a move, and she was part of the school. I did not want to lose all the credits I had earned down there, but she was so sexy that night.

Later as we were leaving and about to get on the airplane, we were giving her hugs and saying goodbye. I was the last in line, and she gave me a very sensual hug and asked me why I did not try to hook up with her. She said it in different words, but that is what she meant. Because she told me that he would have fucked my brains out the night that we were dancing together. I told her that, first of all, she was my teacher and that is kind of fucked up, and second, why the fuck did she wait until the airport to tell me that? I would have totally rocked her world for hours if she would have told me that night. I suggested going and getting it on in the bathroom, and she was down, then the boarding numbers were read, and we had to get on board. I almost wish that she hadn't told me that because I was so pissed off on the ride home I would have fucked the hell out of that teacher.

The group also went on a lot of trips to art museums and had classes regarding the subject. I was an art student, but by this time, I was basically getting sick of it and bored. I still love art and enjoy creating it, but I cannot stand listening to students in the class. They all think that there is so much more than there is within a particular work of art. Sometimes an apple is just an apple; it is not necessarily reflecting on any kind of human emotion, time period. It is not happy or sad; it is just a fucking apple.

I remember spending the majority of my time during the discussion and critique portions of my art classes. I embraced during my freshman year at CU while taking a sculpture course. I worked hard on my first project, which was an accurate reproduction of the Denver skyline. I also carved out the word Denver on one side and a very accurate Denver Bronco on the other. I was asked to explain the meaning of the piece and what it expressed. I said that didn't express shit; it was just the skyline of Denver and it said Denver on the side with a fucking 3D Bronco on it. What more did they want? When it was time for discussion, they said the stupidest shit, like portrayed unity and togetherness and the Bronco was looking over the city like Big Brother and stuff that was even more ridiculous than that. I stuck by what I said and said that it was just a fucking skyline and was not supposed to mean anything; they didn't like that.

I actually fucked up on my second assignment. Well, actually, I was just out partying all weekend. I did have the whole week before to work on it, but whatever. I went to class a bit early and went to the metal shop and grabbed some random pieces from the scrap metal / recycling pile and threw some garbage together. I welded one piece of crap around another one and cleaned it up a little bit, but it was crap. I threw it away after class. When it came time to discuss our "works of art," I was so full of shit. I was just planning on getting an F and probably dropping the class. I proposed that the piece expressed the oppression of the working man and how they are trapped in the workplace; it made absolutely no sense. They ate it up and went off with all their own thought about what it meant. All it meant is that I forgot I had a project due that day and welded together some crap from the garbage. I received an A and lost all respect for fine-art classes in general. I still do art on my own and have done a few big projects, but never again will I try to read into something that has nothing to say.

I was still an art student and did all the regular classes, like life drawing and painting, but ended up majoring in film. People also read too much into some movies, but it is nowhere near as ridiculous and annoying, depending on who was talking. I began taking film because I figured that my homework would just be to watch or go see a movie, and it was. The teachers time the films with the schedules of theaters in Uptown, so we had to go to those theaters in order to do our homework, which sounds like a pain in the ass, but it was actually kind of cool.

The downside to taking these courses was that they basically ruined movies for me forever. I overanalyze everything and look into the film too much rather than just accept it for what it is. I would notice errors in continuity and plotlines to the point where I could not enjoy the movie. I finished all the courses because I still really enjoyed them. I just needed to do a senior project for my painting class and finish my language requirements. I painted my shed for my senior project. I painted one side that faced the east the skyline of Saint Paul during sunrise and the north side a view looking down the Mississippi with Saint Paul on the left and Minneapolis on the right at high noon. The west side was a view of the Minneapolis skyline from the west at night. It was pretty fucking cool. It is still there ten years later; however, it has faded a bit, and the shed is basically falling apart. The only thing left that I had to complete was my language requirement, which is the reason I ended up spending four months in Argentina. After I was done, I just hung out and worked at the moving company. I went to class when I had to, I had no more requirements to fulfill; I just needed a few more credits, and then I would be done. My dad was gradually getting sicker and sicker and taking all types of different drugs and treatments. I wanted to finish school so he could see me graduate before he left. I did graduate on the dean's list with a 3.88 GPA, and I was high every day in class and doing my homework.

   Not long after I returned, the St. Cloud girl from Argentina came back to Minnesota. I did not know that was going to happen. I had already messed around with Flat Tire more than a few times. This was an awkward situation because Flat Tire would always come over whenever, and I liked the Minnesota/Argentina girl. I told Flat Tire that I had met someone down there that happened to live her and she was back and I wanted to continue seeing her. It goes without saying that this did not go over too well with her. She did not run over me with her car or anything, but she was none too happy to say the least.

   I continued to see the big-booty girl from Argentina although Flat Tire would come around all the time. There were many close calls. I didn't get punched in the head or anything, but they both knew what was going on. The worst encounter was at a show I was playing. I was the DJ for Minneapolis Junction, and we were opening for Eyedea, who was in my top three of MCs at that time. I'm not sure which number, but I loved his music.

Big Butt came to see me play, which was okay. A bunch of my friends like my old roommate and his sister and all her friends; however, Flat Tire found out about it and knew that Big Booty would be there, so she fucking showed up. I was spinning and scratching and having fun until Flat Tire walked in and sat at the same table as the other one. I was nervous at first, and then I said, "Fuck it," and just had a good time. After that day, she never stopped giving me shit about her giant ass. After the show, it was very awkward to say the least, and I just got out of there as fast as I could. They both knew who each other were and that I was having sex with them both, but nothing went down.

Big Booty and I dated for quite a while. I met her family, she met mine, and she was really sweet. Everyone liked her. She did just the opposite as when she was in Argentina and was now teaching Spanish at the U of M while I was going to school there, so I guess, looking back, I actually did bang one of my teachers. That's cool.

We would go out to clubs and shit, and she would usually crash at my house, but sometimes I would sleep over at her place, which was actually her sister's place who was in fact a lesbian. I have no problem with that; in fact, it was kind of cool. We would sleep in the living room, and on more than a couple occasions, she would have her girlfriend sleepover, and it was cool as hell. We could hear them fucking or whatever you call it. I know it made me horny as fuck, and we would usually have sex to the sound of her lesbian sister fucking in the next room. That shit was hot. She actually loved it in her big butt, so I would fuck her in the ass all the time, and she also liked to play with toys and could not get enough of sucking my dick off until my balls were drained.

Eventually, she would occasionally say random things regarding me drinking too much and smoking too much weed. I thought it was just her giving me shit and didn't think too much of it. I continued to smoke like a chimney and drink like a fish, which apparently made me smell like a grandpa. I was okay with that; she was not. One day we were just sitting on my couch watching *The Simpsons*, and she told me that I needed to stop smoking so much pot and drinking so much. I asked her if she was serious, and she said if I did not she was going to want to split up. I asked her if she was serious, and she said yes. I took a moment to think about it, and I took a sip of my brandy and looked at her like I might kill her. I would never do anything like that, but that is how I felt at that moment. She met me while drinking excessively, and I smoked herb with her after knowing her for a couple hours. I guess she didn't know that I was an everyday smoker and she only did it occasionally, like special occasions. I was faced with a choice at this moment. She had given me an ultimatum. I could either tell her I would cut back on the intake, which would be a lie, or I could just tell her that I could not do that and it was not going to work out between us. I took another route.

After I had looked at her with evil eyes, I took another sip of my brandy and picked up my pipe, I took a big rip of some really stinky weed and blew it right in her face. I didn't need to say anything, but I told her to fuck off, and she left immediately. I am surprised I did not get hit, but she left, and I never heard from her again.

My girl troubles were far from over. I went back and continued to see the flat-tire girl, but once again, there would be a new conundrum in my life. My girlfriend from Colorado and crush from middle school moved back to Minnesota. We inevitably got back together, and I once again had to push Flat Tire to the side. We dated again for a long time, but that is not to say that there were no infidelities at that time. I did cheat on her, and quite often it was with the flat-tire girl.

Once again, it was a situation where they both knew about each other but didn't really seem to care. At this point in time, my dad was increasingly getting sicker, and he would wake up very early and come over to the house to play in his garage. He didn't do a whole lot because the garage was just a clusterfuck and you could not find anything. He would just stand out there and look at stuff. My dad was somewhat of a hoarder even though that was not a term at that time. This was also around the time that I first yelled at my dad while he was sick. He would come over very early, and I was on an early twenties schedule. I stayed up till four and tried to sleep in until at least noon, and I never had a class before one or two o'clock. He would come over and knock on my bedroom door to wake me up and go do stupid shit that I am not into in the garage.

There was clearly another car at the house, so I had a visitor, but he could clearly not put two and two together. I had to scream at him while I was having sex and tell him to get the fuck out. It was either Flat Tire (the blonde) or the crush (the brown-haired). When they would leave, he was out at the garage and say goodbye, but on more than a few separate occasions, he had called each of them by the other girl's name on many occasions. Both of them had mentioned it to me more than a few times, and they each knew exactly who he meant with the wrong name. He either called the blonde the brown one or vice versa. I had to put an end to that one day when I actually walked the lady out to her car because I wanted to stop in the garage and see what the old man was up to.

As we were walking out, he said goodbye to the blonde one. The only problem was that I was walking the brown one out to her car, not the blonde. I got a very dirty look, and she stormed off, because she knew the deal and she is not stupid by any means. As I have said, they both knew about each other, but they didn't need it rubbed in their face. That was the end of that. I walked up to my dad very fast in a hostile stance and screamed in his face, "What the fuck is wrong with you?" I said that just because his player days were over did not mean that he needed to fuck up mine. He had no idea what I was talking about, and I could see that in his eyes. It was the drugs and treatment starting to take over. He was getting fat, which is weird for someone on chemotherapy, but I did not think anything of it, but when I looked in his eyes, I could see him dying inside. I have seen him drunk out of his brain and hallucinating, having flashback, but I had never seen that look in his eyes. That did not change the fact that I was pissed off at him, and I let him know the deal.

I told him that first of all he is never to come knocking on my bedroom door if there was an extra car there. I also told him not to call anyone by whatever it was he thought there name was. If a girl was walking out and leaving, just say "Goodbye" or "Have a good day," no names. He knew my guy friends all right, but when it came to the ladies, he always managed to shit in my cereal. I forgave him, and we had a couple beers while accomplishing absolutely nothing in the garage. He never referred to anyone by name again.

The three of us continued to switch places every night. I would usually go out to hip-hop shows and parties with the brown one and stay at home watching movies with blondie and fucking like crazy. I would always get down with the brown as well, and in fact, she was much more of a freak, and I was more than okay with that. However, I noticed she was even freakier than when we dated my freshman year. I wondered, *Where did she learn that?* She never did that before, and then I later realized sometimes it is best not to think about it and have fun.

She would do anything and everything. We also did everything together outside of the bedroom. We went to shows and parties, but we also would paint together. She helped me do the Saint Paul and Minneapolis mural on my shed. We even got paid to be DJs at a friend of mine's bachelor party or some shit. I don't know or care what it was, but they gave us money to do something we loved. We had to bring our own tables, mixer, and records, which was always a pain in the ass, but it was fun. She would mix the music and play the songs, and I did all the scratching. My buddy that was paying us made me get on the mic. I wrecked that shit because these cats were not used to the type of shit that I spat. She played the music because she had more records than I did, at least party music that everybody likes. My crate was all instrumentals to freestyle over and random shit to scratch. You might be surprised what you can mix to get a party started if you have what it takes, I scratched "The Little Engine That Could" and "Thomas The Tank Engine" records over N.W.A at a show one time and it was awesome…& hilarious!

I hate to admit it, but she also knew a lot more about music than I did in general. It kind of bugged me, but she would make me mix tapes all the time to listen to on the slopes when tapes were all there really were to listen to when riding. MP3s had not come out yet when I was a freshman, and later when it became affordable, she would make me mix CDs and give or send them to me. She had really good taste in music and had tons of shit. She introduced me to a bunch of new stuff, and I love her for that among other things.

She moved away yet again and was living in Tahoe with some chick that was pretty cute if I remember right. I continued to see Flat Tire, but I also talked to Brown Hair. In fact, we would actually have phone sex all the time. I had never done it before, but she did it very well. So I talked to one and fucked the blonde for a while, and then when winter came, Brown Hair told me I should come to Tahoe and go riding for a week.

I had a free week around Christmas break, so I bought a ticket and flew out there. I met her in Reno, which was the closest airport for some reason, and we hung out downtown Reno for a bit before going to the spot in Tahoe that she was staying.

We went to one bar that was absolutely dead and met some guy who referred to himself as Jonny Reno or some shit like that. That was fun. They had some slot machines, and the place was a real shithole, so the drinks were dirt cheap. He claimed to run the city of Reno or something stupid like that, so I asked him why he was drinking alone in a dive bar. He had no response. We continued to get plowed and had a really good time. Then we drove however far it was to Tahoe and stayed at her friend's house. Obviously, we did the damn thing when we got there, so that is another state of the checklist. Tomorrow was a big day on the slopes; we were set up to ride five days in a row. If I tried that now, I think I would most likely die. It was fucking awesome, somewhat like Utah, nothing but powder everywhere. You could jump off a cliff face-first, and it would not hurt a bit, maybe a little but nothing like falling down in the frozen tundra they call Minnesota.

The nightlife was pretty uneventful because we had to rest up for the next day. However, we found a way to work in some extracurricular activities at night before we went to sleep. We had another session in the back country. We actually took our snowboards off this time and did everything that needed doing.

She moved back to Minnesota, and once again, blondie was the girl on the side, but I was juggling the two. I would usually hang out with Brown Hair during the day, and we would go out at night whenever she could. We went to a lot of shows, many that were very memorable, but nothing to write about, but I did see a lot of my favorite artists. She was my girlfriend again, and we went to a lot of parties, like Halloween and "pimps and hoes" parties. There was a lot of dressing up going on. We did a lot of drinking and doing random pills, usually ecstasy, but nothing was off limits.

We decided to go on a trip, and obviously, we both wanted to go snowboarding. For some reason, she picked Idaho as our destination, but looking back, I am really glad that she did. Once again, it was beautiful. The weather was perfect as well as the snow, and it was a really good time to be there because they had some kind of festival or something going on, and it was pretty cool. There were ice sculptures all over, and we went ice skating and everything; it would probably have been a good place to bring your family or young kids in general.

We just got drunk and had fun. I had a bunch of pictures from that also, but they eventually got lost, which is too bad because I had some really good pictures of all types of different shit, including later that night when we went into town for some drinks. We went into one of the first bars on the main street, and it was totally dead; there was nobody around. Eventually we asked where the hell everyone was, and some random guy was like, "Oh, you don't know? 2 Live Crew is playing across the street at whatever bar it was, that is not important." We looked at each other like, what the fuck? I said to the guy, "Are you sure about that? You do know that we are in Idaho, right?" He said to go check, and if he was wrong, he would buy us a round. There was nothing to lose there, so we headed over, and sure as shit, the place was packed. 2 Live Crew was there, and it was no wonder there was no one around outside; the whole state of Idaho was inside of this bar. The show was everything I thought it would be, a whole lot of big tits and fat asses all over the place, as well as full on nudity and some of the nastiest dancing I have ever seen in my life.

I got pictures of all this, but they are nowhere to be found. I remember at one point I got hit with a pair of some girl's panties. I have never been grossed out by underwear before, but I did not want these things touching me, and I screamed like a little girl as I brushed them off. Perhaps that show wore off on us because I swear we did that same dance on the mountain the next day. It was super warm out, and it was basically unsaid, and we just rode into the back country and got off our boards and got down to business without a word.

We put in some good work, and I remember I was sweating my face off, and it was so cold riding down the slope as the sweat dried. I also remember watching the other skiers going down the hill just a few feet away, and we were sort of loud, but nobody noticed. I find that shit really fucking exciting. I even got her to try something new that she said would never happen. That was the last day of riding, and we had to go straight to the airport in the morning, so it was back to Minnesota for us.

She had moved into an apartment in Minneapolis, which I helped her move into because apparently if you ever work for a moving company, every person you know will ask you to help them move. And it doesn't help to have a pickup truck because it is hard to say no, especially when it is a cute girl or an old friend. I helped her pick out colors and paint her whole apartment, which I later realized was time that I really should have used working on my house not some rental that she was going to move out of in a year. I did not know that at the time, but it was beginning to become a pattern with her. She could not stay in one place for very long. My main problem with this was that she always wanted me to move around the country with her. She did not understand the fact that I did not have a disposable income and was living in a house with so many things that belong to my mom and sister as well as a ton of my dad's stuff that I could not just leave, let alone the house itself. This would become a detrimental problem for us in the future.

My dad was gradually getting sicker and sicker every day, but he was sticking in there. However, his mother, my grandma, was not doing so great she had developed Alzheimer's disease, and it was progressing pretty fast, so we went down to Arizona to see her basically for the last time. The last time I saw her, she didn't have a fucking clue who exactly I was. It was hot where they lived, so I wore a tank top, and she probably just saw someone with tattoos and facial hair in her house and thought that I was robbing them. It was really hard to see her look at me and really not know who I was. I had to stop throwing a pity party for myself because my heart broke when she did not recognize her firstborn son, my father. As I saw the look on his face when his mother did not know who he was, he crumbled inside and eventually on the surface. He was a big strong man and a Marine, so they don't cry, right? Not true. That must have been the hardest shit in the world to deal with, and I could tell he knew that he would never see her again.

My grandpa took care of her and did literally everything for her until her last day, which came not long after we returned home. As difficult as it was, I am glad that my dad got to see his mom one last time and basically say goodbye even though she probably had no idea what he was talking about.

My dad basically developed a bucket list, and he wanted to get out and travel a bit again. My mom had a conference in New Orleans, so she used her frequent flyer miles to get my dad, my sister, and me tickets to fly down there with her well before her meeting, so we had plenty of time to hang out and have fun. This was before Hurricane Katrina, so we spent a lot of time by the coast and went on a bunch of tours because apparently it is the most haunted place in the world.

I didn't see or hear anything haunted, but the stories were interesting, and there is really interesting architecture throughout the city, not to mention the cemeteries. It was weird to learn that everyone was entombed above ground because when the town flooded in the past, the dead would rise out of the ground and float down the street. That is a disturbing thought, and I would never want to see anything like that ever. We stayed on Bourbon Street, which has somewhat of a reputation. It was not Mardi Gras, but it was plenty wild all the same.

The parents (which include my sister) would go to bed early around ten, so I would leave and roam the streets until two or three. There was no shortage of tits and loud drunkenness, so I just stumbled around and had fun, all the while looking for someone to sell me some weed. As always, I found someone right away and set something up. What he had was less than spectacular to say the least; in fact, it was crap, but it was weed, and I really wanted to smoke. I weighed my options and realized if I didn't find any for the rest of the trip and I turned that down, I would have really wanted that shit weed. I bit the bullet and bought the poop weed. It was actually probably about as good as what I smoked when I was thirteen, but it was not what I was used to then or now.

I spent the week with the fam, doing the tour stuff during the day and roaming the streets by myself at night. I was also told not to do this down there, but I felt no danger, and I had fun. There were flyers with naked girls on them all over the street as well as real naked girls all over the street. We got a really good picture of the whole fam at the coast, which I really like because my dad looks very healthy—a little chubby but healthy. This would soon change.

It was back to the frozen tundra, and I continued to work for the moving company and was working my ass off and eating a lot of protein as well as working out. My friend at the company worked just about every day with me. We would work the same hours and eat the same food. We weighed exactly the same and were the same size, except for the fact that my feet were bigger. We began a battle to see who could break two hundred pounds first. We would weigh ourselves every other day, and every time we weighed exactly the same. It took like a year, and we were always the same, but eventually, I got ahead and broke the two-hundred-pound barrier first. I topped out at 213 pounds, but I was not fat.

I only remember this weight exactly because it was the last time I cared because I had won the competition, and it was the last time I could use a normal scale before our next family vacation. They didn't have regular scales there. They measured weight in stones. I figured out how to figure it out, but I didn't want to do equations to find out how much I weigh. I was able to figure it out because I took 213 pounds and compared it with the number of stones I weighed, and it was 213 pounds in stones. I felt like a genius, but what the fuck is a stone?

If you know what the whole stones weight thing is, you would know that I went back to Europe. My dad wanted to go on yet another trip, but he had planned this one out much more thoroughly, and we had a full itinerary. It was not quite like when I was nineteen and I would just grab a tall can at every corner store, walking around the city drinking my face off, which I thought was legal, but it apparently was not. The police don't even have guns there so who cares. I would roam the streets at night and passed out in a doorway on one occasion and get kicked out of a casino in Manchester at one point; I am good at that. This trip was much different. We had a plan, and it actually sounded kind of cool. My dad had everything in order chronologically and even figured in the travel time. It was a mixture of castles, haunted places, and one of the wonders of the world.

We did go to London initially as we did when I was nineteen, and I did grab a tall can at every corner store. I also made a funny drunken mistake that day. I really had to pee, and I went into a pub and asked if I could use the bathroom, and this woman gave me the dirtiest look in the world. I tried to explain and said that I just really needed a restroom. The dirty look got much worse, and I knew what she was thinking. She thought I either wanted a place to take a shower or a place to take a nap. I remembered the proper English word and said "Loo, loo," while using the universal sign language for "I have to pee" and grabbed my crotch, jumping up and down. She understood.

After I was done, I explained to her the meanings of restroom and bathroom, that I just forgot to say loo and that I was not a freak. We had a laugh about it, but I still thought I was creepy. I stayed out walking the streets all night and talked to local vagrants just as I did before, but we had to leave the next day, so I only stayed out till around 2:00 AM. I wanted to be able to just sleep on the plane, and my plan worked.

When I woke up, we were in Dublin, Ireland. This was the worst-smelling place I had ever been to at this point in my life, but it fucking reeked. The smell came from the Guinness Brewery. It was all the smell of barley and hops, which makes beer, so I can't hate on it that much, but when it is that concentrated and overthrowing the air of entire city, it is a little gross.

The first thing we did after we got our rental was go to the Guinness Brewery and take the tour because the whole family knew that was all I wanted to do. It was interesting, and I liked how much the hops looked like chronic buds. They smelled almost like it, too, but not after they have fermented. Then they smell like a baby's diaper, not really, but that town smells like shit. The tour was about an hour long, and you work your way up this tower where there is a bar at the top. They give you a token for a free beer, and that is the end of the tour. We went and got our beers, which were cool because when they poured them, they moved the glass around all weird and somehow poured either a harp or a shamrock into the foam. It was cool, and I basically drank the whole fam-dam's supply of beer.

My dad was not allowed to drink, my sister doesn't really like beer, and my mom is a lightweight. I finished my pint along with my dad's and my sister's before my mom was even halfway done. I drank the rest of that and went to get another one when I heard some shit that made my jaw drop. You can only have one beer at the Guinness Brewery, and I believe that is bullshit.

We dipped out and got the hell out of stink town to drive to Cork, which is basically the closest city to the Blarney Stone, which my dad really wanted to kiss. I was not opposed to it, and they were going to bring me there whether I liked it or not, so I might as well make out with a rock. I don't know anyone from Minnesota that can say that they have done it. So we drove God-knows-how-far to Cork, but it took a long as time. I try to sleep as much as possible during any type of travel. When we got there, we were close to the stone, and our driver was tired, so we stopped at a quaint little coffee house for coffee and food. This is where I would make an ass of myself on this trip and all within around twenty-four hours.

A woman came around and took everyone's orders, but I just wanted some good Irish whisky, and I was pretty tired, so I ordered an Irish coffee. The woman looked at me like I was fucking retarded and said, "So you want a coffee?" I realized that I was an idiot and said, "No, I would like a coffee with some classic Irish whisky mixed in." I explained that in the States we call that Irish whiskey. She looked insulted, said, "That's nice," and walked away. Maybe she spat in my coffee, I don't know, but it was strong as hell and delicious, so I was happy.

We continued on to the Blarney Stone. It is basically a tower with a magic rock at the top that at some point in time someone said if you kiss it you would be blessed with the gift of gab. My free-styling has improved since then, but I think I will chalk that up to experience rather than kissing a bacteria-covered rock. You have to lay down on your back and lean over the edge of the tower, which is pretty high up there, but considering I had just recently become deathly afraid of heights, it was pretty scary even though there were bars to hold on to and spotters to hold on to you. I kissed the dirty rock, and for some reason, it felt gross as I looked at all the people around who had kissed it and thought of the number of people who have kissed it over the years. However, I bet it was cleaner than some of the girls I have made out with over the years.

After the rock, we drove all around Ireland and saw a bunch of random things, but nothing was eventful enough to remember. We did spend more time there in a little town, and my sister and mother got violently ill, puking out of both ends and complaining to no end. My dad and I were just fine and had to play nurse for a little bit. I am now convinced that the Blarney Stone does not like women and it only gives men the gift of gab. We had to leave in the morning, and they got better for the most part, considering they are always difficult in the morning. We got back to semi-subnormal before we left.

We went to the airport, boarded a plane, and flew to Glasgow, Scotland. We ran into a bit of a clusterfuck when we arrived in Scotland. The airline had no idea where my luggage was. Not just that, it got routed to the wrong place, and they would get it back to me soon, but they just fucking lost it altogether, and nobody knew anything. I was beyond furious; I had no clothes to wear. I do usually wear the same old shit every day, but I usually change when I am on vacation. Besides that, my contacts stuff was in there, and I had a little something to sip on if the bars were closed, which is for only like two hours a day, but you never know. We eventually left, and the airline assured us that they would get my bag to me by the next day. I wasn't buying it.

We drove forever; it felt like driving to Duluth, and I would later find out that it basically was. We got to the place we were to stay for that first night. It was like a really old house with a pub in the basement. There were only a few rooms. My sister and I had our own room with separate beds because we would not sleep together. I may have mentioned this, but I would always sleep in the same bed as my dad and had to repeatedly punch him hard throughout the night to get him to stop snoring. Nudging or pushing him was simply not enough. I was still irate and needed to blow off some steam so to speak, so I went down to the house bar.

I was in Scotland, so I ordered a Scotch and whatever local beer the barkeep recommended. I have no idea what it was, but it was strong and delicious. The man asked me if I was paying cash or if I wanted to charge it to the room. I did a double take, and my jaw dropped. I asked if he was serious, and he said to just show him my room key, and it was all good, not in those words, and it was really hard to understand, but that is basically what he said. I was all about it, and that was the beginning of the end of me that night. I kept ordering Scotch and a different beer for the night, and I got hammered.

It all gets a little fuzzy after that, but I do remember a few things. I met up with a group of Scots and was talking it up with them, although I could barely understand a word they said. I had to analyze what they were saying through context and try to figure out what the fuck they meant. I got a hold of it after a while, and after a few hours of drinking nothing but Scotch and beer, I think I started to sound like them as well.

I apparently made friends with them and hung out all night. I remember going to some sort of camping ground and being very rowdy. I specifically remember that at one point I had grabbed an umbrella from somewhere and climbed on top of some building at the site. I remember that I said something stupid, but I don't remember what. I probably yelled something really dumb like, "I can fly!" I jumped off the roof, and it became apparent that in fact I could not fly. I did not get hurt, but I remember falling pretty hard. I would do this a few more times throughout the night. I have no idea who these people were, but they had herb, and I had not smoked for a while, so they were cool with me. I talked with everyone, including a few girls who seemed to be flirting with me, but I was not sure because I could not understand a word they were saying.

If you mix the way a drunken girl talks with a Scottish accent, you get something that is completely inaudible and impossible to understand. I apparently made friends with this one cat, or he just took a liking to me because he said, "Hey, do you like hashish?" I obviously said yes, so he was like, well then let's smoke some. He pulled out a bar of hash that I can only describe as looking like a Hershey bar. It was fucking huge. I had never seen so much hash. He broke off a chunk, and we just blazed it up. I got so wasted. Not only did I drink copious amounts of Scotch and strong beer and was already really fucked up, but I hadn't smoked in four to five days, so smoking straight hash on top of that knocked me off my rocker. That cat was really nice.

I actually freestyled with him and his friends, and they loved my shit. Not to toot my own horn, but they thought I was Eminem or something, probably because they could actually understand what I was saying. A few of them were pretty good, at least I could tell that they were on beat and rhyming, but I could not understand a fucking word that they were saying. The guy whom I initially smoked asked me again if I liked hash, so I thought he was going to try to sell me some, and I didn't know if I even had any cash on me, let alone the correct currency. I was trying to think of the conversion rate so that I did not get ripped off when he pulled out his Hershey bar of hash and took a huge bite out of it. He handed it to me and told me to have a good time during the rest of my holiday (vacation). My mind was blown; this would never happen in the States. I didn't even know if I could smoke this much hash in the week and a couple days before we left. Then I remembered that you can do anything if you put your mind to it, and that is what I planned to do. I vaguely remember the rest of the night. I know I drank and smoked a lot more, and I am pretty sure I jumped off the building a couple of more times.

After that, everything goes black, and I woke up at around 10:00 AM in Glasgow, lying next to a girl with some huge-ass boobies. I had no idea where I was or who she was. I was still ripped out of my gourd and did not give a fuck. She was cute, and her tits were incredible. I rolled over and went to town. She gave amazing head as well, and her boobs were big and perfect for a good titty-fucking. She was really good at everything and did everything. After I was spent, I had to ask where I was and what time it was. I didn't care what her name was. She said that I was in Glasgow, and I said that didn't mean shit to me, so I asked her how long it would take to get to the bar that I met her at, and she said about two hours.

I remember all this verbatim because it was tragic. I said, "Well, put your big-ass tits away and bring me back there, or I will be kicked out of the family." That is exactly what I said, word for word. I would never be kicked out of the family, but I had crossed a line this time. We were supposed to check out and be on our way by 8:00 AM in order to stay on schedule, and it was already past ten. I fucked up. She drove me back to the pub where I met her and the hash man, which was awesome because I had no phone and if I had to try to make my own way back there, I would have had no clue where to tell the driver to go.

We drove for what seemed like forever, and I talked to her the whole time. She was actually pretty cool, but I still don't remember what her name was. Her car ran out of gas about thirty or forty miles from our destination. I was fucked, but she said, "Just put your thumb out." I thought she was joking because no one would ever stop to help you where I live. I never put my thumb out, but someone stopped after like two minutes. These random people just gave us a ride to where I needed to go with no question, and they were very nice. I have no idea how she got back to her car or got gas for that matter, but at that point, I did not care because the family was sitting in the car, in the parking lot, and they all had a grimace on their faces that clearly said they wanted to kill me.

I was in deep shit, but I did not know how deep. I gave the girl a kiss, grabbed her boob, and ran to our rental car. When I got there, there was a silence for a while, and then once we got out of the area, all hell broke loose. They really let me have it, and pretty much all I got out of what they were screaming at me was, "What the fuck were you thinking?" They also mentioned about being nervous and scared wondering what could have happened to me. I understood that, but I really don't know how I got where I ended up. I have a very good idea of why I don't remember, but I would not have gone that far away if I had my head straight. They said that they knew that I was okay when the police came to the place looking for me. I don't know what else I did. Apparently, they had video footage of a young man in a black hoodie with a white stripe climbing and jumping off cabins at a local campsite. They said that I had done other shit, but I don't remember what because my jaw dropped when I heard that, and I was speechless. That was exactly what I was wearing, and it basically sticks out like a sore thumb if that is what they are looking for.

This is when my mom surprised me, which was actually pretty fucking gangster, at least for her—a woman who I would probably compare to Donna Read if I had to pick someone famous. She told my dad to gun it and get the fuck out of Dodge before the fuzz came back. She did not actually say anything like this because she doesn't swear and does not talk like that. She is always very polite and grammatically correct. That being said, I could tell that was what she meant. She was just brought up not to speak like that and has lived by it her whole life. The only times I have ever heard her swear is when I trick her into doing. If I am going off on a rant and I let a *shit* or a *fuck* slip out, she will basically tell me to watch my mouth. And even though I know exactly what I said, I will say, "What did I say?" and she will repeat it almost every time and then gives me a dirty look because she knows I got her again.

Back to the escape, my mom continued to surprise me. From the beginning, I couldn't believe my mom didn't fuck up and somehow turn me in because she knew exactly what I was wearing. She does not break the law for anything; she is that person that would find a bag full of thousands of dollars and try to find the rightful owner. This was the person heading up the getaway, and after we pulled out of the parking lot, she ordered me to take my hoodie off because that is what they were looking for and to take my hat off as well. My mind was blown. Was my mom a career criminal on the side living a double life? I highly doubt that, but if she is, she hides it well. She even made me fully change all the way when we got out of the area.

It seems that the airline brought my luggage to where we were staying first thing in the morning, but they let me think that I was going to have to go over a week more wearing the all the same shit. I think that was my punishment. If it was, it worked because I was very upset, and some of my favorite clothes were in there. I also received another "little" talking to about my bar tab, which may also have something to do with my loss of time that night. Sometimes I can drink forever and the only reason I stop is because I am actually tired. Well, that never happened that night. I wasn't buying rounds for my new friends or anything, but somehow I raked up somewhere between a 150- and 200-pound bill by drinking nothing but whiskey and local beers.

At the time, with the exchange rate, this was anywhere from $225 to $300. The exchange rate is much better these days, but it was not back then, and it goes without saying my parents were pretty fucking pissed off. I know my dad was upset about the money, but I could tell my mom was upset and worried because she saw the tab and how much I drank, which probably blew her mind. I brushed it off and was just fine, and I would say a red flag that I was already a seasoned veteran at the whole drinking thing, just like her husband.

I was in the doghouse, but my family does not usually hold a grudge for very long, usually. We had to be together for the next week and some change, so we might as well get along, right? We drove all over hell through Scotland and saw a bunch of castles. This is one of the main things my dad wanted to do as well and the look on his face when we were at these places was like looking at a young boy when he gets his first bike—it was priceless. The castles were really interesting, and we obviously learned a lot about William Wallace. I had no clue who the fuck he was, and I guess, looking back, maybe I should have watched *Braveheart* before going to Scotland. That is a joke, but it seemed to be the only source of any knowledge that people in our tour groups had about Scotland. We saw a lot of famous sites, and that was all very interesting as well. I don't remember the name of any of the places or castles. We stayed in a castle one night, and I don't remember the name of that either, but it was cool. We drove around Scotland, looking and random cool old stuff and places following our route.

We were now going back to England, but we had other missions in up north that my dad had planned out. I remember we stayed a few days in a couple different castles. Once again, I do not remember their names, but I did see the exact same castle we stayed in on the History channel for some ghost show. The first castle we stayed in was Mary Tudor's residence. She was the daughter of Henry VIII and the first queen regent of England and Ireland. She was given the name Bloody Mary for her persecution of Protestants, which I don't really understand, but I guess that is what they did.

Every kid knew about Bloody Mary when I was growing up, not the story of Mary Tudor but that if you turn the lights off and say "Bloody Mary" three times in front of a mirror, she will appear and scare the shit out of you or kill you, I don't remember. When my sister and I got our room, I was happy as hell. It was the Tudor room and obviously where Bloody Mary stayed, because the room was big as fuck, a lot nicer than where my parents were staying, and considering she was a queen, so it made sense. We later looked it up, and it was. There was a decanter of port on the end table, and I snatched that up, considering we had been driving through the countryside for a few days and I don't remember seeing a liquor store at all. I grabbed a couple single beers at gas stations, but I know my mom would not approve of pulling over to stop and get me alcohol. That is why I thought it was so funny when I would open my beer in the back seat and slam it.

There was really nothing she could do. We were in the middle of nowhere, and nothing was going to happen, so she just ignored me. I grabbed the port and went to town. It was strong and tasted like it had been there since Bloody Mary was alive. My sister took a little sip and almost threw up. I knew what I had to do, and I downed that shit like a fucking forty-ounce. I had a smoke, I was fucked up, and it was time to do the other thing that I knew I had to do from the moment I read the name on the door. I was going to call out Bloody Mary and either see her and die or just be disappointed. I was not expecting to see her, but if there was anywhere in the world to summon Bloody Mary, this was it, and part of me was hoping that something crazy would happen.

I tried to get my sister come in with me to do it because she is a pussy and I knew she wouldn't, and she would not. I took a couple of drags from her cigarette and went to meet my fate. I turned off the lights and said the line three times. Nothing happened, so I did it again, and once again, nothing. I eventually was screaming at the mirror, yelling for her to show herself. My sister eventually came and told me to shut the hell up. I came out and eventually went to go to sleep, but I stayed up, hoping to hear or see something, but there was nothing all night. I was disappointed, but I was also not surprised by any means. It just would have been cool.

We basically left first thing and went to another place that was on my dad's bucket list, Stonehenge. I knew a little bit about the site at that point, but nowhere as much as I have learned since visiting the site. I could tell that the stones where obviously pretty heavy, but I had no idea how heavy. We have a hard time moving these rocks even with modern machines. I also did not contemplate the fact the stones themselves cannot be found anywhere around Stonehenge and they had to travel a long fucking way just to get there. It is already hard to lift one of these things and moving one inch, let alone hundreds of miles. I also did not know that its shape and layout had celestial origin. There is a lot that can be read into the monoliths of Stonehenge and their meaning. It was really cool to be at such an iconic location, and I don't know too many people who can say that they have been there either.

There are other areas in the world with a similar compilation of monoliths configured in in a circle in much the same way that Stonehenge is, but they can be found on opposite ends of the earth and constructed centuries before the possibility of international communication. It makes you wonder, Who really built this shit and what purpose did it serve? I really wanted to walk up and just be able to touch one of the monoliths just to say that I did. I was very disappointed to find that it was roped off, and you couldn't get closer than ten feet from the stones. I did not see any security around, so

I was going to just go under the rope and go touch a rock for a second. I did not announce my plan, but before I could make a move, my mom simply said, "Don't even think about it." That was all she needed to say, and I stopped dead in my tracks.

Normally, I would not have listened and did it anyways because I wanted to, but I was already in the shithole, and I did not want to upset her anymore and ruin her vacation, so I declined to do it. It was still really cool, and I am glad that I got to see it because I cannot imagine the scenario where I would ever find myself back there.

We moved on to the next spot, gradually making our way back to London. Our next stop was another castle that my dad had learned was supposed to be one of the most haunted in England. I actually saw a documentary all about it a few years later, which was crazy because everything looked familiar, and the "ghost hunters" did exactly what my sister and I did. In the middle of the night, we went out into the courtyard and used the night vision on our camcorder. We sat out there for a couple of hours and didn't see a fucking thing just like on the show. I was starting to think that maybe ghosts were just a figment of overactive imagination. That was sarcasm if you didn't catch it. It was a really cool castle though, and I had a good time.

We kept moving on toward my dad's next stop, which I was not aware of, and it was really dumb, but in hindsight, I am really glad that we went there. We made a bit of a detour to drive through and visit a town that bore our family's last name. It made sense because my last name is English. I am mostly English, and we were in England, so I figured that we were going to own the town, but to my disappointment, the town was a real shithole. There was one crappy road which I guess you would call main street and crappy houses on either side. When we got into "downtown," there was a gas station on the left and a restaurant on the right. There was nothing else in the entire town. It was clear that the gas station had been abandoned probably twenty years before I was born, and that was no joke because I was thinking it and my dad said the exact same thing to a few seconds later. He loved everything car related, especially the classics, so I believed him.

We went to the only restaurant and in fact only building that was not a house that appeared to have electricity. I could not make this up if I tried, but the name of the one restaurant was the Cock. When I saw that, I said that we had to eat there because that was fucking awesome. There was a picture of a rooster on the sign as well, so it was not so risqué, but it was still funny. We ate there obviously because it was the only open establishment for at least fifty miles (whatever that is in kilometers), and we were obviously the only people there, so the service was quite prompt. I have no clue what I ate. All I was concerned about was getting a beer.

Driving through the European countryside is very beautiful, and I loved it, but when you are taking a road trip with your parents and are used to drinking and smoking pot all day, a sober road trip is not that fun. I couldn't wait to get to the next gas station. As my family sat down, I went straight to the bar and ordered a 1664. They did not sell that in America at that time, but I think they do now. She carded me, and I happily handed her my passport with a smile. She obviously just looked at the birthdate and handed it back to me. I handed it back to her and said "Read the name, I own this town, so I feel that this drink will be on the house." She laughed and said that it was the funniest shit she had heard in a long time. She really was laughing, and I grabbed the beer, and her face went stone cold in a second and said, "Seriously though, I'm going to need that money." I tried and I lost, but it was funny.

Once again, we got back on the road heading south to London, and we happened to come across what I called a carnival, but my sister tells me it was an amusement park. If that was the case, then the amusement parks in whatever city we were in sucked ass. It all looked like state fair rides that can be packed up and driven down the road to the next hillbilly town. I wanted to stop there no matter what because that is one place I will stuff my face with deep-fried garbage food because it is so delicious. I also love to play the games. I know all the prizes are complete junk, but I just like to win. Unless it is something I like, if I see a kid that clearly can't win a thing, I give it to them and pride myself on my good deed for the day. I also give away my extra tickets and coupons to people who enter as I leave because I know I am not going to go back.

I did not win shit at this fair or whatever the fuck it was, but my sister and I did get something else. I don't believe that they have any real tattoo booths at amusement parks or carnivals in the States, but they had one at this place. We decided to get something, considering we were at the closest thing to civilization just down the road from the town of our surname. We would just tell everyone that we got them in an English town bearing our last name but that I found out later that it was basically still in the same place; it was just not in the booming downtown district of the Cock.

We did not have anything drawn up, which I prefer to do because than it is truly your own, but there was no time for that. We looked through the Flash designs and found a circular design that looked somewhat like a Celtic cross, so I asked the guy what it was, and he said that it was an English cross. The story checked out, and I suggested that it was perfect and that we should get matching tattoos, which we did. I got mine on the underside of my right wrist, and my sister got hers on her leg like a pussy, but we do have matching tattoos now. We hung out at the carnival or whatever it was for a bit, and then we had to get back on the road. We stopped at a few cities on our way back to London, and I remember getting kicked out of another casino in Manchester. I don't know what it is with me and casinos, but I think it is clearly their fault. They just don't like me because my skin is darker and they are all racists. Either that or it is because I act a fool sometimes, one or the other. We visited some more churches and famous landmarks along the way, but I just wanted to get back to the big city.

I was so happy to be out of the car and have the ability to walk half a block and buy a tall can at the corner store. There have so many different beers in Europe. I refused to drink anything that they sell in the States, and I had only had the same beer more than once, except for a couple of times, but those beers were exceptionally good. I still had the chunk of hash that the Scotsman bit off for me. I bought some tobacco and papers to smoke it because I was not about to get busted smoking hash out of a pipe in a different country. I would break up the hash, mix it with the tobacco, and walk down the road, smoking hash in front of my mom as well as the Bobbies. No one had a clue and if they did smell it; by that time I was long gone. I did some walking around on my own as always because I wanted to find some local hip-hop. I am a sucker for the accent.

I found a couple of guys selling their CD on the side of the road. I talked to them for a minute and heard some of their music, which was actually pretty good. They had a CD player with them and played some beats and started to freestyle. They were all right, but I knew that I could trump them. I jumped in, and if I remember correctly, I came correct and blew their shit out of the water. They stopped me and said that it was dope, but I was talking way too fast and they could not keep up. I take that as a win because I was articulate as fuck and said some funny shit and was able to get a few laughs and a couple "oh, damns!" They showed me the way to the nearest record store, and I bought a mixed CD. It had a bunch of classics as well as a variety of local London artists. It was actually really good. This CD would provide the family with an inside joke that is still funny.

An old song came on that everyone knows where the chorus is a back and forth between the performer and the audience which said, "Can I kick it? Yes, you can." It repeats the chorus many times, and about half way through the song, my dad turned down the volume, and in an inquisitive tone he basically asked, "Cheddar chicken in a can?" Even my mom knew what the words were, and we all laughed out loud at him for the remainder of the trip as well as the rest of his life. We did more shit in London for a bit and got a room to stay in. However, my dad, my sister, and I had planes for the next day and night. My mom was actually going to have to do some work that day, so we got out of her hair.

The next day, we decided to go to France, which was a lot easier than I would have thought and more terrifying than I could have possibly imagined. It was worse than flying over or boating across the open ocean, which scares the shit out of me. I did not know that there was a tunnel that went across the English Channel from England to France called the Chunnel. Apparently, it is common knowledge, but I had never heard about it. It did not help that my best friend had installed the unbearable fear of deep waters in me, and we were literally under the open ocean in a fucking tunnel whose durability I did not have much faith in. Looking out the windows, I noticed small spaces in between the stones that made up the tunnel, and there was water leaking in. Needless to say, I was scared as hell. That was a horrifying experience, and I would never want to do it again, although we did have to take it again to get back to London. I was not happy about that. We went to Rouen, which had a vast history and a ton of information on Joan of Arc, which my dad was really interested in. I didn't know shit at the time, but after learning the story, I found it very interesting. It is a compelling story. I have seen several documentaries about her since being there, and I am really glad that I went there.

    A statue of Joan stood in the middle of the town, and I think my sister and I got a picture next to it, but once again, that picture is nowhere to be found. I rolled up a day's supply of cigarettes chalk full of hashish and walked around France high as fuck, smoking right in front of whatever they call cops over there and drinking their local beer. I think my sister was shopping but I was so dusted I don't remember anything but I know I was having a good time. We took the Chunnel back, and this time I smoked myself stupid before we entered the death trap, so I just slept the whole time and avoided the thoughts of the Chunnel collapsing, being submerged in the deep ocean, and then getting eaten alive by sea monsters that have not yet been discovered by man. I passed out, and we made it back to fog town safe and sound.

    My mother and I visited a few museums, but my favorite was the big one. I honestly don't remember the name, but it was right off of Tower Bridge and by the London Eye. I still want to call it London Bridge because it has its own song, but now it is in Arizona, which makes no fucking sense. The exhibit was of Salvador Dalí, and that changed the whole way I looked at art. He was amazing. I had previously learned a bit about him, but I did not know he did sculpture or that he was actually kind of a pervert and definitely a really weird motherfucker that acted like he had taken way too much acid in his day.

I have no idea what my dad and sister did that day, but they met up with us later, and we went on the London Eye, which is just a glorified gigantic Ferris wheel. It takes forever to get on, but then it is pretty cool. There is a really good view of the city as far as you can see. The next day, we went back to the bridge and saw Big Ben as well as all the other iconic buildings in that area. Even though we had seen them all the last time we were there, it was still cool. We later took the car out and went to some other places we did not see the time before, but I could not name them to save my life. That was more or less the end of the trip because we had to leave in the morning.

I just had one problem; I still had a big hunk of hash, and I was not about to try to sneak it past customs. There was no way I was going to waste really, really good hash, so I made the executive decision to smoke it all before we got on the plane. It took some dedication and hard work, but somehow I pulled it off. I crushed up all the hashish and rolled as many cigarettes as it took to smoke all of it. I made two with a little more hash because they were for smoking in the morning and right before entering the airport so I could sleep through have a few cocktails and pass the fuck out, either waking up in Minnesota or dead. By this point in my mom's frequent-flyer shit, she had access to the Platinum club or whatever the fuck it was called, but instead of waiting in uncomfortable plastic chairs at the terminal, we would go into an area that had glass doors that would open for you. I know it is not amazing, but I did not grow up like that. I felt like royalty although it was just day-to-day business for my mom. There were all types of fruits, juices, cereal, bagels, all types of shit, but then I found my Achilles heel, which I would succumb to every time I flew with my mom from that point on. She would later tell me that she did not want to fly with me anymore because I almost beat the shit out of the guy behind me. He kept pushing on the back of my seat, and I did not even have it reclined. I let that go, and I put it back a little bit. He started pushing on it somewhat hard, and this was a grown man much older than me. I turned around to see how much room he had, and he had all types of room, so I politely asked him to knock it off because he had plenty of room. He continued to do it, and I got out of my seat and stood over him, and I think I probably would have done something really stupid and possibly caused and emergency landing, but nothing happened. He backed down, and my sister manhandled me, told me to shut up, and put me in her seat so he was not behind me anymore. She is always looking out for me, or maybe she just didn't want to have an emergency layover and wait for me to get out of jail. Either way, I love her.

My dad was progressively getting worse, and I think they altered his treatment because when we returned, he was round as fuck but could barely walk. I remember I had to push him around the state fair in a wheelchair that year. He was a big boy. He started to lose weight, not at a scary rate, but it was noticeable. He was more mobile and would come around the house every once in a while to stand in the garage and accomplish nothing. That would annoy the hell out of me, but at least he stopped trying to say the names of any females coming in or out. Looking back, it wasn't that bad, and I would trade a year of my life to just have him over here for one night to shoot the shit and do nothing in the garage. I realized that day was coming, so I tried to spend as much time with him as possible. He showed me how to ride the motorcycle that we had, and I passed my permit test. We would drink out in the garage, and when we had enough cans, my dad would set them up like cones in the street for me to learn how to weave in and out while going slow and not tipping over.

In hindsight, this was the stupidest idea in the world. If a cop would have driven by, I would have been fucked. Swerving in and out of empty beer cans that I drank was not a good idea. Nothing happened, and as my dad got worse, I had no one to help me work on the bike, and by help, I basically mean tell me what to do because engines and garage-type shit is not my forte.

My mom was angry that my dad and I had bought the bike in the first place because her brother was seriously injured in a motorcycle accident and still walks with a limp. I sold the bike to make my mom happy, and I wasn't going to fix it up by myself anyways. I continued to drink beers with my dad, and sometimes he would come in the house when I had friends over. The house would be fishbowled to the point where some might say you would get a contact high. I don't believe in that theory, but I guess anytime I have been in a smoked-out room or car, I was smoking as well, so I wouldn't know. He never said anything about it and would just drink some beer and shoot the shit with us; all my friends loved my dad.

I had another good friend that needed a place to stay, and I knew my mom could use the rent money, which wasn't shit, $400 a month to live in a house where you can do whatever you want. He had no problem raising those funds and would always pay on time in cash as opposed to my former roommate who had a job and would pay in cashier's checks. My mom never thought there was anything fishy about that; I would have. He was a good dude and a longtime friend; we partied all the time throughout middle and high school. He was also an awesome roommate because whereas before if I needed weed, I would have to get a hold of him and wait, or possibly he would be busy that day. Now if I ran out, I just had to go to the desk drawer and grab what I needed. There was a place for business supplies and a drawer that was community weed that I could smoke whenever I wanted; it was very nice. We had parties, and there was constantly other fun substances coming in and out, which I would always partake in because if I don't have to pay, then pass it my way, no needles though.

I was working at the liquor store at this time, and every night I either had the blonde or the brunette sleepover. Sometimes the brunette first, and then the blonde would come spend the night at around one or two in the morning. My roommate got used to this. I would bring home copious amounts of alcohol every time I worked and was beginning my downhill slope of drinking. I really did not know how to deal with what was happening to my dad, and I know that drinking and drugs is a copout, but that is the path I chose.

It was nice to work in a liquor store at this time; I got to drink all day, and sometimes would meet girls even though I was currently seeing two. One time, I was stoned-ass, and I saw this girl looking for something and clearly did not have a clue, so I helped her out finding what she was looking for and advised her to get the strongest one.

She initially hit on me, and I was game, so I told her I lived close, and it turned out that she lived like two blocks away in the hood, and yes, she was a black girl with a nice booty, big tits, and a cute face.

I gave her my number, and she called me that night. My roommate was out doing whatever and would not be home that night. She came over to the house, and we got drunk as fuck, and then we did. She did not waste any time. After we got plowed, we smoked a bowl, and as soon as that was done, she took he clothes off.

Earlier in the night, she had mentioned that she had a child, so at this point, for some reason, out of the blue, I asked her if she could still make milk. I did and do not have a fetish for lactation, but I was curious. She pulled up a boob, squeezed it, and sure as shit, there it was. I don't know why, but I had to suck on it. It was delicious, rich, and sweet, like the mild in Argentina. I wonder if their milk is all from human females; that would be weird. She kept squeezing and eventually was squirting all over my face and chest. I loved it, and it got me so hard up right away because she was rubbing her pussy and playing with my dick. We were already making a mess, so we just did the damn thing right then and there, and she fucked my brains out as well as hers. She was a wild one and quite vocal.

She was a dirty talker with a ghetto accent; there was something sexy about that. I could tell she was going to pop any second because she said exactly that, and it sounded like she was trying to hold something in. I asked her if she squirts, and she said yes, so I told her to just cum and let me have it. She was riding me violently at this point, and I could feel her tighten up as she came, and when she got it and was rubbing her clit, she got up off me and continued to rub her clit and have another orgasm when she exploded all over me.

This was not my first rodeo with squirting, but this girl was a pro, and we made an incredible mess. She was wearing my T-shirt and nothing else sitting on the couch, and my roommate came home. It is a good thing he was not five minutes earlier, or he would have gotten an eyeful. However, he sort of did because she did not have any underwear on and was not exactly sitting like a lady. As I was talking to my roommate, she spread her legs and her lips and began playing with her clit. She pulled out her tits and basically put on a fucking show for us. It was pretty cool, completely unprovoked; she just started going to town and squirted some more. I was lucky that my other two female friends did not decide to stop by; that would not have been good because she looked like a fighter. I continued to have her over when my schedule was open, and we played all the time until one day another friend of mine stopped over. She barely had anything covering her tits, and I pulled one of them out to show it to him. She put on a full-out spread pussy one-woman show, but this apparently pissed her off, and she left. Maybe she didn't like him, but regardless, she dipped out, and I never spoke to her again. I was okay with that. I had plenty on my plate at the time, and I had gotten everything I wanted out of her. She covered me in milk and washed it of by squirting all over me. I was happy with that.

My new roommate was great for a lot of reasons besides the fact that there was always weed in the house. He was an amazing cook, at least he knew an ass-load about Asian cuisine, which makes sense because he is Taiwanese, so we always had rice in the house, and he would make really good chicken fried rice a lot as well. I had a rice cooker, and I bought a deep fryer so he would make dumplings, pot-stickers, and cream cheese wontons as well. There was always something to eat which I had never really experienced before. He brought me to an Asian grocery store that I had seen before but never entered. I was right not to do so because I would have had a hard time communicating, and God knows I could not read anything in that store. I most certainly have fucked up whatever it was I was trying to make.

I still remember how to cook all that stuff, so it was a really good life lesson. He also taught me how to mix and cook other things, but that has nothing to do with food. We also just got along really well and grew up with the same people, so we had many mutual friends. But not all his acquaintances were very nice.

One night, me and my blonde friend were drinking and watching a movie when all of a sudden there were three black guys I did not know standing in my living room, and one of them had a gun to my head. As soon as I noticed that factor in this equation, I did not pay attention to what any of them looked like although I did see that one of them had cornrows. I was not paying attention to them anymore; I was focused on the barrel of the gun. I was looking for any markings like Daisy or Airsoft as he was yelling at us to get on the floor. Blondie did it right away, but if I saw that it was a BB gun, I was willing to take a shot in the forehead point-blank to keep her safe. This is what I was actually thinking. I was pretty fucking drunk and possibly not thinking clearly. I didn't see anything on the gun that said Smith and Wesson or anything like that, so I came up with a brilliant idea for how to solve the situation. I looked the gunman in the eyes, and in a very stern deep voice, I simply said, "Fuck you!"

As he pistol-whipped the fuck out of me, I realized the gun was very heavy and very real. Common sense kicked in, and I decided to do what they said. Unfortunately, I could not see because I had a fountain of blood coming from my forehead, blinding me. They were clearly not interested in me because they went straight to my roommate's room and knew exactly where to go. As they were pillaging his room, I was forming a puddle of blood all over the carpet that I inevitably ruined, and I could not see. I asked the one guy out of the three that stayed back to hold a gun toward us if he could possibly grab me a towel off of the stove real quick and I wouldn't do anything. I was not beginning to identify with my captors, but this was the nice one out of the trio, and I appreciated him getting me a towel because I needed to apply pressure because it was a pretty big gash.

I was bleeding profusely and feeling a little faint, but I just kept trying to calm blondie down because she had never been involved with anything like this before and she was very scared. I assured her that I would not let anything happen to her. I did not know exactly how I would do that, but I was drunk enough to do something stupid. They did not go into any rooms other than my roommates. They could have gotten all types of shit if they were just trying to rob the place, but they knew what they wanted, where it was, and they found it fast. They were not quite done because they took my backpack, which had some schoolwork and textbooks in there as well as my inhaler, and there was a patch on the bag that said "Underground," which I got in London.

I loved that bag and those books were not free, but they really fucked Flat Tire over. They stole here bag, which was some ridiculous brand name that had like three other really expensive brand name little bags inside, a really expensive purse, her phone, and a bunch of other shit that girls always have with them. I felt really bad when I asked her how much that was worth and she said with everything that was in there it was around $1,000. They also stole my PlayStation and a bunch of games, but I didn't really care because I don't really play video games.

I know that they made off with a fuck-load of pot and God-knows-what other goodies, along with a bunch of money from my roommate along with what I watched them take from me and blondie. They probably grabbed a bunch of other shit as well, but I was pretty concussed at the time and unable to do inventory and figure it out. I kept trying to tell the police that because Flat Tire called them before I was in working order. I remember yelling at her and asking her what she wanted me to do, tell the cops that we had a ton of drugs and drug money in the house that these people stole and we wanted them brought to justice? It doesn't work like that.

The police told me that they were going to bring me to the hospital because I clearly needed stitches. This was true, but I would not go. I did not have the patience to go to the ER or Urgent Care at the downtown hospital on a weekend. There is always a line of people who were shot or stabbed that obviously need to go in front of you, and by the time you see a doctor, your wound is healed or you bleed to death. I have been there too many times, so at this point, there needs to be a bone protruding from my skin or something really deep and big like my chin while playing softball. I was very lightheaded, but I had liquid cure for that, and they didn't get my weed that was in my room, so I smoked that as soon as the 5–0 left.

One fucked-up thing is that right after the police left, someone stopped by who never stops by my house, and he was a sketchy character. He had been to my house many times before but with other people because we were acquaintances at best and only through other people. He said that he saw police at the house when he drove by and wanted to see what happened. I did not believe a word of this.

If he had never shown his face, I never would have suspected him of having anything to do with it, but now I was pretty sure that he did. I had nothing that anyone wanted, so I was never worried about being robbed like that, but I forgot about the fact that my roommate had everything a drug addict needed, and that was somewhat of a liability.

My roommate was very apologetic, and he gave Flat Tire like $700 cash, which really did not really cover the emotional stress she had been put through. She was an innocent girl who had never been or even in a fight, let alone having a gun to her head. I don't necessarily like being held up at gunpoint, but this was not my first rodeo. Although he was not there, this was not the first time that something like this had happened to my roommate, and it would not be his last. He had been robbed and shot at a number of times before this incident. After he re-upped, he hooked me up with a bag for my troubles and some loot. I remember thinking, *Okay, I will take this, but it doesn't really make up for the giant gash in my forehead that is not healing very fast.* It did heal, and then I just had a giant scar on my forehead. It is right on my hairline, so it is usually covered up; however, that line is progressively receding these days, and soon my face will be nothing but scars, but I have not reached that point yet. Back to my roommate, he decided to move out because he did not want to put me in danger again, which I appreciated; however, it was a bit too little too late, and he was not out of the danger zone either.

He moved into a place with a mutual friend just a couple of miles away. He lived with a guy that was pretty big and strong. He kind of looked like Busta Rhymes, and I do not know how what happened would have gone down; it must have been pretty hard to do. When my old roommate returned back to his new house from work, he found his roommate who, as I stated, was not a small man by any means hogtied in the middle of the living room, and the place was cleaned out. I don't think they took TVs and stuff like that, but they clearly knew what they were looking for and got it. I also do not know how long he was tied up like that, but that must have been a really shitty experience. My old roommate came back around because he still felt bad and wanted to give me some assurance that everything would be okay. He did this in the form of a Glock 9 mm. I did not and do not like guns, but I took it because I figured, what the hell, if anything I could get some money for it. Later I thought of all the shit that my buddy and that this gun could have been involved in things that I would not want my fingerprints or name attached to in any way. I gave it to someone at the liquor store for a bottle of brandy, which explains the other reason I got rid of the gun; I simply did not trust myself.

I can be very hot-headed at times as I have been told, and I don't necessarily think clearly while drinking heavily, which happened to be every day. I was really depressed about my dad's progressing deterioration. He did not look like himself anymore; instead of being the fat marshmallow man, he had turned into the epitome of what a chemo patient looks like. He was skinny, bald, and the medication was getting to him because he was not himself. I was very stressed out, and looking back, I was also clearly depressed as well.

Once again, I continued to deal with this by self-medicating with alcohol and marijuana, as well as some other things from time to time. I felt that if I got too fucked up I might seriously hurt myself or, even worse, someone else. I was drinking about a 750 milliliter or liter bottle of brandy and washing it down with anywhere from a twelve-pack to an eighteen-pack of beer per day. I was not in a good way and in no way trusted myself to possess a firearm. I was still partying with Brown Hair, and one day, we went out and then came back to her place and played all night. I remember waking up in the morning and taking a couple of shots when I got up to wake up as she got ready for school or work or whatever it was at the time. That is the last thing that I remember. The next thing I knew, I woke up at HCMC in Minneapolis on a bed, and Brown Hair and my mom were sitting next to me.

I had no idea what the fuck happened. I knew that I felt like shit and I was very confused, and that was about it. The doctors eventually came in, and the dicks wouldn't even give me water. I was only allowed to have ice chips. That pissed me off because I was so dehydrated and my stomach was empty. I just wanted to know why the fuck I was there, and they told me that I had had a seizure. I said why, and they said they did not know, and I would have to see a neurologist and do some tests to figure that out. I did not jump at the chance to spend hours being tested in a hospital on a day where I could be doing anything but that, so I never went.

I continued to have fun with her as well as the blonde and some others, but they were the main two. One time I was doing the damn thing with Brown Hair and thought that she had to leave at a certain time because she had to work in the morning and told the blonde to come over at some time after that. I fucked up. My session with Brown Hair ran a bit long as it always did, but I thought she really had to go at a certain time, but apparently that did not matter to her when she was getting railed like that and would not stop having multiple orgasms. Once again I fucked up because I forgot to lock the door and Flat Tire came in, obviously hearing her screaming in ecstasy. She yelled as she walked down the hall toward my room, which was her mistake because it gave me time to jump up and hold the door closed. It actually saved her a lot of trauma because she would not have liked to see that. She was screaming, and I told her to shut the fuck up and go sit down. She did. We put on our clothes, and Brown Hair ran out of there really quick because she did not want a confrontation. I don't know what blondie was thinking, but she must have been very upset because if shit would have hit the fan, Brown Hair would have whooped her ass from Saint Paul to Minneapolis in a heartbeat. The brownie left, and I was going to have to put some time in with the blonde and a lot of mind-fucking. It did not take long, and I was fucking the hell out of her within minutes in the very bed that she just busted me in, still ripe with the juices of the woman before her.

I would continue to hang out with both of them, often on the same day, but Flat Tire had a hidden agenda. She knew that the brownie had basically stolen me away from my high school sweetheart. She had plans to do the same and told me that straight out. She said, "I am going to win." This scared the hell out of me, but she was not joking, but the game continued. I went to a lot of hip-hop shows with the one and had the other one over late night for round 2. I loved to hang out with Brown Hair because we would play strip poker and shit or just get naked for the hell of it and play like we were in our early twenties. She would do anything and everything; it was amazing as always, but I still had another hole to fill, and she was going nowhere. I was basically boyfriend and girlfriend with the brown and a fuck toy with the blonde, but I was okay with that. I had gotten used to it.

    The brownie got a bug up her ass again and wanted to move to a new city, New York. Once again, I was being asked to move away with her. Out of all the places in the world, the last place in the world I would move to would be New York. Everything is so expensive there. Just a few years earlier, I was paying one dollar for a pack of smokes, and at the time it cost about eight or nine dollars a pack, fuck that. I had never been there at this point in my life, but I knew it was too expensive for me, and my theories were later confirmed. The only plus I can think of is if you live in the city you don't need a car; I liked that about Buenos Aires as well. I obviously said no to moving to NYC for these reasons among others. The number-one reason was that it was a horrible time to leave me alone. I still had blondie to console me, but the brownie was like my best friend, and she left me when I really needed her. Flat Tire was always there for me, and always has been.

H-P

My dad was on his last legs and not going to make it that long. He still lasted for a long time, but we all knew, including him, that we were at the end of the line. I continued my diet of a bottle of brandy and a case of beer a day, and I was fine with that medication, but it did not help anything. I cried every night and just waited to get that fucking phone call. I spent as much time as I could with my dad toward the end, but he wasn't really himself, I remember thinking that it was possibly similar to when his own mother did not recognize him before she died but not quite to that extent. I would come over and drink my face off because it hurt to see him like that and watch whatever stupid shit he wanted to watch on TV, and it was nice to see him smile every now and then. I would sneak him a beer or two when I could. I think that made his day as well. I could not deny him that pleasure when realistically that day could very well be his last, and I wanted to enjoy it with him happily. I let him drink some brandy as well, but he liked vodka better. Toward the end, he was basically immobile but still coherent, yet no, he was no longer the father I grew up with. I say grew up with because no one really raised me. If it was anyone, it was my sister, and then my mom, who still constantly apologizes for not being there, but if she didn't do what she did and travel all the time, the family would have crashed and burned. My mother was the cornerstone of this family, and without her, we would have been fucked.

My dad was eventually placed under hospice care, and it was getting to the point that it was hard to see him. I would still go watch his programs with him every once in a while, and it was fun to talk with him completely candidly and talking to him like I would a close friend. I would tell him about getting high, fucking random girls.

It was fun because I could see in his eyes that he missed those days and wished that he were able to experience that thrill again if even for only one moment. I spent my days working at the liquor store, drinking all day and getting stoned-ass in the backroom only to go home and do the same thing until I passed out. I tried to call my pops every day, but sometimes I would have people over, and by the time I thought to call, it was too late. Shortly after this point in time, my father was completely bed-ridden, so I upped my medication and was drinking a lot more.

One day, I don't remember what time it was, but I think I was either watching *Jeopardy!* or *The Simpsons* because I remember almost not answering the phone. I saw that the call was coming from my parents' condo, and my heart dropped. My mom would call me all the time to talk about nothing, and I never thought anything of it, but this time I was scared. I knew it was not an ordinary call, and something had or was about to go down. It was my sister, and she was crying. I did not need to hear anything that she had planned to say, and I started to cry as well. I thought that the inevitable had already happened, but that was not the case. My sister told me that I had only an hour or so if that to see my dad alive and that she would come and pick me up if I wanted to see him one last time. I am sure that she offered the ride because at that time she knew I would most likely be unable to drive. I told her to get her ass over here, and I packed up my backpack of supplies. I had a liter of brandy and about a twelve-pack of beer along with my smokes and a few grams of really stinky weed, so I was ready for the worst or at least I thought I was.

When I walked in to see my dad, he looked like hell in a hand basket rolled in complete shit. I love him, but it was very hard to see him like that, and I had to leave. I said, "What's up?" and gave him a hug, but I needed a minute to get my shit together while at the same time letting go by drinking and smoking myself stupid. I knew what was going to happen, and I have seen dead bodies before, but I had never watched someone die. I remember sitting in his recliner and drinking that bottle of brandy and chasing it with shitty beer for about an hour when my sister came and got me. She told me that if it was the end and if I had anything to say to dad, that now was the time to put the bottle down. I was almost done with it and good and drunk, at least enough to deal with watching my father die, or at least I thought. I went into the room where my sister and mother left me alone to have my last moments, which was a sobering moment that I knew was going to happen but apparently not ready for. It was like the end of ET, where both the alien and Elliot were so pale and dying, barely able to speak. It was hard to witness; I was helpless.

Everyone always says that they wish they would have had a chance to say what they wanted to say to someone close to them before they passed away. Well, I had that chance, and I took full advantage of it, although in hindsight, knowing that my words would be the last that he would ever hear, I could have been a little nicer. We had always spoken candidly with each other and said exactly what we meant, but looking back, I think that I possibly came off as a bit of an asshole. I meant every word that I said and would not take one of them back, but he possibly did not necessarily have needed to hear that on his deathbed. He had said what he wanted to say and actually wrote me a letter that I did not read until after his funeral and will ever read again. I told him how I felt about everything from the way I saw him while growing up and looked up to him to the point where I lost all respect for him. I updated it to that point in time where I was very appreciative that we could at least spend some time together and have fun, which we did, but I did not ease up about the fact that he had fucked up a lot of shit for the whole family. I knew that they would never say anything, but it is not that kind of party with me. He said that he knew that and to go ahead. I wish I had not continued.

I went into great detail on how he had hurt me over the years as well as his daughter, and most importantly, his wife. I will never say anything more specific about what was said that night because what exactly was said was meant for one dying man and no one else. I said everything I had wanted to say for everything I had wanted to say for years but was reluctant because of his situation, but I just thought that if I had something to say, basically speaking for the whole family, I would regret not saying something.

In hindsight, I regret saying anything. He was no longer hooked up to his machine, which is I guess why they had told me that it was my last chance to have a moment with him. I did not need a beeping noise to stop and go flat to know what had happened. After I was done with my rant, I just held his hand and told him I was sorry about that and that I loved him. I have no idea what he said because he was fading away fast. It kind of sounded like "Fuck you," but I am pretty sure that is not what he said, what I do know is that what he said was, "I Love You" although I do not think that is all what I heard at the time. I don't remember exactly what I heard or said because I polished off an 18 pack of beer and a bottle of brandy waiting for him to die. That sounds really fucked-up and it is, however sometimes that is just how it is. I was three sheets to the wind with a full flask and a jar of weed at his funeral. I was fucking plowed but I remember every second of the service. I still think it was kind of disrespectful to be so hammered and stoned-ass but he never saw me any other way so who cares? If the tables were turned I am sure he would have done the same. Those were the last words he ever spoke. As I said, I did not need a beeping noise to tell me that he was gone, but I could feel the life leave his body. His eyes were still open, and I have seen enough movies to know that you are supposed to close them. I did, and it was one of the saddest things I have ever done.

I called my mom and sister into the room and did not need to say anything; we all just cried for quite a long time and made our way out to the living room. My mom got on the horn immediately, calling his siblings to let him know that it was over because I know they were all awaiting that call. I sat back down and put on some show about animals because I love watching that shit, but I did not listen or learn anything because my mind was racing. I had more brandy left in a flask in my backpack, which I eventually just began referring to as my purse because it had everything I could possibly need for a weekend, even if I was on the street.

I always had a change of clothes, clean drawers and socks, any pills I might need, my inhaler, toothbrush and toothpaste, Kleenex, toilet paper, protein bars, other food stuffs on occasion, a Camelbak full of water, a knife, at least a few lighters and an herb pipe with whatever weed I had at the time to bring out of the house for the night, as well as alcohol, because sometimes one night can turn into a weekend. I still had plenty of room to hold double that, so I always used it to carry shit around. Now that I write it down, it sounds like I was planning to go live on the streets, that or Armageddon. This was not the case. I just liked to have everything with me that I needed, and this day was a perfect example. I had already drunk a liter of brandy and at least six or ten beers while sitting there, and now I was crying. My only thoughts were to drown my sorrows a little more; it couldn't hurt. Luckily, I had some herb with me because I knew it was going to be a long shitty night and I always plan ahead. I smoked myself stupid, and I know that I drank myself retarded because I don't remember anything after this point for the most part, but I do remember them wheeling my dad out of there and blacking out. I know I didn't do anything stupid because I would have heard about it later for sure.

Flat Tire was there for me. I am not sure if she came over that night or not, but I do know seeing her was one of first things I can remember. I talked to my buddy whom I tell everything as well, but I could not really bring myself to talk to anyone else except one other person who was at one point in time was my best friend that I often had nasty sex with, but once again, that was no more.

My dad was cremated, and his service was like a month afterward because everyone in my extended family lives as far away from the frozen tundra as possible. I thought this would be enough time for her to come to the service, considering we had been more than friends for like fifteen years, but I guess not. Some friends that I had not talked to in a very long time came for support, and everyone who met my dad liked him. My heart was broken. I understand it is not free to fly from NYC to Minneapolis, but she had a disposable income, and it was well within the range of possibility. I got drunk as fuck and then went to the service where I had a full flask and enough pot to last me a weekend. It was like twenty degrees below zero, but I spent the majority of the time outside. I came in initially, found out when it was going to start, and then went back outside. My friends came with me, and I just drank and smoked my face off until it was time for the ceremony.

I might have been drunk as hell and high out of my brain, but I remember the service well. There was a little service with some marines where they folded up a flag and gave it to my mom. Neither I nor my sister was able to read the eulogy that we had written, so his brother read it. I remember being really sad, and that is about it until the last line that my sister and I put in for the conclusion. We wrote that we hope wherever he is that they have "Cheddar chicken in a can." My mom and my sister smiled because they knew the joke although nobody else did, and I am pretty sure I laughed, but I am not positive.

Ol' boy-girl with the hanging earring probably smiled as well because I know that I told him that story and he loved my dad. He did an awesome impression of him that no one can top, and I still make him do it because it is fucking hilarious and the closest I will ever get to hearing his voice again. That is unless I call my mom's condo, and she is out of town because my dad is still on the outgoing message on the answering machine. The first time I heard this, it scared the shit out of me, but now, every once in a while, I call when I know she is not there just to hear his voice.

I went and checked out all the old pictures that they always have up on some tag board like they always do, which was sad enough without all the extended family who doesn't even really know me consoling me. What do you say in that situation? Yes, this really sucks, and I am not happy right now. By the way, I am also really drunk and pretty fucking high, but it might be wearing off, so as uncomfortable and depressing as this is, I think I am going to escape again and further my intoxication in the parking lot with people that I am comfortable around. I don't remember saying that, but I sure as shit was thinking it.

I was not doing so good at this time and still drinking my face off. I was by myself most of the day during the week, and I would just take shot after shot, chasing it with beer. I was missing my dad pretty bad, so I was not in a good way. I began to start hearing voices, and that scared me a little bit, but I just kept drinking. I began to see things. At first, it was just random shit out of the corner of my eye, but it soon progressed from there. I began to think that that my dad was trying to communicate with me from beyond the grave. I don't remember exactly what I was hearing, but it was something to that effect. I then began to see these little kids running around the house, laughing and running down the hallway. I believed that they were trying to show me where my dad was and bring me to him. I chased them down the hallway a couple of times and even ran headfirst into the closet door at the end of the hallway. I remember feeling things similar to what happened when my first seizure happened. I was smelling the same smells and having the same visions, but I do not think that I had an episode. I called my girlfriend, and she was busy but could tell that I was truly scared and told me to call my sister. I do not know how I remember this, but I do.

My sister came over and took care of business. She brought me to the hospital because I guess I was clearly fucked. I walked in on my own power and checked in. When they processed me, they asked how I got there. I told them that my sister gave me a ride, and they said, "No, how did you walk in here? With you alcohol level, you should not be able to move right now." My BAC was around 0.40 percent, which is incredibly high considering 0.08 percent makes you illegal to drive. They knew I was jacked up eight ways from Sunday, so they put me in a room. Luckily, my sister was with me, but it was not all good for very long. We stayed in the doctor's quarters or what I like to call the second waiting room for a little bit, and then I began to get antsy.

I remember the walls turning into cobblestone walls like something you would see in Bedrock on *The Flintstones*. I remember jumping up and running out of the room and screaming, "We got to get the fuck out of Bedrock, let's go." That is the last thing I remember. They must have shot me with a tranquilizer dart or something because the next thing I knew, I was in the hospital with an IV, and I had no clue why I was there or what had happened. I was literally on lockdown and not allowed to leave for a week. However, on the first day, my roommate/girlfriend came to visit me, and it was really nice because I still barely even knew who I was, but I knew who she was.

They gave me a daily breakfast of pills, and I have no idea what they were, but I know I was in a different world for a week. I was surrounded by a bunch of people who clearly had some head troubles and were really fucked up. I did not belong there. I made one friend who was just a recreational drug abuser, which I could completely understand. He was not just crazy like the rest of the patients, and we got along. Flat Tire came by the first day and every day after that to spend time with me when it was allowed. We would play the stupid board games from the '50s that they would allow the mental patients. It was not until about the third day when I finally got my head together and began to understand the world around me. After some investigation, I found out that I was being stored in the psych ward and I had extra bracelets on me that said I was a fall risk and basically might possibly freak the fuck out and go crazy. I don't remember what it said exactly, but that was clearly what it meant. So I was apparently batshit crazy, "one flew over the cuckoo's nest" style.

I tried to get Flat Tire to have a quickie with me in the hospital bed, but she is not that kind of dirty birdie. It would have been a good story to tell though. I stayed in that shit hole for a week, and the first thing I did was grab a beer and pound it the second I got out.

I continued to work at the moving company, which I am still amazed I was able to do for so long, but despite the drugs and drinking, I was in pretty good shape. I was eventually fired for bringing a bottle on the job and drinking. I did not bring that bottle, but fuck yeah, I drank some and then some, but it was not mine. I was a little pissed off that they came to me first before asking anyone else. I told them that I did not bring the bottle and it did not belong to me, but I took a few shots while we were working. Nobody else got fired, so I am led to believe that I got sold out and fired for being the only one who was honest even though every single worker on that job was guilty. Whatever, I just needed to find a new job. This is when I returned to my high school liquor store job again and continued to drink way too much until I realized that I needed to find a new, better job. I fucked up my timeline a bit and probably repeated some ish, but it is kind of hard not to when you are typing everything from memory.

One day I got a knock at the door which would change my life. This was not unusual because everyone from back in the day remembers my house and seems to stop by at random, often at the worst possible time. It was an old friend who had dropped out in junior high and I had not seen since. He showed up at my door with a big fucking dog, and I was a little confused. I let him in and gave him a beer and smoked some herb with him because I am a good host. We hung out for a while, and then he asked me if I could watch his dog for like two weeks. This was a big-ass brindle boxer that weighed one hundred pounds and looked like an overgrown pit bull. He said he would give me enough food for two weeks and then come back and get him. After many shots, drinks, beers, and smoking my face off, I said okay. I had never had a dog before, and he seemed pretty nice, so I figured, what the hell, I might as well; he was cute.

I took care of that dog for well over two years and fell in love with him. My friend's sister worked at the liquor store up the street, so I would walk him there exactly at three o'clock every afternoon so she could see him. Their mom would pick her up from work and was so excited to see the mutt every time. He was not actually a mutt; he was a purebred AKC certified boxer, and I had his original pedigree and everything.

My friend's mother lived in the same building as my mom. One day I saw her in the hall, and she told me that the dog was mine now and she would not let her son take him back and she would say that in court. When Flat Tire moved in, she had a Chihuahua that was a little bastard. I hated that fucking dog. He was a yippy fat little shit that would not shut the fuck up and the true definition of an ankle-biter dog. This dog was so protective of blondie and would growl and bite at me any time she was around and try to bite at me. When she would go to work, I would take a nap on the couch and wake up to that fat fuck on my chest, and when I woke up, he would lick my face and shit. That dog fucking loved me.

He would always sit by me during the day and rub up on me; he was nothing but sweet. The second my long-haired roommate would walk in, he turned on me and was 100 percent evil. He was still a really fat little Vienna sausage of a dog. During the day while the lady was away and the dog was nice to me, I would walk him. We started off small, but by the end, we were walking a little over two miles at a time, which I can only imagine would be like a marathon to a Chihuahua. I was able to slim him down considerably by around four pounds, which is like half of a Chihuahua. Everything was cool between us, but he was becoming progressively aggressive even toward his mom, which had never happened before, but she ignored it.

One day I was playing with the little, and I think I had just eaten or something because out of nowhere he lunged at my hand and gripped onto my middle finger. I tried to pull back, but the little would not let go, and he actually bit right through my finger. I kept pulling, and I pulled that fat fuck up off the ground. His teeth had actually penetrated all the way through my finger, coming out the other side. We agreed that the dog needed to be put down. He had to take medication every day, and although he had lost weight, he was still basically unhealthy. I know it was hard for her, but it only got worse because when she brought the dog in to be put down, they asked if he had bitten anyone in the past seven days, and she said yes.

In hindsight, she knows that this was the wrong thing to say, and she will never answer that way again if put in the same situation. They basically said that they would have to cut off its head and she had to bring it to the University of Minnesota to be examined and make sure it did not have rabies because then I might have it. I am not afraid of rabies. I am crazy enough as it is, and this was just pouring salt in the wound of a girl who loved animals more than anything in the world, and she had already been through enough. She was broken up for quite a while, but that would not last.

We were out one day, doing something. I think we were at the zoo. I love the zoo, but it can be depressing, especially seeing animals that belong in Africa forced to live in Minnesota. That is not fair and would be like forcing a person to go live in Antarctica with no warning and having to live the rest of their life there. I think we went mini golfing afterward also; I love that too. After that, we went to the local humane society. These are also very depressing, but I just look at it like going to a zoo for domesticated animals. We look at a bunch of cute kitties and some puppies, and I figured that was the end of that, but it was not to be.

On the way home, we passed a pet store, and she wanted to go in there and just look. I was reluctant, but I said okay. There were a few kitties but mostly little puppy dogs. They were cute, but I wasn't going to bring one home; however, my girlfriend was in love. She found a pack of little Chihuahuas with one little yippy runt of the litter that she took a liking to. I knew what she was thinking, and I said absolutely not. We were not getting another dog; the big one was enough for us.

I made her put it back, and we left with her pouting and talking about how she loved the little one. We went back home, and I did what I do; I drank some beer and smoked some weed when she said she had to run some errands. This was not out of the ordinary because she always ran errands on Saturdays, but I remember that the first thing I said as she left was, "You better not come back with that fucking dog!" I smoked myself out, lay down, and woke up to the sound of two dogs barking, and I have never been more pissed off in my life.

The little shit was plenty annoying, but he was nowhere near the level of asshole that the one before him was at. I knew that my boxer who I now just refer to as the fat one was really good with little kids and even babies, but apparently, he loved little dogs as well. The two got along right away, and they have slept together ever since, and they also look out for each other and play together; it is actually pretty cute.

I did not see my old friend for well over two years when he once again just dropped by out of nowhere. I opened the door, and the first thing I said was, "Don't even think you are taking this dog away from me." That was not his plan; he just wanted to see him and have a drink. We went to a local bar and drank it up. He was hitting on a bunch of girls, which I was not interested in, and it is a good thing he did not hook up or anything because the motherfucker has four or five kids by three or four different girls, so I think he has enough on his plate.

I just sat at the bar and talked with the barkeep and the local bar flies. I was like Norm on *Cheers* up there. The next time I went up there, the bartender asked me if I wanted to clear out my tab, which confused me because they never charged me for beer. I asked what was up, and he said that my buddy was putting drinks and shots on my tab. He said, "You know, the one who started the porn website and has all types of money." That was fucked. He lived with a kid whom, when the internet first came out, he bought the rights to the domain name freeporn.com. He eventually made an ass load of money off it as well as some other sites. Everything that my friend was telling these girls he was trying to hit on as well as the bartender was his roommate's life story. If he had told them the truth, they would have taken their free drink and walked away. Actually, I paid for those drinks. When I paid the tab, I was not charged for any of my beer, but dipshit rang up a $50 tab.

I wanted to kill him, but I paid the tab and coincidentally never spoke to him again. This could be because of the tab or possibly the way he left my house when he dropped me off that night. He was plowed, but he drove me home safe, so I was cool. I just told him to drive safe, and I went into the house. A few seconds later, I heard tires screeching around the corner in front of my house but thought nothing of it until the next morning when Flat Tire told me to go look outside. Sure enough, there were burnout marks around the corner, but then they hopped the curb and fucked up my yard, continuing through the yard where he took out both mine and my neighbor's mailboxes.

My mom told me about some job that she explained as basically grading papers. All you needed was a college degree. Nothing could have been further from the truth; it was a government-run organization, although they never said that. I did eventually find out it was part of the "no child left behind" initiative, which is the shittiest program ever, and it makes no sense. Before we could grade papers, we had to spend a few days doing eight hours of tests that was like a kick in the ass back in time to high school. It is so easy to forget that shit after a decade. Some of the math stuff was pretty like, if you have a round pizza that was eight inches in diameter and one-fourth-inch thick, how thick would a rectangle pizza be if it was four-by-eight inches?

It was ridiculous, but somehow all that shit came right back to me, and I aced the tests. It was seasonal, unfortunately, in the winter, and it was a bit of a drive, but the money was really good. They probably paid so well so people would have the money to pay for the therapy they would need after working there. It was stressful as hell. I quickly learned the flaws in this system.

The schools filled with nothing but privileged children who have everything are getting funding, and those schools that may be in an impoverished community are getting fucked because their papers or tests are not as good as those of the rich bastards. It is not their fault that their school has no funding, and that is the reason why they deserve it. They would study from books made of paper and write on paper with pencils. Apparently, this is a lost art. The rich kids have personal computers at school as well as at home and would learn from PowerPoint presentations in class. No shit, they are going to get better grades, and these are the kids and schools receiving the funding and that is fucked up and bass-ackward.

The privileged ones would write about coming home from school and playing their Xbox on their big-screen TV and then chatting online all night. The less fortunate were real kids. They would write about coming home and playing stickball or soccer. At least it was something outside. Many of them did not even have the internet. They had to learn from books like true scholars while the privileged could just look up the answer to the homework on their cell phone in two seconds.

The reports by the kids who were clearly privileged were well-written reports and then had excellent handwriting while the papers by the children who were clearly not as well off were not as great and the handwriting was a little shaky, but you could tell that they tried hard and put their all into it. I did not need to know their background history to know that these kids were living in shit, yet they made the effort every day to take the shitty bus (which many of them mentioned) and working their asses off. The kids with well written submissions were like the epitome of every rich kid I wanted to kill in school. The money was clearly going to the wrong places, and I hope George W. Bush rots in hell.

Around this time, my mom had a conference that she needed to attend in Hawaii, so she brought me and my sister with her. She had lots of frequent-flyer miles, so it was no big deal, and we just stayed in the same room as her that the university paid for, so it was all good. It was fun. Everyone loved Spam, and you could get it on anything even at a nice restaurant. My dad would have loved it, and he really loved Spam. I mostly hung out with my sister because my mom was busy, but we went out and did some cool shit.

We saw SS *Arizona* that was sunken at Pearl Harbor through a glass bottom boat, and it was really cool. There were a number of people on that ship, and a much smaller number were saved or retrieved. It was weird to think of the fact that there were dead rotted men down there in that ship, but it was still cool. My dad would have really liked that as well.

I was out smoking on the patio one day, and a woman who was one floor down and a room away yelled up to me and asked me what I was smoking, and I told her it was a cigar. She told me to come down to her room and kick it for a little bit, and I had no problem with that. I went down to her room and finished/shared my smoke with her and had a beer. We talked about grabbing some herb because I had not found any yet, which is stupid because this was like the first day I was there. She obviously wanted some too, and it was clear that she was disappointed that I could not help her out in that department. However, she was also clearly interested, and I probably could have gotten down with her, but I had plans with my mom and sister in like five minutes, so I just went and met up with them because I had already fucked up on this trip and did not want to make them any angrier with me. I never went back to her room for two reasons.

Part of me felt bad about my roommate back home, and I just didn't care that much. I made some phone calls because I had a friend from high school that was living down there and tried to get ahold of him. I did get ahold of him, and he picked me up from the hotel one night. We went to a restaurant. It was me, him, and his girlfriend, and we had a great time, at least I did. I drank my face off, and afterward, he hooked me up with a dub of some ill-ass chronic that one could probably smell outside if it was in a Ziploc bag in the trunk. This shit was diesel.

Once again I just crushed it up and put it in my cigars and smoked it. That way, I could smoke in public. I thought about going down to the woman that I had talked with before and smoking with her, but then, once again, I just didn't really care anymore and wanted to keep the weed for myself. She was really hot, but for some reason, I didn't really care. We did all types of shit and of course went to some beaches. I forget which one it was, but I got hurt at one.

Part of me wanted to try surfing, but the logical side of me which rarely comes out told me not to try it, so I did not. I decided to go boogie boarding instead, and I had a good time. The open ocean scared the shit out of me, so I was happy hanging out in the shallows. I like to snorkel and look at stuff Discovery Channel style. This was until I stepped on a sea urchin that stung the fuck out of my foot. I watch a lot of animal shows, and I heard that pissing on your foot is the thing to do if you step on one of those things, so I told my mom to bring me to the ABC across the street because there was a wooded area next to the parking lot so I could piss on my foot. I did want to do that and did not want to do it in the open, considering I have been arrested for that in the past.

There were a million places I could have pissed on my leg, no problem, but it hurt like hell. I wanted some booze, so I had my sister run in the store and get me a tall can. I was happy, but that shit still hurt like hell for the rest of the day and was pretty swollen till I got home.

I returned to my grading job and just said, "Fuck it," and had fun with the job from then on. I would drink my face off before the morning commute and drink beers in my dad's truck during breaks, which at this point was my truck. I hated that truck, although I did have fun in it and on it. I was lucky because there was no traffic either way during the times I had to commute, so I got loaded as hell. Along with that comes the inflated self-confidence of a drunk, and I eventually talked to this Cambodian girl who worked there. Everyone would just walk around the building during break to stretch their legs, and one day, it started raining, and we were right by the truck. We got inside to get out of the rain, and I did not fuck around. I grabbed her by the head and pulled her in. She was all about it, more so than I was expecting considering I was half and half on if I would get slapped or not.

I felt a good vibe from her; otherwise, I would not have done it. She was actually a lot more into it than I had expected. When you have a fifteen-minute break with hot Cambodian with big tits sucking your face and grabbing your business, it goes by really fast. We agreed that she would follow me to my house after work. We went back to my house, and there was no talking, no anything. We just walked in the house, and she tackled me. She was a freak, too, and goddamn, did she have nice tits. She took control and was quite good at it. She was into ass play and talked incredibly dirty with the sexiest accent imaginable. I had an inkling that she just might be a squirter, so I asked her straight out. Without a word, she straddled my face and began rubbing her clit like she was trying to start a fire until she exploded everywhere, and it was amazing.

When I first heard about this phenomenon, I thought it was a myth and that the girls were just peeing. It is no myth, and this woman just spayed hot lady jizz all over my face. I learned that this was a skill that many woman have but are reluctant to display because they are embarrassed. Fuck that, I embrace that shit. It is porno, sexy, and fun.

I was still in touch with Flat Tire, and she still came over every night only to leave early, go home, and get ready then go to work. The lease on her house was up, and she had to move. I still think that this is bullshit, and she just wanted to move in with me, considering she was sleeping there every night anyways. Somehow she convinced me to let her move in, but I told her she had to pay rent the same as the two before her, and that was no problem. My mom really needed the money at the time, so it seemed to fix two problems at once, plus I had a live-in vagina that I could play with whenever I wanted. The best part was that she had so much shit, including her bed, that she had to put it all in the extra room. This way, if we wanted to play, we could do the damn thing and then retire to our separate quarters to sleep in peace. It was basically the same as before, except I didn't need to call her if I wanted some lovin'. In fact it was quite nice because she would cook and clean, although I am in no way a misogynist and never told or asked her to do anything. She just needed things just so, and she wanted it clean.

I thought I had cleaned the house in the past years; it was at least good enough to throw parties which I guess isn't saying much, but she turned the house upside down. It was clear at this point that I had a girlfriend on my hands. My dad got me into stand-up comedy, and I have listened to a lot of it throughout the years. Male comics would always talk about how if you decide to let your girlfriend move in or, God forbid, get married, everything will change. They would joke about the fact that once you let your woman move in with you, you should just picture everything that you love in the house, take a breath, and then imagine it all gone. That is exactly what happened. I had the house decked out like a fucking frat house, and she came and turned it into a respectable domicile. What the fuck? Everything that I loved got the boot, and she replaced it all. I do like having nice shit, but there is something to be said about the fact that you could light on fire and put out with a beer in the middle of your living room and not give two shits about it.

I gave in and let her revamp the joint, and it actually looked a lot better. There was no more smoking in the house (herb is okay). You even had to take your shoes off; it was like jail. Looking back, she really turned the house around. We painted the hallways, the bedrooms, the living room, the bathrooms, and the kitchen. We got rid of basically all the furniture and replaced everything. It was like a brand-new house besides the fact that I could no longer come and go as I pleased without an explanation.

I got very good at storytelling very quickly, but it was cool; we had fun, and it was nice to have a clean house and food. I had forgotten that food was good and that you should eat it every day. I had forgotten that somehow over years of partying. We went to a lot of parties together, which must have been weird for everyone at the parties at one point in time because I was kickin' it with both the blonde and the brown at the same time for a couple of years and they were both friends with all the same people that we would party with.

The people never knew who I was going to come with, and it would change weekly. I am an asshole. But now that the brownie was gone, I just partied with Flat Tire. We went out to shows and all types of different ish, which was awesome because she would drive and I am not going to risk fucking up behind the wheel. I would obviously not want to get into trouble, but if I were to hurt anyone else, that shit would give me nightmares for the rest of my life, and I don't think I could deal with that.

We went to one party, which was a "pimps and hoes" party, and obviously, I was the most pimped out, and I didn't even need to change from my daily wardrobe. We were drunk as shit and probably dancing like idiots when she jumped on me. I held her up, and then for some reason, I lifted her up, which caused us both to tip over. I had to make a decision at this point—go down with her or just let go so I wouldn't fall. I let go. I dropped her over my shoulder right on her pretty little face. She was busted but lucky because she was inches from the top of the stairs to the basement. She was dripping blood down her face, so I felt pretty bad, but I immediately said, "What the hell did you do?" To this day I deny that it was my fault and that she jumped over me; that is not the truth.

Coincidentally, her gash was basically in the same spot as the one on my forehead from getting pistol-whipped. However, she definitely did not need stiches, but she does cry when she gets a paper cut, so it was blown out of proportion.

It was time to get back to work, and the next season of the "No child left behind" began in the winter, but for some reason, they waited until the weather got really shitty before starting. Everyone had to take another week of classes and a few tests. I was not as nervous this time, and I aced them again. This time, I was grading high school seniors, so it was a little more interesting, but it was still depressing. Once again, I just said, "Fuck it," and would get loaded while I worked; I didn't care because it was obvious that the government does not care about these kids, at least not the ones that really need assistance.

I would drink a bunch before work, drive there, and return to my truck on every break to re-up my alcohol level and wake up. I don't drink coffee. It was only a matter of time before I started just drinking at work while I was working. I would always have pre-made gin and tonics to bring to work in my purse. I would just take the coffee cups with a lid and fill it with ice by the water cooler. I would sit down at my station and make a drink right there. It was all clear anyone that saw me thought that I was just pouring my bottled water on ice, but I was getting plowed as fuck and grading high school seniors' tests and papers. I did not fuck up. In fact, I eventually got in trouble for being too good, but that happened later. Before that happened, I had run into another very voluptuous woman while walking around the building on breaks many times but never spoke to her.

One day, I just approached her and started up a conversation about God-knows-what, but it seemed to work. She was incredibly sexy and had all the proportions that men desire. Basically, she was stacked in the front as well as the back. She was also Asian and somehow also Cambodian. I have no idea why they like me, but I guess they do. The same scenario occurred, and I ended up making out with this woman in my truck. Once again, this girl followed me to my house, and once again, shit hit the fan as soon as I opened the door.

This girl took the definition of being a freak to a whole new level. When we got inside, she told me to go grab a towel…NOW. I did, and she placed it down. I knew, to some degree, what was going to happen, but I was not quite sure. She jumped on the towel with her ass in the air in a downward dog position and told me some dirty shit I cannot even remember, but basically, she was commanding me to fuck her in the ass. This girl loved this for some reason, and I began to become curious if you could make a woman cum by fucking her in her ass. I would later find out the answer. She eventually threw me down and had her way with me. I fucked her ass until she came, then I fucked her tits and her mouth for a while. Then she flipped me over and rode me like a horse or more accurately like a mechanical bull.

Once again, I had an inkling that this girl might squirt if you push the right buttons. I asked her if she got down like that, and her face lit up like I just gave her a diamond ring. She rode the pony for about thirty seconds before she could no longer hold it back, and she unleashed the beast; she wet me up like a fucking typhoon. That shit was hot as hell, and she was not done. She rubbed her juice all over and got off another one. I continued to play with her the entire time we were working together at the same place.

I eventually got "laid off" for the exact reason I hated that place, but I did not know the system was as fucked up as I found out that I basically did not fail enough kids, specifically from certain districts, which happened to be those that were clearly from lower-income communities. These were the kids that needed the money, yet the government would rather give the money to children who all have iPhones, iPods, iPads, and God-knows-what-else.

The company told me that they had to let me go because my numbers were not on the right side, meaning that I was not failing enough of the poor and not passing enough of the rich. The fucked-up part is that I saw my numbers, and my accuracy rate was at the very top of the entire business, around 90 percent accuracy. So I was doing better than the majority of the graders, but I lost my job for one reason—I did not fail enough black children. There is no other way to say it, but that was the case plain and simple. There were no names on the papers, but I could tell from what they wrote about and how they wrote it exactly which side of the tracks they were from. I know I was doing the right thing, and that "no child left behind" act should be renamed because it is leaving behind the kids that really need assistance. Needless to say, after I stopped working there, I never spoke to either of the squirt queens again.

I knew I needed to get another job, so one day I took the big dog for a walk around the lake by my house. There was a bar up the street owned by one of the guys I played softball with and a few other people whom I had worked with and some others that were just on the softball team. So I figured I would give it a shot. I actually ran into one of the guys from the team that I would step out with to smoke a bowl or two during the tournaments. He was out having a smoke, and I obviously could not go inside because I had my fat pig-dog with me, but I talked to him and told him I was looking for a job and to ask Lunchbox if he could find anything for me.

Lunchbox was a big fat friend from the moving company as well as the softball team. His mind was always blown at the fact that I could smoke so much herb and still function, and I thought that was hilarious. The cat I was talking to said he worked in the kitchen and he was actually going to quit in a few weeks. I got a job, and it was perfect. I could do whatever I wanted. I had to cook food, and I was really good at it, but when there was downtime, I would smoke a bowl, drink some beer, and do my prep work. I did not smoke cigarettes at that time, so I would literally work my whole shift without taking a break, and I never once ate the food even though we were allowed one meal of whatever we wanted each shift. I would have gotten so fat if I would have taken advantage of that opportunity. Instead I just got high as hell and drank a ton of beer.

There were no worries because I remember the first time I got busted smoking herb in the back by the owner, and he just told me to blow it out of the fans and get back to work. They would give us beers in the kitchen every once in a while so that was no big deal, but one time, early on a Saturday morning after I had been up all night, the owner saw me in the back slamming a beer quite early in the morning, and he simply shook his head at me and walked away. I slammed it and threw it away and never heard about it again. I continued to drink throughout that day, but I was a little more discreet.

I cooked alongside of a few other cooks and then ended up with one guy whom I actually got along with. He was a big conspiracy theorist, and we got along on that tip. We also smoked herb together and hung out sometimes outside of work. We would go to the strip club down the street for happy hour and basically just to play pool, but we had fun and saw a titty or two…good times. I introduced him to hip-hop, and he tried to get me into his hippy music, but no dice. That was not happening. I have love for all forms of music, but that does not mean that I want to listen to it.

We had a good time in our kitchen, which was our own world, and I feel that it went by pretty fast. It did suck that we ended up sweaty as hell and smelling like deep-fried shit, but we had fun. I would go out and have a couple mugs of beer and relax after work, maybe play some ski-ball and whatever other games they had, and occasionally, I would hook up with a girl from the bar, but it never resulted in anything really fun.

Around this time, I decided to finally meet my new roommate/girlfriend's parents. It had been more than a few years, so I am sure that they were curious about me. Her entire extended family goes up north to cabins that are all on one beach every July for one week every year. I decided that I would finally come up there with her because she had been asking me to for more than a few years. I met her parents once before the cabin, and I don't know what the fuck we did. Maybe we ate dinner or just stood around, I don't know, but I know that they were very polite and treated me nicely. I eventually went up to the cabin for the week and hung out with her entire family, and I was pretty uncomfortable. We obviously shared a room in the same cabin with her parents.

They knew we had been living together for a while, and they are not stupid. They had their first kid when they were younger than we were at the time, so they knew what we did behind closed doors. She had a really big family, and I was not used to that. I still don't remember all their names. I was clearly the black sheep of the family although I was not part of the family. When we would go out into town, I looked like I was some foreign exchange student that they had taken in because I didn't look like anyone in northern Minnesota. It was like I was the darkest thing anyone had ever seen, and I think all my tattoos blew their minds. I didn't care. Everyone was always nice to me, and I had fun. We went out on the boats, and all met up by a bridge where it was shallow, and after the last boat came up with people whose names I could not tell you if you paid me, because I have no idea, but I know that "Flat Tire's" niece was on there. When they got off and we were swimming, she told me that one of her cousins asked who the black guy with tattoos was hanging out with the family.

I am a little darker than your average cracker jack, but I don't look black. Maybe that is why they all remember my name when I can't remember half of their names. They are all good people, and it is a good time up there. Every night is a different theme; there is always taco night, an Italian night, and some other nights I don't remember. They would eat a lot. On top of that, they would drink like fish, which was kind of cool because there was always a bottle of rum in the kitchen of our cabin. The first Monday way logging camp day, and the entire family goes up to this breakfast place, and it is like a tradition or some shit. We go with like twenty-five people, and it is stressful as hell, but it is also good, and I always have fun. They have the free-range chickens out there that you can feed and a river which for some reason always has fish at that you can feed and a bunch of other stupid shit.

I usually just played with the kids while we waited. A group of twenty-five was apparently nothing new to this place, and it became apparent that this was a tradition for many other families as well. The place was the epitome of northern Minnesota. The waitress would come around and ask how many eggs you wanted and how you wanted them. You could say a dozen it doesn't matter, but you better eat that shit. You get hash browns and ham or bacon and unlimited pancakes. There is no way you can finish all that food. They also had a gift shop that you basically had to walk through to get in or out of the place; it was basically like a ranch. I really liked the gift shop because it was full of all the stupid shit that you wanted to get when you were little but your parents said no. Well, now my parents were no longer around, so I bought all the stupid shit that I had always wanted growing up. It was always me and the little boys in the family running around in there, and I felt like I was one of them again.

Flat Tire has three male cousins, all brothers, that all smoked cheeba and liked to drink a lot, so we naturally got along. We went out one year and spent the entire day out on the lake, literally. It was sunny as hell and hot as fuck all day. Mix that with the fact that I did not eat anything or drink anything besides alcohol, and it is the perfect recipe for a really shitty tomorrow. We had a blast. We smoked our faces off and put out the fire with fire water, then put out that fire with beer. We were set.

I would dive off the boat wherever we were if I got hot which was enough relief for me, and I love to swim, so it was a win-win situation. I do not get sunburn, but at the end of that day, I could definitely feel the sun on my skin. I was all good in the morning, but I did feel a little sick, and I knew the cure for that. I would time my approach very carefully and wait until the perfect moment when everyone was occupied then fill up a Dixie cup full of rum and grab a couple of beers to chase it. That always worked, although I felt like I was smoking crack in the bathroom at like fifteen years old, sneaking away to have a drink in the morning with a family full of heavy drinkers. I guess I was a few levels above them on the "heavy drinker" scale; I was definitely a 10 on that scale if there was one. For some reason, it was not cool to have a drink before noon; but the second the clock hit twelve o'clock, all bets were off, and every one drank their faces off.

We would also go tubing and whatnot, but I brought my kneeboard, which none of them had tried before. That was really fun because we used her dad's boat, which was big and fast; I actually pulled off some good moves. I wish I had a wakeboard because that would have been much more fun. The lodge also had a nine-hole golf course that was just free, so you could just walk on and off whenever you wanted. There was also a big field with a little playground in the corner. It had a wooden pirate-ship-looking fort thing that I would walk to and smoke out every morning. There was always a game night, which was fun, and we would play with very small denominations, which was always disappointing when you cash out. One time I took the pot, and it was a total of five dollars. Oh well, it was fun.

I would also play games with the cousin that did not involve any of the old people, those conducted highly intoxicated and were for real money. There were always days that we would go into town as well, which always involved a trip to the candy store. This place was awesome; it had all the candy I could remember as a kid that you can't find anywhere, as well as old candies that I knew my mom liked so I would always pick some up for her. They also had really good fudge in town, so we would also get some big slabs of a couple different kinds for my mom, and we would eat some of it too.

I spent a lot more time fishing with her family. I would always wear my swimsuit because if my lure or anyone else's got stuck in the weeds, I would jump off and swim to go get it. I always had a pair of goggles in my tackle box. I would always catch fish, although it was always rock bass, but I didn't care. I practice catch and release, and I just like being outside. And if I catch fish, then all the better. My favorite memory was of playing with the kids in the water, especially my girlfriend's niece because she was terrified of the water.

Her mother had told her that she would sink if she ever tried to swim because black people can't swim and they will drown if they go in the water. I told her that she is as white as she is black and that everything her mom told her was complete bullshit. She was tiny, but I pushed her little ass off the end of the dock. She wore a life jacket, so she was okay, but I jumped in after her and made her tread water the best that she could. I had her swim to where she could stand up and I made her take off her life jacket to try to swim out to where she could not touch.

I have no idea why she trusted me because she did not know me from a hole in the ground, but she did. We swam out into the lake, and she did great for a first-timer. She was too young and doesn't really remember this, but I do. I credit myself with teaching her how to swim and creating her love of the water because now you can't keep her out if we are anywhere near a pool or a lake. She is now a very good swimmer, and it makes me so happy every time I see her swimming and loving it.

I had to go back to work so that happened, and it was pretty uneventful, except for getting loaded, smoking out, and the occasional titty show. I loved to drink my face off for free afterward as well. Around this time, Brown Hair came back into the picture for a month, and that was interesting. She came up to the bar and drank, and I would come out and drink with her and go smoke while I was working. However, the first time I saw her again, I told the other cook that I had to go do some shit, and we boned out. We went to my truck and went to town. She went down on me without saying a word, and it seemed like she had been practicing. We fucked like rabbits in the cab of my truck for quite a while. I have no idea how long, but it didn't matter because it was a slow day. We got done, and she headed out. When I went back into work from subzero temperatures in nothing more than jeans and a T-shirt sweating my face off, everyone knew what went down and had a laugh about it. She stayed in town for a while, and once again, there was a battle between the two over whom I wanted to be with, but I just chose to just do the damn thing with both of them.

Another year went by, and I have no idea what year that was, so I don't know what happened that year, but I know that I still played with the brownie until she moved away again. I know that Flat Tire and I would always get together with my best friend and his old lady for Halloween, Christmas, and New Year's Eve, so we did that, but otherwise, I have no idea.

Summer came, and it was time to go back up to the cabin. I did a lot more fishing and a lot more swimming as well a knee-boarding. I showed Flat Tire's nephew how to do a few tricks, and we had a good time. I remember one day golfing that was really fun; that is because it was just me and my girlfriend, no one behind us and no rush, which is awesome because we both suck. I can actually get pretty close to par most of the time, and I even got a birdie once, but I hate holding up the group if all the men go out golfing.

I like it laid-back so I can drink my beers and smoke some weed. I also started to opt out of the Mexican food night from then on because my stomach just cannot handle it. I would hook up my MP3 to some speakers and have my own little dance party to myself while they were gone, and I had a blast. I actually just freestyled the whole time, listening to hip-hop, but I could have had a dance party if I wanted to. I also played with the two boy ragamuffins that were always up there that came to get me and play with them ever since one year when I brought my pellet gun up there. They thought I was like the cool uncle or something, and I would shoot the gun with them as well as a wrist rocket that I would bring up there every year. I decided to cut them off after one day when they asked me to sneak them some beer, and I swear if those little shits ever ask me for some weed, I might have to tell their dad because I want nothing to do with that.

One day I went out with the cousins again all day, and I may have overdone it that time a little bit. We smoked a ton of weed and drank a hell of a lot, and I jumped in the lake when it got hot, but I think the sun may have been a little too much for me this day. I don't get sunburned because I am already dark, but it is kind of like wearing a black sweater in the sun. I say sweater because I am very hairy.

I got a little bit too much sun, but where I went wrong was I just laid down really early and basically was out for the night. This was not good because my body is used to having a regular intake of alcohol throughout the entire day and well into the night. When I awoke at around 3:00 AM, I felt anxious, and I could tell it was the whole withdrawal thing, so I filled up my Dixie cup with rum and grabbed a couple of beers and went to the room. I went to work and drank as fast as I could, but I was still so nervous and anxious that I was pacing back and forth in the room, which was not very big. Then I remember smelling that same smell I had smelled the last time I had an episode. I began to have flashbacks and see visions of random shit, but most memorably the Nintendo 64. I still have no idea what the significance of that is, but I know that every time I see it in my head and smell those weird smells, bad things happen. I know that I was walking around, and Flat Tire asked me what was up, and I said nothing. I grabbed the top of the bunk bed, and then I completely blacked out. I remember waking up in the living room and having no clue what the fuck was going on. I don't remember much of the rest of the time up at the cabin that year, and I think we might have even left early, but I am not sure.

I apparently stiffened up, and there was a loud cracking sound, after which I fell straight backward and landed flat on my back. I did not know it at the time, but I actually broke my back. I snapped one of my lower vertebrae in half, and now my spine is shaped like a fucking question mark. I sound like a grandpa when I sit down or stand up, and I cannot walk for very long without taking a break. The doctors suggested surgery, but that involves putting a metal plate or some shit drilled into my spine, so I said, "Fuck that." My back just hurts really badly all the time, and I have learned to live with it. I am able to get all types of pain killers but have known too many people who have died from abusing that shit, and I did not want to join that club. I will still take some and drink a bunch, but I don't do it every day.

Through hearsay and hindsight, I learned that I apparently went fucking crazy after we got home. I really do not remember shit about this, but it has been reiterated for me by my mom, my sister, and blondie; and they all said the same thing. I have no clue what I did, but apparently at one point, I threatened to kill my mother and told her that I was going to go grab my gun and shoot her in the face. They said I was very serious and pretty fucking scary. I do not own a gun and do not like guns, and I love my mother more than anything else in the world. Whoever said that shit through my body in my voice was not me; it was something else that I could not control.

I do remember them calling the goddamn police on me to take me away. I went peacefully, but as we were walking out, I remembered that I had my dugout with some really stinky weed in my pocket, and it is a felony to bring any contraband into an institution or jail. I was not put in handcuffs or anything and at that point should have realized where I was going. I was not going to jail because I really didn't do anything illegal besides terroristic threats toward my mother, but they had other plans for me. I was getting hauled off to the crazy house again, and I remember one more thing. I said to wait one second, and I took my dugout and weed out of my pocket for some reason right in front of the police. I was just going to put it back in the house and go peacefully, but as I pulled it out, I made eye contact with one of the officers, and he just said, "Okay, let me have that."

In hindsight, I should have probably stepped in the house really quick and thrown it on the table, but that was not to be. The cop was cool though and didn't say shit, so I didn't get in any trouble. He just put it in his pocket and transported me to the nut house. I guarantee that my herb never made it to the evidence locker. That cop looked like a smoker, and I am sure that he smoked my weed. That's okay because I didn't get in trouble. I hope he enjoyed it. I then have no further memory of this time, but I am told that I spent another four to five days in the psych ward. It was awesome; they have such great Jell-O.

I had to get my head, belly, and back checked out basically because my mom said so, and when it comes to certain things, Mom Dukes runs the show, and you do not question her authority. If she tells me not to drink a beer at 8:00 AM, however, I am quick to ignore that. I went to the back doctor first even though I knew it was broke, and they confirmed everything that I already knew, then I went upstairs to the neurologist. This took much longer, and I had to return many times and was subject to numerous tests like CAT scans and MRIs.

My neurologist wore Crocs with socks on, so I called him Dr. Crocs in Socks; he didn't mind. He showed me a scan of my brain and was trying to explain it, and it was like trying to read brail without hands. The pictures meant exactly jack shit to me. He told me that I had epilepsy and that was the cause of the seizure and I more than likely have had previous ones but just don't remember. I could believe that because I didn't have a clue when I woke up at the cabin and there were more to come. He did not say that, but he implied it, and that was crystal clear to me. He was right. I told him everything about my history trying to find the catalyst for these seizures. I told him that I had basically been using "mind altering" drugs just about every day for the last twenty years although I had some days off in jail or the hospital. I do not consider marijuana a mind-altering drug, but it is classified as one as well as a hallucinogen. I do not agree with that one at all.

I want to know who classified it as a hallucinogen and find out where they get their weed from because it must be amazing; I have never experienced that. I explained that I had also done acid well over one hundred times; I had lost count. The same goes for mushrooms, cocaine, meth, ecstasy, special K, nitrous, GHB, as well as a rainbow of uppers and downers, pills of every sort, which I abused with copious amounts of alcohol. There were others, but sometimes they didn't even have a name. That is really dumb, and I would never do that again.

Nothing bad ever happened, and I always had a good time. But it was still stupid, and I would never do it again. He said that none of that would have anything to do with why my brain is fucked up. I said that I had never been told that before and I have had MRIs and CAT scans and the doctors didn't say anything about epilepsy and asked how I could just develop this after thirty years of being fine. He just said that sometimes it just happens but they could either cut my head open and fuck with my brain or give me a bunch of meds. I was not going to let anybody cut open my back and put shit in it, so there is no way, even if they are doctors, am I going to let anyone break into my head and play with my brain. After I found out a bit about the meds that he suggested, I agreed to take them because they were non-narcotic and not habit-forming, and I know that they are not because I forget to take them all the time, and in fact I hate taking them. My stomach had also been fucking with me for a long time.

I got my ish together and went back to work. I was just working weekend nights, so I just got fucked up the whole time…Maybe I didn't quite totally get my shit together, but I came into work every day and did my job. My conspiracy theorist cooking buddy and I would just get really stoned, and I would pound beers all day while cooking people's food. We did a great job. We just happened to be stoned ass as we were doing it.

I was working the grill and the window one night, and every time that I would put the orders up at the window, I could see this girl sitting at the bar eye-fucking me, and she would not stop. I worked the rest of my shift while she fucked me with her eyes, and I went to have my after-the-shift mug or two of beer. She happened to be sitting at my corner of the bar, so I really had no option but to sit by her. However, I had an alternate agenda because of the way she was looking at me all night. I had no other option; I walked right up to her and simply said, "You have been mind-fucking me all night… Do you want to go fuck in the parking lot or what?" There was no hesitation, and she walked out to my truck with me. I did not even know her name. I bent her over the back of my truck and went to town. I was the last car in the lot and totally visible to the street, which was always very busy. Anyone driving by could have seen me fucking the hell out of this girl over the bed of my truck, but I didn't care, and it made the experience awesome because I had come to realize that I get off on the possibility of being caught.

The bar nicknamed her Back 40 because that is what the parking lot was called for some reason. I ended up talking to her again, and she would come up to the bar and fuck me all the time. Once we even did it on the smoking porch right in front of another couple that was just sitting out there. We had no idea who they were. I went out to the patio with Back 40 and sat down to have a smoke. I poked a couple of onies, and she sat on my lap. After a minute, she was rubbing on me and grabbing my cock, so it was apparently on like donkey. She was wearing a skirt and obviously no panties, so she just stood up for a second and pulled my junk out, sat down, and rocked back and forth as we were looking right at these people and they were looking at us. It was awkward and fun. When we were done, the couple said something to us as we were walking away, but I don't remember what it was. Regardless, they were basically telling us that they watched us have sex the whole time.

I informed her from the beginning that I lived with my girlfriend and she came first no matter what. That seemed to be okay for the time being. We would go to a mutual friend's apartment and use his pool all the time. It was the same apartment building that a friend of mine lived in not long before, so I knew how to get into the pool. We would go there all the time for a couple summers. I remember one time a few friends that also worked at the bar with me came with to go swimming. The girl that came was pretty fucking cute, and I could tell that she was a little trollop. She was playing with one of the bartenders who she was apparently fucking, and he pulled the string on her bikini bottoms, so they fell off. She screamed and announced what had happened. I instantly dove in the pool and swam under her, and I remember it perfectly. I could draw it from memory. I swam up, and I could see everything, and it was nice. She was very well groomed. I returned to that pool a number of times while our friend was out of town, but we just walked right in.

I remember one time in particular where we were in the pool and a family came in. They were swimming in the deep end, and we were wading in the shallows and sitting on the stairs. She was squatting down in front of me and began to play with me. I was watching this family with children across the pool, and she was stroking my dick off like it was one of those shake weight things. It was exciting, and it was obviously doing something for her as well. She began to go to town on her pussy and even pulled her tits out. Keep in mind there was still a family on the other side of the pool that I was watching. She got pretty worked up, and I was hard up like someone with no money who just lost their job.

When we first met, I implied that she go down on me, and she said that she would never put a dick in her mouth. This day she grabbed my cock and gobbled it like a fucking popsicle. She had skills like she had been doing it her whole life. She also told me that she would never take it in the ass, but that would soon change. She turned around, pulled her bikini bottoms to the side, and jumped on my cock like it was a hot commodity. She rocked back and forth like on the porch at the bar and fucked my brains out all the while with that family swimming right there. She got off really good and started squealing. They may have noticed, but they did not say anything. It was clear that we should probably get the fuck out of dodge pretty soon, but she continued to ride me like a roller coaster until we were both finished. We packed up our shit and took off. We went back to his apartment, and as I was smoking some herb on the deck outside, she came out and started fucking with me. I ripped her clothes off and bent her over the balcony. I fucked her from behind hard, and she was basically screaming and telling me to fuck her harder. We were in clear view of anyone walking or driving by, but she still kept moaning and squeezing her tits, begging for more.

She lived in Duluth and would get hotels in the city when she would come down here. She knew I loved to swim, so she would always stay in a place with a pool and hot tub so that I would come and play. It worked. I went over all the time while the old lady was at work to go swimming, but she had other plans. We would go swimming, and I had fun. I also vaguely remember getting a couple of hand jobs in some of the hot tubs. We would go play in the hotel room and did everything. Now that she had sucked her first dick, she could not get enough and would inhale it the second she got a chance. Then all of a sudden, she was more than down to take it in the ass. In fact, she bent over and begged for it. I fucked the hell out of her ass, and she loved every second of it. Ass fucking is the best to do in hotels, especially if you have two beds because if one gets all gross, you have another bed to play on. I love ass play, but pulling out a poopy dick can be kind of a buzzkill. There is nothing like having her suck your shitty dick clean after tearing her ass up; you don't kiss them after that.

    We still hung out and would go out, and she would always buy my food and drinks, which was okay with me. She was a big Gophers fan even though she went to UMD and was primarily a Bulldogs fan. She knew I went to the U, so she bought us tickets to a U of M basketball game. Before the game, we were walking through Dinky Town on the way to the Barn to watch the game, and she said she wanted to stop at the Gopher shop to look at some clothes. When we got inside, she told me to pick out anything I wanted, and I was really confused. I found a Gophers hoodie that was neither maroon nor gold; it was all green and pretty cool. It was also expensive, but she did not seem to care, and I really liked it, so I said, "Fuck it," and let her buy it for me.

    I wore the hoodie to the game, which was somewhat awkward because the hoodie was green and we were playing the Spartans, who wear all green. Unless you looked really close, it looked like I was rooting for the wrong team. I called my buddy from the farm to brag that I was at the game and wouldn't you know it, he was at the game as well. Not only that, but he was in the same section and just a few rows in front of us. He stood up, and we waved at each other. It was kind of cool. We kept watching the game, and then I felt a hand on my leg, and I knew what was going down. I put my other hoodie that I had worn to the game on my lap to cover up what was going on, but she kept going and rubbed one out while we were watching the game. I was getting jerked off with thousands of people all around me; it was awesome.

    I kept working, and nothing too eventful happened, although I do remember one day after my shift I went out to the patio to smoke some herb, and my boss was there with some other people that were of some importance, but I did not know that. I just plopped down and drank my big-ass mug of beer and started smoking my weed like I was at a Cyprus Hill concert. Afterward, my boss pulled me aside and simply asked me nicely to keep my constant pot smoking on the low-down because he was actually having a meeting with his bosses at that time, so it didn't look very good. He just said that he had never seen me before and did not know who I was. My feelings were not hurt. It was just so nice to get busted smoking chronic at work and not get into trouble at all. I actually didn't really get busted because I knew he was there when I lit up; I just didn't care. This was also when I played fantasy football for the first time. It was like a twenty-dollar buy-in, so I said, "Fuck it," I had no idea what I was doing anyways. We did the draft at the bar, so I just got drunk as fuck and smoked out whenever I got a chance. I had no clue what to do I just knew that I at least need players for each position. I just looked all the names and picked the funniest ones. Two players I remember were Woodcock and Woodhead. They both did really good. I ended up winning second place, so I got like $200, and I was stoked. I continued to go up to the cabin, and it was pretty much the same ish every year, lots of alcohol. I smoked a lot of weed, fishing, other water sports, games, and a bunch of food.

I still hung out with Back 40, not only because she would do anything I told her to. She was also really easy to talk to. You could tell that most of her friends were boys growing up. She wanted to bring me to more games. For some reason, I guess she knew I didn't have the money to buy tickets for myself, that and the fact that I am just fine watching it on TV where I can lay down and take a piss whenever I want without crawling up a million stairs to wait in line while urine is dripping down my leg.

I do like going to big games though. It's all good as long as I don't have to drive. She brought me to a Twins game, which was pretty uneventful. Maybe we did some other shit, but I don't remember, so I don't care. The next game was a Vikings game, which was huge for me. If I had ever been to one previous to this, I was really young, and I don't remember it. I was super happy. The game was awesome and the building we saw it in no longer exists.

She got a hotel right downtown Minneapolis by the stadium, which was not a mistake; she had plans. It just so happened that it was a fucking blizzard outside, so I at least had a good excuse for why I was not coming home, but that was a close call. If she would have suggested that she would come pick me up, I would have been fucked, but it was literally a violent winter wonderland outside, and no sane person would want to drive if they did not have to.

I knew she had the room so I brought my purse with me. I had my swimsuit with me, so I jumped in the hot tub the second we got back to the spot. I went swimming after that, but I needed to warm up and relax my back because it was cold as fuck outside, and I was basically standing for the whole game, and my back was really sore; it was a good game. There was quite a bit of debauchery that occurred, and I noticed that she had gotten a room with two beds so we could make one all gross; we made good use of that. Everything on the list of dirty things you could possibly do when we were done, we went for round 2, then round 3. She was unusually loud, but I was okay with that. I knew that I was for sure in trouble, and I definitely got the third degree, but I was able to talk my way out of it.

At this time, the band of Flat Tire's brother was playing a lot of shows, and I went to a few of them with her. Somehow I managed to hook up with random girls, a few of which I later learn were much older than I had expected. I met the majority of them while smoking weed outside. Even though my old lady was right there, I would get their number and just say we should get together and smoke sometime, and it worked every time. This was the beginning of the cul-de-sac days. I would have the women come pick me up, often when my old lady was home, and we would drive down the street to a side road off the lake to smoke.

I would usually start by taking a big hit and then grabbing their head and kissing the hell out of them and blowing my smoke down their throat. It worked every time and usually ended in incredible blow jobs. The old girls really know what they are doing. They were all in the same age group, but I did not know what that was until the last one that I messed with dropped the ball. She was not a cock sucker, but it was the first time I had ever been forcefully made to titty-fuck someone, and then she gave me one of the best hand jobs I have ever had. Curiously afterward, she licked up the cum off of her hands and said that she had to get home to her daughter.

First of all, I could not understand why she would not put a dick in her mouth but she slurped up my cum off her hand like it was liquid gold. I found out how old these women I was messing with when the last one told me she had to bring her daughter to some cheerleading shit, and I asked how old she was and she said she was seventeen years old. I asked how old she was, and it was over forty. I don't remember exactly what the age was because my mind was blown, but she was much older than me. My girlfriend was gone when she picked me up but was home when she dropped me off, so I told her to drive around the block, and I ran through the neighbors' yards, so I was not seen being dropped off. It worked, but I quickly learned the reason why it is damn near impossible to cheat in Minnesota when it is wintertime, because the tracks in the snow are a dead giveaway that you had someone over and exactly what kind of person that was. I got called out for my tracks coming through the neighbor's yard. I have no idea what I said, but I talked my way out of it.

I learned my lesson when my girlfriend came home and asked me who was over that day. I was confused, but I figured that she noticed tire tracks in the driveway, so I told her that my buddy I watch *Jeopardy!* with came over to watch the game. I was fucked because she asked, "Since when does he wear size 6 women's shoes?" He is a big boy and wears size 13 in men's, so my story didn't necessarily work out. I did not get in any trouble, but I learned a very valuable life lesson. I had two other close calls on those back roads, but I was done with the cougars.

One was with Back 40 on the side road and my truck was facing the road that went around the lake. She was going down on me, and I knew I did not have much time before the old lady came home and there would be drama. Just then, as I was about to blow my load in her face, I clearly saw my girlfriend drive down the road, heading home. We were like thirty feet away, and I am so fucking lucky that she did not look down that road because I would have been fucked. The other one was a big clusterfuck of poor decisions and bad timing. It involved the brown-haired girl from junior high and Colorado. She was visiting for the holidays and came to see me at work. After a few drinks, we headed out. The blondie was at the house, so we went down the road by the lake for a ways and pulled into a cul-de-sac. Due to the fact that it was Christmas break, it was cold as fuck, and the snow was really deep. I have no idea how long we were fucking down that road, but it was clearly too long. We did everything, having sex at least two or three times, and left the music on, which was a horrible idea in retrospect. The car died, and we were fucked. My house was about a mile or so away, and the closest route was through the woods. The snow was very deep, and I was in no way dressed for the occasion. I walked back to my house because the only option outside of calling AAA or a towing company that we could get out of there. It was over 3ft. of snow cold enough to freeze your scrotum to your legs and I was stupid enough to call my old lady for help in a situation like this but I did it anyways because I am an idiot. On the other hand, it is also all too easy to get away with murder when you do it out in the open. When you sneak around you get busted eventually. However, it is so simple to lie without lying; you just need to leave out a few crucial facts and make sure that everything you do say is true, if you didn't lie and just left out a few details, who gives a shit? You're innocent. Unfortunately, that only works for so long, you will be caught eventually. Contrary to popular belief it is not just the boys playing the game. Ladies are just as guilty as men. Women are just better at getting away with it and it is no secret. Not only are women slicker than men but they are smarter, they think ahead as opposed to men who typically think with the head in their pants. I went home and told my live-in girlfriend that I was parked down the road with my ex-girlfriend to smoke some herb and the car died. These two hated each other, so it was a bad idea to begin with, but I asked my girlfriend to drive out in a blizzard to jumpstart a girl's car whom she hated and had caught me in the act of having sex more than once. She brought me to the car, and we got it started. The brownie left, and I was just glad that I still had my testicles.

 Back 40 was still around and would come over or bring me to a hotel quite often. I can't imagine driving back and forth to Duluth every week, fuck that. I know why she did it; she knew that I would come over every time if I could get away with it, and there was a nice pool at the hotel. This way, she would inevitably get me naked at some point, and she would have her way with me. I continued fucking her in the ass because she became increasingly fond of it. At one point, she mentioned that she would want to be in both holes at the same time. I told her to grab her dilly stick because I guess I just assumed that all women had dildos. Everyone that I have ever known has had one and was quite skilled at using it, sometimes putting on a show.

I asked her if she wanted to go to Sex World and get her one, and she had no idea what it was. It is a porno warehouse in downtown Minneapolis where we used to go to get nitrous to do whip-its and kill what was left of our brain cells. The last time I had been there was with the guy who played the little boy Brian on *ALF*. It was a random situation, but my roommate's sister had met up with him in California and actually got married. We got along really well, and he stayed over one night. There is no other way to say it, but this kid really liked his drugs. I was hanging out with my girlfriend from high school, and she pretty much slept at my house every night, so she hung out with us the night that we hung out. That was okay because she drove. He wanted to find some heroin, and I told him that was a request out of my capabilities. I told him I could point him in the right direction but I do not fuck with that shit so I could not really help.

We were hanging out, drinking and smoking weed, and he kept mentioning the H, and I came up with an idea. He was also ranting about wanting to have White Castle because they do not have those on the west coast. I remember the first time I went to Cali I had to stop at a Jack in the Box because I remembered it from *Menace II Society* growing up, and we do not have them in Minnesota. I decided that if this kid / TV star wanted to find heroin, Minneapolis was the place to go. I planned out a route so we could stop at a White Castle on the way downtown, and then I suggested going to Sex World because there is always seedy characters around that neighborhood, and one of them is bound to have some black tar or something. If not, we could grab some whip-its and get stupid. We went to White Castle, and the ALF boy looked like a kid in a candy store. We took some pictures of him and me in front of the White Castle sign, drinking Heineken and eating sliders. We went to the porno store, and no bullshit, within two minutes, he was approached by a guy selling black tar heroin. What are the odds? He got pretty fucking lucky, so we just looked at some porn, grabbed some nitrous oxide, and dipped out. I did not touch that dirty drug, fuck that.

 I got a little off track there, but the next time I went to the sex store was with Back 40. She wanted to get fucked in both holes at once, so we went to go get her a dildo because I was not going to slap balls with another dude as we fuck her; I don't play that game. We went to Sex World and looked around for a while and found her something nice that put me to shame. It vibrated, pulsated, had these beads inside that rotated around, and it also twirled around in a way that no human penis could ever possibly match; it was not fair. It was cool with me though because I would just watch the show and then they always want the real thing, so I would always get mine.

 She wanted to get me something for some reason, and I said I didn't care because all the movies are like forty dollars for crap and the rest is like pocket pussies, which I did not really have any interest in. She ended up buying one that had a pussy and an asshole. I did not think I would ever use it, but I wore that shit out like a pair of socks; it did not last very long. She left the merchandise at the counter and wanted to go watch the strippers and see what was in the booby room.

 There was just a bunch of hookers dancing and rubbing their pussies on stage. I was not really impressed. She paid to get me some dances, so I guess that was cool. There were booths where you could watch pornos, and she wanted to go in there. She had a stripper's stack of ones, so she kept feeding the machine and was really into the porn. She got horny as fuck and basically forced me to fuck her brains out. Apparently, she was not wearing underwear, which is always classy. She braced herself against the wall and demanded that I fuck her really hard from behind and do whatever the hell I wanted. I fucked the hell out of her in a porno booth at a sex shop, which would probably glow in the dark if you brought a black light in there. It was probably covered in jizz, and that is gross, but we did it. We also got busted. Luckily, it was after we had both finished, but we were politely informed that there is not to be more than one person in the jack-off booth at a time. We said okay, grabbed the dildo and rubber pussy/asshole combination, and hit the road. That was fun.

One day after I got off work, she decided that she wanted to fulfill her dream of being filled in every orifice. At one point, she wanted to do two at once. We went to a local Frisbee golf course and just plopped down on the ninth hole, which was completely out in the open; we could not have been more conspicuous. She got ass naked in the middle of the fairway and went down on me like my dick was on fire, and she wanted to put it out. She wasted no time. She sucked my cock off for a while, and then she turned around and presented putting her ass up in the air, begging me to fuck her in the ass. I am an understanding person, so I was willing to help her out in this situation. I took care of that ass like we were in a porno. She flipped over and wanted to try her new toy; this was a first for me. So I had her on her back and was fucking her ass as she was stabbing her love canal with a vibrating, twisting crazy rubber cock. I could feel it vibrating on my business through the other side, and it was actually pretty nice; I liked it. I have never heard anyone cum so loud in my life; it echoed throughout the whole Frisbee golf course. I had to ask her if her orgasm was vaginal or anal, and she said it was a little bit of both, but I had never heard her squeal like that before. We were so far out in a very wide open area, but we could still see the street and parking lot, so anyone could have rolled up on us at any point in time on that night. She instantly developed a love for that dildo and loved to use it, putting on shows and whatnot.

I spent more time with my roommate/girlfriend. We would go to shows even though most of them were not her cup of tea, but I had a good time. We saw a lot of people, especially at sound set. Every year, we would also go up north every fall, basically to look at leaves changing color, which sounds really stupid, but it is actually really beautiful up there by Lake Superior. We would usually stay in Duluth, but we went to other places up north as well. I remember one time we went to the spot where the Mississippi River begins, and you can basically just step over it. I really wanted to do this just to say that I had done it, but when we got there, a whole busload of little shits were on a field trip and all over the place. We had to leave because I was getting increasingly anxious and the possibility of me acting a fool was growing, and I didn't want to get arrested for assaulting little children. I pouted and made a big stink about it until we had to leave and basically would not shut up until Flat Tire brought me back there and I got to step over the Mississippi. I was very happy, and I am still glad I got to do it and can say that I did.

I was doing some renovation on the house and had to go get some doors to replace the broken-ass ones that were in the house. I got new doors, but right after that, my shit box of a truck broke down, and I had to get it towed back to the house. However, I did like that truck for a couple of reasons. First of all, it was my dad's truck, and he absolutely loved it, so it had some sentimental value because it would remind me of him when I would drive it. I also made it my own because when he gave it to me it was really ugly. It was two-tone with red stripes on it, and that just had to go before I could drive it. I stripped it and repainted it so it felt like my own truck, and I put a very loud stereo system in with big woofers so it sounded like mine as well. I had to junk the truck, so I took everything out that I had put into it and donated it to charity. I needed a car, but I was only working the weekends at this point, so my roommate would give me a ride and pick me up whenever I worked. That was cool because I could drink a lot more after my shift and not worry about driving down the most police-infested road in the Twin Cities.

The girl from Duluth noticed that I had no truck anymore and asked what I was going to do for transportation. You basically cannot survive in Minnesota without a vehicle. Public transportation is a joke and even if you find your closest stop to get picked up, you will still be walking at least a mile or two in the snow and freezing cold to get there and wait while you freeze to death only to be late to work and lose your job. I told her that I had no idea what I was going to do but I didn't have much money for a new car, and besides that, I only buy old shit boxes for cheap because then if anything happens to it I can just throw it away without too much loss. She told me that she was about to buy a new car and that she could probably sell me her old one for cheap once she found her new car. She found a new car and offered to sell me her '98 Rav4, which still started and ran just fine for only $200. I jumped at the chance to get a car for so cheap because I couldn't go wrong. It had a lot of miles, but it ran fine. I didn't care that it was red, but I had to do something about it. I wasn't going to put more money into painting this piece of shit than I did for the actual car, so I came up with a cheap solution. I was bitching about the fact that it was red, and someone pointed out that it was really maroon. I knew what I had to do. The colors of my alma mater are maroon and gold, so I was halfway there. I decided to turn the Rav4 into the Go4. I found a bunch of big decals of the University of Minnesota's emblem. I had big Gopher M on either side of the vehicle, as well as a giant M on the hood and a U of M tire cover on the spare tire. I didn't bother to put my stereo in this car because it was worth more than the car, and if the car got stolen, I would have probably been more upset about losing my speakers.

I talked to Back 40 all the time because she was fun to talk to. Once again, I attribute this to the fact that all her friends are men and she is basically one of the guys. The guy who loves to suck dicks and take it up the ass, I might as well have been talking to a gay man. She knew about my roommate, and I had told her that I love her and that we would more than likely be getting married at some point because she had told me very bluntly that I was hers and she was not going to go anywhere. She knew that I had a girlfriend when I met her but that she had kind of moved in on the brownie's territory and claimed me for herself.

I have taken enough psychology courses and spent enough time with women to know what was going on in this bitch's head. She figured that if it happened once it can happen again, and possibly she could fuck up shit between my girlfriend and I and step up to the plate and be my new girlfriend. She went about this in a really shitty way. She basically started out by threatening to straight up tell my girlfriend that I was fucking her. I was terrified, and I knew I was down but not out. I told my girlfriend when I got home that there was a crazy bitch at work that thought I was having an affair with her, but I was not. It was a really crappy story, but she let it slide even though I think she knew there was some truth to it. I kept messing with that stupid bitch because I am a moron and she gave really good head any time of day. She would drop anything she was doing, maybe not a baby, but she would stop whatever she was doing and go to town, and she was really good.

One day, she was all horny or something when I got off work because she was over me like stink on shit. I don't really like that metaphor, but she wouldn't leave me alone. I told her that I had plans with my old lady and I was going home to watch a movie. She would still not let me be, so I slammed my beer so I could get out of there. I slammed one more because they were free but I wanted to get the fuck out of Dodge. She was plowed, and when I went out to my car, her old car, she would not let me leave. She got in between me and the door and wouldn't budge. She said she wouldn't let me leave until I fucked her in the parking lot. I was not about to play along because I had plans with my girlfriend and the last thing I needed was for her to smell another girl's pussy on my cock. She did not fuck around. If she was concerned or thought I was up to something, she would demand to smell my dick, no joke. Luckily, I would usually take a quick whore's bath at the sink before going home if I was up to no good, but I did not want to risk it this time. I also just wanted to relax on my couch and see the movie even though I cannot remember what movie that was. She would not get the fuck out of my way and was demanding that I hand over the keys to her car. I said, "Are you fucking high? You sold me this car, and I have my name on the title to prove it, so take me to court if you want just get the fuck out of my way."

She would not budge and was really starting to piss me off. I have never punched a female before, but I was seriously contemplating it. After way too long, I had enough and was ready to body that bitch. I took the keys and held them so there was one key pointing out through each of the spaces between my fingers. I was like a very ghetto makeshift version of Wolverine. They were sturdy, and if I would have punched her in the cheek, I would have made three holes right through her face. I started to get butterflies in my belly like what happens just before you get in a fight and are squaring up with the other guy. I was really going to punch the shit out of this girl if she did not move. She saw the keys in my hand and that I had a clinched fist and got the picture. She was literally two seconds away from getting her cheeks pierced, and then I would have gone to jail. I thought this through, but I just really wanted to punch her badly over and over again. Looking back, I am glad that she moved. Nothing happened, and I don't have that on my record because it would have been a really serious assault, and I surely would have spent quite a while behind bars. She was so drunk she did not even remember this afterward.

My mom had a conference in Phoenix and brought my sister and I along so we could go see my dad's dad, who lived a ways outside of the city, but it was nice, lots of stars. You don't see that in the cities back home, but it was even better than up north. We stayed in Phoenix for a day, and while my mom was doing the work thing, my sister and I walked all around the city. The first thing on the list was to go pound a few beers. After I was done with that, I asked my sister what she would like to do, and I have no idea if she even said anything because she is the most indecisive person I have ever met. I think we just walked around, and I would stop here and there to pound a beer. I suggested that we go to the science museum, mostly because one time when we stopped, I could see the building behind my sister's head. We went, and it was really nice, but that shit is really expensive. I just wanted to learn. I could have bought a good amount of stinky weed for the price of a ticket. I had some more drinks, and then we took off for Grandpa's house, which was basically a trailer there were no houses like in Minnesota, and no one had a basement.

As we drove to my grandpa's house, the three of us were just talking about God-knows-what when we all saw some weird shit in the sky. There was some sort of craft flying above the car. It was dark, which made it stand out even more because it had multiple colored lights on the perimeter of the craft. It was in the shape of a triangle and not really moving very fast for an aircraft. It was basically hovering above and going the same speed as the car. Any commercial aircraft traveling at that speed would drop to earth like a stone, but this thing was just hanging out and clearly had the ability to basically stop and hover in midair without any forward momentum. Humans do not have that technology or at least the government does not tell us about it. Hovering is a possibility and has been experimented with for decades. Even Hitler built a craft nicknamed the Bell, which was able to accomplish this, but nothing has ever been able to do what this thing did next. It was still just above us maybe a little bit in front, but if it was moving, it was going really slow until all of a sudden it took off like a bat out of hell. Not like fighter jet balls to the wall but more like some *Star Wars* or *Star Trek* light speed kind of shit. This thing flew straight away from us in the same direction and did not change direction at all, yet it disappeared in less than one second. We were in the middle of the desert, so that fucking thing traveled really goddamn far in the blink of an eye. If it were just me driving, I would have written it off to me doing too much acid and things of that nature back in the day, and maybe I was having a flashback. The only thing that lets me accept the fact that I had really seen that is that my sister and more importantly my mom both described the exact same thing as me and told me I was not crazy.

That experience was crazy though, but no one got abducted, so it's all good, and I'm glad that I got to see it. It was hot as fuck but nothing compared to the next time I went down there. My grandpa was turning ninety-five years old, and my dad's whole family bought plane tickets to meet up and have a family reunion / "happy ninety-fifth birthday" party for him. About a week or maybe less before we were supposed to meet up down there, he died. We had to make a big change of plans because everyone had already purchased their plane tickets and gotten their hotels set up, so we knew we would no longer be going down for a birthday. Now we would be going for a funeral service.

We went down there, and this was the hottest shit I had ever experienced. It was 114 degrees. That is temperature not the heat index, which is like two hundred degrees in Minnesota. They say that it is a dry heat, and that is nothing but bullshit. It was just flat-out hot as fuck. Minnesota is really fucking humid because there is standing water everywhere you look, but it is often colder than Alaska in Minnesota at certain times of the year. I love being outside all the time, which is maybe why I am darker than the average bear in Minnesota, but 114 degrees is re-goddamn-diculous.

We did not see any crazy spaceships on this trip which kind of disappointed me, but whatever. We stayed at a motel a ways down the highway because the house was full with the first responders that were lucky enough to live on the west coast where they could just drive over and they didn't need to put up with massive snowstorms, which held us back all the time. All they have to put up with in California is massive floods, wildfires that last all summer, and devastating earthquakes. Spoiled-ass motherfuckers.

I know that is my family, but eight months out of the year, I wish I lived there and I am jealous, but I would never want to live in the desert no matter how beautiful it is. The reality of how hot it was down there became clear when my sister and I went to the pool at the motel. We had to walk across the parking lot to get there, and I walked there barefoot mostly because I walk barefoot all the time, but I only had one pair of shoes besides the ones for the service, and I did not want to fuck them up. It was nowhere near high noon. In fact, it was after sunset, but it was still hot as hell. The pavement felt like it was burning my feet. I figured that it was no big deal because I walk barefoot through the snow all the time, but I was wrong. The parking lot did burn my feet. They were covered with asphalt, which burned the bottoms of my feet, and it hurt like hell. That being said, I had a good amount of beer in me, and there was a pool nearby, so I was happy enough and jumped in. I dipped my feet in the pool before we headed back to the room and ran back. This had little to no impact on the damage to my feet. When I got back to the room, it was like I had asphalt insoles plastered to the bottom of my feet, and it hurt like hell. I had to wash them off forever, and I got most of it off, including some of my skin. It was kind of gross and didn't smell very good. My mom actually bought me an eighteen-pack of beer that night because I didn't want to go to the store; I was blown away. What amazed me more is that she didn't smack the shit out of me the next day on the day of the service when I told her I did not want to go to breakfast and that I was going to stay in the room and drink beer instead.

We went to the service, and it was just as I had expected, depressing, sad, and hot as fuck. What the fuck is the deal with churches in the South? They have no air-conditioning even though it is hot enough to cook an egg on the sidewalk outside. There is air-conditioning at the churches in Minnesota even though it is around or below freezing for the majority of the year. I dressed properly and even wore a bolo tie, which I think is ugly as fuck. My grandpa wore them all the time, so I thought it would be somewhat of a tribute to the fallen. The tie actually belonged to him, and he then passed it on to my father.

When I arrived at the service, my dad's brothers had one of my grandpa's other bow-low ties for me to wear because they probably thought I was going to show up in a hoodie and baseball cap turned to the side. That is how I dress, but I know how to be respectful when it is necessary. They were blown away that I was wearing the tie because all the brothers and in fact every man there was wearing one. No one had told me that this was to be the theme of the service, so they were really surprised that I wore one on my own without anyone telling me to do so.

The service sucked as do they all. There was a lot of singing, which I do not partake in because my voice is so deep it carries very well, and I am pretty sure that I do not have an even decent singing voice whatsoever. However, my cousin who was right behind me has an amazing voice and was very vocal. She was belting out like the fat lady at the end of an opera, and she was really good, but it was kind of annoying. She was obviously very proud of herself and her voice as well. She should be, but it was the fact that it was directly in my ear and very loud. I let that go because she had a great voice.

During the ceremony part of the service where they put his ashes in a wall next to his wife, I had a little eagle on my leg. This eagle contained the ashes of my father, and it was really little, so I thought I would bring it with so that my dad could be there in spirit. I don't really believe in that shit, but it is the thought that counts. I was sitting next to one of his brothers and pointed out the bald eagle on my leg; he did not understand. I guess my dad never expressed his fetish for bald eagles to his brother, but I explained the situation and told him that his brother was there with us. I made a grown man cry. Every man in the family was wearing sunglasses, and I am positive that it was to hide the fact that they were crying because that is how my family is on both sides. No one ever shows emotion or talks about anything that is hard to talk about; it just gets swept under the rug and ignored. However, I could see through the tears falling from under his sunglasses a slight smile, and there was a moment of bittersweet happiness.

    We took pictures with the family afterward, which seemed awkward to me because we were not celebrating anything but the polar opposite. I know people say not to look at a funeral or service as a loss but as a celebration of that person's life. Fuck that, it is sad no matter what. You can remember all the good times, and that is great, but then you have to remember that it will never ever happen again. I just don't know how you can look on the bright side unless they were like 120 years old, and everybody was just wondering why they weren't dead yet. Then it is probably a blessing as they say. If I ever can't wipe my own ass, I want to be shot in the face. My sister broke down, and it was just like after my dad's service, but I was not in the same boat. We only saw him every few years if that and not for very long, so I was not as close to him as my grandpa on my mom's side, plus I had not been around as long as her, so she probably had more memories of him than I did. I am also pretty positive that she was thinking of our dad throughout the whole thing. I was straight-faced, so I figured I should console her, so I gave her a hug and rubbed her head, telling her to shut the fuck up and relax. That is not a joke. That is verbatim exactly what I said because that is who I am and that is how I talk. I held her, and it was like her emotions punched me in the chest, and I started crying like a baby.

    My mom got into it, and we cried it all out, which was good because the shittiest part of the trip was coming up. We all had to go back to his house and more or less dig through all his things and everyone would pick out what they wanted. I wanted to throw up. It was sad enough that he was gone, but now we were going to raid his house and take everything. It seemed really morbid and kind of fucked up to me. I did not want any part of it and just sat in the sun until my sister explained that anything that we don't take will end up being donated to charity (joke). Well, I couldn't let the less fortunate get this stuff, so I looked through some of it.

There was a pocket watch that he apparently said that he wanted me to have when he died. This really caught me off guard, but it was really cool. The only thing I wanted was the picture with my dad in it where he looks exactly like me or vice versa, whatever. I got other shit, too, but I didn't ravage the place like everyone else. The rest of that side of the family was a lot closer to him, then we were probably because they lived half of the country closer to him and saw him more frequently. I figured they should have first dibs on whatever they wanted. I didn't want any material things, which might be of great monetary value. I just wanted the two things that would remind me of and make me feel close to my father and grandfather even though they were gone.

I had continued to talk to my ex-girlfriend who now lived in NYC, and we would have really dirty phone sex quite often. She had talked dirty to me in the past, but that was while we were fucking. I had never done the phone sex thing before, but she seemed very skilled and experienced in the art of talking like a dirty slut. I almost got caught a few times, but one time was a little too close for comfort but ended up being a good experience. My girlfriend was asleep when she started talking dirty. My voice carries very well, and I would be busted in a heartbeat if I tried to do that shit in the house with my girlfriend down the hall. I went out to the garage so as not to be heard; I had all the lights off so I thought I was in the clear. We talked or mutually masturbated whatever you want to call it for around an hour when I heard a knock at the garage door. My heart dropped, but it brought about the same excitement of being caught but not to the same degree because all I was doing was sitting in the garage with my dick in my hand.

I have had many close calls in similar situations, and I have been busted a time or two or three, but who is counting anyways? For some reason, when a woman catches you in the act of cheating on them, they turn into Wonder Woman and punch you in the face. One time, I lucked out because I was able to avoid all the drama, but the whole experience was scary as hell. In hindsight, it does make for a good story, so I guess it was worth it. I had one of my regular "naked friends" over for some good old-fashioned dirty sex. I knew that another "naked friend" was going to come over to play later, but she said she would call first. I told the first one that this could happen at any moment, and she would have to get out fast. I was not planning on her calling when she was about two blocks away. That was a really shitty fucked-up warning call if you ask me because I had absolutely no time to get out of this safely. Even worse, this girl in my room was butt naked, because we were in the beginning stages of a freak fest, and she was practically sucking my dick off so I had a boner hard enough to shatter a car window.

    I used the age-old technique of tucking your dick upward in between your belly and your belt. I needed to hide the naked girl in my room and convince my wiener to stop being rock hard before taking care of the other girl as quickly as possible. I told the naked girl that the girl coming over was a fucking nut job and that she would probably kill her if she saw her naked in my room. I told her to hide in my closet for a second and I would take care of the other one. To her, I think it sounded like I would be getting her out of the house, but I really meant I was going to take care of her because I knew that is what she came over for. I got the naked one, who had an amazing rack by the way, into the closet and went to the living room to meet the other one before she got inside. I was too late. She had already come in as I walked down the hall and cut me off, grabbed me, and pushed me into my room and onto my bed, where she proceeded to force-fuck me.

    It was very memorable for two reasons. First of all, I got her off three fucking times before I even had a thought of busting a nut. Second, there was a naked girl hiding in my closet who was most likely terrified and scared for her life because the crazy girl that was fucking my brains out would kill her. I was correct, and it was clear what old batshit crazy bitch came over to do. There was nothing else on her agenda. I gave her what she wanted, and she jumped up, said she had plans, and boned out. I was okay with that even though she came three times so fast I didn't even get a chance to get close to getting off once. Then I remembered the naked girl in the closet who was probably shaking like a wet dog and thought she was going to die. I made sure that the crazy one had left, and I rescued the poor naked girl from my closet. That is funny because they are both crazy. What happened next caught me completely off guard, but it was all right with me. I expected a much different reaction than what I received. I do not know if it was that she got off on hearing me fuck someone else and the sounds of her screaming for more. I have a feeling that it might have just made her really horny, and she was very quietly rubbing one out in the closet, at least that is how I like to remember it.

I got tackled again, except this time the woman who raped me came charging at me out of a closet, and she was literally dripping wet. I could see her juices were running down her legs, and she clearly knew what she wanted and she wanted it bad. She was going to get it no matter what. I must have put on a good show for her because from the way she was acting, she wanted to upstage the previous client. I know she got off at least two times, maybe three, but once my work was done, she went down on me, and I blessed her with one of the biggest loads I have ever produced. You know it is a lot of jizz when you cum and it is so much that she gargles and chokes on it.

My cousin who sang the churchy songs like it was a job right into my ear at our grandpa's funeral service had landed a position as an understudy in the Broadway play *Cinderella* and was living in New York. She was getting married, so we all went to attend, but I think my mom just wanted to travel for pleasure for once instead of flying around the country and never leaving the airport because the conference was at the Airport Hyatt. I never know where she is. One time I called her for a ride home, and she was in fucking Russia, which was news to me, but it was nothing new to me. She did that shit all the time, but it is okay because she brought my sister and me to NYC for the wedding and also to see all the shit you are supposed to see when you are there.

We weren't there all that long, and there is way too much shit to try and see it all in a week, and we weren't even there that long. We did see a lot of the staples; however, there were no more twin towers, and the new World Trade Center was not completed yet. We went to the Empire State Building, but the line to go to the top was long as fuck because it was a really nice day, but I couldn't give a shit less. I told what was left of the family that I would be at whatever bar was close to meet me there when they were done. I did not find a close bar right away, so I grabbed some booze and walked around the streets of NYC, drinking my face off with my good buddy Jack (whiskey). They clearly did not want to leave me alone because they hunted me down and did not even go up the building either; they could not watch me forever.

I had one primary objective, first and foremost before anything else and just like every other time I have traveled out of state since 9/11. I have had to find my weed in new areas, sometimes from sketchy characters. I can always find it when I am out of town, and it always works out, but I prefer my buddy in town who will come over to my house within minutes. I answer the door in my pajamas, and he sells me a bag for a good price (he is a very honest person). Then I listen to some music and watch some animal documentaries with the sound off and smoke a bunch of chronic. It doesn't get any better than that. He is a good friend.

I have been friends with everyone I have gotten cheebah from in the past, but it was not really the same because my buddy was a neighborhood kid from back in the day, and he has always lived down the street so he could be there in a heartbeat (freestyle). I am really fucking high right now, and I might have drunk around ten too many beers beyond drunk, but I am okay. I think my train of thought may have ran off the tracks and crashed in a clusterfuck of too many ideas in my head at one time just then. There is no rhyme or reason to whatever it is I am typing here. I just get really high and drink a lot of beer every night and just freestyle. I write off the top of the head. I have no outline or notes; it just flows.

In hindsight, I realize that this is a horrible approach to writing something if it is going to be this long. I did not know it was going to end up like this. My friend with the hanging earring simply asked me to write down a few of the stories I tell him all the time so I don't forget them and he wanted to read them again. I figured I would type him two to three pages, maybe five, but all these true stories kept on coming to mind, so I just continued typing and staying up till like 8:00 AM, drinking and smoking my face off. If I ever decide to write something again, I will have a very thorough outline and plans for everything before I start.

I wasn't joking. I am stoned ass right now, and I got a little distracted, so I guess I let my mind wander a bit. I was in NYC before I trailed off and my parents (my mom and sister) did not trust me and for good reason, but still I did whatever the fuck I wanted. I understand the protective parental point of view, and it is perfectly understandable for my mom to be concerned if I were to walk around in NYC at night by myself. Well, I did it anyways. We were only there for three nights, so I had to make the best of it. My parents were watching TV. It was not that late, and we were in fucking New York City, and I was going to make the most of it. I just got ready and grabbed all my supplies, and you always have to make sure you have the cell phone, so I dipped out. I just said, "See you later," and I walked out the door. I think they may have said or asked me something, but I didn't care; I was going out regardless.

I had been out in big cities all night in many different states as well as countries, so I was not concerned. Manhattan is really a lot like fucking Disney World because there is absolutely nothing scary about it with muggers and all the shit; they show on the news nonstop. I walked all over hell, but the first order of business was to get some strong drink. I can sniff out a party store like a bloodhound, so I found what I wanted in no time. I grabbed a pint of Jack Daniel's and hit Times Square.

I called the boy-girl and talked to him for a while as I was walking around, drunk as fuck, and I did not have a worry in the world. Nothing happened. I had planned ahead and had a bag waiting for me, so I talked to my old girlfriend and set up a time and place to meet the next day. She lived in Brooklyn, so unless I wanted to spend all the money on a cab, I had to take the subway to go see her and ultimately weed some grass.

I was pretty confused with the subway system and was not too sure about it, which she could tell over the phone, so she said she would meet me in Manhattan and bring me back to the BK. I have ridden many subways in many different cities, but I really did not want to get lost here because the wedding was the next day and my mom would have killed me if I disappeared. I met her at some bar downtown, and we had a drink before heading to Brooklyn.

We were going to a bar/coffee shop or whatever it was where she was doing an art show and selling some of her work. We took the subway, which I was taking mental notes of the entire time because I wanted to make sure I could make it back to my parents without getting in trouble. We went and had drinks and checked out her show, and I finally got a taste of some stinky herb, which was such a relief. I was quite a ways away, and I said I did not want to take the subway home in the middle of the night. I was not scared; that was bullshit. I just missed her and wanted to play. We drank a bunch, and I got really stony. It is amazing how high you can get if you just take a couple days off from smoking. I have known this for a while, but I still prefer to smoke every day, which works for me.

We went back to her apartment and bullshitted for a while and smoked some more herb until inevitably we started making out like we were fucking teenagers. I remember everything about that night in great detail even though I was loaded and high as hell. It was like we were eighteen years old and back in Colorado when we first started messing around. After a while, it gets a little hazy, but I know she got her rocks off because she passed the fuck out right away, which was okay because I knew I would hit her up in the morning before I left. I did, and I definitely remember every second of that. I got her off again, which was easy because I knew how to push all her buttons and they were easy to find.

Now that I had satisfied her about half a dozen times within eight hours, it was time to look out for number one. I almost fucked up because I started thinking too much. I was thinking that I had better bust a nut so I can say I have done that in New York, but over the years, I have learned that when you start thinking, you fail. When I was a teenager, I would just focus on the girl. Tits, ass, and pussy were all that was on my mind, and I had no problem cuming, but I always made sure I got them off. The awesome part is that I would have a smoke or something, and then I was all types of ready for round 2, then 3, and so on.

My twenties were just about the same, except there were a lot more victims on my hit list. Now I have found that I just need to go into a Zen-like state of mind and be void of any thoughts or problems happen. I do not have ED or anything like that. The wang is always ready to go until the job is done, but usually I realize that I am not going to finish, so I will let her have another one or two, and then I am just not into it anymore, so that is the end. That is how I knew that I was getting old.

When I was twelve years old, I would have cum in my pants if I got to touch a boob or, even better, the long-sought-after vagina. Now I can have big tits in my face and a girl riding me telling me to fuck her harder, and I might notice that it is time for *The Simpsons* or *Jeopardy!* and now I will just finish her off then go watch my program. I was not going to let this happen. I wanted to cum in as many countries and states as I could, so I went to my happy place and just had fun. I exploded in a big way. This was most likely partially due to the fact that we had not been together in quite a while. It was amazing, and I remember shaking and having to chill out for a while before I could even stand up.

She had to go to work or something, so I had her escort me to the correct subway line to get to where I needed to go. She told me the route, and I had made a transfer, but as long as I knew what letter the route was on, I was golden. It was not my first rodeo, and I actually like taking the subway when I am in new cities; however, if I lived there and had to take it every day, I can guarantee I would hate it. I found my way back just fine and felt like I was a big boy! When I got back to the hotel, I think my parents were a little upset with me, but I did not give a fuck because it was truly worth it. We went around and looked at some more random shit that you are supposed to see when you are in the NYC. I have no reelection because I only slept for an hour or two and I was still fucked up. The wedding was not far away, so we had to get ready and I had no idea what I was in for. I will only go to church for a funeral or wedding, but I can't stand that shit. It makes me uncomfortable; maybe that is because I am the antichrist.

I don't really remember the wedding, but I know that it was very churchy and not my style. However, there was one aspect of it that was right up my alley. There was an open bar, and I can still see the look on my mom's face when they announced that and how she looked at me. The look simply said, "Don't even think about it." It was too late; I had already thought about it and knew what I was going to drink and I had a couple of cigars with plenty of really good weed mixed in.

It was an open bar, so I wanted copious amount of strong drink. I was drinking Wild Turkey on the rocks when I ran into my dad's brother. He asked me what I was drinking, and I told him, and to which he replied, "No shit, I am drinking the same thing." His was mixed with soda, but I know that I can't expect everyone to be as hardcore as me. Between me and my uncle, we killed that bottle and then some more random shit, but I really don't remember what. I am not very close to my dad's side of the family, so I did not do a lot of schmoozing, but I made sure to congratulate my cousin and her new husband before I got too drunk. I made it just in time because shortly afterward the bar closed, and I was well beyond a state of severe inebriation. The party was shutting down, so I went outside and said that I was going to have a smoke and wait for my mom and my sister to come meet me and catch a cab.

I sat down against the wall outside the place and smoked some herb and a cigar. They took forever, and I basically fell asleep on the curb, and aside from my wardrobe, I probably looked homeless. I was obviously drunk off my ass, and now I was really stoned, so I just took a little nap on the sidewalk of NYC. What's wrong with that? My mom didn't think it was very cool, but I didn't care. While I was smoking, I talked to my Brooklyn friend, and she wanted to get together. One of her roommates from Seattle was in town, and they both wanted to hang out. I saw pornographic possibilities for that night. I told the parents to let me know if my phone rang in case I did not notice; I was fucking plowed and kind of did a face plant the second we got back to our room. I can only assume that I started snoring within seconds, but I know for sure that they made no attempt to wake me. They got me in trouble, fucking jerks; they did that shit on purpose because they did not want my drunk ass wandering around the city again. I would have been fine, but that was my last chance to see my friend, and I missed out on that and managed to piss her off at the same time. This was fucked up even because seven years later I have still not seen her since Brooklyn. We talked for a while after I returned to Minnesota and still did the phone sex thing, but I began to think that she had a man-toy out there, which I suspected while I was out there, but it didn't change anything. One day out of nowhere, she just said that she thought we should not talk anymore, and I was positive it was because of some new guy in her life. I took her very seriously. I hung up, and I never called her again.

    Back at home, after I returned to my house with my roommate/girlfriend, everything returned to normal. I continued to work at the bar up the street and have random indiscretions, but I was beginning to stop being how I have been my entire life. Even when I was out with her and some other girls at the strip club, after the bar and I saw her looking at my junk and grabbed her hand and put it on it, and even though she had huge tits and was a freak, I did nothing to seal the deal. I saw the look on her face, and I could have pulled it off. However, I was beginning to get sick of all the sneaking around and then the guilt afterward (sometimes), so I did not. She had been bugging me for some time now that she wanted to get married and it is all her friends' fault because if they were not all married with children and she was not the last one, it would not have been a big deal.

    Women are mentally challenged that way. I would say *retarded*, but that is a bad word. After a while of realizing as well as verbally hearing directly from her that she was not going anywhere, I figured that I would think about it. I realized that although we met through sexual relations and maintained that as the main reason that we got together for years in the beginning, she had begun to grow on me, and we had a good time together. It was no longer about sex every time we saw each other because she was always right there; it was a very different scene. Having separate bedrooms probably helped with that, but I would change that for the world. It is so nice to have a bed all to yourself sometimes.

In addition to taking trips up north and spending a week together with her family every year at her cabin, we just actually talked more and really actually get along. I say *actually* because we are polar fucking opposites and do not really have anything in common. I like a lot of her music because she is old and I heard a lot of it from my sister while growing up, but she does not like the majority of what I listen to. There were many other differences, but there was one thing that I noticed that I had never experienced before. She actually and genuinely cared about me and not just my penis. Even though that was all she wanted for a few years after we met, we actually became friends, and she really did care about me. She would take care of me when I got sick or had seizures and bend over backward to make me feel better, not in a sexual way. She was just very nice and took care of me.

I always joked that if I ever told her that I wanted a Denver omelet she would drive to Colorado and get me one in a heartbeat. That makes her sound stupid, but that was never what I meant by that. It simply meant that she was always looking out for me. I had way more in common with Brown Hair, but when it came down to it, she was not there for me, which became clear when she did not show up for my dad's service.

I had made up my mind, sort of, but not all the way. I decided that I would I would let her join the married old ladies club with her friends, but I was not going to say anything for sure as far as actually getting married. I figured I would tell her that if we were still together after a few more years or five that we would do it then. I knew what kind of ring she liked, which was awesome because as engagement rings go what she wanted was very simple and not expensive at all. Some of my friends have paid many thousands for theirs even to the point where one needed to get a loan to pull it off. I paid one hundred dollars, and I knew it was exactly what she wanted. It was actually very nice. This was a few months out from when I was going to "ask." I really didn't need to ask because she had made it clear that she wasn't going anywhere and I couldn't get rid of her, so I basically just needed to submit.

I had my plan, and it was good that I had time because I needed to find the perfect onion ring. Homer proposes to Marge with an onion ring on *The Simpsons*, so I figured that it was a no-brainer. I was going to do it on our birthday with an onion ring and nothing more. I must have gone to Burger King a dozen different times and just got onion rings until I found the perfect one for a real ring that was just the right size and flawless, for a fast food onion ring, I mean. I found the gem, so I wanted to preserve it; however, I learned from the other contenders I had selected throughout my search that they do not go bad. They simply get petrified because they do not mold, rot, or anything, probably because they are deep fried in nasty shit which makes it no longer organic material. I decided to spray a shellac coating on it, which I did a couple of times, and when I was done, it was shiny and sealed in a hard clear coating. I waited until our birthday, and there was nothing really going on, so I said I didn't want to go out and that we should have a bonfire, make some s'mores, and have some drinks. It was all a part of my plan. None of my friends stopped by, and it all worked out perfectly.

I wanted to ask her at exactly midnight when it is sort of both of our birthdays at the same time, so I brought out my cell phone. I always have my phone with me camping, but I keep it off to save battery. It is just for emergencies. No, you don't need to talk to anyone when you are being one with nature. However, in the case of this bonfire, my house was about fifteen feet away, and I had a landline so there was no reason for me to have my phone out there. I only mentioned that because she noticed that when around midnight I was looking at my phone every two seconds. I realized that it was to buck up or bail out, so I took a big rip off my piece of some sticky icky and slammed some beer and said, "Cannonball," like in *Caddyshack*. Just then, it turned midnight, so it was time. I have no idea what I said, but I know it was not the traditional way that you are supposed to do it, and I know that I said something stupid like a really bad joke, but I don't remember exactly what it was. Maybe I said that I was the burger king and asked if she wanted to be my queen. That would have been funny, but I really don't know what I said. I remember that I pulled out a ring box and opened it for her with only an onion ring inside. She fucking cried like she just won the lottery, and I put the onion ring on her finger.

In *The Simpsons*, Marge wants to take it off after a second because the hot oil was burning her finger, but this one was well preserved, so she had plenty of time to take pictures of herself with the onion ring on her finger and put it on Facebook within seconds. I hate Facebook. She was fucking stoked and never asked about a real ring. She had passed the final test. I kept her dangling all night until we were going to pass out and she was still busting nuts over the situation. Before we crashed, I gave her the real thing, and it was like a little girl at Christmas. I was really drunken and pretty dusted, so my recollection of anything after that does not exist. We probably fucked or something, but I have no idea. My job was done, and I could relax…for now.

I went back to work, and I did keep talking to one of the girls from the bar and mostly for one reason that I do not feel great about, but it was her idea. She loved to spend money on me. She would buy me shirts and other things that I would not buy for myself, but that were totally my style. I could not turn them down. I know that somehow psychologically she figured that she could buy me away from my girlfriend; she would do these things to try to get me alone. In addition to my free beers after work, she would buy me drinks and shots to get me to stay late and maybe play. She would also buy me beers and bottles of hard alcohol, which I was no longer supposed to drink in excess. I also got along well with her and had good conversations until she would get crazy, which inevitably happens to all women once in a while. I have learned that over the years. Not to mention the fact that she could suck a golf ball through a garden hose and would do so at the drop of a hat and would get wet in two seconds and be ready to fuck at any time anywhere.

We did actually talk about real shit a lot, and I was trying to figure out what to do for work because I did not want to work at the bar forever, and a liberal arts degree doesn't really do much. She mentioned that she noticed I was really good with math so I should do something along those lines. She suggested going to school to be a pharmacy technician, and it sounded like a good idea to me. There is a pharmacy on every street corner and a new drug coming out every other week. It was way cheaper than the university and would not take as long because I only needed an associate's degree, then I would have that as well as my bachelor's, which looks pretty good on a résumé. I enrolled in a program and began classes. However, I took them all online. This was a blessing because driving to class is always a pain in the ass (freestyle), but in Minnesota, it really sucks assholes.

I did all my classes basically the same way I have written everything here thus far—drunk, high, and very late at night into the morning. There were a few classes involving mathematics and learning prescription names which nowadays doesn't mean dick because there is always a new or better one on the market or coming out. The majority of the classes and assignments were based on ethics and laws related to prescribing medication and how to do it properly. The mathematics shit was just like high school and the classes that were all about writing essays was a fucking cake walk. It was exactly like what I am doing right now, I had nothing written down to type from aside from a couple of notes, and I would just freestyle the whole paper usually seven to ten pages; I never got less than an A.

I wrote my final thesis and paper the night it had to be turned in, and I sent it in about ten minutes before the deadline. My thesis went against everything that the course had taught; I proposed that there was an epidemic of children being misdiagnosed and overprescribed unnecessary medication in this country. Parents are way too quick to just give their children a pill rather than do some actual parenting. If a kid is always running around and playing with an active imagination, it could mean that he or she is just a child and doing the things that kids do. Why would you want to deny them of their childhood? I know from personal experience because I was a little spaz and was diagnosed with ADD at an early age; they hadn't made up ADHD yet, but I am sure they would have said that I had that as well. They put me on Ritalin, and I guess it helped me study and get my shit done, but it also made me feel cracked out like I had done a bunch of nose candy.

What do you expect when the first four letter of the medical term for the medication parents are shoving down their kids' throats is *METH*. College kids snort Ritalin and whatever else they are prescribing now to stay up all night. Some use it to stay up and get their work done, and others use it to get high because it is literally pharmaceutical speed. When I was taking it, my friends noticed a difference in me and did not like it. They said they did not like the new me because I was boring and they wanted the old me back. I stopped taking that shit, and I still graduated on the dean's list in high school and two colleges. My professor loved my paper and basically told me that I had big balls but I pulled it off. That was cool. I graduated with a 3.91 GPA, pretty fucking good if you ask me. I did good, but it was mostly ethics and writing. I didn't learn shit about pharmacy, which is what I wanted to do, but I did learn that it is a corrupt evil compilation of companies that don't give two shits about the people who are sick; they just want to keep them sick so they can keep selling them pills and taking their money.

I was still working at the bar and continued to have sex in the parking lot. I figured that if the waitresses get to go out and smoke ever five minutes, I can have some fun for a minute if there are no orders up. I lost the cook whom I worked with every day; it was always just him and I in the kitchen and we had a good time. We did not listen to the same music, but we would bring in stuff to introduce the other one to. He turned me on to some old hippie rock shit, and I turned him on to some good independent hip-hop. He was also a big conspiracy theorist, so we would talk about that shit all the time, and then he started bringing me all these burned DVDs which were all very interesting, but they also made me feel that all these conspiracy movies could be the source of his craziness.

He was cool though. We would smoke herb while we worked. I would drink, and sometimes we would go to the booby bar down the street to play pool during happy hour. I remember the first strip club I went to. I was only eighteen, so I couldn't drink, but you had to drink to be in there, so I got a soda. It was eight fucking dollars.

The nasty strip club a block away from my house gives you two cans of beer for five dollars. We would always play pool and just that; we never fucked with the girls, but if you happen to see some titties out of the corner of your eye, I had no problem with that. Sometimes if some perv would be tipping good and you could see a whole big gaping pussy show, I think we stopped and watched that, at least I know I did more than a few times. They removed the pool tables at one point to put in a VIP room, which is fucking ridiculous because in that neighborhood other than drug dealers and pimps there are no high rollers. Now that I think about it, that room is probably always packed because that is all there is around there.

We never went back there again; I have been back with girls but obviously not to play pool. We would hang out after work, and he would come to my house because it was really close and get drunken high. I went to his place once because I was hard up and he had some weed to sell, so I stopped by to grab it. I learned a lesson when I went there. People who have multiple cats are fucking crazy. I later told this theory to my cousin when he was staying with me from California, and the look on his face quickly told me that he clearly had multiple cats. I felt like an asshole, but what can you do?

So my crazy cat cook friend left the bar to work at another spot for better pay, and it was just nicer, I guess. I was not happy. They brought in some scraggly old bitch that I couldn't stand. I tried to play nice for the most part, but she was such an old nasty snatch-hole, and she bugged the shit out of me. We got into it one day because she threw the sharp knifes in dirty dishwater, which is just stupid, and I cut myself because I had always told everyone to leave those on the side. I guess she did not get the memo. I bitched her out and made her dig them out, and she never did it again. Everyone knew this rule after I yelled at my pool buddy for doing the same thing. We had already made friends, but it pissed me off, and I bitched him out too.

About half a year went by without incident, but she still bugged me when she did something and I cannot for the life of me remember what it was, but she really pissed me off. I made a big stink over something she did, and I was fed up. I told he that her food sucks, that she was worthless, and that she should just fucking leave because I could do a better job by myself. We were no longer scheduled together, and I did pretty much work by myself, but that was okay with me. I was good, too, because I was the one that made the meat and everything needed for the coney dogs that we would sell on whatever day that was, and my Coney dogs got voted best in the Twin Cities by *City Pages*. My name wasn't attached to it, just the bar, but it was still pretty cool.

One day I got a phone call, which was weird because anyone that I know would probably call my cell first. If I had to describe the man on the other line just by his voice, I would say he was some sort of Mexican hit man and he was pissed off. He said that he was the brother of the scraggly bitch I was working with and he said that he was going to stab me in the parking lot. The nasty bitch was Hispanic, so it didn't seem too farfetched, so I wasn't going to take any chances and I did not confront her. I just came into work ever time with a big fucking bowie knife on my belt, which I had sharpened the hell out of and could access in the blink of an eye. Nothing ever happened, but I was ready to stab a motherfucker if shit went down. I mentioned the situation to the boss, and nothing ever happened. I noticed that the bar was going downhill, and I had heard through the grapevine that they were having some financial troubles. I knew I should just get out of there. I put in my two weeks' notice like a good boy and got the fuck out of there.

After I quit, I still hung out with Back 40, and we really were just friends. It just so happened that she would go down on me every once in a while and tell her to fuck her in the ass. Other than that, it was a completely plutonic relationship. She still did everything she could to get me alone, and she came up with a really good idea. She bought two tickets to the Vikings vs. Packers game, and she knew I would want to go to that shit. I had never been to Green Bay, nor had I ever seen a NFL game played outside. I really wanted to see that while being a dick and wearing all purple to a Green Bay game. They don't like us very much.

I really wanted to see a game in the snow where everyone is falling down all over the place. It had been a really cold shitty winter, so I thought for sure it would snow for the game, but no dice.

She got a hotel room right in "downtown" Green Bay, if you can even call it that. It was tiny (my hometown is bigger), and the whole place smelled like hot rotting shit. It is now number one on my list of smelly towns before Dublin. At least Dublin stinks because they are making beer, and Green Bay smells because they are Packers. The whole place smells like wet cardboard, and it is really strong and fucking gross.

The hotel had a pool which was awesome, so I hot-tubbed it up every night that weekend, and then in the room, it was a fucking freak fest. She brought her toy and wanted to do everything. She immediately jumped on the bed and stripped, jamming that rubber phallus in her business and demanded that I fuck her in the ass. And who am I to judge? I jumped in there and took care of business. Wouldn't you know it, she had another anal orgasm, and it was crazy. It is a good thing there were two beds in the room because we destroyed that bed. After we took a breather, and I thought we were done. She got up and bent over the dresser in front of the mirror and told me to get over there because she wanted to watch while I fucked her brains out. If I didn't mention it before, she had tig ol' bitties, or huge boobs if that makes more sense. I remember watching them hang as she spread her butt cheeks while yelling at me to slide in. I went to town, switching holes, and she came multiple times, both vaginally and anally. I will never forget that image and the way she was screaming, demanding that I fuck her harder ever though I was giving it all I had. My legs and back were about to give out, but I couldn't say no to that.

The next morning was game day, and I woke up in the best possible way. I was totally asleep, and I thought I was having some sort of porno dream, and I don't really remember what it was all about, but I do know that when I woke up she had my entire penis in her mouth and was sucking on it like a fucking popsicle. I had been woken up like this before, but this was really, really good.

We went to the game very early to tailgate because we were meeting people there. Two friends from the bar that she had known for years from Duluth had recently moved there, and they went to the game. They are married now. My boss and cat that I worked with at the moving company forever was there with his old lady, and there was a bunch of other people that I knew, so it was cool. I am not much for brats and chips before the game. Just give me some beer or a strong drink. I dressed up for the occasion. I had dark blue and gold sneakers on because that was the closest to purple I could buy without wanting to punch myself. I will wear the jersey, but shoes go year round, and I will not were purple if I don't have to. That being said, I had on purple Vikings pajama pants on over my jeans. I also had long underwear on because it was fucking cold as whatever the opposite of hell is. I had a hoodie with a Chris Carter jersey on, also purple, and a purple Vikings hat. I walked up to the game in a sea full of green. It was awesome, and I felt like a badass.

It started off good because as we walked to the stadium we went past a radio station who was broadcasting live. When I walked by, he called me out and said, "Carter? He is a dinosaur. Why would you wear that?" He said this over a loudspeaker while everyone is walking into the stadium. I got gangster and turned around and charged the booth yelling, "You're a fucking idiot. He will be in the Hall of Fame next year." Guess what, he got inducted into Hall the very next year. I kept shouting, and my old boss had to hold me back. He weighs about three hundred pounds, so it was like running into a brick wall, but I got my point across because apparently I could be heard on the radio, so I consider that a moral victory.

It was a good start to the day, but it got better. There was a guy a few seats down from where we were sitting which were very good seats by the way, fifty-yard line, and he was being obnoxious. I let it go, but at one point, he started yelling at these kids wearing Vikings gear every time they would stand up if the Vikings made a good play. One of the kids had glasses that were thick as hell, and I am pretty sure he was special needs, so now that guy was really pissing me off. At one point, we sacked the QB, and they stood up clapping and cheered. This douchebag screamed at them to sit down or go back to Minnesota. I had enough and decided to have a chat with the gentleman. He was an older man with gray hair, and he was pretty loud, but he did not know who he was fucking with. I have a very loud, deep voice that carries very well. I stood up and screamed in my pro wrestler voice, "I am from Minnesota [which was obvious from my attire]! Leave those kids alone. They are just trying to watch the game like everyone else. They paid for their tickets the same as you, so sit the fuck down, shut up, and watch the game that you paid for, or I am going to beat your ass." He sat down and properly shut right the fuck up, but what was surprising was that everyone in the rows behind me apparently agreed with what I had said, but when I looked back, they were all wearing green and I was in all purple. I guess we found a common ground because I might have said or screamed what everyone was thinking.

I kept my eye on him for the rest of the game, and he did nothing. He would not look at me, and we were forced to go our separate ways when the game was over. It was a good time. The rest of the weekend was filled with more debauchery, the same as before, and once again, it ended with fucking in the mirror, listening to her scream for me to fuck her harder while she squeezed and sucked on her tits. I can't forget that image.

Lucky for her, the Vikings made it into the playoffs, and the first game was in Green Bay. This trip was much different because I had the booze flu big time, but I was not going to miss the game. I had never been to a playoff game, and since it smells so bad and is a long ways away, I could not see myself ever going back to Green Bay again in my life. It was also even colder, and the possibility of snow was good, so I was stoked. I was throwing up like every couple of minutes or so, and I felt like death. I lay in the back seat and held my composure as long as I could until I threw up in my mouth. I rolled down the window and spit it out, and I'm pretty sure it got all over her car, but whatever.

I told her to stop at a gas station and get some plastic bags, so she did, and as we pulled up, I hit the wall. I opened the door and just unloaded about a gallon of bile; it was fucking disgusting. There was a girl standing right there watching me, so I just waved to her, said hello, and lay back down. I got my bags and threw up all the way there, which only got worse once we got into stink town. Hotels in town were now over triple the price as they were before. This was obviously because of the playoffs, but one room at the same place we stayed at before was $350/night, which is literally jacked up.

 We stayed with her friends from Duluth that I knew from the bar, the couple who moved there. I was still fucked and spent the night puking into my gas station plastic bag, but I knew I would be okay for the game. Somehow I got fucked that night and in the morning, but I remember throwing up in the middle of one of those sessions. That must have been hot. They all went out for breakfast, and I stayed behind because I still felt like I was rotting from the inside out. They had a big Jacuzzi bathtub, so I said I would take a soak and get ready for the game.

 I drank some beers really quick to get my levels back to normal and soaked. It was awesome, and then I just lay around the house, drinking my face off until they got back, and when they did, I was right as rain. Back 40 also had a bunch of cocaine so that woke me up, and I was more than good to go. We went to a few bars before the game and had signed up for a beer trolley or something like that. It looked like a trolley car from San Francisco. It drove us around to a bunch of different bars, and it was really cool because the bars would give to-go cups for your drink, and you could bring it on the bus and to the next bar. I had never experienced this before. There was also tailgating before the game and a bunch of tents where they were selling food, which I don't care about, but they had beer and hard alcohol as well, which is more up my alley. I got a lot of comments on my outfit, and the majority of the people just said that I must have steel balls to wear something like that to a Packers game, which I do, and a lot of people in Packers gear actually told me, "Good luck."

 We went to the game but sat separately. We had really good seats, which I am sure she paid out the ass for, but I didn't care. Once again, I wore the same attire because it was fucking freezing cold, and once again, it did not snow. And once again, the Vikings lost. I was not surprised. It is very hard to be a true Vikings fan, but I am going to stick with them. They have to win it all eventually. I might be dead, but it will happen. After the game, I really had to piss and somehow made it to the bathroom before the stampede. They have urinals in Green Bay, which is much nicer than the troughs where you are elbow to elbow with another man who has his dick in his hand, which is uncomfortable.

That being said, one Packers fan managed to break every rule of urinal educate in less than a minute. He walked out and pulled out his dick and began talking to me, and that is okay but the rules are you face the wall in front of you and do not look over. He instantly broke this rule and crossed the line when he made eye contact. I could feel him looking at me, and I wanted to make sure he wasn't looking at my junk, but he was staring right into my eyes, and it was really creepy. He commented on my Vikings gear and how I was brave to wear it, which is something I had heard all day and it was getting old. He said that he was sorry that they had to whoop our asses, like he was on the team or something. As he was "consoling" me, he broke another cardinal rule of urinal etiquette when he put his hand on my back. You simply do not touch another man while he is holding his penis and in the process of urination. I should have turned and peed all over him, but maybe he would be into that; he seemed like a freak. When he was done with his rant, he slapped me on the ass. You shouldn't even need to be told that playing grab-ass is even more unacceptable at the urinal. I really wish I didn't have to pee so bad because it was taking forever, and toward the end, someone behind me started chanting, "Fuck the Vikings," over and over. I continued to piss, but without looking back, I simply held up my middle finger facing whoever was saying that.

Toward the end of what I was doing, I noticed that all the urinals had filled up, and the douchebag was still chanting, and I still had my finger up. I figured that he was directed at me, and then a whole choir joined in, and the entire restroom was filled with drunken fucks chanting, "Fuck the Vikings." I had to check my business, and since I always hang low and lazy, everything was secure, and I could finish up no-handed. I raised my other hand with my middle finger up, so I was giving the double. My dick is out, and I am pissing middle finger to this crowd talking shit about my team. I finished up and put my business away only to turn around to see a packed restroom of Green jerseys. My heart dropped, but they all just kind of smiled when they looked at me. Regardless, I got the fuck out of there quick.

After the game, the parking lot was a zoo, and they still had the tents with drinks, and they had live bands now. It was crazy, as it should have been. They just won the first game of the playoffs, but I felt like kind of a dumbass with my all purple Vikings pajamas on. I said, "Fuck that," held my head up, and wore that shit with pride. I was surprised once again by the Green Bay fans. There were a few comments about how they handed our asses to us and whatnot, but what I remember is that the majority of the people I spoke with were very nice and said that we gave it a good shot or better luck next year. For the most part, they were all very polite, at least I didn't have to be separated from anyone or kicked out of the function at any point. I would say that a good 99–98 percent of Packer fans are genuinely nice people; I guess the Minnesota nice crosses the river.

We drank a ton and went back to the house to do a bunch of coke, but first, we had to hit some more bars. That was a great idea. I had never really seen double before in my life, but I started to after those last few lines. We went to a bar and drank it up. I am not allowed to drink hard alcohol at home at this point, but I can when I'm out doing something, so I take full advantage every time I go out. I drank a bunch of Jack and coke, but I was still so high on powdered coke and weed that I could barely see. I signed up to do karaoke to a song that I know every word to. I was so fucked up I was trying to read the words, and I couldn't see shit. All I saw was doubles of everything. If I did not try to read that shit, I would have flown through the song with no problem. I have done it before and actually got tipped after I was done, but my high ass tried to read the words that I already knew, and I got confused. I started to freestyle a little bit and talked some shit about Green Bay because I was the only one that was not wearing green in the whole place. I said that I didn't have my glasses and couldn't read. I said, "Fuck it, you all, and you can go wipe your asses with those green jerseys." Nothing happened.

We did a bunch of more coke and probably some other shit in the parking lot, but I can't remember for sure but something dirty probably happened. We did not close down the bar, but we got drunk as fuck and headed back to the house. We were high as fuck and drunk as hell, so we retired to our room where she proceeded to do a line off of my cock, suck it off and have her way with it. I remember that I performed excellently, but I could not finish because I did way too much coke that day/night, but I took care of that in the morning for like an hour.

It was time to go back to the cities where you can breathe the air without gagging. I had a few drinks, and we hit the road for what would become my most memorable car ride to date, and I don't know how you could top it. I have received road head in the past from various girls, but this was a whole new kind of road head that I didn't even know was possible, and I think I invented it. I was smoking chronic and drinking beer when she grabbed my crotch and started stroking my wiener. I was okay with that, but it caught me off guard. She kept playing with my business and obviously getting wet because she pulled one of her big-ass boobies out and was playing with it and looked like she was about to cum from simply playing with my dick and her tits. I figured that I had better inspect and see if my assumptions were correct, and they were. I reached my hand down her pants, and there was literally a puddle in her panties. She looked at me and told me to pull it out, so I did, and she was planning on jerking me off, but I had a better idea. I suggested that she give me head instead. She was really good at it. She mentioned the fact that she was driving down the highway, and that was not possible. I mentioned that her car had cruise control, and if she put it on, I could steer. It did not take her more than two seconds to put the car on cruise and inhale my cock like it was much-needed oxygen. She did not have any control of the car. She leaned over and was titty-fucking me and sucking me off like it was the end of the world. The thing keeping us on the road was just my hand on the wheel driving 65 mph with my dick out and barely conscious. She actually finished. I was bone dry and very impressed. I returned the favor, although it was pretty tricky. I must have done something right because she squirted all over my face.

My Body Hates Me!

My stomach issues were getting worse, if I didn't mention that I was having wicked stomach problems. Every once in a while, I would get the hiccups and they would not go away. The only thing that would fix it was making myself throw up. I had no problem doing this. After years of drug and alcohol abuse, I was a pro. I just had to flex my stomach muscles, and I would produce. The thing was that even if I had just eaten a bunch of food and/or drank half a case of beer, all that would come up was foam—no food and no beer, just foam.

This had been happening for a few years, and all the women in my life (my mom, my sister, and my girlfriend) knew about it and wanted me to see a doctor. This eventually progressed into making me an appointment for a doctor then more or less kidnapping me and forcing me to go through this shit that I was not ready for. They shoved a long-ass tube down my throat to get a look at my belly; I swear it was like ten feet long down my throat for a little less than an hour. The doctor had some internet music or something because he asked me what I liked to listen to, and I told him the truth, thinking there was no way he had it, but he played a sick mix that lasted the entire time of the procedure. It was really nice, and I just zoned out, which might have to do with the fact that he gave me an ass-load of drugs. I told him I had a high tolerance, and he did not fuck around, and I was out.

My sister had brought me there and obviously brought me home. She recorded the whole thing, and it was hilarious and a lot like some video that went viral about a kid after the dentist who had gotten all doped up. I was loopy out of my brain. It might have helped that I knew whatever I was going to was going to suck ass, so I smoked my face off beforehand. I eventually got the results like two weeks later, and they basically just told me that my insides were fucked. They wanted to do more tests, and I did the usual scans and annoying crap that I have done many times before, but they also wanted to do some new test that I had never heard of. I was stony when they told me about it, so I just said, "Whatever, make the appointment."

When I went in, I had no clue what exactly I was going to do, but it ended up sucking big hairy sweaty balls. I had to drink a radioactive slime concoction that tasted like puke that had been eaten and then thrown up again, mixed with the nastiest thing you can possibly imagine and heated up. I also had to stand up for half an hour and stand still. I am not good at that, and I wasn't too excited about the idea of radioactive shit that I have no knowledge of flowing through my body. At the end of this, a nurse came up to me and said, "That wasn't so bad, was it? Did you have the strawberry flavor?" I was doped up again, so I was blunt and asked her what the fuck she was talking about because what they gave me tasted like hot shit. She looked at what they gave me and told me that it was the original formula and that she had heard that it tasted terrible. She went on to tell me the vast selection of various flavors that they had to offer; it was like salt in a wound. Why the fuck did she tell me that?

A few weeks later or so, they called me to come in and talk about my results, and they would not tell me over the phone. When I finally meet with the GI doctor, he basically just told me what I had heard before—my belly was fucked. I had heard this before but not definitively. This added up to three surgeries that the stethoscopes wanted me to have done—my knee, my back, and now my stomach. I don't know how much money these medical fucks think people have, but I am not going to pay off some shit for years that will still hurt me for the rest of my life. I have enough foreign medical objects in my body as it is, and I do not need any more. The total of those surgeries could have bought me a house, farm, and thirty acres in the Dakota's. I still need those surgeries, and I am in extreme pain every day. But it is what it is, and I can only pay for what I can afford, so I am okay with the pain even though it really, really sucks ass.

I would still get the hiccups all the time and could not eat any of the spicy stuff that I have always loved. My knee and especially my back kill me all the time, especially when we do the charity walks. My mom, my sister, my girlfriend, and the dogs would usually come on the walks; there were two a year, for butt cancer and epilepsy. I used to lead the pack, but I soon found myself falling behind and needing to take a break to stretch my back and get my shit together every five minutes, and then I started to need to sit down. Oh well, I would crawl every inch of those courses just to finish them and support ass cancer and epilepsy. That is not a joke.

I messed with Back 40 a bit here and there, but I began to realize that I did care about my roommate/girlfriend a lot. I played ping-pong with the blondie, the brownie, and the Back 40 until it got old, so I had to cut it down. NYC was easy because she was busy doing her own shit, but the freak show was a little tricky to get rid of.

We planned a trip up north with the boy-girl and his old lady near Brainerd and close to a ski resort. It was two stories high, it was so much more than we need. Before we went up north I was under the impression that everyone was down to party so I figured that I would grab a little bit of coke. I asked Back 40 to grab me a bit of blow. I figured that everyone would be happy, especially me because I was planning on getting dusted ass! and riding down the hill. We don't have mountains in Minnesota. She was taking too long, so I called my old roommate, and he was over in a heartbeat. We made the exchange, and I was happy. I had not done this in a long time, and I trusted him, so I just gave him money for whatever he handed me. After he handed me one package, he paused and said, "Here, take two. I am in a good mood." I was cool with that, so we headed up north.

I had misinterpreted the situation because I thought that I hinted at bringing shit up there and everyone was down, but apparently, they did not know what I was referring to. Everyone did some at one point or another, usually late at night.

One night was great. I was coked out of my cranium, and we all went to the hot tub. They also had a big-ass pool with a bunch of balls and toys in it. When I get around water, I turn into a little boy again, so I sat in the hot tub for a bit, but I had to jump in the pool and play because there was even a basketball hoop I had to play but I couldn't just jump in. This place had a waterslide, and I was so high there was no way I was going to turn it down. No one else went down it, but I did. It was awesome, which is funny because I have been on waterslides ten times bigger, but this was more fun. My theory is that before I was really young, with my family, and sober. This time I was basically drunk but also high off my ass on some really good coke and good herb.

I played by myself in the pool for a while because everyone else sucks, and then I went back to the hot tub. Why is it that at the end of the night a really hot girl comes into the pool by herself and you are there with your girlfriend? I fucking hate that. We stayed until they closed, and I went down the slide one more time; I had to. The day that we were to go riding, the girls did not want to go because they wanted to lick each other's pussy. Maybe it was shopping, but either way, they were not going. The boy-girl and I went to ride, which he had not done in a long time, and I was broken. I made the decision to do a bunch of cocaine and have fun on the hills. I did that in Colorado, and it was awesome.

This was not Colorado and a real buzzkill. I knew that we would only be riding on hills, but you just make the best of it. My buddy did a little powder, but that was it for the day. That was the best powder we saw all day. Fuck, I miss the mountains. It was the single worst experience I have ever had snowboarding, but I still had a great time. Maybe it was the coke and weed, or maybe it was because I was with my best friend, but I had a good time. We got separated on the first run for about half hour, but I found him. I stayed close after that. The hill was windy as hell and sheer ice. You could have literally gone down the hill in ice skates. We found solace in the woods, and there were some toboggan-like trails through the trees. We were going pretty fast, but I know we were not going the speed that I was experiencing. I was so fucking high; it was like a goddamn video game.

I made excuses to go to the chalet few times to do a few lines (freestyle). I had fun and made it down the terrain park three times and hitting every obstacle without falling, which was good because my back hurt like hell and that would have been really bad if I had fell down. I did some pretty ill shit for someone who has not been on a board in years and was more or less broken. The whole trip was awesome. Up north, there is a roller-coaster ride right by the shores of Lake Superior, and it is the shit. It isn't really a roller coaster, but you sit two people inside this little car that looks like a revamped go-kart or bumper car that is attached to some rickety rails made out of old coat hangers or something; it didn't look too safe. I said, "Fuck it," because if I die I won't remember it, and if I get hurt, I could sue there ass just like every other douchebag in America.

I swear, people get hurt on purpose just so they can profit from an organization that they know has a lot of money and would rather pay out than have any cases publicized. If I would have broken all my limbs falling off that track which was rickety-ass hell and terrifying. I think they might have been able to compensate me for the price of one pillow during my hospital stay. It was a small place, and I doubt that they had much money because they didn't have any business. The track went all the way down the "mountain," which is what they called it because it was the tallest point in the state, but it was still just a fucking hill. It is a long drop, and it was scary as hell, but nothing like the mountains, and it was only scary because it looked like it was built in some hillbilly's garage. It also took a lot of sharp turns over high cliffs, and I have no idea how that thing stayed on the tracks. However, it was right over Lake Superior, so it was fast, fun, scary, and beautiful. When we got to the top, I said that I would not leave until I had gone down again, and she knew I was serious. That thing is fucking awesome. Anytime I make it that far up north, it will be mandatory that I and whoever I am with stop by that place because it was incredible for something built by a hillbilly with scraps from the junkyard.

When we got back home, I heard from Back 40, and apparently, she did go and get me the powder I had asked for. I had not heard from her because she was in jail. Her dumbass drove a few blocks away and picked it up only to be pulled over for shitty driving. She had "a few beers" and got busted for that. If anyone is suspected of being intoxicated and they say that they only had a few beers, you should just take whatever number they give you and multiply it by at least tree, in my case ten. Like last night, if I told you I drank a few glasses of wine while I typed all night because the old lady was out with friends for the night, that would be bullshit because I drank a bottle and a half along with about a dozen beers. So I apologize if the previous pages are a bit cloudy, but I was drunk as fuck. I also had some really stinky weed.

Back 40 said that she received a DWI, and they also searched her car. She was jailed for a few days for possession of a controlled substance. I heard from her once afterward, and she told me what happened. I told her that she was stupid, and that was the last time I ever spoke to her. It was incredibly good timing because I had been trying to figure out ways to get rid of her for some time, but nothing was working. She lost her car and most likely her job. I don't care, but she could no longer stop by and see me, so I was free.

The next time the local police proved that they are completely worthless was around this time. My girlfriend was helping my sister and I do some landscaping stuff in the front yard. We had to dig up some old bushes that died and plant some new ones. It took a while, so we were out there for a long time. Some of the people across the street at the shithole apartments were having a get-together of some sort. They hadn't busted out the piñata yet, but they did. First, they had to mutilate some poultry. While we were putting in the new bushes, we heard what sounded like chickens, which seemed weird until my sister noticed and said to look across the street. There were a couple of guys walking out of the apartments holding live chickens by their legs. They brought them down to the grill in the yard on the side of the apartments, which was right in front of our faces. The chickens were placed on the picnic table by the grill, and they held them down, at which point they repeatedly bashed them in the head until they were dead. It was really hard to watch, but we couldn't look away. They threw the whole chickens on the grill with the heads and feathers, everything. It was gross.

I was pretty sure this was illegal at least the part about keeping live chickens in an apartment building, so I called the police. I explained my story, and they asked me the typical questions: what were their skin, hair, eye color, and their size? Every person in whole little ghetto across the street has dark hair, brown/black eyes, dark skin, and is around the same size. I was annoyed, so I kind of snapped at the lady on the phone and said, "Look, just go to the address I gave you and look for the people burning chickens. It's not rocket science."

I think I pissed her off, which may have had something to do with why they took forever to not show up. I waited for around half an hour and decided to run up to the liquor store before the rush and before the police came. I drove up to the LQ, and I passed a DQ with two local police squad cars in the parking lot. I assumed that a unit would be at the apartments at this point. I got my beer and headed back to the house, and when I passed DQ on the way back, the two cops were just hanging out, eating sundaes, so I knew that there would be some police there when I got back. I was wrong, and there was no one. We finished the bushes; they finished off their chicken and disappeared, all before the police never showed up.

I called the local police back and asked why no one had showed up, and they said that they were really busy and all the squad units were out doing important shit. I asked if eating Dairy Queen was considered an emergency to the police department. She was rightfully confused and asked me what the hell I was talking about. I am writing all this in my own words because it is how I remember it. I told her that a half an hour after I had called the station to report the situation, I drove to the store and saw two squads at DQ eating ice cream, so she was full of shit, and their department was negligent and good for nothing. No police ever showed up until the next day when I called back. They sent some young girl who looked like she was right out of high school. She had no idea what she was doing, and she had a tiny little notepad that she scribbled on. I don't think she even wrote anything down.

I continued to go up to the cabin with my roommate/girlfriend, but things began to change. There was always a shit load of people up there, but things were changing. Her niece who stayed in the same cabin as us was getting older, which is going to be a nightmare in a few years, but she will be there all too fast. She loved to swim now, so I would have lots of fun with her and the other little girls in the lake all the time, and it was fun. All the adults would sit on the shore and drink, and I love to swim, so I figured someone should play with them. They would all attack me and make me come and play anyways. They would also kidnap me and paint my fingernails. I didn't mind. My sister did that to me throughout my childhood. The cousins had also gradually changed year by year. The three brothers that I would party with all got girlfriends. Each one would bring a new one up every year so it just progressively got worse. One year the cousin that loved to smoke a lot and drink his face off all day every day, so we got along really well. He eventually had to go to treatment. He met a girl there, and they hooked up.

I don't think that treatment is a great place to meet someone because if one of you falls off the wagon, you are both fucked. They got married within a year, and the first time the majority of the family met her, she was part of the family. That was weird, but it must have been awkward for her as well. My girlfriend's whole family talks so much behind the backs of the rest of the family; it is not even funny. It was the consensus of the family that he was always the fun one out of the three, and now he was the no-fun one. I felt bad for him. He was not the same person as before, but he was still a good kid, and I got along with him. The three of them all got married in no time. I did the math, and between the three of them, if you added up the time from when they met their wives to when they got married, all three of those relationships does not add up how long I was messing with my girlfriend before I even met her parents or even how long we had been living together.

I was a complete idiot to point this out to her because it only made her push for the whole marriage thing even more; I am really stupid. The cousins were still fun, and we fished together. But they always had baggage around, and we haven't gone out with just the four of use since the invasion. I found solace in hanging out with her dad. I requested to go out with him really early in the morning, just the two of us. I would see him go out all the time at around six when the sun came up. I was up as well because my schedule is always fucked, but I also liked to get up and burn one as I watched the sunrise over the lake, have a smoke, and then go drink some alcohol, so I did not have an episode and watch *The Simpsons* on my tiny DVD player. I don't even watch it anymore. One reason is that the screen is so small it is pointless, but it is really because I know every episode front to back, and I can just relax. I see the whole episode in my mind every time, and I fall asleep to it.

When I got the balls to ask the big guy if he would bring me out with him in the morning when he goes out, he said yes. I was nervous because that was kind of his alone time to get away from the wife and her family, and I understood that, but I wanted to go with him because he was the closest thing to a dad that I had, and I really missed mine. We had fun. He treated me like an equal, like a man, and I was always honest with him. I didn't tell him about stuff I had done with his daughter, but I think it was best to leave some things out. It made me so happy the first time we went out that when we got back, I ran up to the cabin and cried in my bunk. It made me so happy, but it made me realize how much I missed my father. I love the big guy, but I don't think I could ever bring myself to call him dad. It seems like blasphemy to me. I know that is probably not the correct word, but it just wouldn't feel right to call another man dad when I still miss my real dad every day.

I love those mornings, but I would never smoke in front of him even though I really wanted to. I would pregame my ass off though, so I was always dusted ass. I would roll up cigarettes and smoke those like they were going out of style, and that was cutting it close because he loves his boat more than his children. That is not true, but he just really likes his boat. I hung out with the little boys that were up there because they hounded me like the little girls did. When they were just little ragamuffins, I made the mistake of bringing my pellet gun up to the cabin. I made sure it was okay with their dad first, but I let them shoot a bunch, and after a while, I started to feel like I was babysitting and was wondering if I was going to get paid for this time or at least compensated for all the pellets that they used.

Once again, hindsight tells me that I had made a poor decision. I should never have introduced them to that shit because from then on they expected me to bring various tools of destruction because I guess I was the "cool uncle" at the cabin even though I was not an uncle at that point. It might have had something to do with the tattoos because no one else had them, and I have a lot I guess. So they wanted menacing toys, and like a little bitch, I would bring them shit each year like wrist rockets and whatnot.

I was denied a few of them because my girlfriend would not let me bring them up for the boys. I realized that I had made a mistake years earlier by handing them an air pistol when they asked me if I would grab them some beer from by the campfire. I said that I did not have the authority to do that, but if their dad told me it was okay, I would steal all the beer they could drink. They were like twelve, so it would not have been a big heist. They did not end up drinking any beer. Sorry, little guys.

The next year, the whole family was doing the breakfast thing at the annual spot, and for some reason, they sell all types of knifes and crap like that in the gift shop that you are forced to go through in order to get to the place where you eat. They had butterfly knifes there, and the boys were trying to get me to buy some for them because you had to be eighteen to get them. Naturally, I bought one for myself because I am still just an immature little at heart. Later I found out that their dad did buy them some, so I had to teach the boys how to use them so they wouldn't cut their fingers off. They weren't that sharp, but you can still cut yourself pretty good.

I would go to the golf course in the mornings by myself because I hate playing with other people. They have always been playing golf their whole life or something because they are always really good, or at least they keep it in play and not in the woods. I don't do that all the time, and I can keep up, but it is stressful. I have more fun when just my old lady and I go while we are up there because we both suck, and we just take our time and suck together. There was never anyone on the links up there. Whenever I have been to a real golf course, there have always been good golfers behind us, so we end up letting them play through and drinking a beer. It is sad and embarrassing. However, along with the other changes that had occurred up at the cabin, the golf course changed as well. It was now a Frisbee golf course. It was also a soccer golf course, whatever that is. I don't know, but it actually looks kind of fun. I want to try it one of these years.

I used to go and smoke weed at the swings and in the playhouse they had out there, but now I had a new agenda. I would take my girlfriend's car and drive up to the golf course by myself and go Frisbee golfing. I fell in love with Frisbee golf one year, and I cannot for the life of me remember who introduced me to it, but I love it.

When I started, I had a broken right hand, and I am a righty. I had to learn how to play with my left hand, which in hindsight was a Godsend. I got pretty good and could keep up even though my good hand was in a cast. When the cast came off, I had to wait for the snow to melt, but I had collected quite a few discs, and I hit the links. I was now ambidextrous, so I could throw a curve either way; it was sweet. I was literally equally good with whatever arm I was using. I have tested this theory a few times now, and I have proved it to be true.

One day I made myself a day pack filled with all my Frisbees that I would need. I had plenty of beer as well as a pipe, some good stinky weed, and my smokes. I went to the course at around six thirty and had the course all to myself all morning. No one ever came. I got high as fuck and pretty tipsy; it was a good time. I played twice using both hands; I used one disc for my left and one for my right. I used different discs at times like when I needed a putter, but I kept track of which hand was for which disc. After thirty-six holes, I was dead even between my right and my left hand. I was also drunk by this point and super-duper high, so I drove back to the cabin.

I don't remember many more episodes, but I guess they have occurred. Supposedly, I had I few more up at the cabin. I don't know why I wait all year until I am at a place where I am just supposed to relax. That sucks, but I do recall one episode which was somewhat like the first except I didn't break my back again. I remember waking up and feeling nervous. I could see the Nintendo 64 again, and I have no idea what the significance of that is, but I know that every time I have experienced that, bad things would soon follow.

There are also smells that I cannot describe or compare to anything, but I know that when I smell it, I get very scared, and it never ends well. I knew that I needed to get some alcohol in my system to even me out and calm me down. I poured a drink and had a beer, but I could not bring myself to drink them. I know I took a shot of rum and a few sips of beer, and that was all I could do. Then whatever happened went down, and I woke up to the same old shit. People huddled around me, asking me if I knew my name or where I was. As soon as I wake up and shake it off, I know everything—my name, address, social security number, bank account number, insurance card number, whatever you want. I used to know my driver's license number but they changed it, so now I don't have a clue what it is I just know it starts with a *V*.

I got up and I knew something happened and was pretty pissed off because it is not fun. When you have a seizure, everyone wants to force feed you and make you drink liquids to get hydrated. This is bullshit because even the thought of food could make me puke and anything I drink is not going to stay down for that long. I really needed something bad because I was dehydrated beyond belief. I tried to drink water, and my predictions were confirmed—it all came right back up. I could feel my body shrinking and my bones protruding. That is an extreme exaggeration, but I was really fucking dehydrated, and I needed to be hydrated somehow. I was stuck between a rock and a hard place because I needed water but I could not drink it. I was fucked.

My girlfriend wanted to bring me to the hospital, and I reluctantly agreed. Normally, I need to have a bone literally broken and sticking out of my skin before I would go to the hospital, but I felt like hot death, and I knew I needed hydration right away or I would be in trouble. We went to the hospital, and I think I needed some help walking. I know I was shaky as fuck, but my old lady told me it would all be all right. She always calms me down.

They hooked me up to a "banana bag" to hydrate me, so that was cool. I was fucking thirsty, and my mouth felt like the goddamn Sahara Desert. They would not let me drink anything; they said that the bag was feeding me. I said, "Fuck that, I want something wet in my mouth." I didn't say exactly that because that sounds kind of porno, but that is what I meant. They would only give me ice chips, and I ate a ton of that shit. At the time, it tasted like frozen gold. The bag must have worked wonders because before it was empty I started to have to pee, and it just got worse because they did not come back even though I was yelling. I was very adamant about the fact that I had to pee or I would do it on the bed, so they told me I needed to stay on the IV and I could use it to walk to the bathroom for support and stability. I walked to the bathroom, but the second I stood up, I felt it—I was not going to be able to hold this in. I could barely walk, so I wasn't moving too fast. I was wearing the gown that they always make you wear at the hospital, so I had no coverage, and as soon as left the room and started walking down the hallway, I just started pouring piss like a bottle of pee that was suddenly turned upside down. I could not stop it. I hobbled my drunk ass to the bathroom, leaving a huge trail of urine behind me. When I got there, I did not have to pee anymore and did not want to make the walk of shame back to the room. Sure as shit, they had a crew down the hallway cleaning up my mess. I apologized as I walked by and got back to my room as soon as possible.

The episodes usually happen in the morning, and I thought it had something to do with alcohol and going through withdrawal, but that theory has been debunked. I went to Sound Set with my girlfriend and her hot friend on the boy-girl's birthday. We were there all day, and I must say it really made me feel old. Snoop Dogg was there, and I looked around. All the kids that were attempting to sing along were not even born when the song came out. It was sad. I knew that it had sold out when I saw slug with a really long line to come up and take a picture with him for like five dollars.

I remember freestyling with him at the 7th Street entry when I was fifteen, and now he thinks he is a fucking rock star. He is really talented, and I like his stuff, but this was getting out of hand. Maybe it was because Snoop was opening for him, which is fucked up too. We decided to go because it was really fucking hot and there was no shade anywhere. It was basically cheaper to drink beer than water, so we were all dehydrated and way too hot. We decided to skip Atmosphere (Slug) because I had seen him a million times before, so it didn't matter. We stopped at the Porta Potties on the way out so her hot friend could take a piss; this is where I checked out. I woke up, and it was no longer superhot outside.

It was no longer daytime, and I was inside of a medical tent on a cot. I was really fucking confused until some dude who looked like a doctor came up to me with that goddamn flashlight, and he was holding my ID. He asked me all the regular shit, which I spit out in two seconds—name, address, and even the first part of my driver's license number, which I didn't even think I knew.

Just then, my girlfriend and her friend walked up, so I just said, "Look, it is my girlfriend and her hot friend. I remember them." He basically said that was good enough for him and that I could go if they stayed with me. I stood up, and my pipe fell out of my pocket. I looked at him, who was looking at it. I picked it up and looked back at him. He said to just leave, so I put it in my pocket, and we dipped out. We were parked really far away, and I could barely walk, but one of the women EMTs noticed this and offered us a ride on her golf-cart-type thing; it was very sweet of her. I really do not remember this next one or even if I had one because I don't remember shit, but my girlfriend swore that I did have one even though she wasn't there. She says that she can tell when I have had an episode.

I was alone at the house, doing probably absolutely nothing, and I know that I lay down in the middle of the day to take a nap because I had been up all night doing absolutely nothing. I lay down on the couch, and when I woke up, I was on the couch, but the glass coffee table was shattered. I had no idea what was going on. This was not my first rodeo, so I checked all the signs to see if I got robbed or not. My pot was still on the table, and it was all there along with my pipes, and the doors were all locked. I was really fucking confused, but I did have a big lump on my forehead, and my chest was sore. I did some forensic work, which I only know because my girlfriend is constantly watching murder documentaries. I saw exactly where I fell, and if I would have dropped a few inches in either direction, I would have been impaled through my chest or my face.

My head was a bit sore to the touch, but I have a high tolerance for pain, so that doesn't mean much. I am just surprised that my face did not get all cut up and that I was lucky enough not to land on one of the metal table legs. I still have no idea how that happened, and I really don't understand how I got back onto the couch and fell asleep with no recollection of anything. These were big ones, or grandma seizures as I call them (the real name for them sounds similar, but I don't know how to pronounce, let alone spell it, so I just call them grandma), but there are many little ones as well. I don't know what I call those, but they are annoying, and it is usually when I am sleeping which sucks.

I continued to do the epilepsy walks every year, and now I had my own team. It only consisted of my mother, my sister, my girlfriend, and I. I also walked for the daughter of my sister's friend. One year, I actually had team shirts made up and raised over three hundred dollars. It is not a lot, but every little bit helps, and I didn't really do shit. My girlfriend set it all up, and it was mostly her friends that donated. When I first started doing the walks, I would walk up in front with my mom because we would walk really fast, but after I broke my back, I started to gradually slow down a little bit each year. Eventually, I was dragging ass in the back with my sister holding on to my knee and my back. We took pictures with her friend's team, and no one in her family believed that my sister and I were related because she is pasty white and I am brown. I think it is funny.

A few days after that walk, I went to the thrift store with my sis because that is what we do. When we got back to the house, we were talking in the kitchen, just shooting the shit, and out of nowhere, she says that she has something to tell me, but she doesn't want me to get upset. First off, that is a horrible way to start a statement. Right off the bat, I know that I am going to be offended by something or pissed off. I know my sister very well, so I looked at her face, and it took me about one second to know what the deal was. I said, "You're fucking pregnant, aren't you?"

She was, and I was going to be an uncle. I asked how far along she was, and I don't remember exactly what she said, but she was well along. I never noticed because she was already a big girl and she always wears really baggy clothes, so you couldn't tell even up until she gave birth. She just looked like a fat girl. I talked to her a lot, which was good because she would soon disappear. I hated the baby daddy and actually had volunteers that would kill him at the drop of a hat if I just said the word. But I did not because I knew that it would hurt my sister, and I did not want to do that. Just like my dad, everyone loved my sister, and some were apparently down to kill someone for her—that's love. I asked my sister why she didn't just "take care of it," and she said that she was way too far along. She was like halfway or something, I don't remember. This is when I get pissed off. I was upset that there was a child in my sister's belly that was fathered by a complete piece of shit, but what really made me mad is how long she waited to tell me. I asked her if Mom knew, and she said yes. They had both been keeping this a secret from me for like four months or some shit.

She said that our mother and she were worried that I would freak the fuck out. They were right. I was pissed off, but there is nothing I could do about it now, so I just said okay, but I was really mad about the whole situation. In fact, I was more upset about the fact that they kept it a secret from me for so long like I was no longer a member of the family. Beyond that, my sister lied to my face when I asked her about the situation. I asked why she did not get it taken care of because she could not afford it. She told me that it was already too late and she did not know, so it was an accident. I can't wait to tell that little girl that she was an accident. That is fucked up. I would never do that, but this really pissed me off even further.

I know how the whole lady cycles work and when the window closes for taking care of such issues if you are not ready for a child. I asked her how she could possibly miss three periods and not realize that something was up. I told her that she was either lying through her teeth or she was fucking retarded. You should never use that word, but in this case, it is completely applicable and the best word to use. What woman over thirty-five is not aware of their cycles or would not get concerned if they had missed one period, let alone three? I called her out and said that I knew she was having a baby on purpose even though she could not support it. She eventually had the baby, and of course, I went to the hospital because it would have been fucked up if I did not.

My soon-to-be wife and I went there, and it was really awkward because King Dip Shit was there. He did not say one word, which was probably a good idea because I would have bodied him right there in the hospital and went to jail. Goddamn it, I hated him with every ounce of rage I had in my soul down to my core. To put it lightly, I simply wanted for him to not exist anymore. I cannot do this because when I heard the news, I asked me sister one simple question, "Do you love him?" She said yes, so I was fucked. I hate him so much, but I love my sister more, and her happiness is more important, so until she starts to hate him, my hands are tied. She had the kid, and it was a little girl. I knew it was going to be because she asked what she should name her a month or so before. I picked my sister's middle name because it is a nice name and there are many nicknames she could use if she doesn't like her full name when she gets a bit older. Fuck, I changed my name a bunch of times. I was blown away when I learned that that was the name she picked, and I was even more excited to hear that she would have our family name and not Capitan Douchebag's last name.

I was terrified of the baby because I got nice and high before we went there and I had been drinking quite a lot. Whenever there is a new baby that I am supposed to hold, I have images in my head of me dropping it, then it dies, and everyone hates me, so I don't like to hold newborns all that much. Blondie grabbed the baby and held it first, although I am sure my mom held it forever before we got there. I think that she really wanted to be a grandmother. I said I would hold it but only if I was sitting down. I say "it" because newborns look like aliens, and I have no idea how people can look at them and say they are cute. They are always disfigured and weird-looking. They don't get cute until they have a head of hair and are not all slimy. And when people say they can see their dad's nose or their mother's eyes on a newborn child, those people are morons and just trying to say something nice just like when they say that they are cute.

My mom bought a ton of shit for the little girl, but we had been stocking up little girl outfits for the last four months. If she has another kid, I will not do that again because they grow out of them in like a week, fuck that. I did buy her a bunch of old Dr. Seuss books and a cat-in-the-hat stuffed-toy thing that I guess she loves. It was kind of annoying that she was there every time I hung out with my sister now because "dad" was just sitting at home, playing video games. There was no reason he couldn't watch her. I missed just hanging out with my sister, and now there was this screaming stinky shit machine everywhere we would go together. It sucked. I understand that it is an infant, but she didn't need to bring it with her.

Boner Boy was back at home doing nothing. He could have watched her. Dr. Dickhead was not allowed at any family functions, so the scream machine was always there as well. She was gradually starting to look like a human being, so it wasn't so bad. It would be a few more months before she would shut the fuck up, but even now, she still makes a lot of noise.

One day, I told her to just admit it and I would let it go. She would not admit to anything and stood by the fact that she did not know she was pregnant. I went on to tell her once again that she was either lying or that R-word that you should never say. She left without saying a word, and we did not speak for over a month. It was the longest I had ever gone without talking to my sister, and it fucking killed me. She was my best friend. We talked on the phone all the time, sometimes for too long because she doesn't shut up and we would go to the thrift store every week. I felt like I had lost her. She literally did not answer my phone calls anymore. My heart was broken, and I was really bummed out. I had to tell my mom that I wanted to apologize, but she would not answer my calls. She must have told her because a week or so later she answered when I called her. Everything was all peace again, but it still sucked because I never saw her, and Lt. Dingle Berry was the cause of it. For the most part, we only saw each other during family shit, which is pretty few and far between. I hate that baby daddy. I lost my best friend, and I still get sad about it.

I had my back against the wall with the whole marriage thing, and it was apparently crunch time. I was not going to get out of this alive until I put a ring on. She had her damn ring. I didn't get what the big deal about getting married was, especially because I have absolutely no money and am not worth shit. I have no idea why anyone would want to marry me. I am not throwing a pity party; I just honestly don't have shit to offer. That's how I know she truly loves me, but she was pretty adamant about the fact that she was going to marry me and she wasn't going anywhere. I agreed to set a date, but I was firm on the fact that I was not stepping foot into a church. She is Catholic, and I don't believe in shit, so I figured we could compromise and just go to Vegas. She wouldn't agree to everything because I wanted to just do a drive-through marriage if any, but it was clear that was pressing my luck. We were also pretty clear about the fact that I did not want a big wedding because I get nervous enough even when I am just at the wedding for the drinks afterward. We agreed that we would just invite our immediate family and three friends.

Her immediate family happens to be about much bigger than mine, so with my friends and family, I was inviting six people, and she had about sixteen. It was still going to be really small, but it still made me nervous. I knew who I was going to invite for my friends because I had an alternate motive for two of them. Well, one of them was always going to be there because it was the boy-girl, and I had known he would be my best man since seventh grade. He had another falling out with one of our friends, and they had not talked in a few years. They used to be really close, and they even lived together for a couple of years. They would get together with their girls and hang out every weekend, just the four of them and whoever else. It was a ridiculous situation because the boy-girl was accused of hitting on the Ecuadorian's girlfriend, which was complete bullshit. He would never do that, not in a million years. I can't picture him hitting on any girl, let alone one of his best friend's girls, especially not her because she is not his type at all. I still talked to both of them for the few years that they were not speaking and would hang out with them individually, but I was getting sick of it because they were both being really stupid. They were brothers, and it was getting old. I had a good plan. I worked it out so they basically had to stay in the same room with each other. They could have gotten separate rooms, but it wouldn't make any sense, so they got a room and even flew out together. I think that deep down they wanted to patch things up and be friends again.

My third friend was going to be a neighborhood friend who is now a professional photographer, and I wanted him there because he is a good friend and he loves gambling, so I figured he would have a good time in Vegas. I also figured that I could give him a job and have him be the photographer for the wedding. This way, he could come out, gamble, party, have a good time, and get paid. He said he just could not afford it even after being paid for the pictures. Sometimes people just need to save their money for a while. My cousin, the only one I really get along with who stays at my house every summer, came out, so he was my third friend. I needed to pick a date that was a little ways away, so I had time to breathe. We agreed on Halloween, and that was cool because it was a little less than a year away. Everything worked out perfectly for anybody willing pay to go to Vegas, and they must actually must actually like. That or they just like Vegas and have lots of money. I was scared to try to buy weed out there because I have seen one too many cop shows in Vegas, and I didn't want to fuck up the whole thing.

One of the guys (three) in my party knew that I really wanted some herb but was not going to risk it, so he just asked from some young random piece of shit a half a block down the strip. There were cops that had someone arrested for the same shit. The kid kind of jumped at him basically suspecting him of being a cop, so we pulled him away. I knew it was a bad idea because I scoped out the situation and it was run like a business. I could see the lookouts, and I could tell who was watching, who was holding the product, and who held the money. They were on high alert, so the only outcome I saw possible was broke, in jail, or dead. He would have been better off losing his money and taking a punch or two rather that spend the weekend in Vegas, essentially missing his flight and paying out the ass and missing work.

I have no idea what kind of weed the little fuck was packing, but across the street from that same spot at the Bellagio in front of the fountains, the exact opposite happened to me. I don't know if he was an entrepreneur or if people just see me as someone who buys drugs because I have been offered every narcotic under the sun in every country I have been to. Regardless, I remembered my advice to my buddy and figured it wasn't worth it, especially when I saw the same operation going down on this side of the street, except they were black.

These guys could have fucked me up in a heartbeat, but I made a promise to myself that I would not fuck up another wedding, and I kept it, I think. In hindsight, the only thing that sucks about the situation is that it was some of the stickiest stinky beautiful cheeba I have ever been offered while on the road or overseas without going out of my way to find it. I still think to this day how nice it would have been able to get dusted ass like Hunter S. Thompson and wobble around the streets of the LV without a clue.

The wedding took all of five minutes, and Elvis was even there. We, as in all the *cool* people, went out for strong drink before dinner, which was ridiculously expensive, I can only imagine. It had all types of weird shit I have never had, like clams. I like oysters, but clams almost made me spray hot puke and ass all over my new wife's dress. I spit that ish out when I remembered that there was an open bar, and I didn't look back. I had some steak and some other food that had previously been living, but I don't remember what I could not take my eyes off that bar. We still had to choke down cake, which was actually a three-tiered cream cheese chocolate cake that completely went to waste. I had a sliver of that cake which was delicious. That was enough for me and it was off to the open bar. My cousin had the same idea, our eyes met from across the table, and we were both eyeballing the bourbon. I had a couple of Jack and Cokes before I noticed he had his eyes on the Maker's Mark, so we raced to it and split that bottle glass for glass.

We killed that on top of numerous other cocktails of whatever crazy girl decided on. I can drink like two of those until I get a toothache and need more really strong, preferably brown, booze to cleanse the pallet. The old lady and I were supposed to do the traditional dance. Whatever that is, we did not, because my wife cannot dance and I cannot dance with someone who has no rhythm. I am not a professional dancer "anymore," but you need someone to pick up the slack or at least keep up. We could have practiced, but it would have gone nowhere, and I didn't care. It was time to leave the old folks and go waste some money for no reason other than we were in Vegas, and that is excusable.

We had a whole top floor reserved, which didn't really mean shit because it was at dinnertime for me in Vegas. That is if I actually eat in Vegas. My breakie usually consists strong and liquid in that kind of environment. So we drank as long as we were allowed to while still being able to walk…sort of. I might have mentioned this part already, but it is too funny to leave out. And what I have written is too long for me to go back and proofread, and I am a horrible reading guy, so I am a self-diagnosed dyslexic.

Being that it was Halloween, I asked my best man to dress up with me as the Blues Brothers from SNL, so we did, and we had the costume perfect to every detail. We even got stopped a couple of times by couples that wanted their pictures with us because they thought we were performers of something. We complied until it was time to make our way to the Bourbon Room, which was the contentious of the women who did outnumber us because it was more of a dance party atmosphere. What better place to be when everyone is whored out or dressed up? No regrets.

When we walked into the party, it was like Studio 54 if it were managed by slot jockeys and people from out of town. Immediately the DJ passed me and the best man and demanded that we get on stage for the costume/dance contest. He said that the least we would get would be $250, so I found my buddy to get some drink money. The fucked-up part is that he can do the Blues Brothers dance perfectly. I have seen him do it since we were twelve years old, and he would have won us that loot. However, he does not like to dance in situations like that, and frankly, neither do I, but I knew we would win. The DJ promised so all I had to was get his ass on the floor and herd him to the stage. I got him out to the middle of the floor somehow where all the ladies were dancing and got distracted. I ended up in a circle of my bride's drunken friends, grinding on me when I realized my blues partner was missing, and I could not do it myself, but I took off anyways. I checked every restroom, both men's and women's, for a long time until I went back for some help, and the other groomsmen left with me.

I was not going to go have sex without my best friend. He would not have been involved, but he would have been welcome to do so if he had wanted, but I know that would probably be the last thing on his list. He would not answer his phone, and we had checked the strip and damn near every restroom we passed until someone had the genius idea to check the groomsmen's room. Luckily, we had one key or we would never have had closed and put out an APB for that motherfucker because I was worried as hell. More concerned with finding him than I was with doin' the damn thing with the new wifey, who coincidently met us at the door of the club, being carried by her harem of harlots. I told them to bring her to her room and I would be back as soon as I found him. This turned out not to be the case.

So my two other groomsmen and one of the bridesmaids whom I hated for years went out to find my better half. I love the other two just as much, but at this point in time, finding him really was more important than being with my new wife. Fuck, she was coming home with me and has been for years. I hardly ever get to see my "brothers," so I had to find my boy. We got to his room and found him much in the same state as my new wife, except he actually made it to the bed. We taunted him for a while because that is what good friends do, and there was a bottle of expensive whiskey in there so I couldn't leave that alone. I mean…while I was there, why not? We made sure he was safe and drank our faces off, randomly poking him and jumping on the bed. He is lucky that we had grown out of the days of drawing dicks on people's faces. We grew out of that a long time ago, or did we? I didn't. It was down to my last groomsman who was roommates with the best man and one of the wife's best friends. We drank until the roommate and groomsman kicked us out because we drank the booze and they were both slowly dying, so we left.

I spent my wedding night drinking with the one of the bridesmaids that I truly hated, which was cool because she hated me as well, but I have better reason. We actually got to know each other and get along very well. Who would have thought that a dick squeezer to be a chick like me? I hated her because during one of my house parties, there was some boy-girl wrestling going on. This was when we would have keg parties and completely fuck up the house. She is a fisty feisty drunk and will fight a man twice her size without a second thought, which is pretty cool as far as I am concerned, but this time, she went too far because my roommate was a good wrestler and got her pinned.

Everyone else was either pumping the keg, smoking weed, or God-knows-what-else, but I was one of the few who saw the attack. He had her pinned, and she knew she was fucked after years of hanging out with this girl. I know for a fact that she would bite off another woman's clit, squeeze her face, and spit it back in her mouth if it came down to it. So I was looking down, watching this because I wanted to make sure they didn't break anything even though everything was garbage. She and I made eye contact, and I gave her a look as if to say, "I know you're fucked now," to which she responded with her eyes which clearly said, "Oh yeah? Watch this."

As she did this, she properly squeezed his balls so hard I could feel the pain and it hurt, but the look on her face as she squeezed his beanbag was far more disconcerting. She stopped what she was doing to stare at me and give me another creepily hot, scary devil stare with his manhood in her hands as she took it from him. I don't know why this took so long because it bothered me to the point that I still think about it. She smiled at me as she calmly gave him the G. I. Joe kung-fu ninja grip to his junk. She smiled again as she twisted all the way around, smiling and laughing. We get along real well, but that bitch is crazy, and I would never cross her. I have been kicked out of more bars because of her getting in fights over nothing than I have ever been kicked out of on purpose, usually on Saint Patrick's Day. She has gotten me kicked out of just about every bar, every year, sometimes for life, but they won't remember my face.

I go out on a rented trolley with the in-fam every year for the last seven years or so, and she has never failed to get us kicked out of at least a couple bars every year even though I am the one smoking herb in the middle of a busy street next to a cop. That has happened more than once. It is usually just me, my brother-in-law, and around seventeen women on the trolley filled with a million Jell-O shots, sometimes a keg, and usually anything else you could want, and a ton of food, but I can feed myself. I like the hooch! It is a good thing the sister-in-law has disposable income.

Another one of the friends got married first, so he was one of the bachelor parties before mine that I was being forced to go because my neighborhood buddy told me that I don't get out of the house enough anymore, and if I didn't go, he was going to bitch-slap me. I went to the party, and I am glad that I did. It was for one of our Asian friends who was Hmong. I asked my old roommate how he felt about that, because he had previously said that they were dirty mountain people that were the white trash of the Asian community. They were actually good friends, and we had a few other friends who were Hmong as well, so I guess the Hmong rule does not apply to all of them. The party was at a hotel downtown Minneapolis, and it was a really nice room. It was like four rooms; it was fucking huge. There was a huge main room with a kitchen and a patio, then there were two adjoining rooms on the left side and two on the right. They all had their own bathrooms and big-ass bedrooms. There was also a third room on the right side. Any one of those bedrooms alone was nicer than some of the motels I have stayed in before.

My girlfriend brought me to the hotel. She probably volunteered so that she would know exactly where I was. I didn't care I appreciated the ride. I told her I was going to party my ass off and there was going to be a bunch of whores there. I did not know if that was true, but I thought it was funny. She didn't say shit and dropped me off. What a good girl. When I walked in the door, it was like a fucking high school reunion. Actually, more like a high school party. Reunions are stupid. I have never been to one, but anyone from high school that would want to talk to has my number, so I am not going to waste an afternoon telling hundreds of people that I don't give two shits about the same story over and over.

This was just like a party, and it started the second I walked in. There were a bunch of people that I had not seen in many years, so there was a lot of man hugging, and then they basically said "Dig in" as they parted the sea of people. I discovered that there was a table full of nose candy on the other side. I had to make sure that it was coke and not meth because I did not want to be up all night, and it was. Little did I know that it would not matter because I was up all night, at least I wasn't up for three days, and I could eat food. I did take a nap at one point, however, but that was a good idea.

I dove into the powder but was not greedy. It does not take much when it is not your poison. I drank a ton of that and was happy. They had a bunch of liquor and no one was drinking it. I took care of that problem for them. Everyone was going to go out to eat at a nice place before the strippers came, and I had no appetite. I said that I had no money, which was not true, but I just did not want to go. They said that it wasn't a problem and they would cover me. I finally just said that I wanted to lie down so that I could keep up with the crew all night, and they were confused because I had just done a bunch of blow, but they just said, "Whatever," and went to the restaurant.

In retrospect, I should have gone with them because I ended up losing that money that night. I did lie down, mostly because my back hurt, but I was kind of tired, and it was a good thing that I did because I crashed and slept for over an hour until they all got back. That was another reason I did not go. It was a group of like forty guys, and half of them were coked up or drunk. The other half was his family, which was kind of awkward because they just stayed in the third bedroom the whole time while they were there, and there was crazy shit going on everywhere else.

I woke up and tasted a little more candy to really wake up and just poured a drink as we were just shooting the shit, and I guessed waiting for some girls to come show their boobies and dance around. After a while, a man came to the door wearing an all-white suit—white tie, white hat, chains, and rings, everything that would be included in the pimp kit. There is no way this guy was not a pimp. He talked to my neighborhood buddy in the other room for a while. He had set everything up. He paid the man, and I knew then what we were in for. These were not strippers coming here; they would be full-blown whores, and they were.

After Pimp Suit left, the hookers came in, and everyone was standing around like a dumbass, possibly because they were really high. Well, I was high as well, and my first thought was to grab a titty. There was a white girl, a black girl, and then something else that I couldn't quite figure out. They were all attractive and fit, so that was a good thing.

The white girl was talking to everyone and clearly trying to get things started, so I just grabbed her tits. I took about zero seconds for her to start taking her top off; she had really nice boobs. I felt them without the shirt and bra for a little bit, then I stepped back and said "Queue up, lads. She is all yours." She was happy because unlike me they all had money to spend on strange vaginas. I had a free one at home, so I was cool with that. That is not to say I won't play and watch. There is nothing wrong with that.

One of the friends was also a neighborhood kid; he lived a couple of blocks away and was really proud about being Irish. I will call him Kid Irish. Well, the dude went to the bank and got $1,000 in one-dollar bills so that he could "make it rain" on the girls. I cannot think of a bigger waste of money; it makes absolutely no sense to me. However, I have no problem with watching someone else waste their money and reeking the benefits while some poor college girl degrading herself for a roomful of drunken coked out guys. It quickly went far beyond just titties when all three of the girls got butt naked, and from then on, it was a free-for-all, and there were no closed doors.

The third room was packed with Asians and nothing else. They did not want to play at all; it was weird. These girls were running from room to room, doing random shit. Apparently, it was $20 for a blow job and $40 to fuck, and those girls made a lot of money that night I tell you what. There was a lot of fucking and sucking going on in each room. I just walked around and got a little show then go to the next room while stopping in the middle to powder my nose. I was mostly focused on the black girl, partially because I like black girls, but she was usually just dancing butt naked and playing with herself, and she was sexy. There was also the fact that I didn't really have any desire to see my friend's cock and balls.

As the night went on, I do remember doing a couple of lines of coke off one of the hooker's tits and then off her ass and one really close to the honey pot. I was really fucked up and doing some more blow in one of the bathrooms. When I came out, my neighborhood friend came up to me with my wallet in his hand and said, "This is yours, isn't it?" It was, but it was missing the $40 I had in there. I did not suspect him of doing anything dirty at any time in any way; he is one of the most honest people I have ever known. I call him the neighborhood kid because his nickname in high school was Fat Dude, and he is no longer fat, so that is fucked up. I just call him by his name now. I am not putting any names in what I am writing, so for this, he is "neighborhood kid."

This is why I should have gone to dinner. Or I could have used it to fuck a whore and get chlamydia. One of the sluts probably took it, but it wasn't worth my effort to make a stink about it because it wouldn't solve anything and I would just look like a dick. I decided to look at it positively because I had already done a lot more the $40 worth of coke, smoked a bunch of weed, and drank my face off for free, so I let it go.

At one point, I was called into the bathroom of one of the side rooms to do a couple lines for some reason, so I did. I had no idea what was going on. As soon as I did my lines and when I walked out, there were two hookers in the room and two of my friends. One of them was Kid Irish, and I don't remember who the other one was, but one of the girls closed the door and would not let me leave. I said for them to do their thing and I was going to go have a drink. She told me that I was going to sit down in the chair and watch; she was very dominating. Once again, I did not want to see my friend's business, but I really did not have a choice.

There were two beds, so each couple took a spot and went to town. I cannot get the image of Kid Irish's balls, not because they were amazing but because I really had no desire to see them. The white dominatrix girl hopped up at one point because I was trying to leave. She pushed me back in the chair and made me sit there as she rubbed her naked body all over me. She was really good at what she was doing, but I really just wanted to get a drink and stop being in a room with two of my friends' cocks and balls hanging out.

She rubbed on me for a while, and then I said, "Fuck it," and dipped out. I did not give any of those girls one dollar the whole night, except the $40, but technically I did not give that to them. I mingled around for a bit, drinking and sniffing, and then I went into the other bedroom. I walked by the room full of Asians. God, that was weird. There are naked girls running around, and you don't have to pay anything. Why would you not come out and watch? Oh well, it made more elbow room for the rest of us.

The other room had the black girl in it putting on a hell of a show. She was still butt naked and playing with herself; it was pretty entertaining. Kid Irish eventually finished up and was apparently not finished. He came in with his bank roll and was ready with the forecast. He was going to make it rain. She rolled around on the bed, pleasuring herself as he flung bills all over the bed. She just rolled around in the money as she did her thing. She danced on a few people here and there, but I just like watching her have fun with herself.

At one point, someone mentioned that she hadn't got me yet, so they all made me lie down on the bed. I obviously did not have a choice in this situation. I lay down, and Kid Irish made it rain on me, so she would jump on top and rub all over me so fast and hard the bitch almost started a fire. The thought of it is kind of gross because she was rubbing her wet, wide open pussy all over a pile of dirty money. That is yucky, but it would get worse.

This went on for longer than I had expected when my buddy Scare Face put a ten-dollar bill in my mouth. I was not tied down, but for some reason, it felt like I was. For some dumbass reason, I bit down on the bill with my teeth. I think it was because I didn't want the dirty money to touch my lips. I remember pulling my tongue back as well, so that must have been the reason, but it was a big mistake. She was squatted over my face then dipped down on my face and proceeded to pull the bill out of my teeth with her twat. It was amazing, and I was impressed. I still would not put my dick in any one of those girls, but that was pretty cool.

When she was done, she was scraping up her money, and I found something hard on my shirt that kind of looked like a fingernail. I talked to her and told her that I thought she had broken a nail, but hers were painted, and they were all there. She held my arm and said, "Honey, I think you broke yo toof." I felt it with my tongue, and sure as shit, it was busted. I put the extra piece on there, and it fit in like a fucking puzzle piece; it literally snapped in.

I was pissed off, but I took it off and threw it in my fifth pocket so I wouldn't lose it. I went to the dentist that Monday, and they said it was just the composite but it was a good thing that I had it and that it fit so well because it saved me about three hundred dollars. It fit right in, and it only took them about twenty minutes to finish the job. I was really happy and actually didn't have to pay anything because I got that composite within the year. All four of my front teeth are 50 percent fake. I have broken or had help breaking them all.

I don't remember too much of the rest of that night, but I do remember that I was the last one awake. People gradually turned off until I was alone. I was okay I did a bit more blow and helped dispose of some of the liquor they couldn't finish. By this time, the sun was coming up. That always comes so quick when you have been up all night. I guess I woke up a few cats when I called my old lady for a ride. I forget that my voice is really deep and carries, so I guess I was probably being loud, but whatever, I wanted to go home. I also did not recognize the fact that it was super early, and she had not been up all night doing coke, so she was probably sleeping. She was happy to pick me up; I think she was just happy to take me away from the coke and strippers and hookers.

She picked me up, and I brought two friends out with me and asked if she could bring them home, too, because they lived in Minneapolis. She was sweet and said okay even though I am sure she was pissed off. I was busted about five seconds after getting in the car. She can tell if I have been putting shit up my nose in a heartbeat. I move my mouth around like a crackhead, and it is just very obvious if you really know me and how I really am on a day-to-day.

The next bachelor party was for one of the cats and was very unorthodox, it was way up north at his cabin and was mostly about shooting guns and fishing, not very typical of a bachelor party, but it was fun. That is until 7:00 AM every morning when we all awoke to gunshots. I hate guns and do not have one, but apparently every member of the party had one and just had to shoot it at the break of dawn.

We all slept outside in tents. There was a cabin, but it was about the size of my garage, and we had way too many people. The boy-girl and I drove up together, and we shared a tent, which was actually pretty nice. He had a big tent, way better than mine, and he slept on a cot, so it was off the ground. I had an air mattress because of my back. I slid the lower half of that under his cot, so it was like we had a little dorm room tent with a bunk bed.

We had a ton of room in the corner for bags and changings clothes or what have you. There was no running water although they did have an artesian well and an outhouse. I would always pee in the woods, but when you gotta go, you gotta go, and that outhouse was every bit as disgusting as you can possibly imagine and then some. I drank my face off the first day as most people do and stayed up pretty late.

During the first day, we wanted to do some fishing right away, so I put on my swimsuit. I went fishing with the boy-girl and the groom's brother. We went up and down the river for a while and then went to a shallow canal where we docked the boat and got out. This was the shit that I loved. I just swam around to places I wanted to fish, mostly in the reeds, and was often knee-deep or deeper in nasty mud, and I loved every second of it. I usually fish for bass and pan fish because you have a much better chance of actually catching something as opposed to just going for the "whopper."

I was cast into the weeds and was swimming for a better spot to stand when my bobber went down. I set the hook and was reeling in as I was swimming, but the fish was pulling me. I found some footing and began to real in whatever it was. All of a sudden, the fish jumped out of the water, and it was a big-ass northern pike at least three feet long. It snapped my steel leader off and broke the line. Even though I practice catch and release, it would have been nice to at least get a picture with it.

I did land a bunch of bass, so all in all, it was a good day. Although I did not dive in the river and catch any carp with my bare hands or bite the head off a bass like in the past, I still had a great time. I was nowhere near as drunk and overheated as that weekend, at least not yet. We went back to the cabin and got drunk as fuck. It was not that we were not drinking while we were fishing, but that is two things at once, so after we were done with the poles, we just but a bottle in each hand and set our focus on one thing only, getting wasted. We were very successful in doing so. I remember setting up for a bonfire and doing some other shit. There are always chores to do when you get up there, but whatever.

At one point, his uncle said to me, "Hey, you look strong. Come help us move some of these cinder blocks." I just said nope and walked away. Luckily, the boy-girl was there and explained to him that I had broken my back, and I heard him say that he could understand that because he did construction, so he actually felt bad for me.

We got plowed and burned things mostly in the fire pit, but we smoked a ton of shit away from the fire. When you are with a large group, it is important to go off with a small circle of friends to smoke; otherwise, you might only hit the bowl you packed once; it is simple stoner etiquette. During one trip, we were smoking some shit they called wax or something like that. We smoked it out of some sort of vaporizer, and it seemed very similar to hash or hash oil. In fact, I think it was the same thing. I didn't give a shit; it got me high as hell. Then when you walk away from the fire and any source of light, the stars are fucking amazing, even better than Arizona, except I have never seen a UFO up there. I have seen the northern lights, and that was awesome but no aliens.

Everyone was trying to get strippers to come there for the party, so the same neighborhood kid was in charge of that. I said out loud that if I even see one girl there that night I would give everyone $100. I am really glad no girls showed up. You have to understand that this cabin was creepy as shit; it was something out of the movie *Deliverance*. It was far from any paved roads, and there were no lights anywhere for miles. A girl would have to be pretty desperate to come out there, and if they were anything like the girls from the last party, there is no way their pimp would be okay with the whole situation. It looked like the perfect setup for a horror movie. I did not have to pay anyone, and I could not care less that there were no titties around; women were usually not even allowed at that cabin anyways. I was happy enough fishing, getting high off my ass, and then getting fall down drunk and sitting by a big-ass fire. In fact, I am pretty sure I did fall down once or twice. It was very dark when you walked away from the fire even though I had a head lamp; it doesn't really help when you are wobbling all over. I slept like a log (I have no idea what that means, but I slept really well) until the guns went off.

I was cool for a minute and talked with the boy-girl in the morning, and then I felt sick but not like booze flu; it was my fucked-up stomach, and it was pissed off. I got up to piss in the woods and stayed there for a while, throwing up green and yellow bile. One of the kids that jumped me in middle school walked by and asked if I was all right. I said that I was all right but my stomach was a little mad at me, and he said good luck with that, which is exactly what I would have said in that situation. No one wants to talk when they are hurling out their insides. Everyone was going golfing; they had all brought their clubs and were serious about it, fuck that. I only was to golf with people that suck ass. Don't give a fuck about golf and just want to drink eighteen beers on eighteen holes.

The boy-girl did not like to golf either. In fact, he didn't like to do a lot of things. He did, however, like to shoot guns, and apparently, he had two more than I thought. I, however, liked weapons since I was young, probably because I did tae kwon do and was really interested in it. I had every *Teenage Mutant Ninja Turtles* weapon from the crew; I had all four and still know how to use them. In fact, Donatello was my favorite, and I won a few weapons competitions with the bo staff. I love them and collect all types of weapons, like throwing knives, throwing stars, throwing darts, butterfly knives, swords, nunchucks, sais, switchblades, and of course, my bo staff. That is my favorite weapon because it is just a stick you can find one anywhere. All you need to need is a broom or mop something with a stick, break it, and then you can kick some ass.

I do carry my switch or some knife with me when I pass through shady neighborhoods, but I do not think that I could actually stab of slice someone. The situation would have to be pretty severe. I knew he had a twelve-gauge sawed-off shotgun, but I was unaware of the plastic Glock and the .22 rifle that looked like it was from the Civil War.

I was throwing up a bit, but I took a break from that and had some hair of the dog to go handle firearms, always a good idea. I started off with the Civil War relic that had like a bolt lock thing going on. I don't know what it's called, but this was an old gun. I did really good with this one and pretty accurate for someone who never shoots and hates guns. The Glock was fun, and obviously, I held it sideways like a gangster and quoted shit from gangster movies. That is what you are supposed to do. They have way more kick than I was expecting, and there is no way that the chicks in the movies that are busting rounds with a gun in each hand like it ain't shit could do that. Either that or I am just a little bitch. I moved on to the shotgun. I had fired a shotgun before, but apparently, not a twelve-gauge because that thing kicked my ass. I shot it with the butt on my shoulder, and that was okay, but I could tell it was strong, and then I shot it from the hip, which was actually really fun, but not as accurate. I tried to just draw and fire like someone's running at me all of a sudden or some zombie, which I don't believe in, was running at me. And when I fired, the gun came back at my face and got about a millimeter away from my nose, which would have broken it yet again.

I learned that you should always have stability when shooting a big fucking gun like that and that I had no business holding a gun in the first place. We played for a while, and I was okay, but then my belly got mad at me again. I needed to lie down. I went into the cabin, and they actually had a TV and a VCR, so I put in *Fear and Loathing in Las Vegas*. The boy-girl came in with me and hung out. That was nice. I got up to puke up a bit of yellow foam here and there, but I mostly just lay on the couch, watching the movie, and felt like absolute shit for the majority of the day.

Things got better, and my belly was okay for the most part. It was good enough for me to drink my face off again. We had a bonfire again, and for some reason, they threw a couch in it. The fire got fucking huge and almost out of control. That was fun enough, and then it was time for sleep and camp clean-up, which sucks every time, especially when you feel like shit. I slept like a baby once again until the guns began to fire; this is when my shitty last day began. We had to take everything down, pack up, and get the fuck out of Dodge. I had a little canister that held a cooling towel that kept me cool because it was always hot as fuck all day and especially at night. I threw up in that thing all day. It was never a large amount, but I was sick as fuck. I was completely functional, but just like having to take a dump, I just needed to barf every few minutes into my little bottle. I did not spill, and there was no problem. I would be in the middle of a conversation and just say, "Hold on for a second," puke, and then continue talking like nothing happened. I am a pro. The boy-girl and I listened to music the whole way back, and I freestyled the whole time while hurling every few minutes. It was really nice when my best friend told me that he was really impressed with my ability to capture the beat and hold it. He told me that I had gotten really good, and that meant a lot to me.

The wedding that we were pre-celebrating was one that I probably should not have gone to. For one thing, the actual wedding was huge as fuck as hell to hold in a big-ass church. I should have known better than to go to an Irish Catholic wedding in the first place. I was really uncomfortable, and it was no fun because I cannot stand being in a church if I do not have to, but I guess I had to be there because he was a good friend, and that would soon change.

The dinner was nice, and we got a good table, and the food was good. During the reception, there was obviously an open bar, and I did exactly what would be expected of me and drank myself stupid, but I kept my composure. That was toward the end of the reception when I was reportedly plowed. There were two place mats on a table. They did not look like anything special, and everyone was clearly signing them and writing a stupid little message or some shit. When I went up to the table, I had no idea what to write, so I was just standing there like a jackass. The groom's friend from California who we partied with me when I drove him back to school was standing over me and told me to draw a cock. I partied with this guy in Cali and knew him all right, but I don't know why I listened to him. He said, "It looks like you don't know what to write. Why don't you just draw a giant cock and balls?" I did exactly that with great detail, and it was pretty impressive. It had throbbing veins and pubes, and it was even shooting jizz all over and it took up the whole middle of one of the placemats, which I thought was awesome. There was a plus sign between their names, which is where we or I should say he decided that I should create the phallus, and for some reason, I listened to Cali man who destroyed the groom's studio in college, but that is a different story.

I went to town on that place mat; they had a ton of markers, so my cock and balls were immaculate. There was a lot attention paid to detail, so there were pubes, and then I even put in some veins. Then as a topper, I had it spitting drops of cum into a puddle. I really should not have signed my artwork. I had no idea that they had a plan to frame the place mats and hang them up. Had I known that, I am sure I would not have drawn such throbbing cock and balls in the middle of it. It was not long before I got a text from the groom, telling me that he wanted me to leave the wedding. I was okay with that because I understood that he was upset, but I needed to piss as I waited for a cab. I passed him on the way and tried to talk to him, and he just said, "Don't talk to me."

I said that I was sorry and that I had already called a cab, but he basically told me to fuck off in so many words. I went out to the front stairs and sat behind a pillar so you couldn't see me if you walked out of the building. His little brother found me and told me not to stress because he was just crazy over the whole wedding thing. He handed me a bottle of Jameson, and I love whiskey, so I drank up.

His older brother as well as his dad came over and told me not to sweat it, so that was cool. I texted him a bunch of times while I sat outside smoking and drinking, but there was no reply even though I know he looked at the messages. I remember while I was smoking an old man noticed that I rolled my own cigarettes and asked how I did it with only my hands. He said that he used a roller, and it worked much better. I said, "Okay, old man, I challenge you. I will roll one by hand, and you roll one with your little rolling machine, and we will so who is better." We pulled out our supplies at the same time and started. I was drunk off my ass and could not walk a straight line if you paid me, but I have been rolling since I was thirteen, so I knew what I was doing. I finished in half of the time it took him, so we compared the smokes, and mine was perfectly symmetrical and rolled tight as a butthole. His was loose and looked like shit. Sure you could smoke it, but it could not hold a torch to my rolling skills. I said, "Sorry, old man. You might be twice as old as me, but you lose this round."

I really wish that I had actually bet some money on that because I smoked that old man like a rack of ribs. My cab was going to be there any minute, so I was just chillin' on the steps behind the pillar, smoking some herb. The boy-girl and his woman came out, as did my old lady, so we were all sitting out there. Apparently, my voice is really fucking deep and carries for miles. I don't notice it, but people have been telling me that for years. The groom came outside for some reason, possibly because his brothers and dad were out there. They were nowhere near me, but he heard me talking. I was not even being loud, and there is no way he could see me, so my voice must actually pack a lot of bass, I don't know. All I know is that he was still pissed off because I may have a deep, loud voice, but he has a very nasal high voice. I guess they are both very distinctive. He could not see me, and I could not see him, but he apparently, heard my voice and said, "I know you are still here. Get the fuck out." I told him I was waiting for the cab, but that wasn't good enough, so I walked down the stairs. As I left and caught the cab, I simply said congratulations. My girl came with me, and we went back to the hotel. I later found out that he felt like I had disrespected him by coming to his wedding "all coked out." This is bullshit because while I might have had more than the average beer to drink and I was high out of my gourd (that is how I am every damn day), I was not coked out…yet.

Back at the hotel, we got out of our nice clothes and just relaxed for a while because everyone was still at the reception. We had some drinks, and I got stoned ass. I hate hotels these days. There are no balconies anymore, and you can't even open the fucking windows. Beyond that, they don't even have vents anymore. There used to be vents in the bathroom, which I can only assume was to get rid of the stinky poop smell. But they are no more vents or ways to ventilate your stink, and on top of that, the bathroom is always so close to the bed, so if you have to blast ass, anyone in the room is going to hear and eventually smell you. For this reason, I often use the facilities in the lobby after I smoke if I have to drop a bomb. Smoking my medicine also presents a problem because of the smell. This is why I am forced to bring a "bounce tube" even when we go to the cabin.

The concept is that you stuff an ordinary toilet paper roll with fabric softener sheets or bounce and blow through the tube after you take a hit. It works really well. I started doing it at like fourteen, and parents would never notice anything. I would know the second I walked into a room what was going down if I smelled dryer sheets in a room with no washer or dryer, but I guess most people don't make that connection. That is cool; it allows me to smoke my medicine wherever I want.

The room we had was actually really big, and the bathroom was far off, so that was cool even though I never needed to use it, although I did wake up in there. The shower looked like something you would see in a porno. It was about fifteen by ten feet and had like four showerheads all over. It was really nice, but we never used it, and eventually, it would hurt me. People started coming back to the hotel; every one of the friends was staying at the same place. We went over the boy-girl and his old lady's room for drinks and just talked for a while, but they seemed kind of burnt out, as did my old lady, so we went back to our room. Their room was a lot nicer than ours because it was bigger, and instead of a porno shower, they had a Jacuzzi, so fuck them.

We were both on the new side of the hotel, and our neighborhood buddy was on the old side. After a bit, I got a text from my neighborhood buddy whose room happened to be just down the hall, and he said to come over and burn one because he had a patio and he knows I like to smoke. I was on my way in a heartbeat. They clearly did not give two shits about the no smoking policy because the whole room was smoked the fuck out in no time, and it was a two-room suite. These fuckers even had a balcony.

It was an old hotel, so I guess it makes sense, but I was just jealous because I had to go downstairs and outside to smoke because my girl got the room in her name and I did not want to get her in trouble. So it was a smoke-out party, and there was a bunch of the friends from back in the day there. The balcony was really nice as well because I was able to smoke whenever I wanted, which became very important as the night went on. We drank a bunch of God-knows-what, I don't even remember, but I do remember when the snow started falling.

Apparently, everyone had cocaine, and I had no problem with that. I also had no money, but I did have money but not to spend on blow. I only do blow recreationally, which basically means that I only do it when I don't have to pay for it. There was plenty going around, but I never asked. My neighborhood buddy shared with me and was very generous, as was everyone else in the room. I stated and played for a long time and occasionally went back to my room just to say hi, but the old lady was kinda dead, and I was very much awake. I have no idea how late I stayed, but I got high as shit and powdered my nose until it was numb.

I went back to my room because I actually got pretty tired. That is what I like about coke; you can eventually sleep at some point as opposed to glass, which tends to keep me up for what seems to end up being like a week. I lay down and was high off my ass. I remember breathing really deeply, and when I would close my eyes, it was like a collage of visuals and colors morphing and doing all types of crazy shit. I was basically having a flashback, like I had released all the latent LSD in my system. It was crazy, but somehow I fell asleep and had some crazy dreams, although I cannot remember exactly what they were about.

At some point in the night, I apparently went sleepwalking and, it ended up really shitty. I mapped out the path that I walked, and it was exactly how I would get up in the middle of the night to go piss. However, the bathroom was much different than the one at home, and that proposed a problem because I apparently stumbled into the porno shower and must have tripped on the ledge and fell down. I do not remember any of it, but I know I woke up stomach down with my face jammed up against the wall. My head hurt like hell, and the first thing I did was check my eyes and made sure my teeth were all there. I have a habit of breaking my teeth.

When I woke up, I had a big-ass lump on my forehead, and it hurt like hell. I medicated that with some herb and cheap beer before heading home. There was a breakfast, but I didn't feel like running into the groom that morning, so we just boned out. A couple of days later at home, my neighborhood buddy came over to have a smoke break, and by this time, my eye was all types of bloody colors and swollen shut; I could not see out of my right eye. The first thing he said was, "What the fuck happened?" I told him that the groom ran into me in the parking lot as we were leaving, and he punched me in the face. He totally believed me and was like, "Holy shit, are you serious? I can't believe it." I played it out for a while because it was funny, but I eventually told him the truth, and then he just said that I was a jackass.

The most recent wedding that I had to go to and probably the only one I have ever been to that I actually looked forward to, maybe more so than him, was my best buddy, which at this point was less than a month ago. However, not only have I known him and his wife longer than they have known each other. I love them both. Why? My high school girlfriend and I hooked them up because we each had a best friend and wanted a couple to go on a "double date" with. No one else really ever had a steady relationship, so there was no couple that lasted more than a week or two, and that was a long one. I waited till college for the short-term relationship, but those were much shorter than a week or two, more like one night. I hope I never see you again. That is not his kind of party; he doesn't or didn't operate like that at all, so we picked the two out because we knew they were perfect and just so happened that they were two best friends.

The high school sweetheart and I lasted for about ten years until I moved to Colorado and cheated on her with my junior high crush. I saw that as an opportunity I could not pass up. I had wanted that since I was fourteen, and in retrospect, I would not take one second of it back. It was worth it, except for getting hit by a car and flying through the car windshield because she found a picture of me and her together. We weren't even doing anything bad. We were snowboarding, and I have been snowboarding in the mountains. This includes a plane flight, which requires a plane flight if you want to get out of Minnesota before spring, with both of them together at the lodge and everything.

One of them knew I was fucking them both at the same time. Not the same time but often on the same day. The point of the story is that Ol' Demolition Derby and the hippy had different ideas about when and who got to play with me. But if anything good came out of that relationship, it is that I/we found someone for our best friends, and they stuck it out longer than I could hold out. However, if you overlap those two and the time that was going on with my current wife, that is 10 + 10 + 15 = 35. That means I have sorta been in a steady physical relationship for as long as I have been alive if you add up the numbers.

I exchanged boning numbers with a good buddy of mine you probably know if you are reading this. I ran out of fingers and toes to count all the conquests a couple times when I was cut off. He told me to stop there and said something that made me feel like a real asshole. I was told to shut the fuck up for the most part, and he told me that he had only been with three or maybe four girls and that I had slept with two of them that he knew of. It may not seem like I have no conscience, and I do claim to have no shame in my game, but that truly made me feel like a big piece of shit. However, I did only get his sloppy seconds, so he got the goods, but what really hurt was that he told me he would not fuck or even mess around with anyone I had ever been with even if you paid him. I understood where he was coming from, but it still kind of hurt.

I had a stony moment there; sorry, I lost my train a bit, but if you think about it, it is basically like talking to me in person because I jump all over hell and try to tell eight stories at once. Back to the wedding that I had been waiting for since the ex-old-lady and I hooked, these two freaks up. We all knew it would happen, and I might have been looking forward to the wedding just as much as the bride because I saw him marrying her as a moral victory. Because, really, how often does setting up two mutual friends for the purpose of eventually getting naked ever work?

They (Paula and Abdul) say that opposites attract, and these two very much fit that theory to a T. If you were to see them separately, you would never guess that they are soul mates, and I have no idea how my ex and I were able to pick up on that, but it worked, and I consider it to be one of the best decisions I ever had a part in. It changed two people's lives forever.

I am not arrogant enough to take credit for what happened, just for what started it. They did all the dirty work themselves; we just set the table. We didn't know they were going to go for the whole buffet. So our double dates turned into triple dates because now the other groomsman and his woman would join us, and so the six of us would get together as often as possible. At this point, my second long term had moved back to Minnesota and was part of the "group date." This was a hard task to accomplish, especially when you live in civilization and your two best friends live in Bumfuck, Iowa, or at least it seems like it.

After hippie head moved away yet again, *bitch*, I traded her for the girlie I met at the cabin, and she picked up right where the others left off, and we were one big happy family of six drunks. Good times. I got a bit sidetracked, but the point of that rambling was that my new lady and I were and are very different, as were my homie and his old lady that I helped him meet. We all went to the same school, so it is not like we went too far to find someone for him, but the third couple in our little friendly orgy weekends spoke little English. The point being that each one of us had or has very different personalities, but when the six of us would get together, it was total synergy, and we all had fun doing whatever, usually drinking excessively. There were a few fallouts here and there, but we always came back to family, which we are until the third couple gets deported. The thought of that really makes me sad, but once people get married, you almost never see them again anyways, especially when they are shipped to and make a new life in another country. I am just glad for all the time we did get to spend together.

That was a lot of rambling all over the place, but I did have a point. Out of the six of us, we were all very different, but we became a family. The other couple is moving to where you need a passport to visit, which I most likely will do when they get married and that will happen unless the theory (not mine) stands that *mi amigo's novia* is possibly staying here simply because she is illegal and has no passport. She is allowed to stay here because of the common-law marriage situation up here. Some people think that once they get down there she will split up because she will no longer need him. If that were to actually happen and she breaks his heart, I will spend every dime I have to fly down there and beat the shit out of her until she learns to speak English correctly. That being said, I think that the healthiest relationship out of our crew of screw-ups would have to be my best bud and his polar opposite that the first ex and I hooked up.

The proposal was well played—not as cool as my proposing with an onion ring, but it was still pretty slick. He made her cry by breaking up with her, causing her to lock herself in the bathroom. He buckled. I don't know exactly how long he made her suffer, but I think that it is fucking hilarious. He set her free and eventually came clean. I was not there, but this is how I picture it. Hairdo was crying on the floor, possibly scratching at the door, while my bro was laughing his ass off trying to be quiet. He knew that he had won or submitted, depending on how you look at it, but I know for a fact that he would not have proposed unless he was positive about a "yes."

I was the same way. In fact, I was proposed to numerous times before I gave in because for some reason a woman can't propose to a man, but why? Because if you corner a guy with some shit like that, unless you have been together forever, you might as well consider him gone. He will run like the wind into the nearest half-respectable open porthole where he can dock his cock. I know I would. So at this point, I do know that he got down on one knee and properly proposed to her through the door. There was a moment of silence when, without opening the door, she busted through like the crazy cartoon bitch in *Who Framed Roger Rabbit?* So she busted through the door, tackling him through the debris, and properly beat the shit out of him while she hate-fucked him screaming, "It is about fucking time asshole!"

This has been the viewpoint of all friends on both sides; it was about fucking time. We all knew it was inevitable. Now I was not there, so I don't know exactly how it went down, but if I were her, that is how I would have done it. He is a hell of a catch. That might sound really, really gay, but if you knew who I was talking about, you would agree hands down. I do *love* him though…as a brother!

The stage was set, and there was no turning back. As with any man he did not want or need to have anything to do with the planning. All a man wants to do is get the shit over with and shut that bitch the fuck up no matter how much you love her. WEDDINGS SUCK ASS! I think he composed himself quite well, much better than I. He played it off like he didn't care, but I know my boy, and I guarantee he lay awake almost every night, stressing. This is exactly the opposite approach of the one that I took. I simply said it needed to be small and faraway so that only true family/friends could come. I answered no more questions. Though he never said anything, I know my brother, so I just told him to hold his breath and it would all be over soon.

That is easier said than done. I was nervous, but I did not care anymore. I gave in. Fuck, she moved in, told me that she would never go away, and she was not bullshitting. I gave in. I know that my buddy knew it was inevitable, but he was nervous. When it was time for my day, he was more nervous than I was. I walked up to "the chapel" with a Rolling Rock in hand and at least six or seven in the belly. On his day, I had no worries either because everyone there was breathing a sigh of relief that they were able to see them joined before it was too late for them (those who witnessed the occasion) because we all knew it would happen. We all just wanted to be alive to see it. Rather than be nervous for him as he was for me, I was overjoyed and have never been so excited to go to a fucking wedding. Four words brought me there come hell or high water, and they were, "Best friend, OPEN BAR!" I would have crawled there even if there was no booze; I would have just brought my own.

He was unusually calm and collected as we came up to the ceremony at a dope-ass mansion in Saint Paul with a glass of mimosa for me and my women (mom, sister, and wife). I told him to relax by force of habit, but I instantly knew that he had it on lockdown. On top of that, his brother was standing in some kind of military-looking pose from a sniper-shot point of view on the balcony. He looked like a badass. He was my best man, and I did want to be his, but he does have a brother, and I do not, so I just figured that he would be that guy, which is fine. He did say that they wanted me to be a part of the wedding, so they wanted me to be the one to marry them, which would involve me becoming an ordained minister. I did that, and I can now hold prayer groups and marry people among a bunch of other dumb shit that I will never do, but I am now an ordained minister even though I don't really believe in God in the magical way that most religious people do.

I even went as far as to write some things to say with a few off color jokes put in, but it would have gotten laughs. They were tasteful but probably not what you would usually hear at a wedding. They made the right choice to go with the uncle that they did because he did a good job, and it took all the stress off me. I was okay with that and ultimately just wanted them to have a great day, and I didn't want to be that guy who fucked up the wedding again.

Next, I found out that they had gotten a DJ, and initially, I was a little butthurt because I have done DJ shit for years, so why didn't they ask me, right? I thought about it and realized that I would rather be having a good time rather than working, so I was cool with that. I also realized that I spin vinyl and would have to bring all my own wax. Nothing I spin would have been at all appropriate for a wedding, so my feelings were not hurt, and I was plenty happy to walk around, getting drunken ass, having fun with no schedule. Then I got anxiety over the groomsmen, and if there were any and I was not part of that crew, I would have taken my best friend off to the side and punched him in the dick until it ruined his wedding night. He got lucky. He chose not to have a best man or any groomsmen, so he saved his beanbag from a world full of hurt…no joke. I think he left it out because his father was not able to make it, and I understand because I was kind of butthurt that my dad could not make it to my ceremony, but that is how life and death work, and they are both bitches.

I made sure to take it easy so as not to make an ass of myself and ruin yet another wedding, let alone this one. He did awesome, and I am proud of him, considering how nervous he was for my wedding, and he had no family there. The ceremony was beautiful, and I kept my cool until the point that they mentioned that everyone was sad that my boy's pops was not able to be there, and I lost it. I can cry very quietly, but I looked around, and my ladies were all looking over to see if I was crying, and I was. I looked around, and just about everyone else that knew him was in tears. He is clearly missed. What was crazy is that my boy kept a stone-cold face even though I could see and feel him crying inside. He did an awesome job. Once again, I am proud of him. If they would have said some shit like that when I was doing my vows, I would have beaten the shit out of whoever was reading the vows as I cried my ass. I did fuck up a little bit because as they were walking down the aisle after the fact, I gave him a pat on the chest and her a pat on the back as they walked back down the aisle. I didn't think about the fact that they take pictures sometimes at this time; I hope I didn't fuck anything up. If I did, that wasn't my hand in the picture.

 Everything was done, so they both had hours of makin' the rounds to do. Some of the boys and girls and I made our rounds out to the car for some THC-Re-Leaf (relief). I did not do any coke at this wedding, and I was on my best behavior. I did not see a lot of my special little guy because he was constantly making the rounds, but that does not mean there was no drama. My mom and sister stayed around for a while, and I was amazed that my mom tipped for my Jack and Cokes. She hated my dad for drinking so much, but it was a special occasion, and my mom paid to get me drunk. You didn't even have to pay for booze, but that is the type of woman Mom Dukes is, and she loves —— or whatever his name is (the groom).

 She had been driving us around from age eleven to seventeen. Who wouldn't love him? My mom is a stiff tipper, so the bartender was serving me half a bottle of Jack with a splash of Coke until he left. After that, I took care of myself. I did not end up getting belligerent; however, I was plastered ass. At one point, I was out at the car, firing up the "green party," when one of the neighborhood kids from back in the day came out to join me and asked if I was out there to get away. I didn't know what he meant, so he said to take ten steps toward the mansion. I did, and all I could hear was someone with a high-pitched voice screaming, ranting, and raving about God-knows-what, and I knew exactly who it was. It was the kid who kicked me out of his wedding for ruining it, and he was upstaging me. So I went up to where the sign-in thing was that I fucked up for his wedding to prove that I could do it right, but I was not allowed. I got to the book or whatever it was and was immediately cut off by my mom, sister, wife, and a bunch of other bitches. I can't quite remember who, but none of them would let me near the sign-in book.

They, including my mom, said that they knew what I did last time, and they would not let me do it again. How the fuck did my mom know about that? Regardless, we agreed that my better half would write out the message, and I was only allowed to sign my name. No joke, they huddled over me, ready to steal the pen at any moment, so I simply wrote my name, and once again, I adverted fucking up my brother's special day. I felt vindicated even though I would never have done that I fucked up once, but I'll be damned if I do it again.

A little later, the boy whose wedding I did fuck up pulled me aside to "talk." I was ready to throw down if need be, but I am glad that was not the case. All he wanted is for me to admit that I made a mistake. His good buddy is the one who suggested I do it, but the pen was in my hands. I had the power to draw a penis or a heart, and I picked the wrong one. I do feel bad about it, and I truly apologized. I don't think we are going to go bowling any time soon like we used to, but I am glad we were able to squash it. He eventually got enamored and was screaming again, not at me but at the trash can in the middle of the kitchen, where there were more than a dozen partygoers conversing. He screamed his brains out and then his insides in front of everybody. The entire kitchen was filled with the smell of hot puke, and he cleared out the room in a matter of seconds.

He eventually got booted outside, and the groom went out to follow him. The new wife called on me to find them because they had both been missing for a long time. I saw which way they walked, so I went off to find them. I walked around the entire perimeter of everywhere they could have been, but when I found them, it was not the groom consoling the drunky; it was the other way around. I found them both on the front steps of the mansion, and the groom was keeled over in a bad way.

All of a sudden, he whose wedding I ruined and I were working together to save the groom. I was sent on the mission to find him by his new wife, who was freaking out, and told me that because I was his best friend I would be able to find him, but I could not bring him back to her in the condition that he was in. We worked together to get him out of sight; it was like we were friends again. Like I say, I don't think we will be going bowling anytime soon, but it was nice to play with him again. Do you remember when you used to call a friend when you were little and ask them if they wanted to come over and play? It was kind of like that, except our game was "get the drunken groom into hiding before the bride drops a tit because her new hubby has gone missing."

I ended up towing his limp body upstairs, which is fucked because I used to weigh twice as much as him, and it was all muscle. But now I have a broken back, he's got fifty pounds on me, and I got stuck dragging this big lump of dead meat up a ton of curvy stairs so that he would be out of sight from his new bride. I threw him in a room, out of sight, and told the new old lady that we found him and he was all gravy. She was cool with that and continued to get plowed with the rest of the lushes.

The mansion was supposedly haunted, and I wanted to see me some fucking ghosts. I knew our mutual neighborhood pot buddy and his girl would not be down to go looking for them. Why? Because they are black, and black people are terrified of ghosts. Sometimes stereotypes are completely accurate, and sometimes they are fucked, but in my experience, "they" stay away from ghosts, magic, and water. It is not always true. I have seen a white man dunk and a black man swim, but if you did the numbers, everyone is equally equal. My niece who is mixed race or half black (however you want to put it) was told by her mother (black) that black people cannot swim and that they will automatically sink if they go into water. That is fucked. Just because that stupid whore can't swim doesn't mean she needs to ruin her daughter's life.

My niece told me this theory up at the cabin, where she wore a life jacket always. I told her that was bullshit and G'd her life jacket and properly pushed her off the dock. It took me about five minutes to teach her to float and swim, and now you can't keep her out of the water. In fact, since my back issue, that little freak can swim laps around me, and you can't get her out of the water. You would not be able to teach me to dunk though; that will never happen.

I went off on a tangent there, but the fact remains, no one would come look for ghosts with me except for these two girls who had names, but I don't name names. We went throughout the house, top to bottom. The basement was uneventful, but these girls were drunk and still wanted to play. The attic was supposed to be the haunted place, so the three of us went up there in the dark and just sat and smoked a copious amount of marijuana. If it were ten years ago and my wife was not on the same property, I guarantee I would have plowed them both. They were being quite suggestive and touchy. We began talking all types of sex and porno stuff, and to be honest, I was being kind of a pompous asshole. Drunk girls love that shit for some reason. I wasn't really being a dick, but I knew that we all went to the same high school. They were younger than me, so they knew me, but I had no clue who the fuck they were. We kept talking about dirty ish when one of them said, "You have a lot of confidence, don't you? I bet you have a big cock, huh?" At that exact moment, my wife came up the stairs, looking for me, and heard every word. This startled the young harlot, so for some reason, she turned to the wifey and asked if that was the case. The wife responded, "Why the fuck would I tell you that? Then you would chase it." It was unspoken, but it was time to go, and I wanted to find my drunken little buddy anyways. Plus I wasn't planning on doing anything.

We got down to the kitchen, and it smelled so bad I was half embarrassed for the puke master who wrecked the kitchen and half mad because it was fucking disgusting. The kitchen was full of everybody who was loud, and they were all yelling at each other. I have no idea how they put up with that stink. It was a spectacular mix of hooligans, both male and female, and nobody was speaking the same language. It was kind of funny, but the main man was still alive, and that's all I cared about, and then he disappeared. I stuck around because I understand Spanish, and I found it to be funny as hell.

The "wife" of one of my groomsmen was very loud and either telling people that she loved them so much or simply "Fuck you!" An old buddy from the neighborhood put her in her place, and it was fucking clown shoes. He went off about how she has been here for over fifteen years and she can't talk normal. I don't necessarily agree with his viewpoint, but I have stayed in other countries for long periods of time, and I had no problem picking up the accent within a week or two. She is holding on to that shit because she wants to go home and she wants to bring our cousin away from us with her. He is very protective of his women, so I stood in between the conflict, but he just stood back and laughed. I know him very well as well, and I could read his face like a book. If anyone else was saying the things that were said to his girl, they would have gotten sliced. I don't know where he keeps them, but he could be butt naked. And if you insult him, he will pull a razor out of God-knows-where and cut you—that is how Latinos roll.

The kitchen still smelled like puke, and it was really gross, so I went to find the groom once again because he had disappeared. During my search, I found the bride passed out on a futon in the middle of the room next to the bar. I figured she would be all right there for a little while until I could find her man, so I went on the hunt, which took almost as long as the neighborhood search for him an hour or so earlier. I started at the basement, which everyone was afraid of, and scoped the whole house top to bottom. He must have been walking around because I eventually found him in a room I had already checked. I had to slap him a bit and remind him that he just got married and should probably sleep the first night with his wife. This was not easy, but eventually, I was able to drag him downstairs to the lady on the couch. My hope was that she would help me bring them both upstairs to the super-king-size bedroom that was bigger than the top floor of my house, but she just grabbed him and pulled him down onto the futon. I figured that my work there was done and that she would eventually bring him upstairs and take advantage of their bedroom that was worth more than my whole house. I said that I would check on them.

I wanted to do some more ghost hunting. The kitchen still smelled like puke, and there was still a lot of noise, so I grabbed some supplies (sticky weed, pipe, lighter, couple shots, beer, etc.) and everything you could possibly need to go ghost hunting in a pitch-black haunted attic. Everything except for a motherfucking flashlight, I forgot that. I said goodbye to the puke kitchen and told them where I would be in case I got "poltergeisted" and they needed to save me. I had no lights, but I think one of the girls I was up there with before had magic ninja weed sensors, like in cartoons where the character smells it and floats to the source, which is exactly what this bitch did.

I was up in the attic for about two seconds, and she came up right behind me and sat down. She also did not have a flashlight. We stayed up there smoking cheeba for around two hours, and I did not hear no ghosts. I think she just wanted to get high, and I have no problem with that. As long as I have enough, I prefer to smoke with someone as opposed to alone. Once again, the talk turned to porn-type shit, and I could have hit that in a heartbeat, but I realized that I might have actually grown up a little bit. Growing up a little bit from a piece of shit doesn't mean dick. It would have been fun to have nasty dirty porno sex like she said that she was into, but I had to go home in the morning with my wife.

Ten years ago, that would have been awesome, and I would not have felt a bit of regret, but I had the little devil and little angel on my shoulders, and the white one won. I used to have no conscience, but my old lady takes care of me, and I would think about it every day, and I am so glad I did not go through with that.

I said that there were obviously no ghosts and I had to check on my brother to make sure he could consummate his marriage in a "decent" bed that was about the size of my entire bedroom. When I did get there, they were still spooning on the fucking futon and would not move. That's cool; it was their deal and waste of money. Any other day, I would have G'd that bed and sprawled all out, but I had a trollop of my own in a bed somewhere, and I found her. The fucked-up thing is that everyone that planned the shit, including my wife, knows that I do have a history of sleepwalking, and they could not have planned the rooms any worse. Luckily, nothing bad happened, and I am surprised that I did not fall down any stairs at all, not even a slip, probably because I was on high alert to "not be that guy."

Right outside of our room, if you were to walk straight forward, two steps maybe, there was a stairwell, all wood, literally across the two-foot hallway, and then you would roll down the stairs. My back is already broken; I could have been paralyzed. I said, "Whatever," because it had been a while since I had sleepwalked, at least a couple of years. The next morning, I was awoken by a herd of recovering drunkards who had been looking for me for quite some time…I did sleepwalk, and I am extremely lucky I did not fall down those stairs. They found me in some random bed down the hall. All in all, it was the most successful wedding I have ever been to, and I wish those kids the best of luck.

I finally talked to my sister seriously about her baby and the piece of shit that helped her make it, and I finally got her to be honest. I asked her exactly what I had asked her before, and she finally owned up to it and told me that she had the kid on purpose even though she had no way to support it and the worthless video game junkie wasn't going to do dick and was really irresponsible. She did not say the last part, but she at least admitted to the fact that she got pregnant on purpose, knew she was pregnant, and kept it a secret from me because she was afraid of how I would react.

I told her that she was a moron and I was disappointed even though I knew it from the first second that I looked at her face when she told me she had something to tell me. I am always honest with her, and it really hurt my feelings that she would flat-out lie to my face. I realized that she wasn't going to go anywhere, so I just figured that I would have to deal with it. She brought her everywhere, which really pissed me off at the wedding. We had a short list to begin with, but she decided that it was okay to bring her infant, who was not even one year old, to the wedding in Las Vegas for God's sake. We were staying in a fucking casino. If you run out of smokes, you could get your fix just walking around the hotel, secondhand style. Las Vegas is no place for a child, and I didn't want a baby at the wedding, and I thought she was being inconsiderate by bringing an infant on a plane. I told her that she should just know that the second she walks on the plane, everyone on that plane will instantly hate her. I was upset because I could not understand why she couldn't leave the baby home with the dick-sucking homo faggot fucker. I have nothing against gay people; I see them as equal. They should have every right that straight people do and should be allowed to marry, but sometimes those words are applicable and fun to say.

There is no way to describe a thirty-year-old man wearing a fanny pack. I don't care if it is functional and convenient. That shit is gay. All the blondie's friends had kids, and they did not even bring their husbands, let along children. They all agreed that it was suspect and not believable, but whatever, she did it anyways, and she brought the fucking baby. It was not like they were staying in our room or anything, but I specifically asked her not to bring that thing, and she did anyways. I love her, but what a bitch.

The soon-to-be wife and I flew out early so we could get the license taken care of, and that was really uneventful even though going to the courthouse is technically the marriage and the rest is just for show. There was nobody there, and it took like two seconds, so at that point, we were officially married, but we still had to do the fucking ceremony thing to make her happy. The cabby must have seen it in my face because on the way back to the hotel, he asked if we wanted him to stop by the liquor store. My heart dropped. I just said, "Holy shit, it is like you have known me my whole life. Yes, I would like to go to the LQ. Thank you." We went back, and I got loaded, and we played a few slots. I didn't play any tables because it was a really crowded weekend and they were always packed, and on top of that, I don't really know anything about gambling etiquette. I know a little, but I don't feel comfortable in Vegas, and I don't like to lose all my money, so the nickel slots are enough fun for me.

The families all came the next day. It was crunch time, and I felt like hot death. My friends were supposed to arrive any minute. It took a while, but I basically told everyone to suck it up and wait for my friends to get there. They did, and we had a really nice dinner. I actually ate a lot of food. I wanted my sister to come out with all of us after dinner, but she would not because she said she had to take care of the baby. I told her that grandma was there to take care of that so she could come out and have fun, no dice. This is why I did not want her to bring that fucking child. We got into a little argument, which consisted mostly of me talking shit and talking down to her. My mom and my Ecuadorian friend split it up. I simply said, "You know you were wrong," and we went our separate ways.

I was really disappointed. I wanted to hang out with her more and we would, but for the time being, I was really pissed off. I went and hung out with my two buddies and went back to their telly for drinks. When we got back to the room, my little Hispanic friend tore into me like I raped his mother. I understand that in his culture they respect their women much more than Americans and probably most cultures, but this was a family issue, and it was between me and her. I would never lay my hand on a woman for any reason, and this was my sister; we were best friends, so I think that gives me the right to talk shit if we are having a disagreement. We debated for about half an hour, and I told him off. I said that I knew that he grew up in a matriarchal society and had the upmost respect for the women, and I agree with that. But I believe if someone is wrong, then you have every right to voice your opinion. I admit that I am a bit outspoken and might come off like an asshole at times, but I always make my point and am undefeated in debates. I think it might be because people get sick of listening to me ranting and raving; that is still a win in my book. We agreed to disagree, hugged, and ended it all with a bunch of shots and beer—can't go wrong there.

The next day was the wedding, so I figured I should get at least a little bit of sleep. I threw up right away in the morning and knew that I had to fix that situation or I would be in deep shit. A lot of times when I get sick in the morning, I end up being sick the majority of the day, and that would not be acceptable that day. I knew what I had to do, so I started crushing some suds. She went down to the pool, and I said I would meet her there. Unfortunately, I had no weed to calm my nerves because I didn't want to ruin the wedding and everyone's tickets/hotel rooms by getting kicked off the plane before we even got married, so I did not have any. I did have an option at one point, but I didn't like the dude's prices. He tried to sell me an ounce; I told him I was only here for a few days, and he told me a price per gram.

First of all, I did not like his price because I did the math and it was jacked up. Maybe he thought I didn't know what I was doing, so I said no. Secondly, he was a shady character, and I was getting a bad vibe. His buddy was standing very close and making me suspicious. I also had all my money in my wallet; I should have had a smaller denomination in my pocket for such an occasion, but I did not. There were police everywhere. We were out in the open, and there is no way I was going to walk off the beaten path with these two gangster to get a couple grams of weed.

One of two things would have happened—either I pull out my wallet and buy some shit only to be arrested in a heartbeat or I pull out my wallet, dude sees that I have more loot, punches me in the head, and steals my wallet. Either way, I didn't like the possibilities, and it wasn't worth it. Everyone already flew out and had their hotel rooms, and I didn't want to be that guy that ruined the whole weekend for everybody. It turned out to be a god decision because on the way back, after I had grabbed my supplies, the cops were busting some cats in the same area, so I feel like I dodged a bullet. I didn't have any weed, so I just drank it up but tried not to go too far because I did not want to act a fool at the wedding and ruin it. I drank myself up to an equilibrium and was good for the day. It was funny because without smoking pot I was more stable than I had been in years. This only led me to drink a whole lot more, but I tried to pace myself until after the ceremony.

I went down to the pool and met up with the girls; my two buddies were going to swing by. I thought they would want to go swimming; it was a nice fucking pool with a swim-up bar and everything. I told the best man or boy-girl and the other friend that I had invited to meet me by the pool because it was really nice. These deep shits walked up to us at the pool in street clothes. I thought we would go swimming and shit, but no dice. I should have known better; it was too public for the boy-girl. And even though they just reunited and became friends again, they usually stick together.

The bride-to-be and I went and got some beers at to pool bar. It was eleven dollars for a fucking can of Red Stripe. They were sixteen ounce, but still that's a lot of fucking money for one beer. I buy a case of beer for that price in Minnesota. I do drink cheap shitty beer, but still that is really pricey, so I decided to limit my bar drinking and load up on supplies from the store.

I found it funny that the only place on the strip to get milk, bread, cheese, as well as beer and hard alcohol was Walgreens. They don't have anything like that in Minnesota; you can't even buy alcohol on Sunday. We had our drinks, and I went back to the room to pack up some beer that I had previously bought. I drank four more beers for less than the price of one; I had beaten the system.

I was sitting with my old lady and her friends when her father came up to me, put his hand on my leg, and said, "There is no turning back now, it's all over now." He didn't say the last part, but I could see it in his eyes. I told him that I knew what I was in for, and he told me I was part of the family now. Well, not yet, but as long as I didn't leave her at the altar. That is not possible because the groom waits at the altar, not the bride, and I had no plans of doing that anyways.

My two buddies came to meet me before the whole thing; they came over fully dressed, and when they came in, I was still in my pajamas. They were kind of pissed off, but I got dressed in under five minutes. I had trouble with my tie because it needed to be tied just right for the costume, and I could not do it. My Ecuadorian friend helped me out because it needed to be perfect. The best man and I were going as the Blues Brothers. We were the only ones in the wedding dressing up, and he never would have done it if I hadn't made him. Her sister rented a limo for the wedding party, which was a little disappointing because there was no liquor in the car, but that was okay because I had some beers packed in my tux somehow.

We got to the shitty "chapel," which was actually shown in *Fear and Loathing in Las Vegas* and right next to a pawnshop that has its own show for some reason. The old lady actually watched that show all the time, and I tried to tell her, but she did not want to. She regrets it now. When we got in the building, we only had to wait a few minutes for the couple before us to be done. There was an Elvis impersonator there that we could have paid to do the wedding, which I wanted to do because my mom hates Elvis and it would have really pissed her off because she would have known that I did it to bug her. I decided not to do that, and we just did the regular ceremony, which only took about five minutes once we got in there. We did have to take pictures afterward, but it was no more than ten minutes with everything. The second we got done, I lit up a smoke and headed for the beer. We had the reception at a really nice place, and the meal was unbelievable.

Her sister (or I should say her sister's husband) paid for everything, and I was okay with that. I ate stuff I have never had and some that I had only heard of, but it was too pricey for my pallet. Everything was awesome, but I don't think that I liked the clams. We had a wicked nice cake. I say that because it was Halloween-themed, and but it was also wicked cool. It was all black with a spiderweb, a spider on it, and the cake was chocolate and cream cheese. It was fucking delicious, but there was something much more tempting on the menu, and it was free, so I could not turn that down.

I don't fuck around when there is an open bar; I can drink beer all day and be just fine, but at times like these, my kind seeks strong drink. I started out with Jack and Coke. I actually drank all they had, which was only like half of a bottle, but I killed it. I asked my cousin what he was drinking on, and he said he was going to drink Maker's Mark, so it was on like Donkey Kong because we killed that bottle. We opened it, drank equally, and were done with it in no time. The crazy thing was I could stand and walk perfectly fine, and I had more to drink than anyone else at the wedding. It was probably because I did not have any herb, but I don't care. I will tip over now and then if that is the price to pay for smoking that sweet, sweet cheeba.

That second bottle was not the end of the party. I killed a few more drinks, and then all the girls wanted to go out and dance. Goddamn, that shit is annoying, especially when they can't dance, and it really is embarrassing to be seen with them. We went back to some casino; I think it was Caesar's Palace where we were staying, but

I have no idea because I was plowed. I did not really want to pay for drinks at the bar; I would rather go the LQ and get a case of beer for the same price because I would just walk around with my can of beer and no one would say shit even though it is illegal.

As long as the drunks are pouring money back into the city, they turn a blind eye. As we walked around, the boy-girl and I kept getting stopped simply because we were the Blues Brothers and people wanted to take our picture or a picture with us. I guess they thought we were performers or something, it was funny. I had a few Jack and Cokes before we went out to whore it up. We went to the Bourbon Room, which was really popular for some reason. The place was poppin' and it was a lot of fun. There was a Rocky Horror Picture Show theme going on, but we were not aware of that. We just went there and danced. I had fun.

I went on the floor and was dancing with every girl that was not my new wife. I mostly danced with her friends. They were grinding their butts on my crotch like sluts in a rap video, and I was slapping asses like a wicked school mistress; it was a good time. I got off the floor for a while to grab my friends, my cousin, and the Ecuadorian. They came out and danced, but I could not get the best man to get on the floor. We were wearing fucking matching costumes; he had to come out and dance with me. Beyond that, he knew the Blues Brothers dance and had it down pat. It was perfect, but he would not budge.

At one point, the MC left to go take a piss or something, and on the way back, he stopped me and asked if the boy-girl and I were together. I said yes but not like that. He said that there was a costume/dance contest and that if we entered we were guaranteed to win at least $250, so I was all for it. I told my buddy that we had to go up there, and somehow I got him onto the floor. Well, actually, I was pushing him. We were all out on the floor dancing, waiting for the next contest to start on stage.

I was grinding and slapping ass as the kids do these days, and when the contest was starting, my best man was nowhere to be seen. He got scared. My heart dropped like I had lost my only child. I ran to the nearest restroom and checked every stall—men's and women's. I even checked everyone within like a mile radius, but there was no sign of him. I went back to the club and found my Ecuadorian friend. I told them that the best man was MIA and we needed to find him ASAP. I told one of the girls that we were dipping out and why. I don't know if she even heard me, but we went out to the strip to begin the search. We walked up and down, checking all restrooms and benches. He was plowed, so we figured that he got sick and passed out. My buddy's phone had no service, so he kept trying my phone for about twenty minutes until we finally got through to him. That motherfucker went back to their room to lie down and didn't say shit to anyone. I was furious.

We went back to the club to let my cousin and the girls know what was going down and it was that it was time for them to head out as well. They were all pretty fucked up, but my new wife was fall-down drunk, and it was hilarious. They all decided to head back to their rooms. I made sure that my wife's sister would make sure she got back to our room because I needed to go find my friend. This was on our wedding night…I had my priorities in order. I would jump in front of a bus for that kid. The Ecuadorian, my cousin, and my girl's friend with huge tits walked to his hotel to make sure he was still breathing. He was, which meant I could let him know how I felt about him, leaving me alone on the dance floor without telling me where he was going.

He is not the type of person that should be left alone on the streets of Las Vegas, especially when he is drunk-ass like he was. He has a short temper and a big mouth. He could have easily gotten himself into a lot of trouble with the law or worse, so I was scared. We got to the room, and sure as shit, he was passed out on the bed, and I was relieved, but then I remembered how angry I was that he just boned out without a heads-up. I knew what I had to do.

I jumped on the bed and smothered him. I shook him like a horrible parent or babysitter would shake a baby. I knew I might get puked on, but I didn't give a fuck. I was pissed off. After I had gotten my point across, I hugged him, and we spooned for a minute. I love him and was just glad that he was safe, but I was still upset.

Now it was time for strong drink. We drank a bunch of whiskey, and I picked on the boy-girl while he was trying to sleep. He doesn't remember any of it. My cousin bitched out first, which makes sense because he is forty years old and then some. It is also funny that he did not know how to drive a manual car. I taught him how to drive a stick, and I thought it was funny teaching someone ten years older than me how to do something you should learn when you are fifteen. If you got stuck in some shitty situation and there was only one working car and it was a stick, you would be fucked if you did not know how to drive it.

So my cousin went back to his hotel. His girlfriend was there, but I never met her. It was just me, my Ecuadorian, and Big Boobs taking shots and me occasionally fucking with the boy-girl. Boobies and I left after a while because it was way past late. It was kind of odd hanging out with her because I had previously hated her for a long time. This was a result of a party my first roommate and I had at the house and she was there. For some reason, she began wrestling with my roommate, which was all in fun, but he had her pinned, so she grabbed his cock and balls. I looked at her in the eyes, and she knew what she was doing. I said, "What the fuck?" She smiled, squeezed his balls, and twisted them. I could not let that shit go because I couldn't believe she actually did it.

After four or five years, I just let it go because she was not going anywhere seeing as she was one of blondie's best friends, and I was not going anywhere either. We had a talk, and it is all peace now. We actually have a lot in common. We are both big drinkers who will fight at the drop of a hat. She walked with me back to the hotel, but I was so drunk and casinos are constructed in a way that you basically get lost, keeping you there longer. I asked here to help me, and she walked me to my room. I gave her a hug and went to the room. We have been friendly ever since. I returned to our "wedding suite," which was crap, and I found my bride in a pretty shitty way. The first thing I did was go take a leak where I found her leg bracelet thing, which I was supposed to take off her after the wedding on the floor in front of the toilet along with her panties. The leg garter I was supposed to bite off or some kind of dumbass tradition.

I am still glad that she was passed out because there was puke everywhere over her drawers and hooker gear, everything. I walked into the bedroom; my mind was blown because it was nothing like I would have pictured my wedding night to be like even though I never really wanted to get married in the first place. I walked into a bedroom with my new wife sprawled out on the bed coved in potato chip crumbs and snoring like my dad. At least she put pajamas on, so I was able to get a memorable wedding photo I showed her parents in the morning. She was a hot mess, but I still fucked her brains out in the morning. I bent her over the bed and went to town.

I spent some time with my sister while my mom watched the little shit machine. We stayed up pretty late, but did not spend much money, just nickel slots, but we had fun. Earlier in the day, the horse of the husband of my new wife's sister was racing in some derby, which is where he gets all his money from. I put five dollars on it, but it ate a giant shit sandwich.

There was also a wild game, and they were playing my cousin's team. I wanted to bet on that, but I knew that Minnesota was going to lose the game. I really wanted to rub it in his face if they did, but they did not, and I am glad that I did not bet even though I just lost the money with my sister on the slots that night.

We flew back to Minnesota the next day, and I guess I was an ass on the plane. I know my voice carries, but people were staring at me, and some bitch hit me in the head with her bag as she was walking by. I guess I was making a big deal about it. Now my wife does not want to fly with me anymore either, oh well. We returned to the frozen tundra, and I had one thing on my mind. There was a pipe and a couple bowls of weed in the car, and I could not wait. We gave the boy-girl a ride back to his house since he lives in Iowa, closer to the airport than us, so it made sense. I got so high with only taking like two rips of that delicious cheeba. It is amazing what taking three days off from smoking can do.

We came back home and nothing had changed. We picked up the dogs because the boy-girl's wife was watching them for us. They were not married, but they will be. We returned home, and in the following months, I was asked multiple times how my life was different now that I was married. There was no difference whatsoever. We had lived together for six years so, and everything was exactly the same, except for the fact that she changed her name. We still go to hockey games and lacrosse games even though I don't think she gives two shits about the games, but I have fun, and we go to shows because we do agree on some music, but if it is hip-hop, I think she just goes to be nice and spends time with me.

We went up north every fall to look at the leaves and ride the scary ass roller-coaster thing that flies down the "mountain" and seems really unsafe, but that makes it fun. It's just a little go-kart on rails, and it goes really fast with sharp turns. We go to a new place every time, usually Duluth, but there was one bed and breakfast that was really cool. It was old as hell, and I cannot believe it wasn't haunted, but it was still cool. The north shore is always beautiful, but somehow leaves changing color makes it really pretty for some reason the leaves changing colors and the overall atmosphere of being "Up Nort" along with the whole Minnesota nice factor makes a very beautiful place even better…It smells really good too. **More Loss.** By this time, I had realized that I truly had lost the best friend I had in my sister. I had already boycotted her baby's daddy, and since he is no longer allowed at any family functions, I could no longer go over to her house because it would not be a pretty scene. I might need a step-stool, but I would punch that tall motherfucker square in the nose before he even had a chance to say hello. Since she always had the fucking baby, she rarely came out, and when she did, the little one came along. I see her every once in a while, but I really miss my sister.

The dad of the boy-girl with the dangling earring died this morning. It was the saddest moment in my life since the day that I got that horrible phone call. His father did not like me at all to say the least. He saw me as a drug-dealing, drinking bad influence to his son. He was probably correct in that assumption. After high school, when I graduated on the dean's list and went to a university, once again graduating on the dean's list, he warmed up to me and actually showed me some respect.

Unfortunately, on this shitty day, my buddy had plans to come into civilization from his residence that I basically refer to as Iowa. It might as well be he lives so far away I never see my brother anymore. He had plans to meet up with his father to go get new tires for his car and go out for a Sunday drive. He drives a Monte Carlo, which was his dad's favorite car in the world, and he was very obsessive about it. He loved his Monte until one day someone broke into the garage, jacked it, and stripped it. They found it in a cornfield or some shit, and it had been strategically disassembled. We joked about it, but it really did seem that he loved that car more than life itself. He would sit out in the garage and drink Bud Light and just stare at his awesome car.

My pops did the same shit except he was staring at a clusterfuck of God-knows-what all over. It has been eight years now, and I am still digging through endless shit, and I have no idea where or what anything is. Now I know why he stood out there so long doing nothing. It is like a tornado blew through a hardware store and threw it up into the garage. Old men are funny. The boy-girl's dad got a new car, another Monte, and he built a fortress around it. He tore down his garage and made it twice the size, turning it into the most gangster man cave ever made. There was room for like three cars with an additional twelve feet covered with checker box flooring for watching car racing and whatnot, and it was fully furnished with everything you could possibly need—couches recliners, fridge, big-ass TV. It was the ultimate safe zone for any married man.

My buddy called me on Super Bowl Sunday and gave me the news. It really sucked because I was stoked for this game, partially for the commercials, but Denver is my number-two team after the Vikings. I had everything set up—good beer, just enough stinky ass weed to get me by, and nobody coming over. I was happy, and then I got that call. He called his work first and said that he would not be in for a few days, but I was the first one that he called and actually said it out loud and began to come to terms with the shitty situation. It was the first time he actually let go and expressed his feelings, and I knew how he felt to some degree.

I basically hated my father for the majority of my life. We did have good times and memories, but for some reason, I tend to always remember the bad shit. The boy-girl and his dad had a great relationship, so I can only imagine that what he is and will be going through must be ten times what I experienced. I only regret that I didn't spend more happy time with my old man, whereas my buddy and his dad had a great relationship. I envied that.

People can think whatever they want in this situation and that maybe I should not get so broken up over the death of a man who was not even my father. I did not go see him every day, but I did bring him some homemade beef jerky every once in a while, and we would watch car racing and drink some Bud Light. His dad was a fucking G and always had a strap on his belt. He pulled his steel on some gangster trying to get in his garage. This was an old man who was G'd up from the feet up and was not going to take it anymore. Taxi driver style.

The fact is that when I heard the news, it was like my dad died all over again. I was obviously sad about the news and the loss in general, but I cried like a little bitch because I knew what my brother was going to have to go through. I could only just promise to be there for him no matter what, as well as his mom if she needed because she lives like a block away from me and he lives in fucking Iowa or at least he might as well.

Hindsight

The following are afterthoughts that I came up with while writing and could no longer find a chronologically correct place to put them, so I figured I would consolidate them at the end. I have never read anything this long before, let alone write it, but that is okay because it is confusing and all over the place, much like my mind state. I wish I had strapped a tape recorder to my skull like the late great Hunter S. Thompson while trying to recall the stony drunken haze that is my childhood and beyond. Had I done so, I would never finish what I am writing, and it would be far too long to read, maybe I need to do volume 2.

    I stayed in touch with my high school sweetheart even thought I cheated on her, and she ran me over with her car, we stayed friends that occasionally got naked and did the damn thing, no big deal. She even stayed with me for about a week while I had a live-in girlie. The reason was that her boyfriend punched her in the eye and pushed her down some stairs. Drugs were definitely involved. She still won't tell me the name of the asshole, but if I ever find out, I will cut his dick off and shove it up his ass. It was really weird, but it all worked out, and she and my old lady actually get along, and it was all peace. They bonded over their hatred of the girl who was my first crush and the one I hooked up with in Colorado.

    The period of my relationships with these three girls overlapped, spanning over a decade. They all knew each other because we went to the same school and they all hated each other with a passion because they all knew what I was doing yet they all continued to fuck me. Girls are crazy. There were many, many others during this time, but these were the ones I truly did love and still care about to this day.

I love fishing and have caught huge fish in the ocean, but I just love being out on the water. My high school girlfriend and I would fish all the time. She loved fish to the point that after she would unhook her catch, she would kiss it and say, "I love you," before setting it free. I won't go that far, but if a fish gets caught and stuck in the weeds, I have a pair of goggles in my tackle box, and I will dive in and swim to the fish, save it, and set it free, saving the fish and the lure. I don't kiss the fish thought.

I do have two bad catches throughout my fishing career, however. My fist was in Montana when I was probably eight or nine. I was fishing off the dock, and the neighbor's dog was standing behind me, and I did not know. It was a black Lab. I went to cast, and after I drew back and went to cast, I was stuck. The Lab had jumped at the lure and ate the lure. I freaked out and dropped the pole. The dog freaked out and ran back to the cabin, which was up a steep rocky hill, dragging the pole behind him. If I remember correctly, the neighbor wanted to kill me, but I think I was too young to be held accountable.

The next incident was on the lake down my street at a friend of mine's property. He told me to fish there any time I wanted as long as if I catch a carp I kill it, basically by bashing it with a blunt object until it stopped living. Luckily, I never caught a carp on his property, but one day, I had the catch of a lifetime. I went to the dock, and my buddy's little brother was fishing there, so we hung out and fished for the afternoon until I made one cast I will never forget. It was a one-in-a-billion shot that I could never do again if I tried my whole life. I caught a blue heron in midair; it swallowed my lure and flew off. It was strong and almost pulled my rod out of my hand, so I held on and tried to reel it in, not to catch it but to set it free. The bird was trying to fly away, but it was tethered to my pole and basically flying in place, trying to get to the tree line, which would have been a bigger disaster, so I kept reeling it in to no avail.

An old man was walking around the lake and saw this, which really pissed him off. He yelled, "What the hell are you doing? Leave that fucking bird alone!" Why the fuck and how the hell could I catch a heron with a fishing pole on purpose? The bird was suffering, but I didn't want to cut the line because it might eventually choke it to death. I yanked on the line one last time, and somehow it unraveled, and the bird flew away, probably terrified but alive, and I know I didn't hurt him too bad because my line didn't break, and I still had my lure—no one got hurt.

However, I have not always been so nice while fishing. I do practice catch and release, but sometimes, every once in a while, I drink too much and don't think too much what will happen. Once we were fishing on the Mississippi "up nort." For some reason, a lot of people from Minnesota say "up nort" instead of "up north." I think it is because we are so close to Canada. There were four of us at one of the cat's cabin, and we were fishing off a fork in the river, which made it sort of like a little island. I got shit-canned real quick. We started drinking at dawn, maybe a little before that, and continued to do so all day. I drank way to much brown liquor, which is bad news for me. It makes me punchy and mean. I got way to drunk and dehydrated, plus it was hot as fuck out, so I did the only sensible thing and started rolling around in the mud until my whole body was covered.

Wild animals got it right; covering yourself with mud is an impenetrable sunblock and better than any bug sprays. I think I passed out for a minute or twenty, but I remember hearing thrashing in the water and ran to the riverbed. There was a carp flopping around in the shallows. Maybe it was too big for that part of the river. I knew what I had to do, and I dove off the riverbank like a fucking superhero and tackled that bitch. It was only like a three-foot drop to the water, but I had to jump pretty damn far only to land on the sewer rat of Minnesota lakes.

It was a white carp. I had never seen one before, and after I pounced on it, I had to wrestle it a bit. It was a hell of a fight, but in the end, I won. The fish was not killed by me or any of the crew, but we did see the same carp floating down the river a while later. I feel horrible in retrospect because I think I killed it, but what I did next was far worse. We fished up and down the river and were doing pretty well. In fact, I caught my first northern pike, which is to this date the only northern I have caught. I have also only caught one walleye. I have caught many a bass in my day, and unfortunately, one bass met me on the wrong day.

After a full day of heat, sun, whiskey, and some herb, I was a bit feisty. I don't remember if someone dared me to do it or if I am just a jackass, but I caught a medium-sized smallmouth, which is very fun to catch, and after I unhooked it, I bit its fucking head off while it was still alive. I spit the head out, threw the fish, and then I felt like the biggest asshole in the world.

That shit was fucked up, and even though I am not a believer, I probably deserve to go to hell for that. Sorry, fishy. I will always love fishing and will never bite another fish in half, but I can also never shoot, kill or harm any animal in any way ever again. I shot a bird in the throat with a pellet gun when I was around thirteen. It fell right out of the tree, but it wouldn't die. I shot it a few more times, and I ran out of CO_2, so I refilled the gun, stood on the bird, which had a perfect hole right through its neck that was pouring blood, and emptied the clip. The bird would not die, and I could not watch it suffer anymore. I stomped on its head to put it out of its misery, but it has caused me to feel like a dick for the rest of my life since that day. You should not kill animals unless it is for food and you really need it; otherwise, wobble your already overfed ass to whatever fast-food garbage food dispensary you frequent and leave the animals alone.

There are many animals that would and will eat you in a heartbeat if given the chance, but that is because they have to in order to survive. I hate guns, but I know how much bullets cost, and they are not cheap. Take that money and buy your meat from a grocer who gets their meat from a slaughterhouse where they kill hundreds of cattle and poultry every day. It sucks that these animals are bred simply to become our food. The point of my rant is, if you do have to kill something, it should only be to keep yourself alive. Is that selfish or survival?

Here are a few short memories that do have long stories, but my hands are getting tired, so I am just going to throw down the gist of it; they are pretty self-explanatory. The majority of my fronts (teeth) are fake or composites. I had a little too much fun growing up, doing stupid shit that was out of my league or running my mouth to someone who was out of my league. I also managed to hurt myself doing the most asinine things. One of my favorites was inspired by the boy-girl. The day before picture day in seventh grade, he dove off the diving board doing what he referred to as a sailor dive. He put his hands to his sides and dove headlong into the pool, which I think was about nine feet deep. That seems deep enough, but somehow, he managed to plow his face into the bottom of the pool. He fucked up his face pretty bad, and in his seventh grade school picture, it looks like someone put a power sander to his face. Over twenty years later, I would recreate that moment, but mine was a little more spectacular.

My sailor dive incident happened while playing with my niece at my soon-to-be-sister-in-law's pool. I love playing with her. I have known her since she was born and watched her grow up. She is the daughter of Flat Tire's brother and happens to be half black. I don't know if that is the politically correct way to that, but I don't give a fuck. People get pissed off if you say "mixed," and if something like that honestly bugs you, then you are too sensitive and should probably not be reading anything I write.

Regardless, my old lady's side of the family go up to a cabin every year in July, and the little ragamuffin was terrified of the water and would not get in even if you lit a fire under her ass. Her whole life, I have always been the one to play with her and her friends. She seemed to like me as did the rest of the kids, so I guess I took some of the stress of the "adults" while they got plowed. They drink a lot. This was a very new concept to me because my whole extended family is very straight-edge, not conservative per se, but they don't party or talk like my in-laws, and there is a ton of them. There is like thirty of them every year, and it's weird watching the kids grow up.

I have watched them from diapers to puberty to being as tall as me. It makes me feel old, but that's okay. I got a little off track, but my point was that I was always playing with the kids, especially the little girl who would eventually be my niece. We got along really well, and it seemed like she had a bit of a little girl crush on me. I ignored that because I just had fun playing with her, but I couldn't get over her fear of water, so I had a talk with her to figure out what the problem was. She informed me that her mother told her that she should not go in the water because she is black and black people cannot swim, and if she went in the water, she would sink like a stone.

We had a long talk, and I explained that it was the stupidest thing I had ever heard and threw her in the lake. She was still at the age where she needed a car seat, so she had a life jacket on, and it was shallow enough for me to stand, and I jumped in right after her and held her until she started treading water. She got the hang of it right quick, and now you can't keep that girl out of the water, and she is a great swimmer. So whenever we are near water, we swim and play. She likes to roughhouse, which was fun when she was little, but she is getting big and I am getting old. I just can't throw her around like I used to. I credit myself with helping her overcome her fear of water and teaching her how to swim.

I am never going to have kids of my own, so that is about as close as I will ever come to raising a child. She grew up so fast. I remember her in diapers, and she is thirteen now. While we were wrestling in the pool, I was dragging her around by her legs, and I noticed they were starting to get hairy, they had not always been that way, so naturally I said, "Hey, your legs are getting hairy." Without a pause, she explained that she knew and that her armpits were getting hairy as well. She then proceeded to say, "It is called puberty, duh." I knew that was going to happen any day now at this point, but I worry about when she grows into herself. She is a really pretty girl, and at thirteen, she is already getting a ghetto booty, and the front is starting to fill out. I feel really bad for her dad because if I were in his shoes, I would be that shotgun dad and she would be on a tight leash. I digress.

I found the fact that she mentioned the whole puberty thing so freely interesting. I asked what she knew or if she had taken sex ed. classes yet, and indeed, she had. And apparently, they teach it a lot differently these days. I remember seeing cartoons or drawings; she said they saw real pictures of everything, as well as STDs. That is a good scare tactic; however, I don't think it is working, especially because now fifteen-year-olds are trying to get pregnant to get a gig on some fucking MTV show. That shit makes me sick. I know she is not going to go that route though. I pray to something I don't believe in that she does not take that route because she is a real smart cookie and has mad potential. I know how I was at her age and what I was doing. She is not my daughter, but it makes me sick to think of her doing the type of dirty shit I was into at the tender age of thirteen.

I must say I knew much more than her when I was at that age; however, I found my dad's stash and was watching hard-core porn at around ten years old—shit that I still find kind of off-putting even though I got calluses on my hands from watching those movies every day. My parents were never home, so I watched that shit all day and night. The best part is I knew how to find and hit that clit before I was twelve. From what I remember, just about every girl I have talked to about the subject has said that at a young age, guys don't know what the fuck they are doing. I was a pro before I ever even saw a pussy in real life; I knew how to hit that spot before I had even kissed a girl. However, as with anything, you need to practice, and mistakes will be made. Every woman is different, and sometimes you have to explore before you find what makes her cum. Yeah, the clit seems like the fail-safe way to go, but sometimes it might take doing something completely different—something you never thought of and maybe don't want to do. But what the hell? I will try anything once, maybe more, no guys though. I am not homophobic; it is just not that kind of party.

The five-way was one thing, but it was dark, and there were two beds so my buddy and I were never on the same bed at the same time. The girls just kept going back and forth from bed to bed. I preferred just two girls until I turned thirty, and now it just seems like too much work. My record was having the old in-out-in-out with four different women in one day, all separate occasions. It took up my whole day. I should have doubled up with two of them and saved some energy, but I was twenty-something, and I had plenty of love to give. I would rather just take care of business, have a smoke, and pass out. No matter what, it is mandatory that you make your partner cum before you go; otherwise, you are just being selfish. I say partner because it doesn't matter what team you play for; the same rules apply.

I have been hit on by gay men before, but it never really bothered me. I would just say, "Thanks but no thanks." Every once in a while, long ago my friends and I would actually go to gay bars because there is a surprising surplus of straight women there who go there so they won't be hit on all night. If you just play it cool, the women that are interested will come to you, and the guys catch on and will leave you alone. Leave you alone as in not hit on you, but gay guys are awesome conversationalists. It is hard not to have a good time with a party of "queers," and I can say that because a gay friend of mine told me that word is okay now. The LGBT community has such power because they embrace who they are and don't give a fuck what anybody else thinks.

I would compare it to a fat black woman wearing something way too small and hanging her gut out, dancing at the club, but you know what? She don't give a fuck because she just got her nails and hair did, a new dress, and she is going to flaunt that shit because she knows that she is beautiful and that confidence does make a person more attractive. Confidence is very sexy, but you can go too far and then you just come off as a conceited asshole or cunt. Why did I call out fat black woman? Because white girls are so stupid when it comes to body image. They don't realize that true beauty really is within. It sounds cliché, but if I met the hottest woman in the world—big tits, fat ass, and the whole package—but usually complete moron or at least a bit daft, I couldn't do it. Yes, I would fuck the hell out of her and the next one, probably multiple times on separate occasions, but I would never have any emotional attachment or respect for her if sex is all she is good for. I need someone I can wake up with sober and have a meaningful conversation or no conversation at all and be content. My point is simply that it doesn't matter what for fix is as long as it makes you happy and happy for the right reasons. It is still fun to have random sex with someone you don't give two shits about because then you can do all types of dirty shit that you would probably not do with someone you love.

My advice would be to get all that shit out of the way while you are young and then find the one that you love and stick with it. I would suggest that you do as much as you can before you do find the one because if you do get really crazy while you are young, you will never need a porno again. You will have plenty of memories to masturbate to for the rest of your life. Masturbation is very healthy.

So if you do find the one who you feel that you love, I do have one theory about how to know if it is true love. A healthy relationship is based on communication, and if there is no conflict, there is really no communication. Couples do not agree all the time, and keeping problems pent up only leads to inevitable problems that usually end relationships. Being honest and speaking your mind might get you slapped in the face, but it may also save or even strengthen the bond between you and your significant other. I told my wife about my infidelities before we were married so I could go in with a clean slate. My mother told me that you only get married once, and I have always remembered that. What I have realized over time is that fighting is somewhat the cornerstone of a healthy relationship. If you keep your emotions and opinions to yourself, you not only prevent any progress in whatever issue there is, but you put yourself in a subservient position where you have no power. Power struggles can be the end of relationships, so there needs to be a happy medium. Stand your ground of some things that you really do care about, and don't back down, or you come off as a pussy. However, sometimes you need to just back down and let your significant other have their way, because sometimes it is really not that important and sometimes it has benefits.

The intention of this rant was supposed to be my definition of true love or at least an example of it. True love is when you can truly speak you mind and have a full-on pull-no-punches argument, which might possibly end in "Fuck you, I hate you," and then you walk away. You each take a breather, and five minutes later, you both approach each other on your own accord and apologize, regardless if you were right or wrong and simply say, "I love you," end of story. Maybe you have makeup sex, who knows? But it makes for a healthy relationship based on honesty even though sometimes you have to lie. White lies are important sometimes if it saves someone from hurt feelings, but you should tell someone if they look like a train wreck.

This is true love. If someone is wearing a horrible outfit or has a booger sticking out, you let them know. If you don't, you are a dick.

When my father passed away, he did have one dying wish, which was to have his ashes dumped into a particular lake in Glacier National Park. We fulfilled his wishes to some degree. It was a long steep climb to where he wanted to be and then a long steep descent to the lake, which just means more hills both ways. It was not close, and my sister could not make it. I gave her a ton of shit for that, but with my current back and knee and whatever else is wrong with me, I would have been the little bitch of the family. We did find a little waterfall that actually led right into the lake and poured his ashes in there, close enough.

As mentioned, my writing is all over the place, and I am constantly reminded of new things. As with my love of fishing, my love of bowling has many stories that arise. One of which I was just told about and would never had remembered it if Hanging Earring did not reiterate the story for me.

I have a stern policy and code of etiquette when it comes to bowling, and I don't fuck around. The first and foremost rule that I will not back down on is that you respect the bowler next to you. If the person in the next lane is about to roll, you do not walk up and throw your rock. You wait your fucking turn and roll your ball appropriately and politely; everyone wins. It seems to always be teenagers that fuck this up. I love rolling next to old people and little kids, but teenagers fucking suck. I was probably annoying as well when I was at that age, but I knew not to roll my rock when someone in the next lane was about to bowl; it's common sense. I have been known to have a few choice words with my neighboring bowlers for breaking the rules from time to time. Threats have been made and followed through, which is why my wife will not go bowling with me anymore unless it our birthday or some special occasion or something. There is one bowling alley that for some reason makes me fight or at least get into one. I believe I mentioned it earlier when on Christmas we got into a fight because my buddy yelled, "Jesus is the reason for the season" and a bunch of guys rushed us so I had to get the girls in the car first then get everyone split up and into the car. I did not throw one punch that night.

However, one night at the same bowling alley, my fellow hooligans and I were rolling next to a pack of post-pubescent, just-got-their-driver's-license cocky fuck heads and their bitches. This is what pissed me off. These hoes kept throwing the ball around like a fucking toddler with some sort of mental health issue, and I would just stand there and stare. After a few times, I looked at them and raised my hands as if to say, "What the fuck?" One of the boys on the asshole squad kept staring at me and would not take his eyes off me. I stared him down to the point that my eyes got dried out and lost interest. I really didn't care that much, but my buddy did.

My friend noticed him staring at me and asked him if he thought I was cute because he would not stop looking at me. I do not remember what was said next, but I do remember hearing, "Well, let's go do this," and without a word, the benches cleared, and we headed out to do the damn thing. My bodyguard railed him before I could get down the steps, and it was basically over, but that did not necessarily mean it was over. I threw in a couple of blows, and my buddy Chunky was stomping on his face with his Timberlands. At this point, the police arrived, and the kid claimed that we jumped him and stole his chain. My best bud got some mace to the face and hit with a blackjack (baton) by those who are meant to "serve and protect." He could not see or walk, so I had to carry him to the car. Later I found out that the police picked up his necklace right away and asked him if it was the chain we robbed him for, and it was end of story. He went to jail, and we all walked away.

I later found out that one of the girls whom I was apparently flirting with was the security guard's girlfriend, and he had it out for me and my crew the whole time. Something was said about getting a hotel room. I don't really remember that, but there is no doubt in my mind that this could have come up as a possibility. It sounds like something I would do. There is no way the police would have been there that fast if he was not on alert to the situation and we would have killed that kid.

I am on vacation right now up north (Minnesota), and I brought my laptop even though my wife told me not to because we're on vacation, but fuck her, I do what I want. Plus I figured it would give me something to do if it was a shitty day and everyone was being a bummer, and it just so happens that today is that day. Everyone is being either a crab ass or a bummer or is tired, so I walked away and locked myself in a little room. I come up to the same set of cabins every year on Big Sand Lake, and her whole family on her mom's side is there. It is a shitload of drunk motherfuckers and a bunch of rowdy little shits that get bigger every year.

I was reluctant to come up here for years even though the flat-tire girl asked me every year. I had not yet met her parents, so I wasn't going to get stuck for a week, five hours from civilization with a family of nutjobs and no way to escape. However, that is exactly what I eventually did. They drink a lot and they are all batshit crazy. I fit right in. I am usually the one that gets stuck playing with the kids—usually the little girls, they like me. They make me bracelets and paint my nails; it is awesome.

One of the daughters of my wife's cousin is a really smart cookie; she asked about and talked to me about my writing because she wanted to know what I was doing. I explained to her my writing style, and she totally understood. We also talked about random philosophical shit, and she was as good as or better than anyone in my college classes. There should be more kids like that; the world would be a better place.

There is also a pair of boys who have grown up now, and I know that at least one of them will serve time at some point, probably sooner than not. A couple of years back, I was shooting my pellet gun with them because they asked me to bring it up the previous year. One of them asked me to get them some beer. I started drinking at an early age, but not ten, so no dice on that little buddies, maybe in a couple years. I love it up here because it is quiet. Aside from the loons and other birds and, of course, the daily drunken quarrels, it is very peaceful. There are no cars driving by, no police sirens or gunshots; it is quite nice.

As far the family feuds go, wife's parents are like George's parents on Seinfeld; they wake up and go to sleep, yelling at each other and arguing over the stupidest shit. It is pretty funny sometimes, but it does get annoying. Her brother and sister all get into it the whole time, but it's all peace. At the end of the day, everyone loves each other even if they can't stand them. They are all very liberal, but they always manage to start some debate with the whole family over politics. They are all on the same side, but they all have their own opinion. I throw my two pennies in every once in a while, but for the most part, I stay out it, and sometimes I throw my hands up and walk away.

There are like thirty some people here. Here family is big, just her mom's side, and they all live in Minnesota. The only family I have in Minnesota is my mom and my sister. I only see my extended family if someone dies and possibly if someone gets married, but that depends on where the wedding is. It is kind of nice, but I can only remember so many names. They all know who I am, but I only know a couple of them by name, and I've known them all for years. I just say hi. I gave up trying to get people's names right a few years ago. They all know me because I stick out like a sore thumb in this family. They are all very fair-skinned, so I am the darkest person up here in northern Minnesota right now, including my half-black niece. I also have a bunch of tattoos as well, so I guess that makes me stand out, and none of them have any.

One year, all the boats met up at a channel to a connecting lake and one of the young girls who was new apparently said, "Who is the black guy with the tattoos in that boat?" referring to me. I thought that was funny. I enjoy hanging out with my father-in-law, especially after my dad died.

One year, I made a request to my new father-in-law to go out with him fishing, just me, and it was awesome. We didn't catch shit, and the weather was crap, but we just talked, and he filled a void that I did not realize was there to that degree. I was crying inside in a good way, but I did not let him see this. He actually just went into town to fix my fishing pole that my nephew's friend fucked up. What a nice guy. Although I know he used that as an excuse to go to a bar with my wife's uncle (and that is exactly what they did), he did fix the reel. When my wife's uncle heard that the reel needed to be fixed, he jumped at the opportunity to go into town and get a drink even though he said he just wanted to go to the bait shop. He is a good dude too.

Last year, he saw me walking up the beach, and I heard him say that it hurt his back to watch me walk. Apparently, he has a fucked up back as well, and he could feel my pain. It is not a secret in this family that I smoke pot like it is going out of style, and he was probably a party guy back in the day, so he asked my wife, not me, if I would smoke with him because his back was killing him and that seemed to help in the past. I was ecstatic; I love smoking with old people.

I brought up two kinds of chronic, one for daily/morning use and some super-duper sticky-icky for when it's time to get down with the get down or blow someone's mind who isn't used to the flavor of the funk that I bring. It was some really stinky crystal-covered chronic, so I set the old man up for a rip of something that would make the weed he used to smoke seem like ginger beer. I told him that it was not what he used to smoke in the sixties. I specifically said that it was going to knock him on his ass, but he took a good rip, just one, and said he was good. I went inside to put my supplies away because it really stunk, and I get shit for stinking up the joint every year. They even bought me a shirt with a skunk that said "It wasn't me" on it because I fishbowled the whole cabin while they were out doing something I didn't want to do. So I am the token pothead of the family vacation.

I put everything away, and as I was walking up, someone said to me, "What the hell did you smoke with him?" I told her it was the good-good, and she said that it must have been because he was just standing up and fell straight over on his back. I didn't see it, but he apparently got up and did not complain about any back pain; that was some good fucking weed.

I smoked again with him this year because his back was giving shit, and this year, I could feel his pain. It could have just been my own back because I feel it right now and he is nowhere around. This year, I brought up a vapor thing with some kind of hash oil or something in it that is basically like an e-cigarette that pumps out THC; it is pretty cool. I brought it so as not to rub my addiction in the face of the family. They know I am high all day, but they don't need to watch me get high. I offered the old man the choice of some really good chronic or the electric thing; he chose the vape. I warned him once again that it was stronger than anything he was used to, but he proceeded, and once again he was in a new world he had never experienced. I know he got high back in the day, but he wasn't quite ready for this. However, instead of keeling over and being incoherent, he was just incredibly high and giggling like a schoolgirl; it was fucking hilarious.

I get plowed every year and am high off my ass from sunup to sundown, and it's beautiful, so I always have a good time, and if the family is going crazy, I just clap my hands, walk away, and go do my own thing. My schedule is fucked because my dogs wake me up early as hell every day, so even on vacation, I am up before everyone else and have to be quite. There is no rule about that, but it is just common courtesy.

The family has some dumbass unspoken rule about drinking before noon as well, so I have to hide a cooler in the room and drink in private if it is before twelve o'clock. But as soon as it hits noon, it's on like Donkey Kong. There is a free Frisbee golf course here, so I just go up the road with a few beers and enough ganja to last me eighteen holes, and I'm good for the morning. It is only a nine-hole course, but when I learned about Frisbee golf my right hand was in a cast, so I learned how to play with my left hand. I am good with both hands now, so I play one Frisbee with each hand and see which one does better. I always am within one or two shots; I am ambidextrous!

During the day, I don't wear any shoes or socks, no shirt, just a swimsuit, and I try to be by or in the water at all times. Unless we go into town and then I will put clothes on. Sometimes I will even dress nice because there are a few nights and mornings when we go to the same place on the same day every year. One is the Logging Camp; it is set up like a military mess hall and is always busy as fuck. We go there with thirty-plus people in our party, and they go around and ask, "How many eggs?" and "Do you want and sausage ham?" You can say as many eggs as you want, and there are unlimited hash browns and pancakes. The place is nuts, and there is a gift shop that you have to go through in order to leave that sells all types of random shit. I got a butterfly knife there one year, and this year I bought brass knuckles that also has a knife in it, how useful. We go to a bunch of other mandatory stops like the candy/fudge shop and stores that sell cheesy up-north shirts and other restaurants and bars, one of which I fucked up at this year—the Royal Bar and Grill.

I had purchased a bottle of apple whiskey and proceeded to drink damn near all of it before we went out for a family dinner. There were only about twenty-five of us, so it wasn't as bad, but I feel for the waitress and cooks.

Everything was cool until some fuck in an American-flag cowboy hat came and turned on some country music. I flipped the fuck out. I was yelling and crying out, "What the fuck is this garbage?" They were a lot bigger than me, but I did not care. Eventually, I had to leave. I did get to eat all my food though. Dad-in-law just shook his head at me because he has previously referred to me as a "hothead" because of an incident on this lake. We were at the channel, and I was fishing with my blue bobber that I love. I have a few of them because I love blue, and I can always tell which one is mine. Don't fuck with my blue bobber. This little punk was parked in the boat launch playing loud garbage rap music that no one wants to hear. I love hip-hop, but I don't know what you call the crap he was listening to. It was just annoying. His little boy was in the water, throwing rocks, which is fine, but he was specifically throwing them at my bobber, so I wasn't catching shit. I asked the kid multiple times to quit, and he kept doing it, so I blew up at the dad. I threw my pole, threw my arms up, and let go a laundry list of curses and threats. The shithead packed up and sped away, honking like a douche. I won that round.

I thought those flip-outs made me look bad, but my nephew took the cake this year. He is twenty-one or twenty-two now, so he feels that he can do whatever the fuck he wants. He came up here with his girlfriend and his fat friend who doesn't wear deodorant, and all hell broke loose. They drank way more than they should have and stepped out of line. My nephew and Stinky were fighting very loudly on the beach and almost came to blows over politics; the fat boy was a right winger. Later, some fight broke out between him and his uncle (my brother-in-law) over who starts the grill or some shit; they don't get along. The argument grew, and he walked into the cabin a threw a full Corona at the wall inside the cabin, which caused his mom to come in and lay down the law at a volume that I am sure you could hear across the lake, and it is a big-ass lake.

She pushed the fat boy off his feet and kicked her son out and made him take his spoiled ass, his harlot, and the stinky pig-boy back home to their spoiled lifestyle. His mom married a millionaire, and that little brat is so spoiled and does not appreciate it one bit. He cursed his mom and the whole family out for not treating them like adults. His girlfriend did as well, and she just turned twenty-one three days ago. Who the fuck does she think she is?

Once again, I steer clear of these situations, and I either walk away or watch and laugh. They all had to leave and drive for hours to go home and have nothing to do for the next five days. My sister-in-law left today because she has had enough. Two of the three male cousins that I usually hang out with left, and a bunch of other people left because everybody just got sick of it. I used to go out with them all day, smoking and drinking our faces off.

One time, I even went overboard and got a bit too much sun and drinks. I had a seizure the next morning, and that really sucked. They are all married now and are too busy with their old ladies to hang out anymore. I will leave mine at the cabin to go do some drinkin' and fishin' with the boys, but whatever. The crew is thinning out, but I don't care because I got my pot, my beer, and something to write because I remember something new every day. We went up to Itasca today to the headwaters of the Mississippi because there was nothing else to do, so why not walk across the beginning of the river. It is only about ten feet across at the headwaters, and there is a line of rocks you can skip across if you are young. I was not going to fuck with that. I have done it before, but I think my time has passed for shit like that. The rocks are wicked slippery, and nobody was falling, so I did not want to be that guy and then be wet for the rest of the day. There is a log a few feet down river that you can walk across where the river is just as small, so I did that. I am going fishing and swimming tomorrow no matter what the weather is.

I fucked myself with that closing statement because I would fish no more that week. I am back in civilization now, and I missed out on the fishing. I got up around 7:00 AM and was going to Frisbee golf a few rounds, come back, take a nap, and then go out and fish it up, perfect day. I was walking to the door to go have a morning smoke before I packed up and went to play when my niece stopped me to point out a bee. I stopped dead in my tracks because bees scare the shit out of me, and the last thing I remember is her saying not to worry because it was on the other side of the glass. The next thing I remember, I was waking up on the couch, and everyone was looking at me. I had no fucking clue what was going on for about five seconds, and then I just said, "Fuck, not again." I knew what had happened but not exactly how.

Apparently, after I saw the bee, which was actually a wasp, I blanked out, smashed my knee on the fireplace falling forward, then fell straight back, rigor mortis style, like Frankenstein with my arms stiff up in the air. I fell through the screen door and landed flat on my back on the concrete steps, and my head apparently flopped over the side and got banged up a bit. I passed out there. Luckily, the owner's wife was walking by, and she is an EMT, and she helped out. She said I was coherent faster than most seizure patients she had come across in the past.

I knew who everyone was and what happened; I was just disappointed. I knew what would come next, and it did on the best day of the week. I got up eventually and stumbled around until the inevitable happened—I had to puke. I can control my stomach just fine, so there were no accidents, and if I need to, I can barf on command without the use of any fingers or foreign objects. I took care of business, but I knew I would be out of commission for the day and extremely pissed off. I retired to the bedroom and threw up in a bucket for the next eighteen hours or so before I could finally keep water down. At this time, everyone was asleep, and there was nothing to do, so I watched/listened to *The Simpsons* for hours until people woke up. I felt like a hot roasted piece of shit served in a bowl of bile. Eventually, I put some booze in me to get rid of the chills; I knew I would not be able to eat until I did so. I got my drink on and eventually put some food in my face, so I was okay. I did get to go out on the boat one more time, supposedly to go fishing, but that never happened. I swear I am the only person in that family who knows where to go if you actually want to catch fish. We did go to a little sandbar, the little brown girl, and I did some swimming, but we were the only ones. That's cool; I like her. That was basically the end of the trip this year. I might have done better had I not drank a bottle of whiskey and two pints of brandy on top of three and a half cases of beer. Maybe I will tone it down next time but most likely not.

Enough about the cabin. Time to reflect on other shit that I would probably forget if I wasn't writing it down. In college, while I lived in dinky town, there were many adventures with many people, but one that I just remembered was of an infamous keg stand. I was at a party that I was not invited to—that is one awesome thing about living in a college town in your twenties. I was talking to whom I would say was the hottest girl at the party. She was smoking hot, and I was trying to hook up or at least get her number. They were doing keg stands, and the whole party (or at least a circle of it because it was a pretty big party) was doing the count for how long each douchebag could drink.

The bar was set pretty high to break the record at around a minute or more, and the girl told me that she would only give me her number if I could break the record. I laughed at the challenge because I was in my prime, and there was no question in my mind that I would put all the little frat fuckers to shame. I got lifted up, did a handstand, and started to chug. After a while, they had to pump up the keg and had to continue to do so. After around two minutes of upside-down beer slamming, the keg tapped out, and I won whatever dumbass contest that was, and I got the hot girl's number. Unfortunately, I lost it, and all I was left with was a belly full of beer and no pussy.

Later that semester, I went to a party at a kid's house from my class in high school who lived on campus. I met another smokin' hot chick and apparently pissed off the host of the party because I think he liked her. I was once again forced to leave the party, but the joke was on him because she came home with me and I continued to bone her for at least a year or so. He called me on my cell later that night and accused me of throwing a soup can through his picture window at his place in Minneapolis. By this time, I was at my sister's house in Saint Paul, so I laughed at him and told him to fuck off. He made some pretty bold threats, but I was not concerned, and nothing really ever came to fruition.

Funny story about that girl, however. After a while, she brought her son around every once in a while who was about ten years old, and yes, we did fuck while he was around. She was a horrible mother. But one time when he was acting up, she brought him in the other room, and all I heard was her yelling his name and then a really loud smack followed by a blood-curdling scream.

Months later, the boy-girl was over, and she stopped by after swimming at the lake by my house, which is fucking disgusting, and apparently, he had a bit of an accident in his shorts at the beach. That'll happen, but you don't need to bring some shitty pants kid to my house to change his drawers when he is almost ten. He was making a scene, so she brought him in the bathroom, and I told my buddy to shut up and listen because some beating was about to go down. No joke, two seconds later, we heard her scream his name and then a loud smack that hurt just to hear. We laughed our asses off, I called it.

Once again, I lost another no-fail source of vagina to the loss of a cell phone. Her number is in the bottom of a lake, and it will never be seen again. This was the same girl that got me punched in the forehead when my girlfriend walked in on us fucking, and it was reasonable for me breaking my hand on a door after she caught me fucking some other girl. I don't have the best track record when it comes to getting away with infidelities.

When the 35E Bridge collapsed in Minneapolis, I was on a weed trip by which I mean I was going to get weed. I could have taken that route, but I took 280 instead, and had I taken that bridge, I might not be alive today. I came home to find my dad and about five of my friends watching TV and just glad to see me, and I had no idea why. I was buying right around the Federal Reserve, which is still the location of my skateboarding highlight. It was the biggest set of stairs that I ever jumped down. I fell many a time and would laugh my ass off, run back up, and do it again. I miss being young and resilient. They called me skittles in those days because I was a fat kid with different hair color every week.

Around this time, I started drinking, and I remember being stuck up north with some family that I barely knew for some reason. I was probably twelve or something, but I was bored as fuck, so one night, I G'd a bottle of whiskey and something else, went down to the lake, and sat in the boat and drank my face off. Looking back, I can't believe how much I drank at that age. It was a stormy night and windy as fuck. The boat was out of control, but I was having fun. I would have been kicked out of the family if they found me, but I just got plowed, passed out, and woke up in just enough time to sneak in the cabin before I got beaten.

I never drive. I do have a driver's license, but if at all possible, I do not drive. This is mostly due to the fact that I am always intoxicated, but I also just really don't like to drive. It was fun when I was seventeen; but it has gotten old. I will throw down for gas money, but if I can avoid driving, I will ride in the trunk, fuck it.

I used to hang out, and we were very friendly. That would soon change, but one year on Halloween, there was a wicked snowstorm over thirty inches, and my dad walked me around the neighborhood even though there was nobody out trick-or-treating. I got all the candy in the neighborhood. Most people just left out buckets of candy that said, "Take 'em all," so I did. Nothing was plowed, and it was impossible to get around, so my dad was either a really nice, caring father or he was drunk and didn't care that it was negative twenty below and impossible to move because he was drunk.

I remember a letter that he wrote to me as he was dying that I will never read again. I really don't remember it that well, but it let me know what a piece of shit I was growing up and that I was no good. I don't think that was necessarily his intention when writing the letter, but I understand what he meant. We had our falling out, and I said things to him that I wish I could take back. But it is too late now, and the only thing to do is try to remember the good times. Everyone says that there were things they wish they could have said to a loved one before their death; I wish I could take some of mine back.

I wish that I could remember more from my past, but surprisingly, I remember a whole lot, although the memories are clouded in somewhat of a drug-induced coma that I somehow managed to live through. I started out with weed at age twelve, and it was down or uphill from there, depending on how you look at it. It quickly progressed to cocaine and methamphetamines, which were appealing. However, I never became addicted. I would go on a binge and be up for a week or so, but then I would recoup and go back to my old ways of smoking weed all day and maybe some beers at night. Freshman year of college, I started really drinking. I worked in a liquor store throughout high school, so I always had access to alcohol, and I had a fake ID, so I could basically do whatever I wanted whenever I wanted.

In Colorado, I hung out with a bunch of cats who were all of age. I was the only white one, not that it matters, but I held my own. I was known as Rob Tiggah the White Niggah. I was okay with that. I had that group of friends and then a group of white boys that I met around my apartment complex. They introduced me to a whole new world of drugs and delinquency. There was even a meth lab in my building. I went to a unit on the bottom floor with my buddy, and it smelled like cat piss. One of the guys asked me if I wanted some "breakfast" and handed me a cooking pot with about an inch of crystal meth in it. This pot had at least a thousand dollars' worth of meth in it. This was at around five in the morning after a weekend of candy flipping and God-knows-what-else-I-did.

I had to go to school in a few hours, so I had to take a look at my situation and make some changes. I really didn't make many changes; I am still the same fuck-up I ever was. They say that if it isn't broke, then don't try to fix it. Well, I think that I came to the realization that I am broken and I am not worth fixing. I would go to raves every weekend or big house parties; I have no idea how I got my homework done. I would never drive. Because I was the only person with a car, I would let them use my ride to get the crew to whatever was going on that week. I got a free ride to the party, free drugs, women, and a ride home with a full tank of gas. I would usually candy-flip, which is when you take ecstasy with acid and then go party like a retard.

Retard is a bad word, by the way, and you should never use it to describe a person, but there is no other word to describe my behavior at this point in my life. I am headstrong and always in control of what I am doing, but with the drug cocktails that I was indulging in, I have no idea how I am still alive. That is the closest I ever came to doing heroin. I have never used a needle. I research every drug I put into my body, and I could tell when the ecstasy I had ingested was cut with heroin. Sometimes I prefer that cut because that is the horny, fuck-anything-that-moves cut, and you can eventually sleep. When it is cut too high with speed, you get all jittery and stay up all weekend. I would rather get all fucked up, get fucked, and go to sleep.

I was introduced to a whole new world of intoxication. I had already done all the powders under the sun, or so I thought. I had done all the party drugs I had heard of to that point, but there was more out there that I had no idea about. Special K was the first to cross my path, and I learned how to acquire it in its raw form and cook it into a powder. It is an animal tranquilizer and has the same effect on humans. Once it is cooked up, a tiny little bump will send you into what is referred to as a K hole, and you are completely incoherent and incapable of even the smallest task. It is awesome…if you are young and dumb.

GHB was the next new drug to me. It is known as a date-rape drug and for good reason. It is a liquid that consists of some kind of hormones or something like that. That is how much I knew about what I was putting into my body at this point in my life. It tasted like sweat; it was a nasty salty brew that might as well have been piss because it was so fucking foul. You only need a capful, and you are out of your mind. I drank a few caps with Walt Disney's granddaughter one time. I did not rape her. She was really hot though, and I have many hazy memories of fucking around with her and her friends.

That came around to fuck me in the ass when my girlfriend found out about it, but it was worth it.

I had tried every drug that I had ever heard of at this point (ninth), including the dobber. I still have no idea what that was, but it was some sort of powder and had the effect of heroin loaded ecstasy; it was awesome. Once again, I was putting shit in my body and had no idea what the fuck it was. This led to a sexual encounter with someone I had lusted over for years. That was cool. We boned in a motel and got busted by a girl with ginormous tits who actually used to be my girlfriend…small world.

There were also these pills I found at the house of my friend's uncle. They were in a bottle that was labeled as Viagra, but it clearly was not. They were not pressed in any way and clearly homemade. They tasted like coke or speed or something. Regardless, it was some form of narcotic, so I grabbed me a handful. There were some orgy-like incidents, and my friend's sister grabbed my cock in the hot tub, but we made eye contact, and it was too weird so that was the end of that. I always had a crush on her, and it would have been awesome to bone her, but there was something not right about it and I just could not do it. I did, however, fall asleep in between her and another one of my friend's sister and ended up fucking the hell out of her in the middle of the night. I had those pills for a while and used them with multiple women, and I still have no clue what the hell it was. All I know is that it made me fuck like a rabbit and induced a euphoria like nothing I had ever experienced before. It was somewhat comparable to candy-flipping or meth but so much more. I wonder what it was.

I do remember one time I was at my girlfriend's apartment in Minneapolis when an ex-girlfriend got a hold of me and apparently lived just down the street. I fucked the hell out of my old lady, and then I said I was going to split so I could sleep in my own bed and she had to work in the morning anyways, so I boned out. I met up with Jawbone, the chick I met at some rave then dated for a while and went to Mexico with. She was a bit of a druggie and was always holding, so we instantly blazed up a bowl of the sticky-icky, but that was not enough. She busted out the glass dick, and it was on like donkey. We got butt-ass naked and smoked a handful of crystal. We smoked and humped in a daze for hours until I came at least three or four times and was spent. She asked me if it was okay if she used her little toy, which was not little at all. I said no, and she put on a show that would put the porno industry to shame.

I smoked, drank, and watched the show of a lifetime until my buddy woke up, and then I plowed her until like eight in the morning or something like that. I like to smoke powders rather than snort them because that shit hurts your nose forever, and when you are done smoking, there is still resin that you can light up afterward and get dusted all over again. I also prefer "huffing" powder to snorting it.

After years of research, I realized that people snorted powders because it "goes straight to your brain." That is bullshit. You are inhaling the narcotic. It does not literally go into your brain; it goes to your lungs. By inhaling the substance like you would a cigarette, 100 percent of the drug gets into your system. Nothing is lost. When you sniff powders, the cilia in your nose trap a vast majority of the drug, which causes the "drain" of the coke or whatever and constant sniffling. By huffing, you get all the dope, and none of the telltale signs of a dope user.

I was curious and tried just about every pharmaceutical you could possibly imagine. The thief in Denver supplied me with any pill you think of, and I continued that habit for quite a while. I tried oxy, which is supposedly ridiculously addictive and has led to the death of more than a few of my friends and multiple celebrities. I got really fucked up, but it was nothing I would walk through a snowstorm to obtain. However, if I run out of beer or weed, I will run through a blizzard. I have never been addicted to anything but beer and stinky cheeba. I could cut out the weed if I had to, but if I don't have a drink for more than eight hours, I get sick as a dog, whatever that means, but I eventually puke all day for the rest of the day.

I have no idea why I began and continue to drink the way I do, but I am pretty fucking good at it. I can put down a liter of whiskey and wash it down with a twelve-pack and still be coherent and even propose philosophies and intelligent ideas. I freestyle at my best, and I seem to be able to pull any tail that I set my sights on. I have debated with the smartest woman on the planet (my mom) and won on numerous occasions while plowed. I know I have won the issue we were debating when she stops the debate and says that she doesn't want to talk about it anymore. I know for a fact that if she knew she was right she would put me in my place and lay down the law. She has done it many times in the past, but I, too, have had my moment in the sun and made the most intelligent person I have ever known see the light in a way that they had never seen before.

When my family did the whole family tree thing for the Thurlow side, they found that my paternal roots are basically English; my mother's side was Irish and German. So I am an Englishman, and I hold my head high representin' that ish. I also like the way that they speak. An ugly English woman can sound so sexy if you close your eyes.

My wife looked up my name on the internet before we were married, not because she was interested in my history but wanted to know if I was some kind of creep-show rapist guy. She found that there were numerous people named Robert Thurlow throughout the world with the majority of them living in England. There was one, however, that stuck out. His name was Robert Thurlow Vanderbilt, who had a son named Paul. My name is Robert Paul Thurlow. What is fucked is that this cat died on February 23; that was my dad's birthday. My father's middle name was Paul as well. I think Vanderbilt is a name synonymous with a rich-ass family swimming in piles of money. I wonder if we are related. Would his fam at least buy me a drink? I don't care if that is morbid; I think it is funny.

Just a few quick stories here for gits and shiggles. I had a good night planned with the boys, and we were going to trip our balls off and do God-knows-what. We got really dusted on who-knows-what and cleaned my room. We realized that the rest of the acid, which was the plan for the night had disappeared, being on whatever it was we were on. We tore the fucking room apart until one of the burn units pointed out that we might have knocked it on the floor and vacuumed it up in our high-ass cleaning frenzy.

The little stoner was right! We dug through a full bag of foul-smelling ish that looked like a collection of something that you would dig out of a fat man's belly button. We found the four hits of acid, and I have no idea what happened after that. I do remember some shit about playing out in the snow and seeing some crazy shit, but I really have no clear recollection. I also remember doing a bunch of acid on various things; there were Froot Loops acid, liquid and paper, and of course, sugar cubes because we loved to embrace the '70s and basically lived like hippies when you think about it. All we did was ditch class, smoke weed, have sex, and rebel against mainstream society.

Some More Random Stories

I love the northern lights. Minnesota is incredibly beautiful up north, and every once in a while, the northern lights happen. They are amazing! You cannot describe them, but they are truly breathtaking. There is no need to be intoxicated, but I must say from personal experience there is nothing like it on acid or mushrooms. I love going up north in general, northern lights or not. It is beautiful, and you can see stars. I live in the city which is polluted with light; the stars are nonexistent, and you hear more gunshots and police sirens than birds and frogs.

I have a fond memory from my brief stint at a Catholic high school. It was when the yearbook came out. I was in there for being a fashion statement. We had to wear uniforms, so any day that we were allowed to wear any normal clothes was apparently a fashion statement. The yearbook crew tapped me on the back and got the worst picture of me turning around, looking special needs, and they put that picture in the book because I had bleached hair and two pierced ears. The part of that yearbook was that in one guy's senior summary, he stated that his life's ambition was to search every restroom in the world for the "phantom smoker." That was me. I smoked weed every day in the bathrooms, but I never got busted. I sold weed in the bathrooms all the time, so there were people that knew it was me, but no one sold me out, not even the seniors that I blatantly shorted by fingering the scale to look like it weighed more than it did.

I lived with my sister for a number of years while I was finishing college because I was sick of living in Minneapolis and I missed having a yard and air-conditioning. After the parents moved out, I moved back to my childhood home with my sister. I made her life a living hell. I was still doing the DJ thing, so I set up my tables on a big ass old desk in the basement that turned it into a suburban/ghetto party room. I spun/scratched records all night, and I had a microphone hooked up so I would freestyle as well. My voice carries enough when I talk with my normal speaking voice. I usually have to whisper because my voice is too loud and I always say stupid shit and I curse like a sailor.

There were a number of issues and roommates. One was her ex-boyfriend, and we did not necessarily get along. I really had a problem with his girlfriend who slept over every fucking night. I got pissed off one night, and needless to say, I was piss drunk and high out of my mind. I started some shit over absolutely nothing and then proceeded to go outside and beat the shit out of his car. He moved out shortly after. The next douchebag who is still around and is now the daddy of my sister's baby moved in. *I hate him!* I don't know what it was that he did, but he pissed me off one day, and I had to kill his fish. I love animals but I hated him so much more.

He had a really nice and big oscar; it was beautiful. I was pissed off for God-knows-what and poured a bunch of alcohol and bong water in the tank. I put something else fucked up in there as well, but I don't remember what. I am an asshole, and I still feel bad about killing that fish. I should have killed him. That piece of shit is still around, obviously because of the kid, but he doesn't contribute to anything. He has no identification and no record at all. He might as well not exist; I wish he didn't.

He has an eighteen-year-old son that he hasn't seen in over ten years. Now he doesn't do dick for my niece, no job, no car, no driver's license, nothing. I even went out of my way to get him applications for a job within walking distance of their house at a liquor store and a convenience store, easy jobs, but he never got off his fat ass to even apply for a job that a *retard* (bad word) could get in a heartbeat.

My anger stems from the fact that he does nothing to take care of my sister or even his own child. I offered to take a day off work to bring him to the DMV and let him use my car to get his license, but he simply said that he didn't want to. He is hiding something, and if my sister ever disappears, he would be the first person to question.

I don't trust him any further than I can throw him, which is not far because I have a broken back and he is a big fat fuck.

I don't know if I mentioned my doggie, and I have written way too much to read. I can write like a motherfucker, but I read at a fourth-grade level, very slow. I am a self-diagnosed dyslexic. I mix up the words, and then I have to reread everything, and it takes forever. That has nothing to do with my dog or anything for that matter… Damn, I got my hands on some really good weed, I can barely see. Anyways, my illegitimate puppy who was dropped off by a friend that I had not seen in over a decade and asked to watch for two weeks that turned into well over seven years, he is my dog now. The other day, he cut the shit out of my foot, and I needed stiches. He is the gentlest giant in the world, and he does not bite. You can put your fist all the way in his mouth, which is gross, but he will not bite. He will just lick your hand. On this occasion, I kicked him right in the fucking face. That sounds bad, but it was an accident. He didn't even notice.

He likes to play soccer, which we do with basketballs. You wouldn't think it possible, but he is so big he can pick up basketballs in his mouth and run around with them, and then he wants you to kick them around, so I just call it playing soccer with the Rock Star. This particular day, Rocky and I were playing "soccer," and when we had a stand-off with the ball between us, we both ran at it simultaneously, and I got there first. I kicked the ball with my left foot for some reason, which is weird because I am a righty. Rock Star decided to jump at the ball at the same time, and my follow-through went right into his mouth. I didn't notice anything, and Rocky simply wanted to keep playing ball, so I kicked the ball again. There was a big slash of blood, and I realized something was wrong. There was a football-shaped gash on my ankle about an inch long and half-inch wide and God knows how deep. I do know that I could see my bone, so it was deep enough for me.

I hate the hospital, and I have had so many injuries I know how to take care of myself. I have reset broken bones and noses. Never done stitches, but I just taped it up, and I am all good.

My dog has a head like a brick both mentally and physically. He gave my wife a black eye once, and one time, he ran up on me and didn't stop. He ran his brick-house skull into my nose, and I had a bloody nose for over two weeks; he was not fazed. He also likes to play baseball with the basketballs. This is when I throw up the basketballs and hit them with a baseball bat, which he then chases down and brings back, sometimes. He does love to chase them though.

One time, while smacking the balls around, he did the same thing and jumped at the ball as I was about to hit it, but I had already swung the bat. I hit my dog directly in the face with a softball bat. I damn-near cried, and he did not blink. He is, as I stated, a brick house, but he is getting old and deteriorating. I don't know how I am going to deal with it when he dies, but it is going to happen, and he is my first dog. I don't plan on having kids, so he is basically my son. I have an image of his skeleton on my leg, so he will always be with me. I do have a plan to get a new puppy before he passes so he can train him like he did with Baxter. Baxter is the other little shit machine that hangs around my house. My old lady had a Chihuahua that was a complete dick. He was a fat little piece of shit that hated everyone and everything on earth. When his mom was away, he fucking loved me and would sleep on my chest. He was fat as fuck, but I would take him on walks. He dropped almost five pounds. That is almost the whole weight of some Chihuahuas. I do kind of miss that piece of shit even though he was an asshole.

What I feel the worst about is the way that he passed. He was put down, but unfortunately, he had bitten me a few times and the last one was about a week before he was put to rest. Neither of us knew that this was an issue, but apparently, it was. The little shit was named Chico, fitting name for a little Mexican. I was fucking with him, and he nipped at my hand and happened to bite through my finger all the way. I pulled back and actually pulled him off the ground because his lower tooth was completely through my finger. I had to pull it out, and I could feel it rubbing against my bone, and now I have scars on both sides of my left middle finger. The worst part of this story is the aftermath. When the puppy was brought in to be put out, they asked if he had bitten anyone in the past few whatever how long. It doesn't matter my wifey is too honest, so she told them the story, so they cut off his head. No bullshit, they chopped off his fucking head and made her bring all his remains to the University of Minnesota for analysis to see if he had rabies. Fuck that! That dog was just an asshole. I wish that it didn't have to come to essentially killing the dog, but I know that he was going to die soon, and this was a far better option than finding him dead someday.

I do a lot (or at least I did do a lot) of walks for various causes before my back started making me want to die every step I took. I would do walks for colorectal cancer in honor of my father and epilepsy walks in honor of my sister's best friend's daughter. It is kind of weird because I completely supported the cause and walked every year. She died from an epileptic seizure at a very young age. I had no idea that I would later be diagnosed with the same "disease." So years after her death, I was now walking for myself as well as her, "God" rest her soul.

One day, the old lady and I did a walk for animals or some shit. Afterward, we stopped by the humane society for some reason, and my first words were that we were not going to adopt anything, so everything was cool. We stopped at a pet store on the way home for some stupid reason, and once again, I clearly said that we were *not* going to get another dog. After we got home, she said she was going to run to the store. We did need groceries, and she goes shopping every Saturday, so no big deal. I did, however, specifically say, "Do not get a fucking dog!" before she left.

A couple of hours later, she walked in the door with this tiny little piece of shit white Chihuahua, and I wanted to punch her in the face. She pulled a really dirty trick that I still hate her for but have to respect because it was quite cunning and manipulative. She told me that the little ankle-bitter was named Baxter, which was not true because I saw his name when we saw him at the puppy mill. This was not a pedigree dog like my fat-faced slobber hound; he has papers. God only knows where this fucking thing came from; all I know is that he was purchased in a shitty strip mall. He is clearly a pure-breed Chihuahua; he just doesn't have papers. The dirty trick was renaming him Baxter.

My sister used her money at camp one year when I was still a little baby and bought me a little stuffed animal, a puppy, and his name was Baxter. Thirty years later, I still have that dog in my bedroom; I love it. I had to accept the dog because of the name, and I guess he has grown on me, and the fat one loves him. They are the best of friends. He is basically like Chico; he loves me until the old lady comes home. He does not turn evil toward me once she comes home; he just pays more attention to her. It is a bit of a slap in the face, but I don't lose any sleep over it. If I do sleep on the couch or even just lay down to watch TV, he will jump up and sleep on my chest with me. He also occasionally likes to sleep right on my face. I have woken up to that many times. I think he is like one of those cats that sleep on babies' faces and steals their souls.

I have one other little buddy, Mr. Bo Jangles, my leopard gecko. I have had other lizards like Jub-Jub, my iguana (named after the iguana on *The Simpsons*). He died. And Skink-Box, a blue-tongued skink, but I gave her back to my ex-girlfriend. Bo J. is the man. I first met him in Colorado. I was about fifteen or sixteen years old. Goddamn, my lizard if fucking old. I went out there to go snowboarding and my buddy's older brother lived out there, so we stayed with him and went snowboarding every day. That is why I went there and to smoke some really stinky weed. The mountains and the weed is why I decided to go to the University of Colorado. I didn't look into the academic aspect of the school whatsoever; I just wanted to be close to the mountains and a place where I could get a home-cooked meal.

Bo J's original name was Premiere, and I thought that was stupid, so I renamed him, and I have no idea where I came up with that name. I just checked, Bo J. is still alive, but wow, they don't usually live this long. He is huge for his species and a gangster to boot. I did have a cat for a bit, Mao. I called him that because he would never shut up. He was constantly meowing all day and night. He was an outdoor cat, and one day he didn't come back. I liked that cat. I have a tattoo of his skeleton with crossbones, all anatomically correct, on my leg. I also have the same tattoo but of my boxer on my other leg; everything has to be symmetrical. I have the characters for water and fire on each bicep and the sun and moon on either shoulder, all symmetrical. I am OCD in that way. Back to the gangster lizard; he fought off my cat Mao and lived.

I was feeding him live mice, just little pinky mice, but mice nonetheless. The people at the reptile store could not believe that I was feeding them to a gecko, but he loved them. I just feed him crickets now because there is only one place in the Twin Cities that sells live mice, and it is in Minneapolis, fuck that. The last time I went there to get a mouse, I took 280 home instead of 35. When I got home, it was all over the news that the 35 Bridge had collapsed. I would have been on that bridge when that happened. I got sidetracked a bit, but the point of my rambling was that my gecko is a big brutish bad-ass that fights cats.

I did not have a lid for the terrarium, so I just put my skateboard over the top of the cage. One day, I apparently forgot to put the board back after I fed him, and when I woke up, he was gone. The old lady and I looked forever until we found his tail wiggling on the floor, and my heart dropped. The cage was all fucked up, and I knew what happened and chased that cat all over the fucking house and booted his ass out. I was furious.

The flat-tire girl found Bo J. under the couch in the computer room; he was missing his tail, but he was alive and eventually his tail grew back! His new tail is kind of bulbous and not the same color as the rest of him, which sucks because the people at the reptile shop would always compliment him on his size and his "large original tail." They said he would be perfect for breeding. I have no idea how, but I found a female leopard that was about the same age as Bo that happened to be owned by a close friend of the guy I got Bo from. I have known him forever but only see him at parties or whatnot, but everyone is too old now so that doesn't happen too much anymore. He gave me his female gecko. I don't remember her name, but I had to give her a new one, so I had to go with Lady Lay. I love Bob Dylan. Fuck, he was from Minnesota, but I am not a diehard fan. I have no idea why I chose to name Bo J. after one of his songs, but it only seemed fitting to name his new girlfriend after another Dilly song.

They did not necessarily get along at first. I can understand some young bitch comes into your territory and thinks they run the place.

This reminds me of when my wife moved in. Random thought...I once heard some comedian say that if you are going to get married, just picture everything in your house that you love and then picture it *gone*! Whoever that comedian was he was dead right. My house looks nothing like it did when I met my wife. It used to be a happy smoke-filled, bottles-and-cans-everywhere, people-passed-out-all-over, keg-in-the-yard type of home...good times. Now my house is completely refurnished, and there are a lot of rules that I was never aware of. The first one was that there was to be no smoking. That is cool with me because I have noticed that I do breathe better now, and the house smells better—until the scented candles come out that all smell like shit to me. It might say apple cinnamon, but all I smell is rotten butthole.

I disagree with the no-smoking rule when it comes to marijuana. Herb is always allowed, no questions asked. Unless you are going to blaze a blunt, then you gotta take that shit outside, or sometimes in the winter when it is like negative twenty below, we smoke in the basement. Once again, I have had a stony moment and flew off on a tangent, but I did have a point to the nonsense. I am stoned out of my mind right now. Lady Lay and Bo J.'s relationship was similar as in she came in and kicked him out of his room. There were two rock houses in the cage, and she booted him out of his and took it over. After a while, they made up, I guess, and did the damn thing. I did not know this, but apparently, when they mate, the male will bite down on the neck of the female to subdue them and have their way with them. Unfortunately, Bo J. was a little too big for Lady Lay, and he bit off a giant piece of her neck...She died. I knew a guy who put himself through college breeding reptiles, and he said that I could make a lot of loot off those two, but it was not to be. Bo J. is still alive, but he is still on his last legs.

More Random Thoughts

I hate school because it has ruined art and film for me, and I love art and consider film to be an art form. Fine art, for example, is complete bullshit, and anything can be considered art even a piece of shit, literally. I don't remember what country it was, but some dude got critical acclaim for smearing a bunch of elephant scat on something and called it art. As long as you can sell your piece of crap piece of "art" with some bullshit explanation about how it reflects of society or some bullshit, apparently it is okay. I have brought in drawings that I pieced together fifteen minutes before class and came to class drunk. I would just ramble about what the drawing meant and all types of random shit that did not mean anything to me, but I passed with flying colors every time. Apparently, you can sell anyone a bag of hot shit if you tell them it is filet mignon; you just need to sell your story.

I do still like a lot of fine art, but for the most part, I feel that it is often overrated and overanalyzed. There is some very fine artwork out there, but spending an hour of my day in my early twenties discussing the meaning behind a drawing of a bowl of fruit is a waste of my time and just fucking ridiculous. The next art class that was completely pointless was photography. I spent so much money (or I should say my mom's money) on cameras, film, photo paper, and my time in the fucking dark room. I don't think they even have dark rooms anymore. Anything I did in my photography classes can now be done on a goddamn cell phone, and not everyone had a cell phone at that time. The one art class that upset me the most was film. Fuck film class!

More Random Thoughts

There are many important moments in your life that you may have missed or are glad that you did miss. Nobody remembers being born or growing up; few people know when they are going to die, but I hope everyone remembers the first time they got laid. I hope you can remember the first time you swore at your parents without getting slapped, but none of these milestones require you to wear a suit or dress. There are two that do, and they both make you cry, at least I do. Yes, I cry at weddings now. Funerals or weddings are it, unless you go to church or have to wear that kind of shit for work, I like to feel comfortable, and I have no shame in my game. I have walked around downtown in my pajamas and slippers. Suits look nice on some people. Some wear them very well, and it looks nice, but they make me feel either obligated or saddened anytime I have to put one on. I cannot feasibly think of any situation where I would dress up like that on my own accord. I only do ish like that to make other people happy or to be appropriate and/or not look like a jackass. I hate being that guy.

I think I need to quit this shit now because I have done way too many drugs in my life. Not necessarily recently but overall. All I do is smoke weed and drink way too much; other than that, I am sober. I will do some blow if it comes around and is free, but other than that, just pot and beer for me. Maybe some hard Ls if the wife isn't around, but that's it. When they diagnosed me with epilepsy, I was unsure and wanted to be clear with the doc. After they did numerous MRI and CAT scans, he showed me the results, which meant absolutely jack shit to me. He pointed out areas of my brain and explained a bunch of nonsense. He might as well have been pointing out a map of Guam or some other place I have never been and asked me for that I had spent the last twenty-plus years ...uld get my hands on as long as it didn't involve ...hat would not have led to my current condition, so ...nd explained that I have done acid more times than I ...nt, no dice. I explained all the other drugs, but he stood by ...t that I simply have epilepsy; I don't buy it. I hallucinate all the ...ne, not just little shit but full-blown hallucinations. Things that I know are not there but look real as day to me; it is fucking freaky. I hate it.

Writing this, whatever it is, has made me realize to what extent in the last couple of days, but I have had fun. I stayed up all night many times while writing this, but within the last couple of days, I have spent an average of seven to eight hours typing through the middle of the night into the morning, and when I stop, my hallucinations are worse than anything I have ever experienced. I would lay down for a bit, enough to get some rest, but when I get up, my whole world has been fucked. It could just be from staring at the screen for so long, but I sincerely doubt that a straight-edge person would suffer the same fate.

The last few days that I have stayed up typing, I have spent the next day in a sea of hallucinations, mostly the vision of every solid object melting. No joke, fucking melting, and it is scary as fuck, as well as shit jumping out of nowhere and shadows playing all types of tricks on me. It is no fun.

When I was young, like fifteen through college, I would take copious amounts of hallucinogens because I had heard of the miracle of flashbacks, so I figured that the more LSD among others that I did, the better the chance that I too would have flashbacks and enjoy the pleasure of tripping my balls off for free! Fuck that, it is no fun. I enjoyed tripping my ass off, knowing I ingested a narcotic and had plans of being fucked in the head until the next morning and then some. It is no fun when you have plans that you need to have your head on straight for and then all of a sudden the walls are melting and large solid objects are moving even though you know it's not possible. This has happened to me way too many times. Once is too many, but I am able to compose myself. If you know me, you have probably seen me in this predicament but had no idea that it going on.

The fucked-up thing is that it got a lot worse after they put n on the epilepsy medication. I asked about those side effects, and Dr. Dickhead's response was, "Oh yeah, that can happen." He tried to give me different drugs, so I asked about those and I have done my research, and just about every drug they have for epilepsy causes similar negative side effects. Fuck that, I would rather live normal and just hope that I don't have a seizure. I have a degree in pharmaceuticals, and I know what he was doing. He was making sure that he kept getting paid by keeping me sick. That is what they do and why I have not gone into that field. Although I do have the paperwork to have a steady job doing the same thing, I don't think that I could do it (morally) and sleep at night. So my head is kind of fucked, but it still works better than most people I meet daily. I am the smartest person I have ever met. That is a joke but only half of one; I will debate with anyone over anything.

Conclusion

I am also going to bring this little project to an end because I just realized that I am around four hundred pages, and I have never read anything that long in my life. I have written papers on books that long, but I usually pick through it and get just enough hard points to focus on, and I have never gotten less than an A while reading maybe twenty pages of a four-hundred-plus-page work. The longest novel I have read was around 250 pages, and that took me years to complete. I am not a good reader. I have gone through my notes, and I could probably write another, second edition of whatever this is, with those notes; but I don't want to repeat shit that I have already written. It is too long as it is, but I have many more stories. I did over eighty times what I was asked to do, so I think that is okay for now, then maybe I will write round 2 if the one who asked me to write this likes what I wrote. If he doesn't, fuck him, it is what it is. It is all true, and no names were named.

    I had fun writing this, most of the time, probably because I just got drunk and stony the entire time and reminisced about old shit that I probably would not have even remembered if not told to write down something. In hindsight, I wish that I would have written it down a little bit at a time so I could have made it a little easier on the eyes, but I just wanted to get what I have written printed out and given to the person who requested it before I die. Who knows, that could be any day, and then no one would ever find what I wrote. I don't like to think that way, but I have come to learn that you never know when you are going to lose someone you love or even your own life. All the material things that people focus their lives on don't mean dick, at least not to me. If you look back your life and focus on what has made you smile including the people that make you happy, those are the things that are important. If you want to climb mountains and travel, then do that, but if you are happy just watching *The Simpsons* and smoking weed, then knock yourself out!

What Robert Paul has written was done very late at night while highly intoxicated as well as very, very high. He chose not to edit because he felt that it should be read, "As fucked up as he was when he wrote it". He has a bizarre sense of humor. It was meant to be simply a compilation of random stories that his buddies were sick of hearing. This was never intended to be published but now that it has, Robert Paul, after soberly reading his own drunken ramblings, has remembered more than enough for a bigger and better round two of hindsight.

About the Author

Robert Paul was born on August 13th 1981 in Minneapolis Minnesota. He was immediately transported to St. Paul MN where he would spend the majority of his life. Robert Paul has seen and done many things and traveled far and wide, some things that most could not even imagine and some things that many people would never want to experience. This is the story of Robert Paul.

CPSIA information can be obtained
at www.ICGtesting.com
Printed in the USA
FFHW022005010419
51443756-56886FF

9 781644 628676